The ORGANIC FOOD SHOPPER'S Guide

WHAT YOU NEED TO KNOW TO SELECT AND COOK THE BEST FOOD ON THE MARKET

Jeff Cox

D0631986

John Wiley & Sons, Inc.

This book is printed on acid-free paper. ♾

Copyright © 2008 by Jeff Cox. All rights reserved

Published by John Wiley & Sons, Inc., Hoboken, New Jersey

Published simultaneously in Canada

No part of this publication may be reproduced, stored in a retrieval system, or transmitted in any form or by any means, electronic, mechanical, photocopying, recording, scanning, or otherwise, except as permitted under Section 107 or 108 of the 1976 United States Copyright Act, without either the prior written permission of the Publisher, or authorization through payment of the appropriate per-copy fee to the Copyright Clearance Center, Inc., 222 Rosewood Drive, Danvers, MA 01923, (978) 750-8400, fax (978) 750-4470, or on the web at www.copyright.com. Requests to the Publisher for permission should be addressed to the Permissions Department, John Wiley & Sons, Inc., 111 River Street, Hoboken, NJ 07030, (201) 748-6011, fax (201) 748-6008, or online at http://www.wiley.com/go/permissions.

Limit of Liability/Disclaimer of Warranty: While the publisher and author have used their best efforts in preparing this book, they make no representations or warranties with respect to the accuracy or completeness of the contents of this book and specifically disclaim any implied warranties of merchantability or fitness for a particular purpose. No warranty may be created or extended by sales representatives or written sales materials. The advice and strategies contained herein may not be suitable for your situation. You should consult with a professional where appropriate. Neither the publisher nor author shall be liable for any loss of profit or any other commercial damages, including but not limited to special, incidental, consequential, or other damages.

For general information on our other products and services or for technical support, please contact our Customer Care Department within the United States at (800) 762-2974, outside the United States at (317) 572-3993 or fax (317) 572-4002.

Wiley also publishes its books in a variety of electronic formats. Some content that appears in print may not be available in electronic books. For more information about Wiley products, visit our Web site at www.wiley.com.

Library of Congress Cataloging-in-Publication Data

Cox, Jeff, 1940-

The organic food shopper's guide : what you need to know to select and cook the best food on the market / Jeff Cox.

p. cm.

Includes bibliographical references and index.

ISBN 978-0-470-17487-6 (pbk.)

1. Cookery (Natural foods) 2. Natural foods. I. Title.

TX741.C73 2008

641.5'63—dc22

2007024558

Printed in the United States of America

10 9 8 7 6 5 4 3 2 1

Contents

Acknowledgments

So many folks deserve recognition for the information in this book that it is not possible to list them all. But these people must be thanked:

Special thanks to the entire team at Wiley, especially editors Linda Ingroia and Adam Kowit, who labored hard to keep me focused, to production editor Ava Wilder for her thorough management of every detail, and to Andrew Miller, who copyedited the manuscript. Thanks to designers Renato Stanisic and Elizabeth Brooks for making this wealth of information accessible and attractive. Thanks to the folks at Oak Hill Farm in Glen Ellen, California, who gave generously of produce and time to make sure we got the resources we needed. Thanks to my agent, Fred Hill, who got this ball rolling.

Thanks also to J. Z. Cool, chef extraordinaire, Lynn Donches at Rodale Press, and to: Anne Bertinuson and Allen Moore, USDA; Gene Kahn, Cascadian Farms; Ben Faber, Elizabeth Mitcham, Janet Caprile, Louise Ferguson, and Adel A. Kader, University of California–Davis; John R. Clark and Curt R. Rom, University of Arkansas; Paul Vossen, University of California Cooperative Extension; Chris Deren and John Duval, University of Florida; Robin Siktberg, Herb Society of America; Dan Pratt, Organic Trade Association; Dave Hill, Connecticut Agricultural Experiment Station; Robert Stebbins, Oregon State University; chef John Ash; Dr. David G. Holm, Colorado State University; Greg Miller, Empire Chestnut Company; David Brenner, Iowa State University;

Randy Wirth, Caffe Ibis; Glenn Roberts, Anson Mills; Jerry Tenenberg, The Great Spice Company; Gemma Claridge, Albert's Organics; Tricia Belcastro, Washington Apple Commission; Mark Farnham, PhD, USDA Agricultural Research Service, U.S. Vegetable Laboratory; Eileen Weinsteiger, Rodale Research Institute; Manny Flores, Jaleo Restaurant, Washington, DC; Constance Jesser, Wine Country Cakes, Sonoma, California; Nancy Civetta, Civetta Comunicazioni; John Lewallen, Mendocino Sea Vegetable Company; Stephanie Kimmel, Marché Restaurant, Eugene, Oregon; Claire Criscuolo, RN, Claire's Corner Copia, New Haven, Connecticut; Birkett Mills, Penn Yan, New York; Nicolas and Laura Catena, Bodega Catena Zapata, Agrelo, Argentina; and all those who helped but aren't mentioned here.

A special acknowledgment to J. I. Rodale, whose organic epiphany started the movement.

Finally, thanks to my wife, Susanna Napierala-Cox, for her love and support, and her forbearance as I spent many a late night at my desk.

Introduction

The perfect dish requires perfect ingredients. That doesn't mean blemish-free produce. It means that the variety of fruit, vegetable, nut, or what-have-you is the right one for the dish being prepared, and that it's as ripe and full of flavor as it will ever get on the very day that the cook is inspired to use it. And yes, it should be organically grown. Why organic? It tastes better. For the cook, organic produce sets the standard of quality. There are three reasons for this.

First, organic growers are primarily concerned with quality, so the varieties they select to grow are known for their flavor impact, rather than their shelf life or ability to ship well.

Second, these extra-flavorful varieties are grown in soil rich in all the nutrients plants need to develop maximum flavor nuances. The effect of organic techniques on the overall quality of plants and animals cannot be overestimated. Your triumphal, masterful dish needs the kind of intense flavor expression that organic ingredients provide.

Third, organic food tends to be fresher, and food that's fresh contains the maximum amount of flavor and nutrition. Flavor and fragrance molecules begin to break down and disappear soon after most foods are picked from the field or tree, so one of the goals of organic farmers is to keep the distance between farms and consumers as short as possible. The increasing popularity of organic food sold at local farm stands, at farmers' markets, at specialty markets, and in supermarkets with organic produce sections means fresher food is becoming ever more available.

More flavor to begin with, and more of this flavor preserved because of freshness—that's a winning combination for any cook.

Another crucial fact about organic food is that it has been grown without agricultural chemicals; animals that produce organic meat, dairy, and eggs are not fed growth hormones or antibiotics, and genetic modification of crops is not allowed. Your meal will be made of good, clean food with the genes that nature gave it. That's reassuring, especially for families with small children, who are more vulnerable than adults to the deleterious effects of agricultural chemicals, and for everyone concerned about the effects of genetic manipulation of their foodstuffs.

This ain't just talk. I had my first organic garden in 1969. I've grown an organic garden just about every year since and have probably grown every type of crop imaginable. Having all that abundance of good food at hand tempted me into the kitchen, where I began to remember the delicious meals my mom made when I was a kid. Slowly—and with many treks to the pizza parlor when my cooking didn't turn out very well—I learned to cook. Eventually, the increasing availability of organic food, coupled with a desire to create something delicious for my family, began to result in dishes even I was satisfied with. Cooking also became key to becoming a better gardener, because I learned which varieties of each crop tasted best in a given recipe, and so my garden began to suit my taste more and more. I've spent most of my life—both at work and at play—acquiring the hard-won knowledge that this book represents. Sharing it with you feels very much like sending over a basket of fresh-picked produce from my garden. As you would with a gift basket, take what you want now and come back often to sample all it has to offer.

—JEFF COX

How to Use This Book

A large portion of this book consists of entries covering over 150 foods grown, raised, or produced organically. Each entry covers the significance of the food's organic provenance. It discusses what farmers do to make sure the food is the cleanest, most nutritious, and most environmentally sound it can be.

Organic farmers select health-giving and tasty varieties of produce. They put a premium on raising healthy animals. They want the distance from farm to consumer to be as short as possible, and they know that food tastes best in season. They sell these products in a range of venues—organic aisles in supermarkets, farmers' markets, and even directly from their farms. With this in mind, the entries discuss when and where to find the foods, what to look for, and how to use them. Topping this off are recipes that evince the best aspects of top-quality organic ingredients.

Because organic farmers grow the healthiest and best-tasting produce varieties (many of them delicious, unique, varieties you won't find in conventional supermarkets), I've listed the best varieties for each fruit and vegetable in the book. You'll find many of them at your local farmers' market or organic market. Shop for them: more and more are turning up in more places every day. It's so important to understand which food varieties will yield the best gustatory payoff. Your insistence on the best varieties will improve the food you put on the table and encourage growers to plant (and retailers to carry) the better varieties.

Organizationally, you'll find vegetables in one section, fruits in another, the dry seeds of plants (grains, seeds, and nuts—and beans, too) in another; animal foods (meat, fish, dairy, eggs) are next, followed by kitchen staples (oils, sweeteners, coffee, and flavorings).

In some instances, I grouped like ingredients together. For example, while there are many Chinese greens, they tend to be various members of the mustard family, so I placed them together in a section. Winter squash share enough similarities that they could share a section—ditto for summer squashes. Citrus is a huge subject, so to simplify it, I discussed the various citrus fruits at the same time.

A few foods are missing—coconuts, and jicama, for instance—because the state of organic farming has not yet caught up with them, as far as I can detect. Whenever possible I included either organic foods that I know can be procured, or foods that I know are produced without the use of agricultural chemicals. If I couldn't find foods that met those tests, I didn't include them.

The organization of the food entries in each section of the book should be self-evident from the category names: season, good varieties (or brands), nutritional highlights, what to look for, storage and preparation tips, organic advantage, uses—and then recipes. I wanted each entry to give you a sense of what the ingredient is like when it is top quality, how you can use it in your cooking, and why you can feel good about eating its organic version.

The suggestions in this book for identifying fresh, high-quality organic foods are meant to be guidelines, not hard-and-fast rules. This is ultimately common sense, not rigid ideology. I'm sure many readers may want to eat only organic food, no matter what. Others may want to eat as much organic food as possible. Still others may be curious and want to try some organic food—just to see what all the talk is about.

I try to eat as much organic food as possible, and as much in season as possible, but if perchance the organic broccoli is sold out, I'll grab a head of conventional broccoli without worrying that I'm condemning myself to organic hell. But the more you know about conventional farming methods and the conventional food supply system, the more inclined toward organic you tend to become. As I've worked on this book, I've kept you—the reader—in mind. I want you and your whole family, your kids, your grandkids, to thrive and grow healthy from your food. There are so many reasons to eat organic food, and they all point directly to you. *À votre santé!*

1

Why Buy Organic Food?

When I worked at *Organic Gardening* magazine during the 1970s, the company had a lunchroom in a house on Main Street in Emmaus, Pennsylvania, called Fitness House. Clients and special guests were taken there to sample real organic food and healthy cooking. It served the most unpleasant food imaginable: unsalted buckwheat groats, sweet potatoes without butter, potatoes boiled in milk, musty-tasting sprouts. At that time, organic food was thought of as good for you and good for the environment—clean, pure, and nutritious—but not all that tasty.

I usually passed Fitness House by and went to Richard's Market for a really delicious Italian hoagie or one of Richard's hot ham sandwiches on a sesame bun with horseradish sauce and melted cheese.

Granola and groats became synonymous with organic food in many places in the 1970s. I ate many an awful meal at back-to-the-land communes from Maine to California. Thank goodness that era is long gone.

Nowadays organic food has come to be appreciated for its richness of flavor, its freshness, and its purity. But as the years passed, I wondered if a special organic cuisine would develop—something that could truly be called organic cooking. And I wondered what it might be. Would it be in the gourmet style of organic cooking found at some trendy restaurants? Writing in the *New Yorker* in 2003, Dana Goodyear described the fare at Counter, an organic restaurant in the East Village in New York City:

> This is a meat-and-potatoes kind of joint, if by meat you mean "meat loaf" made of portobello mushrooms ground up with almonds, macadamia nuts, and cashews in a porcini-mushroom-and-cabernet gravy—and by potatoes you mean cauliflower and pine nuts whipped into a fluffy cumulus and seasoned with parsley and a few shards of uncooked garlic.... The menu attracts a loyal crowd of long-haired sirens so eerily happy-looking and outgoing they might be mistaken for members of a West Coast religion.

While such creative dishes can certainly be tasty, connecting such fabrications with organic food is limiting. This isn't how most people cook at home every day, and it hardly reflects the range of organic cooking.

Organic cooking is real food for real people—good, solid, everyday food made with organic ingredients. It's no longer about faux potatoes made from whipped cauliflower and pine nuts or imitation meatloaf made from portobello mushrooms, and you won't find recipes like those in this book. Good organic cooking can mean cooking in any style, if only because we live in an age when ingredients once found only in ethnic enclaves in America, or in the homelands of different ethnic groups, are available to us fresh, in season, and often in organic form. In fact, organic cooking is most interesting when it is inclusive.

To understand how organic food can enhance any sort or style of cuisine, the organic cook needs to take a good look into the heart of the organic method of growing food, because it's there that the secret of its quality lies. So please bear with me as I condense the knowledge I've gained over thirty years of writing and gardening into a few paragraphs that I hope will be enlightening.

Compost

Healthy soil makes healthy plants makes healthy people.

—Old organic maxim

Put simply, "organic" is a method of growing food using only naturally occurring substances. Properly done, it recycles all wastes and improves the soil as it increases crop yields, working *with* nature's laws and tendencies, rather than attempting to counteract or defeat them. Practitioners of the method conceive of all life in an ecosystem as an interrelated whole to be strengthened, rather than as a group of creatures to be selectively supported, suppressed, or chemically eliminated.

Compost is the heart and engine of the organic method. The rotted remains of what was once living tissue is both the source and destiny of life. What was alive dies and decays to form a nourishing seedbed for new life: the concept is as old as life itself. Go into the woods and look closely at the forest floor. You'll see the leaves and twigs of past years decaying to form a rich, spongy duff that nourishes the trees and plants currently growing there, which will in turn eventually die, decay, and nourish yet another generation of plants. William Shakespeare articulated it well when the friar in *Romeo and Juliet* proclaimed:

> The earth that's nature's mother is
> her tomb;
> What is her burying grave that is
> her womb.

Compost is the perfect fertilizer. It contains plant and animal remains, which have the elements needed for the construction of new plants and animals. But compost is much more. It is teeming with microscopic life of many kinds and functions. A teaspoon of fresh compost may contain billions and billions of living microorganisms. They tear apart and digest the remains of old plants and multiply in a tumultuous explosion of life. A well-made compost pile can reach temperatures of 140 to 160 degrees Fahrenheit as these tiny bits of life colonize the feast of organic matter laid out for them.

Within each microorganism is a fluid that's slightly acidic. When these tiny single-celled organisms die, this acid spills into the soil, where it dissolves various elements, forming soluble mineral salts that further enrich the compost. Some of these soluble mineral salts, such as potassium nitrate, are plant nutrients, which get absorbed by root hairs; without the acid from the compost, much of the soil's mineral content would remain trapped in its insoluble state, of no benefit to plants.

Meanwhile, as the old plant matter (dead roots, leaves, and stems) is chewed up by the life in the soil, it eventually becomes a substance called humus. If you could shrink down small enough for a particle of humus to seem as big as an automobile, you would see a dark, almost black lump with deep crevices, nooks, crannies, and channels creating an enormous surface area in a compact space. If you could stretch the automobile-sized particle out flat, the surface area would cover several acres. This humus particle is negatively charged, and it attracts positively charged ions.

Now nature, being the wonderful mother she is, has given the soil solution (as the soil water is called) a remarkable property called its cation exchange capacity. As plant roots absorb and deplete positive ions from the soil solution, the cation exchange capacity replaces the ions to keep the cations at a fixed, balanced level. The replacement cations come from the humus particles, where they are stored on those negatively charged surfaces.

There's something else remarkable about the soil cations. Because they are the product of biological activity, their molecules are configured in a special way; soil scientists describe them as "left-handed." This is exactly what growing plants require to build healthy tissues, because plants, being biological entities themselves, must have left-handed molecules to work with. Fertilizers made in a chemical factory, on the other hand, contain a random mix of left- and right-handed molecules, which throws a chemical monkey wrench into the whole process.

As soil temperatures rise in the spring and plants start growing rapidly, they need more nutrients from the soil solution, and the cation exchange capacity doles them out. Warmer temperatures also stimulate the growth of a whole range of soil microbes, such as nitrogen-fixing bacteria. These little guys live on the roots of legumes—a class of plants that includes beans and peas. You may remember from high school chemistry that nitrogen comprises four-fifths of the atmosphere and that a nitrogen molecule is N_2, or two nitrogen atoms linked strongly together. Nitrogen-fixing bacteria have found a way to move an electron or two around and unhook the bond that unites the two

THE BENEFITS OF GOOD SOIL

In the not so distant past, people used to ingest beneficial soil- and plant-based microbes with the food they ate—food once grown in rich, unpolluted soil. During the past fifty years, however, our soil has been sterilized with pesticides and herbicides, destroying bacteria, both good and bad. Our modern lifestyle, which includes antibiotics, chlorinated water, agricultural chemicals, pollution, and a poor diet, is responsible for eradicating many of the important beneficial microorganisms in our bodies. Researchers have recently discovered that microorganisms found in soil influence the maturation of the immune system. Our lack of connection with these organisms through soil may be the reason why many allergies, bowel diseases, and immune disorders, as well as chronic fatigue syndrome, are now reaching epidemic proportions.

Source: *Better Nutrition*, October 2003

nitrogen atoms—like taking apart one of those metal Chinese puzzles. The free nitrogen atoms then combine with oxygen to form nitrates, and the nitrates feed the beans and peas. It's a neat, symbiotic arrangement that costs the farmer or gardener nothing.

If, however, you fertilize your soil with chemical nitrogen fertilizer manufactured in a factory using costly fossil fuel (and lots of it), the soil becomes flooded with nitrogen, which turns off the nitrogen-fixing bacteria permanently. You end up destroying a free, natural system and replacing it with a costly, pollution-causing system for which you pay dearly. And yet this kind of wasteful substitution of industrial chemicals for natural processes happens all the time on factory farms.

To put it simply, compost feeds plants what they need, in forms they like, at just the rate they require. And nature is just full of simple cycles and processes like that.

Farming without Agricultural Chemicals

Chemical fertilizers, herbicides, insecticides, fungicides, nematocides—there are thousands of agricultural chemicals that fall into these categories, and a few others as well.

According to the Environmental Protection Agency, 60 percent of all herbicides, 90 percent of all fungicides, and 30 percent of all insecticides are carcinogenic. The organic grower avoids using any chemicals that can harm people, the environment, or the ecology of the diverse creatures that are a part of it. Organic food is also free from genetically modified organisms, hormones, and antibiotics. Land can—and is—being farmed all over the world quite well without these substances.

Importantly for the cook, organic food is thrifty. That's not a reference to the cost of production—*thrifty* is a grower's term that means the plant or animal is well-built, sturdy, and compact, without a lot of weak, watery, excessive growth or spindliness. Thrifty plants and animals are healthy because they get the care and nutrition that they require. Plants have proper color and well-developed roots from being grown in healthy soil fertilized with composted plant and animal residues. Animals are lively and lean without being scrawny; their health derives from eating a nutritious diet of plants raised within this natural system. For people, a healthy diet consists of organic grains, vegetables, fruits, nuts, fish, cheeses, milk, and meat that are all raised within the natural system.

The organic grower works within this system to strengthen and intensify it for the betterment of the crops. This leads to ecological diversity, among other benefits. The more participants in the growing system, the healthier the system becomes. One reason that organic growers can do without chemical pesticides is that a naturally occurring mix of insects will include beneficial insects and other animals that feed on pests. Surviving pests target weak and sick plants first, just as a pack of wolves targets a weak or sick animal. This culls the crop, and the strong, healthy plants persevere and reproduce. The surviving healthy, organically grown plants tend to resist pests and diseases, just as healthy human beings resist diseases. One definition of health, after all, is freedom from illness.

Without pests, what would the beneficial insects eat? Without beneficial insects, who would pollinate the crops? Without compost plowed into the soil, what would the earthworms eat? Without earthworms, what would nourish the plants? Without the plants, what would the pests eat? The interwoven web of life forms circles within circles, great and small, that add up to health and—in the case of organic food—good eating.

Similarly, organic growers can do without fungicides. Organically amended soil is so thoroughly colonized by beneficial microorganisms that a fungus—or a disease-causing organism of any kind—often finds the competition too tough to gain a foothold. A myriad of other little creatures destroy it or hold it in check, multiplying and causing problems for it.

Most herbicides target weeds with broad leaves; grasses such as corn and wheat are left with a free field in which to grow. (Much genetic engineering has been devoted to making them able to

WHY PAY MORE FOR ORGANIC FOOD?

On a large organic farm, broccoli may be interplanted with other crops, such as onions and spinach, to confuse broccoli-loving pests as they search for their favorite food. And some crops planted in the fall to winter over may be plowed under in the spring rather than harvested, in order to enrich the soil for the broccoli. On conventional farms, huge fields of broccoli require pesticides to prevent infestation by broccoli-loving pests and herbicides to keep down competition from weeds.

A local producer of organic chickens must pay a premium for organic grain to feed the birds and then provide them with access to fresh air and sunshine. Contrast this with a conventional farm, where chickens are crowded into cramped spaces and fed antibiotics to prevent disease.

Organic food is grown—and delivered to stores—with great care. This takes more time, and time is money. That's why the cost of organic food is higher. Conventional food has many hidden costs that we pay for in other ways, however. Toxic chemicals harm the environment and cause human illness. With organic food, there are no hidden costs—only benefits.

grow in the presence of toxic herbicides.) This creates a monoculture: a single type of plant over broad acreage—and a feast for pests specific to that plant type. Organic growers deal with weeds by tillage and by interplanting crops with many other crops. This confuses pests. Instead of finding a field filled with its favorite dinner, a pest must search in order to destroy, and the level of destruction is therefore much lower.

Conventional Agriculture

Choosing organic food creates benefits in two directions. In one direction, the choice supports sustainable and beneficial farming practices that protect the environment and make for healthier, more varied, and tastier food. In the opposite direction, the dollars spent on organic produce do *not* support some pretty terrifying developments in conventional agriculture. Although nonorganic (conventional) farming is said to provide more food to people at lower prices, the practice poses various hazards.

GENETIC ENGINEERING

We're constantly being reassured by the biotech industry that genetically modified crops are safe and represent a boon to mankind. But experience gives us pause.

One genetic engineering technique causes new plant varieties to develop at evolutionary hyperspeed, which allows farmers to select for more "efficient" crop varieties faster than ever before. This technique is accomplished by splicing genes that cause colon cancer in humans into a plant's DNA, where they cause a chain of mutations that can produce thousands of mutated offspring very quickly. The offspring are then screened for useful characteristics.

Once these genetically modified varieties of plants (called genetically modified organisms, GMOs, or just GMs) are introduced into a crop, their dispersion is hard to control, as their pollen can spread and pollinate non-GMO plants, turning their offspring into GMOs. Genetically modified corn was inadvertently harvested along with soybeans for human consumption in Nebraska in 2001. That corn contained a gene to produce aprotinin, which belongs to a class of substances called trypsin inhibitors, known to cause pancreatic disease when fed to animals. It also acts as an insecticide, which made the corn poisonous to insects.

In a separate incident, a strain of genetically altered corn that contaminated soybeans in Nebraska was found to produce a glycoprotein found on the surface of two strains of HIV and the closely-related simian immunodeficiency virus. Injection of the glycoprotein into the brain of rats has been shown to kill brain cells, while injection into the human blood stream results in the death of white blood cells.

The U.S. government ordered this corn crop destroyed, but a day after that order was given, it was discovered that the biotech company that had developed the corn had contaminated an additional 155 acres of corn in Iowa. That, too, was ordered destroyed. "This is just the tip of the iceberg," reads a report on the incident by Dr. Mae-Wan Ho of the UK-based Institute of Science in Society. "The true extent of the contamination remains unknown owing to the secrecy surrounding more than 300 field trials of such crops since 1991. The chemicals these plants produce include vaccines, growth hormones, clotting agents, industrial enzymes, human antibodies, contraceptives, immune-suppressive cytokines and abortion-inducing drugs."

One of the leading developers in GMO crops and other agricultural chemicals is a company called Monsanto. Monsanto sells dairy farmers a hormone that greatly increases cows' capacity to produce milk. An international committee has found that this genetically engineered bovine growth hormone (rBGH) may produce chemicals in the cows' milk that could cause breast or prostate cancer in humans who drink the milk (see Dangers in Conventional Dairy Products, page 257).

It's becoming harder and harder to get away from genetically modified crops. Corn, soybeans, and canola seeds available for sale to American farmers may have genetically modified seeds mixed in with them, according to a study released February 23, 2004, by the Union of Concerned Scientists, an independent, nonprofit alliance of more than one hundred thousand concerned citizens and scientists that augments rigorous scientific analysis with citizen advocacy in order to evolve a healthier environment. Transgenic DNA contamination was found in 0.05 to 1 percent of the seeds studied. Those proportions indicate that as much as 6,250 tons of genetically modified seeds entered the U.S. food supply without proper labeling that year. One genetically modified variety, Star Link corn, which has been banned for human consumption, was found in more than 1 percent of samples of corn for human consumption submitted by growers and grain handlers in 2003–2004.

Meanwhile, the use of genetically modified crops has increased the use of pesticides—the direct result of genetically engineered crops that can better withstand them. In *Impacts of Genetically Engineered Crops on Pesticide Use in the United States: The First Eight Years,* a November 2003 report for Ag BioTech InfoNet, a watchdog organization, Charles M. Benbrook wrote, "Herbicide tolerant crops have increased pesticide use an estimated 70 million pounds...[and t]otal pesticide use has risen some 50.6 million pounds over the eight-year period studied."

China, Zambia, India, and the European Union (EU) refuse to import genetically modified foods from the United States. The EU has even passed a labeling law requiring that all genetically modified foods must be so labeled. In the United States, however, the situation is just the oppposite: the government has refused to allow the labeling of genetically modified foods as such. However, when foods carry a USDA (United States Despartment of Agriculture) organic seal or are certified organic by another legitimate certifying agency, you can be assured that they do not contain genetically modified foodstuffs.

HERBICIDES

Herbicide manufacturers assure us that their products are safe if used as directed. But news reports and scientific studies raise doubts.

For example, an herbicide called Roundup is 41 percent glyphosate weed killer and 15 percent "inert ingredient," identified as polyoxyethylene amine (POEA), which acts as a detergent, allowing the glyphosate to penetrate the waxy surfaces of leaves more easily. (The rest of the ingredients are undisclosed.) Japanese physicians investigating fifty-six cases of Roundup poisoning found that POEA is three times more lethal to humans than glyphosate, according to the *Lancet*, a British medical journal.

To increase sales of Roundup, Monsanto has developed "Roundup-Ready Lettuce": lettuce genetically modified to withstand applications of the company's glyphosate weed killer. Yet those herbicides aren't doing the environment—or us—any good. Herbicides may emasculate wild male frogs, according to *Science News*. And men living in rural areas have significantly lower-quality sperm than men living in urban areas, most likely due to exposure to herbicides and fertilizers, according to the National Institute of Environmental Health Sciences. And it's not only males whose reproductive functions can be compromised.

Herbicides are ubiquitous: they evaporate and contaminate moisture in the air. Herbicides occur in rainfall all around the world. In Canada, the herbicide 2,4-D was found in rainfall at levels potentially harmful to plants. The bottom line may be good for Monsanto's Roundup, but it doesn't look so good for the rest of us.

ANTIBIOTIC-RESISTANT PATHOGENS

The widespread routine use of antibiotics in animal husbandry results in antibiotic-resistant strains of pathogens. In fact, disease-causing bacteria may be evolving more quickly than scientists can develop the drugs we need to fight them. For example, antibiotic-resistant strains of bacteria found in meat, such as salmonella and campylobacter, are beginning to appear.

A Minneapolis study by the Institute for Agriculture and Trade Policy found that 95 percent of supermarket chickens tested were contaminated with campylobacter and 45 percent of ground turkey was contaminated with salmonella. About 60 percent of each of these bacteria, which can cause infections in humans, were found to be resistant to one or more antibiotics, including ciprofloxacin and tetracycline. According to *WebMD*, the online medical information site, "Antibiotic resistance in chickens is caused by the widespread practice of putting antibiotics in feed to make them grow more quickly or prevent illness."

A 2002 investigation by *Consumer Reports* tested 484 whole broiler chickens from twenty-five cities around the country; it found nearly half of them to be contaminated by salmonella or campylobacter. Investigators also found that 90 percent of the campylobacter and 34 percent of the salmonella showed resistance to at least one antibiotic usually used to treat people. "There is a growing consensus among the medical community that we have a problem with antibiotic resistance, and that we don't need to use antibiotics that are commonly used to treat humans in animal production," a spokesperson for the Institute for Agricultural Trade Policy told *WebMD Medical News*, which reported on the study when it came out. (If an agricultural trade group is admitting that, you can bet it's an understatement.)

The routine use of antibiotics is not allowed in organic animal husbandry—in fact, if an animal is treated with antibiotics to cure an illness or save its life, the animal may not be labeled organic until it has recovered and the antibiotics are out of its system.

PESTICIDES

Pesticides are ubiquitous around the world. Swiss researchers found that much of Europe's rainwater is so contaminated with pesticides it would be illegal to sell it as drinking water, according to the Summer 1999 issue of *Analytical Chemistry*. But Europe is relatively clean compared with the United States. America is awash in pesticides. In the year 2000 alone, nearly one billion pounds of pesticides were sprayed, dusted, or dumped on America's farmlands and orchards. And this assault continues. About 20 percent of the U.S. food supply is contaminated with toxins from pesticide residues, according to the November 2002 issue of the *Journal of Epidemiology and Community Health*.

Many pesticides accumulate in fatty tissues, such as that found in female breasts. Women with breast cancer were found to be more than five times as likely as cancer-free women to have detectable levels of the pesticide DDT in their blood and more than nine times as likely to have detectable levels of another estrogen-modulating pesticide, hexachlorobenzene, according to a study of 409 women done at Belgium's Sart Tilman University Hospital. DDT has been banned in the United States since 1972, but because its residues are stored in body fat, it can remain in the body for decades. It is one of the organochlorine pesticides known as hormone disrupters. Exposure to these chemicals has been implicated in birth defects, immune disorders, and certain cancers.

There probably isn't a person in the United States who doesn't carry some pesticides in his or her body. That includes children who, because of their less-developed immune systems, developing bodies, and lower body weights, are more susceptible than adults to the effects of toxic pesticides.

A 2005 study by the Environmental Working Group showed an average of 287 contaminants in samples of umbilical cord blood provided by the American Red Cross: human fetuses are beginning life in a stew of toxic chemicals. Among the 287 contaminants were mercury, fire retardants, pesticides, and perfluorooctanoic acid (PFOA), a chemical used in the manufacture of Teflon.

In a full-page ad in the *New York Times* on June 5, 2002, physicians at the Center for Children's Health and the Environment of the Mount Sinai School of Medicine in New York City said, in part:

> We are deeply troubled that an estimated twelve million American kids suffer from developmental, learning, or behavioral disabilities. Attention deficit disorder affects three to six percent of our schoolchildren.... [C]ertain pesticides cross the placenta and enter the brain of the developing fetus where they can cause learning and behavioral disabilities.... Exposures to organophosphate pesticides during pregnancy can result in abnormally low brain weight and developmental impairment.... A University of Arizona study found that children exposed to a combination of pesticides before birth and through breast milk exhibited less stamina, and poorer memory and coordination, than other kids.... There is much that parents can do to protect their children, beginning with the elimination of many pesticides both outside and in the home. And [through] the choice of a wise diet.
>
> (For more information, see www.childenvironment.org.)

How bad is the problem of pesticide accumulation in our bodies? In May 2004, the Pesticide Action Network North America released a national study called *Chemical Trespass: Pesticides in Our Bodies and Corporate Accountability*. The study found that children between the ages of six and eleven years old were exposed to the nerve-damaging pesticide chlorpyrifos at four times the level deemed acceptable by the Environmental Protection Agency (EPA). The

TWENTY FOODS YOU SHOULD BUY IN ORGANIC FORM

Here are twenty common foods and the problems associated with them that should compel the wise buyer to look for them in organic form.

1. **APPLES:** pesticide and fungicide residues
2. **BEEF:** growth hormones, routine use of antibiotics, poor conditions in feedlots, excessive fat from grain feeding before slaughter, possibility of mad cow disease
3. **BELL PEPPERS:** pesticide residues
4. **CARROTS:** pesticide and fungicide residues
5. **CELERY:** pesticide and fungicide residues
6. **CHERRIES:** pesticide residues
7. **CHICKEN:** inhumane conditions during growth and slaughter, bacterial contamination, routine use of antibiotics
8. **CITRUS:** pesticide residues
9. **COFFEE:** exploitative worker conditions, negative environmental impact on plantations: loss of bird and animal habitat, damage to soils
10. **CORN:** genetic modifications, herbicide use, damage to topsoil, pesticide residues
11. **EGGS:** inhumane conditions for the birds, routine use of antibiotics
12. **GRAPES (IMPORTED):** pesticide and fungicide residues
13. **MILK:** use of bovine growth hormone, routine use of antibiotics
14. **NECTARINES:** pesticide and fungicide residues
15. **PEACHES:** pesticide and fungicide residues
16. **PEARS:** pesticide and fungicide residues
17. **POTATOES:** pesticide and fungicide residues
18. **RASPBERRIES (RED):** pesticide and fungicide residues
19. **SPINACH:** pesticide residues
20. **STRAWBERRIES:** pesticide residues

report also said that women carry significantly higher levels than those the EPA considers acceptable of pesticides called organochlorines, which are known to reduce birth weight and disrupt brain development in infants.

Scientists have compared pesticide residues in the tissues of kids eating a conventional diet and those eating mostly organic food. In 2003, one such study by a team of scientists at the University of Washington School of Public Health and Community Medicine found that children on a conventional diet had 8.5 times higher average levels of organophosphate pesticide metabolites in their urine than children eating a mostly organic diet. The researchers concluded that "consumption of organic produce represents a relatively simple means for parents to reduce their children's exposure to pesticides."

CONVENTIONAL ANIMAL FARMING

The fact that organic meat animals are raised humanely would be reason enough for most compassionate people to eat organically. But there are still plenty of other reasons to purchase organic meat.

Ninety percent of all nonorganic beef raised in the United States contains up to six growth hormones that are banned in Europe because of health concerns. One of those hormones, 17 beta-estradiol, is considered "a complete carcinogen" by the European Union's Scientific Committee on Veterinary Measures relating to Public Health. According to its 2002, 139-page report, all of the hormones "may cause a variety of health problems, including cancer, developmental problems, harm to immune systems, and brain disease. Even exposure to small levels of residues in meat and meat products carries risks." As a result, the Europen Union refuses to import most American beef.

Dr. Samuel Epstein, a professor of environmental medicine at the University of Illinois, told the *Los Angeles Times*, "The question we ought to be asking is not why Europe won't buy our hormone-treated meat, but why we allow beef from hormone-treated cattle to be sold to American and Canadian consumers." The U.S. secretary of agriculture, however, called the EU report "unsubstantiated."

IRRADIATED FOOD

It seemed like such a good idea: bombard food with nuclear radiation and all microorganisms within the foodstuff die. No microorganisms, no possibility of spoilage as long as the container remains unopened. Proponents of food irradiation claim that irradiation leaves no residue in the food. But the reason why nuclear waste (the substance used to irradiate food) kills pathogens—or any other living creature exposed to sufficiently high doses of it—is that its streams of radioactive particles literally tear molecules and atoms apart, leaving all sorts of residues, including free radicals that can cause cardiovascular disease and cancer. Radioactive bombardment of foodstuffs also alters DNA and RNA in the foods' cells and creates a whole range of toxic substances—formaldehyde and formic

MAD COW DISEASE NOT FOUND IN ORGANIC BEEF

The discovery of cows infected with mad cow disease in the Pacific Northwest in recent years focused a huge amount of attention on the problem. But people who eat only organic beef need not worry.

Cattle are fed bovine body parts to increase their dietary protein levels. When those beef parts are infected with bovine spongiform encephalopathy (BSE)—mad cow disease—it is recycled into the cattle's food supply. Infected beef can then spread the disease to humans who consume the infected beef. But organic rules prohibit feeding bovine body parts to bovines: organically raised beef has no potential for spreading BSE to humans.

In addition, organic beef is fully traceable: from the market meat case all the way back to the animal's mother and the plot of land it was raised on. Traceability for conventional beef production is sketchy at best.

"The green-and-white USDA organic seal may be little, but it carries a big message: the organic product being purchased is fully traceable, has passed rigorous inspections, and, in the case of organic beef, has never been fed any animal by-products in any form," says Katherine DiMatteo, executive director of the Organic Trade Association, the business association representing the now nearly $20 billion organics industry in North America.

Organic beef must come from animals raised organically from three months prior to birth. In other words, organic beef is born from animals that have received organic feed from at least the last third of gestation.

The organic production system provides traceability of each animal from birth to sale of the resulting meat. Each cut of organic meat and meat by-product can be traced back to its origin. If there were ever a question about the safety of an organic meat product, removal from the food supply would be swift and efficient.

The guiding philosophy of organic production is to provide conditions that meet the needs and natural behavior of the animal. Thus, organic livestock are given access to the outdoors, fresh air, water, sunshine, grass and pasture, and are fed 100 percent organic feed.

Other practices allowed in conventional beef production are forbidden in the organic system, including using plastic pellets for roughage, formulas containing manure or urea, antibiotics, and growth hormones.

acid among them—from what started out as perfectly wholesome and edible substances. No irradiated food can legally be sold as organic.

Had enough? These items are just a handful among literally thousands of news stories, scientific reports, magazine articles, and books, all describing the dangers and decrying the abuses of chemical and biotech agriculture. Many more studies and news reports are posted daily on the Organic Consumers Association Web site (www. organicconsumers. org). This advocacy group is well worth investigating if you are interested in the on-going struggle over the safety and cleanliness of our food supply.

And Now for Some Good News...

American agriculture is a huge business and, like most businesses, does what it must to protect itself from critics, especially lawmakers who would institute rules that would cost it money. But change—though slower than many would like—is happening.

The U.S. Congress now has an Organic Agriculture Caucus, currently chaired by Representative Sam Farr, Democrat of California. It was Farr who authored the nation's first organic standards, the California Organic Foods Act of 1990, which became a model for the USDA standards. In 2002, North Dakota State Senator Bill Bowman, a Republican, introduced legislation to allow farmers to sue biotechnology companies if their genetically modified wheat contaminates farmers' conventional or organic crops.

Americans are not just knuckling under to the GMO lobbyists. In 2003, the city council of Vedic City, Iowa, unanimously passed a resolution making it illegal to sell genetically modified or nonorganic food within the city limits.

Meanwhile, in Europe, the EU Agriculture Council has agreed that no unlabeled genetically modified products will be allowed into the EU market. All genetically modified food, food ingredients, and animal feeds—including sugars, refined oils, and starches produced from GMOs—must be clearly labeled. Another regulation sets up a traceability system for food and food ingredients consisting of, containing, or produced from GMOs across all stages of food delivery, from farm to processor to market. "No GMOs can enter the European market unlabeled," said Lorenzo Consoli, Greenpeace adviser on GMOs. "This sends a strong message to commodity exporting nations such as the United States of America, Canada, Argentina, and Brazil: the times when you could sneak millions of tons of GM soybeans and corn unlabeled into the food chain are definitely over."

ORGANICS HAS ITS OWN CONGRESSIONAL CAUCUS

The Congressional Organic Agriculture Caucus, which held its initial meeting in Washington, DC, on April 10, 2003, was formed as a bipartisan association of United States representatives to "enhance availability and understanding of information related to the production and processing of organic agricultural products."

At its formation, it included sixteen Democrats, five Republicans, and one Independent. It has since ballooned to thirty-one Democrats and eight Republicans. "Organics is one of the fastest growing sectors in agriculture," said Sam Farr, its chairperson. "With new organic standards now in effect, consumers are demanding greater availability and farmers are seeking solutions to their organic production problems. This caucus will give us the chance to discuss ways of enhancing the standards to make them workable for producers and consumers."

"The formation of this caucus is a major step towards getting organic farmers their fair share of federal agricultural resources," notes Bob Scowcroft, executive director of the Organic Farming Research Foundation, based in Santa Cruz, California. "Organic farmers and their supporters should call their representatives and ask them to join the caucus. When it comes to Capitol Hill, there is strength in numbers."

For the current makeup of the caucus, visit the Organic Farming Research Foundation Web site (www.ofrf.org).

Genetically modified foods are still not allowed to be labeled as such in the United States. United Natural Foods, one of the largest wholesale distributors of organic foods in the United States, sponsors the Campaign to Label Genetically Engineered Foods. Its purpose: to pressure Congress and the president to pass and sign legislation that will require the labeling of GM foods in this country. If you're interested in aiding this cause, visit the campaign's Web site (www.thecampaign.org).

There's no doubt that the production of organic foods is exploding. In 2001, worldwide sales of organic food reached $26 billion. It's estimated to reach $80 billion by 2008. Europe is leading the global push. Germany's goal is to make 20 percent of its farmland organic by 2010. Belgium, Holland, and Wales are shooting for 10 percent by then, and Italy and other countries aren't far behind.

Organic farmland in the United States doubled in area in just five years, between 1997 and 2002, and current organic acreage in the U.S. is over 560,000 acres. In 2002, the USDA's National Organic Program issued strict

CALIFORNIA COUNTY BANS GMO CROPS

Mendocino County voters have always been in the forefront of food health issues. In the 1970s, they adopted an initiative to ban aerial spraying of pesticides—but within two weeks, the state legislature stripped counties of the right to institute such a ban.

Three decades later, on Tuesday, March 2, 2004, Mendocino County, California, became the first county in the nation to ban genetically engineered crops and animals by passing a ballot measure sponsored by the county's organic farmers. This time, agriculture officials began to enforce the ban the day after voters approved it.

A consortium of the country's largest agribusiness interests calling itself CropLife America had spent $500,000 on a two-month campaign to defeat the measure, fearing it could set a precedent. But a coalition of organic grape growers, businesses, and local political figures, which spent only about $70,000 on an educational campaign, convinced voters that they should take a stand against genetically modified crops.

CropLife's fears were well founded: environmental groups in neighboring Sonoma and Humboldt counties immediately began preparing drives to qualify similar initiatives on the November 2004 ballot. Those initiatives were defeated, but there are plans to reintroduce them—and expose the falsehoods advanced by CropLife, which was supported by local and state farm bureau leaders and members of the county's conventional agricultural establishment as well.

But there is good news. Supporters of the GMO ban are prepared for an assault on the ban by agribusiness. "We've had this ordinance reviewed by top lawyers, who say they're confident it will stand up to any challenge," said initiative spokesperson Laura Hamburg. And CropLife appears to have given up in Mendocino County. That ban stands.

rules for foods that can be given the department's organic seal. From a one-page flyer called "Organic Gardening in a Nutshell" distributed by the thousands in the 1970s, the rules for organic agriculture have ballooned to sixty-three pages of government regulations covering every aspect of organic food production. What started in 1990 as the Organic Foods Production Act, sponsored by Senator Patrick Leahy of Vermont, has turned into a program of nationwide rules defining organics and issuing seals of certification. Unfortunately, many small farmers are being left out, as big corporations, hand in hand with the USDA's huge bureaucracy, move forward to fill supermarket shelves with organic versions of everything from fresh vegetables to junk food.

Organic Certification: Large vs. Small Producers

The original goal of organic farming was to create sustainable local agriculture. Consumers would know and trust the farmers; farms would protect the environment; supply lines from farm to table would be short. (The average distance food travels from farm to plate in America is 1,300 miles). Certification agencies like Oregon Tilth, California Certified Organic Farmers, and Northeast Organic Farming Association began as regional groups dedicated to assuring the authenticity of local, seasonal organic foods. Today, certification agencies like Quality Assurance International in America and EcoCert in Europe are global in scope. Linda Baker, writing in the online journal *Salon* on July 29, 2002, described an American certification agent for EcoCert who found himself in Japan inspecting a food processor who was importing soybeans from China to process into goods for export to Europe. "Isn't this a little bizarre, a little...unsustainable?" he commented.

He was right. The expenditure of fossil fuels to move foods over long distances and fly certification agents around the world is expensive—and the cost of certification reflects this. It is not sustainable as environmentalists think of that term.

The idea of sustainability had its genesis in a 1910 book, *Farmers of Forty Centuries*, which describes how Chinese truck farms near large cities recycled every scrap of organic matter—including night soil—through composting processes. By doing so, the farms remained fertile and productive, year after year, for forty centuries. Sustainability became a goal of the organic movement as it developed in the 1950s and 1960s. If food production were kept local and organic wastes were captured and recycled, the terrible destruction of America's topsoil that was then occurring (and continues on conventional farms) could be halted and reversed.

For my part, I started something called the National Soil Fertility Program in the mid-1970s. It aimed to have the USDA identify all the sources of compostables in America and steer them to composting centers for eventual return to the land. I remember importuning the Texas commissioner of agriculture as he left a meeting in Washington, DC. I wanted to hand him information about the program. He refused the pamphlet and brushed me aside, saying, "I'm not interested in that[expletive][expletive]."

A deep conflict has arisen between the big organic producers who ship food globally and small, local farmers who find the cost of complying with the USDA and paying for certification prohibitive. (Some organic certifiers, like the New Jersey–based Northeast Organic Farming Association, charge on a sliding scale. Small farms are charged a few hundred dollars to be certified and large ones, a few thousand plus a percentage of sales.)

In addition, many feel that now that the government is involved in defining what's organic, the race to lower standards is on. But unless organic standards are kept strict, the term *organic* will become meaningless as more and more compromises are made. And the lower standards will not apply only to the USDA's National Organic Standards—they will apply to every certification agency in the country.

The enabling legislation is written so that no local group—such as the Maine Organic Farmers and Gardeners Association or California Certified Organic Farmers—may impose stricter standards than those imposed by the USDA. By contrast, most federal safety regulations set minimum standards. The Consumer Product Safety Commission, for instance, encourages manufacturers of products covered by its regulations to exceed federal standards and promote themselves to consumers for doing so.

Many small organic farmers smell a rat—including Bill Duesing, president of the Northeast Organic Farming

USDA BACKS DOWN ON ORGANIC RULE CHANGES

Big agriculture never stops trying to chip away at the national standards for what constitutes organically grown food. One recent attempt came in April 2004, when officials in the National Organic Program and Agricultural Marketing Service—both agencies within the USDA—released changes to the federal organic standards. The changes included expanding the use of antibiotics and hormones in dairy cows, allowing the use of more pesticides and, for the first time, letting organic livestock eat potentially contaminated fishmeal. Administrators of the National Organic Program also said seafood, pet food, and body care products could use the word *organic* on their labels without meeting any standards at all. These "Statements of Clarification" were issued without any public input.

The outcry against these "clarifications" from the public, Congress, the National Organic Standards Board, Consumers Union, media outlets, and many other organizations and individuals around the country was so great that within a month, Secretary of Agriculture Ann Veneman rescinded the changes. She said the USDA was "awestruck at the size and the fury of the protest" against watering down organic standards in favor of nonorganic agribusiness practices.

The moral of this incident is that agribusiness will continue to try to dismantle the nation's organic standards and that the USDA can't be counted on to prevent it. Only the organic community—large and strong and growing stronger—can. Be watchful.

Association Interstate Council, which includes chapters in Connecticut, Massachusetts, New York, New Jersey, Rhode Island, Vermont, and New Hampshire:

> In the long run, the USDA may so debase the meaning of "organic" that growers won't want to be involved unless they grow for markets—like big stores or processors—that specifically require the USDA seal. The federal takeover of organic presents a very large challenge: to define and communicate the values important to Northeast Organic Farming Association members but aren't addressed in the federal standards—local eating, family farms, low and solar energy use, labor issues, polyculture, sustainability, connection to community, knowledge, and control. Although it would be good if all food were grown organically, that still won't address these important issues if we just end up with industrial organic food, which continues to put great distance between growers and eaters while increasing ignorance in the general population about our relationship with the earth.
>
> —Bill Duesing

In the UK, by way of contrast, the Soil Association's organic standards are stricter than those in the United States: farmers can't use peat moss for fear of destroying the environment, and they can't use dried blood because it's too high in nitrogen. For years the British have worried that transporting food long distances—or "excessive food-miles"—will damage the environment.

Patrick Martins, the former head of Slow Food USA, has long been an active communicator about this situation. He wrote the following in *The Snail*, Slow Food's newsletter:

> One word that has been totally lost by the people who created it is the word *organic*. Slow Food USA hopes we can soon return to a purer definition of the word—not a federal definition, but one that embodies the ideas of sustainability, preserving the land, and preserving the small independent family farm. With many Americans now demanding organic foods, huge factory farms have been quick to churn out products to accommodate. But are these foods what Americans are really clamoring for? While organic factory foods do fall under the umbrella of the new federal standards, we choose to support foods and companies that fit a more holistic definition of the word *organic*: one that embodies an ethic that doesn't exist on factory farms. This ethic is not motivated

by profit, but by taste—a love of food.... [We are] asking Americans to think about what *organic* means to them—is it a formula or a philosophy? The future of our planet depends on the answer.

As large corporations move into organic agriculture, many small farmers are seeking ways to avoid the paperwork that comes along with federally regulated organic certification. "Certification is only necessary when you're not dealing directly with the consumer," according to Rose Koenig, a member of the National Organic Standards Board, the group that drew up the definition of what's organic and what's not for the USDA. Some organic farmers who do deal directly with consumers through farmers' markets and Community Supported Agriculture are resorting to terms such as *pesticide free, natural,* or *authentic* to describe their produce—rather than *organic*—simply because by labeling their food organic without certification, they risk a $10,000 fine.

For most purchasers of organic food, the most visible aspect of this wrangling is the emergence of the USDA's green and white organic seal. But that seal can actually be used on products that are only 95 percent organic. John Fromer, an organic farmer who operates Appleton Ridge Flower & Vegetable Farm in Appleton, Maine, quips, "What's the other five percent? Heavy

IS IT TRULY ORGANIC? FROM A BIG FARM OR SMALL FARM? LOCALLY PRODUCED?

If a product is given the little circular green label that reads "USDA Organic," you can bet it's organic and has been certified as such by a recognized certifying agency. If a food isn't labeled at all, and you are unsure if it's organic, ask the person who runs the market to show you some paperwork that guarantees the product's status.

There are three types of sellers at a farmers' market: organic producers, conventional producers, and purveyors. Organic producers will know the variety of fruit or vegetable they are selling, what they did to protect it organically against pests and weeds, and how they improve their soil. Conventional producers will know the variety but won't be able to give you much if any information about organic pest and weed control. A purveyor is someone who buys produce wholesale and sells it retail at a farmers' market. He or she won't know much about the produce. You can always tell if a product is locally produced. Just ask the seller where his or her farm is located and how to get there.

BEWARE OF THE MISLEADING LABEL

Be wary of the label that says, "Earth Friendly, Farm Friendly." According to Chefs Collaborative, an organization of organically-minded professional chefs nationwide, "The label, which professes to be an alternative to the USDA's National Organic Program label, is put out by the Hudson Institute's Center for Global Food Issues. Under the terms of the certification requirements, most conventional dairy practices are acceptable. The label does not have the same standards as the USDA's organic label." The Hudson Institute is a right-wing think tank that grants large sums of money to support conservative causes. The Center for Global Food Issues supports the use of bovine growth hormone. Its director's most recent publication is *Saving the Planet with Pesticides and Plastic.*

metals? It's either one hundred percent organic, or it's not organic."

And although large organic farms can use the seal, that doesn't say anything about freshness. Eliot Coleman, a Maine grower and author of organic gardening books, says, "I don't care if elves and fairies grew it in California, it ain't fresh by the time it gets to Maine."

Coleman avoids certification and the use of the USDA seal altogether in favor of labeling his produce "authentic." But Barbara Haumann, a spokesperson for the Organic Trade Association, thinks creating another word is the wrong way to go. "There is no 'beyond organic,'" she says. "That would totally confuse consumers."

Two others levels of "organic" have been set up under the USDA's National Organic Program. A package can state, "made with organic ingredients," if between 70 and 95 percent of the ingredients are organic, although the USDA organic seal can't be used. And for products containing less than 70 percent organic ingredients, the organic ingredients can be labeled as such only on the ingredients panel.

But the standards set by the USDA's National Organic Program "aid larger farmers and retailers over smaller ones," observes Bob Scowcroft of the Organic Farming Research Foundation. "Wal-Mart is one of the largest purveyors of organic foods in the country. A national standard allows large chain stores to buy year-round from many states and sources according to the same standard."

On the other hand, national standards—and the certification fees they engender—also provide funding for organics-related research. In a press advisory dated April 16, 2004, Scowcroft wrote that in a historic development, the USDA had announced

LABEL LINGO: WHAT *LOCAL, ORGANIC,* AND *NATURAL* REALLY (AND OFFICIALLY) MEAN

The word *local* has no official meaning, but usually refers to your foodshed—the region near your home that produces the foods that show up at nearby farmers' markets, and sometimes in large supermarkets. It can be represented by anything from the person who sells a few dozen eggs from his small flock of chickens to a large farm nearby that produces quantities of fruits, vegetables, meat, or milk. Locally produced foods are generally fresher, sold in season, and are often artisanal—but they are not necessarily organic.

Organic is a term defined by law and enforced by the U.S. Department of Agriculture. It guarantees that the food:

- Is produced without the use of toxic agricultural chemicals
- Has no preservatives or other man-made additives
- Has not been genetically engineered
- Is raised humanely
- Has not been treated with antibiotics
- Has not been irradiated

The soil in which the food is grown is improved by composted organic matter and cannot have been amended with sewage sludge. Rules about organic farming were developed by organic farmers themselves. Organic food may be local, artisanal, and seasonal, or it may have been shipped from a large farm thousands of miles away. When foods are local *and* organic, they are at their best.

The term *natural* has no official meaning at all.

the availability of $4.7 million in 2004 and $15 million through 2008 to fund projects designed to enhance the ability of producers and processors to grow and market certified organic food, feed, and fiber products. That the USDA has funded organic agriculture at all shows what a sea change is underway. It's a far cry from the days when I had to conceal my affiliation with *Organic Gardening* in the hallways of the USDA just to get an interview with a plant scientist.

Scowcroft sees two tiers of organic produce developing side by side: the big guys and the family farmers. "In this new organic world, concerns over social justice and the distance the food has traveled lost out; taste and freshness came up as most important with the general organic food–buying public," he says.

"This is going to spread to the entire general public. The taste and freshness possible with artisanal production is the next great wave in food marketing, and it's coming soon to a much larger audience."

Mark Dierkhising agrees. Now the executive chef at Dierk's Parkside Café, a Santa Rosa, California, eatery, he was for many years the executive chef at Sonoma State University in Rohnert Park, California. I asked him whether the kids at the university were asking for organic food. "The student demographic has changed enormously in recent years," he told me. "Kids from Southern California are well traveled, food savvy, and making demands for more sophisticated dishes than just burgers and pizza. We had pizza, of course, but it was made with fresh dough starter, not powdered yeast. We made organic chicken, fresh ocean fish, prepared the way our better restaurants here in Sonoma County prepare them. But it wasn't just the kids," he noted. "Everyone demanded better organic food—the kids, the faculty, the staff, and the workers."

The good qualities of organic food are being brought to the attention of larger audiences through marketing orders, which are essentially a tax on growers and producers of specific commodities used to advertise those commodities to the general public. The "Got Milk?" campaign was the result of the marketing order levied by the dairy industry, which spent hundreds of millions of dollars to keep milk at the forefront of American consciousness through print and TV commercials.

The Organic Farming Research Foundation's Scowcroft says that in the 1980s, the Table Grape Commission used marketing-order money to savage the notion of organic table grapes. Steve Pavich, a large California organic grower, was forced to pay into a fund used to denounce his own growing method. But now that large companies and big agriculture are going organic, much more money can be garnered from them than from small family farmers to promote organic food.

Scowcroft calls the USDA's $15 million for organic agriculture research—0.1 percent of its research budget, according to some estimates—"a drop in the bucket compared with conventional chemical agriculture." But all in all, he is sanguine. "It's a start," he adds. "Still, it's obscene that land-grant colleges—the big agricultural schools—don't do more organic research."

Current Research

When I went to *Organic Gardening* magazine from the Allentown, Pennsylvania, newspaper I wrote for, I was still in investigative mode. The magazine was great at telling people how to compost and grow tomatoes, but not much had been done to see whether there was a firm scientific base under the

TWO WAYS FOR BIG ORGANIC TO MARKET LOCALLY

One way to market organic milk is to do what Horizon Organic has done: create large dairies several places in the country and move the milk to stores from there. It uses ultrapasteurization to prolong shelf life, but that destroys enzymes and "cooks" the milk. Another way is to do what Organic Valley has done: form a co-op of 1,010 farmer-owners that produce certified organic milk, cheese, butter, spreads, creams, eggs, produce, juice, and meats. The products are sold locally. The farmers in the co-op benefit from the overall marketing effort and publicity that the Organic Valley brand generates. George Siemon gets the credit for developing this idea, which supports family farming and rural communities as it protects the environment. To learn more, visit Organic Valley's Web site (www.organicvalley.com).

organic method. Over the next ten years, I read books and research papers on soil science, entomology, molecular biology, mycology, ecology, plant pathogens, and other agricultural and horticultural sciences and discovered, to my surprise, that there was a ton of information supporting the basic tenets of the organic method—and even expanding them into unforeseen areas. I was never at a loss for subjects for the articles I wrote.

Such scientific research continues today and bears on organic agriculture. The more mainstream organic becomes, the more research gets underway. Here are just three from among dozens and dozens of studies I unearthed in a recent survey of ongoing organic research at large universities.

- At Michigan State University, a Department of Entomology study carries the title *Safeguarding the Supply of Specialty Crops for Consumers*. The goal of the project is to reduce the need for synthetic chemicals in the production of fruit, dry beans, and sugar beets. "We will concentrate on reduced chemical input, good farming practices, and alternative pest control methods," according to the researchers.
- At Cornell University, organic farm and food systems research is underway to develop certifiable organic strategies for controlling weeds and pests in farm crops.
- At North Carolina State University, horticultural researchers are studying farming system sustainability and research support for organic agriculture production. Their goal is to determine the optimal economic and biological strategy for making the transition from conventional to organic production.

RETAIL RULES

The advent of organic foods in supermarkets has created the need for some special rules, defined by the USDA's National Organic Program, about displaying organic and conventional items together.

Large retail chains that carry both organic and conventional produce (such as Whole Foods, Wild Oats, and Albert's Organics) must avoid commingling. Bulk products, such as bins of nuts or oatmeal, baskets of produce, or packaged goods, must be separated by some sort of barrier. There must be an organics-only area of the storage room, separate from the conventional storage area. When boxes have to be stacked on top of one another, the organic boxes should be placed on top so that no falling product or melting ice with pesticide residues can leak into the organic containers. Retailers are even urged to hold on to their empty organic boxes to move organic produce, because as soon as organic produce goes into a conventional box, the produce is considered contaminated and can no longer be sold as organic.

The National Organic Program has also laid down rules for cleaning and prepping organic greens and other produce. The sink basin has to be washed with a cleanser to remove any pesticide residues from conventional food items. Tubs or trays used for storing produce must be thoroughly cleansed as well if they were previously used for conventional items. Prep knives must be cleansed after use on conventional produce before using them on organic produce. In fact, the USDA recommends having separate tubs and knives for organic and conventional produce.

It would be wonderful if these rules were followed and enforced; one wonders how closely they are monitored.

But Is Organic Safe and Healthy?

A telling report by the United Nation's Food and Agriculture Organization (FAO) has a reliable summation of the safety

STICKER SAVVY

You know those annoying little stickers you sometimes find on fruit at the supermarket? They are price-lookup stickers. They're not mandatory and not used in all stores, but they contain some useful information. Conventional produce has a four-digit code. Organic produce has a five-digit code starting with 9. Genetically modified produce has a five-digit code starting with 8.

ORGANIC FOOD NUTRITIONALLY SUPERIOR

Results of a four-year European Union study on the benefits of organic food suggest that fruit, vegetables, and milk are more nutritious than nonorganically produced food and may contain higher concentrations of cancer fighting and heart beneficial antioxidants, according the Medical News Today, November, 2007.

The results suggest that eating organic food is equivalent to eating an extra portion of fruit and vegetables a day, according to the researchers.

Early results of the study show that organic fruit and vegetables have up to 40 percent more antioxidants than nonorganically grown produce. Even greater contrasts were found for milk, with organic milk containing up to 60 percent more antioxidants and healthy fatty acids.

The study was conducted at Newcastle University in the United Kingdom, where researchers raised cattle and grew fruit and vegetables on 725 acres of organic and nonorganic farms situated next to each other. The research project, called Quality Low Input Food (QLIF) project, is funded by the European Union and is the biggest ever to research the pros and cons of organic farming and food.

The study's findings contradict advice by the UK government's Food Standards Agency, which states that organic produce is no healthier than nonorganically produced food. The same claims are made in the United States by the agricultural chemical industry and their associates.

benefits of organic food production. Here are a few excerpts.

Cattle are ruminants naturally meant to eat grass, not grain. But most American cattle are "finished" on grain diets to add fat quickly. Virulent, disease-causing forms of *E. coli* develop in the stomachs of these cattle but not in the rumens of grass-fed cattle. One of the most important goals of organic beef production is keeping the nutrient cycles closed, so the animals are fed diets of hay, grass, and silage. "It can be concluded," the FAO said, "that organic farming potentially reduces the risk of *E. coli* infection."

Aflatoxin is a carcinogen produced by a grain fungus. According to the FAO, "Two studies found that aflatoxin levels in organic milk were lower than in conventional milk. As organically raised livestock are fed greater proportions of hay, grass, and silage, there is reduced opportunity for mycotoxin contaminated feed to lead to mycotoxin contaminated milk." The FAO went on to praise organic agriculture's

TEN GOOD REASONS TO BUY ORGANIC

1. **ORGANIC PRODUCTS MEET STRINGENT STANDARDS.** Organic certification is the public's assurance that products have been grown and handled according to strict procedures, without toxic chemical inputs.

2. **ORGANIC FOOD TASTES GREAT!** It's common sense—well-balanced soils produce strong, healthy plants that become nourishing food for people and animals.

3. **ORGANIC PRODUCTION REDUCES HEALTH RISKS.** Many EPA-approved pesticides were registered long before extensive research linked these chemicals to cancer and other diseases. Organic agriculture is one way to prevent any more of these chemicals from getting into the air, earth, and water that sustain us.

4. **ORGANIC FARMS RESPECT OUR WATER RESOURCES.** The elimination of polluting chemicals and nitrogen leaching, in combination with soil building, protects and conserves water resources.

5. **ORGANIC FARMERS BUILD HEALTHY SOIL.** Soil is the foundation of the food chain. Organic farming uses practices that build healthy soils.

6. **ORGANIC FARMERS WORK IN HARMONY WITH NATURE.** Organic agriculture respects the balance demanded by a healthy ecosystem. Wildlife is sustained by including forage crops in rotation and by retaining fence rows, wetlands, and other natural areas.

7. **ORGANIC PRODUCERS ARE INNOVATORS.** Organic farmers have led the way, largely at their own expense, in on-farm research aimed at reducing pesticide use and minimizing agriculture's impact on the environment.

8. **ORGANIC PRODUCERS STRIVE TO PRESERVE CROP DIVERSITY.** The loss of genetically diverse, open-pollinated crops on our farms is one of the most pressing environmental concerns. Many organic farmers and gardeners have been collecting and preserving heirloom seeds and growing unusual varieties for decades.

9. **ORGANIC FARMING HELPS KEEP RURAL COMMUNITIES VITAL.** The USDA reported that in 1997, half of U.S. farm production came from only 2 percent of farms. Organic agriculture can be a lifeline for small farms because it offers an alternative market where sellers can command fair prices for crops.

10. **PURCHASING ORGANIC PROMOTES THE ABUNDANCE OF ORGANIC FOODS AND NONFOODS ALIKE.** Today, every food category has an organic alternative. And nonfood agricultural products such as wool, linen—even cotton, which most experts felt could not be grown organically—are now being grown in accordance with organic principles.

Source: Organic Trade Association

contributions to cleaner drinking water, biodiversity, indigenous crop recovery, landscape regeneration, and general environmental quality, concluding that it "contributes to sustainable agriculture and therefore has a legitimate place within the UN's sustainable agriculture programs."

SAFER AND HEALTHIER

Organic foods are far safer than conventional, according to a study published in *Food Additives and Contaminants.* The study team included analysts from Consumers Union (the publisher of *Consumer Reports*) and the Organic Materials Review Institute. The data covered more than 94,000 food samples taken through the 1990s. About 80 percent of conventional foods showed pesticide residues, but only 27 percent of organic samples did; multiple residues were ten times more common in conventional foods. Where residues

BUYING ORGANIC FOR YOUR BABY

The demand for organic baby food has grown considerably, as parents' health concerns extend to their decisions about what to feed their children. According to the Nielsen Company, organic baby food sales increased 21.6 percent from 2005 to 2006, reaching $116 million. Supermarkets and specialty retailers are responding to this growing demand by expanding the space allotted to these products in their stores. And manufacturers continue to offer new organic products and introduce organic versions of their conventional items.

Why buy organic baby food? All organic food significantly reduces exposure to chemicals and pesticides used in conventional food production. But the Environmental Working Group reports that commercial baby food is the largest source of unsafe levels of pesticide in food, particularly for children ages 6 to 12 months. Infants and children are especially sensitive to health risks from pesticides because their internal organs are still developing. For example, many studies indicate that toxins in our food and environment are risk factors for the development of allergies and asthma.

In addition, children consume more food in relation to their body weight than adults, which increases their exposure to chemical residues and additives. And since baby food is generally made from condensed fruits and vegetables, the levels of pesticides and chemicals in conventionally manufactured products may be concentrated beyond the levels found in regular food.

The best solid foods for babies—particularly for babies without molars—are pureed organic fruits and vegetables. Read labels carefully, and look for products low in salt, carbohydrates, and sugar.

were found in organic produce, they were at much lower levels than in the conventional foods.

Why were there any residues at all in organic food? The research showed that some were long-banned but persistent bioaccumulative toxics (or PBTs), such as DDT; some contamination occurred from pesticides that were blown onto organic acres; and some conventional items were possibly mislabeled as organic.

Levels of minerals in organic produce were about twice those in conventional produce, according to a 1993 study by Bob Smith printed in the *Journal of Applied Nutrition*. And a recent review of all the available valid research comparing organic and conventional produce conducted by nutritionist Shane Heaton on behalf of the UK's Soil Association concluded:

> Collectively, the scientific evidence supports the view that organically produced foods are significantly different in terms of food safety, nutrient content, and nutritional value. Consumers who wish to improve their intake of minerals, vitamin C, and antioxidant phytonutrients while reducing their exposure to potentially harmful pesticide residues, nitrates, GMOs, and artificial additives used in food processing should, whenever possible, choose organically produced food.

For years people scoffed at the idea that organic food could have more nutrients than conventional. "A plant doesn't care where it gets its nutrients," they'd say. "There's no difference in the foods produced by these growing methods." But Theo Clark, a chemistry professor at Truman State University in Missouri, proved otherwise. Clark and his team of undergraduate students polled households in Miller, Missouri, to assess people's expectations of organic oranges. Eighty-five percent believed that organic oranges would have a higher nutritional content than conventional oranges.

Clark and his team then used chemical isolation and nuclear magnetic resonance to analyze the vitamin C content of organic and conventional oranges. He presented his findings to the Great Lakes Regional meeting of the American Chemical Society, the world's largest scientific society, in June 2002.

The conventional oranges looked better. But when Clark and his team determined their vitamin C content, the organic oranges had 30 percent more than the conventional oranges, even though they were half the size. How could that be? "With conventional oranges," he speculated, "farmers use nitrogen fertilizers that cause an uptake of more water, so it sort of dilutes the orange. You get a great big orange, but it's full of water and doesn't have as much nutritional value."

AN OVERVIEW OF WORLDWIDE ORGANIC AGRICULTURE

The International Federation of Organic Agriculture Movements (IFOAM), headquartered in Germany, issued a report on the state of organic agriculture around the world in February 2004. A fair amount of our food supply comes from outside the country. Here are some important points:

- Professor Ulrich Hamm, a respected organic market analyst, has forecast annual growth rates of 20 to 40 percent and, in some countries, up to 50 percent per year.
- The largest organic trader in the UK expects today's $11 billion U.S. organic market to go to $100 billion in the next ten years.
- In Switzerland, the organic market share is already 10 percent and growing, with the largest canton, Graubünden, having around 50 percent. Austria, Sweden, and Finland have reached the same level of Switzerland.
- The latest statistics from Italy showed 18,000 farms either fully organic or in conversion in 1996. That figure grew to 30,000 by 1998, and has now reached about 60,000 farms.
- Uganda, Egypt, Mexico, Argentina, Japan, Poland, and Australia are all involved in organic agriculture and report growing consumer demand.

I don't think Clark's theoretical explanation is complete. Remember the concept of "thrifty"? And how organic crops get the nutrients they need in the amounts they need at the time they need and in the form they need? Organic plants are growing optimally, and whatever the biological limit on the amount of vitamin C—or other nutrients—they can produce, they are closing in on that limit.

A lot of this kind of information is finally breaking through. Agribusiness can no longer stem the organic tide, or churn out disinformation about organics, and in many ways is starting to follow the old bromide, "If you can't beat 'em, join 'em." And so we have the spectacle of organic strawberries from California and Florida being sold in winter in the Northeast, grown by who knows who—but certified organic by Quality Assurance International.

It's heartening, though, to an old organic hand like me to see the entire national food system beginning to move toward organic. After all, organic acres are cleaner and more ecologically diverse than conventional acres. But the best acres are the ones close enough for me to see with my own eyes ("Eat Your View" is a popular bumper sticker in Europe), farmed by a human being I can talk to.

I most fondly remember the local farmers where I bought my eggs, bacon, and milk in Pennsylvania. And now here in California I meet the farmers at one of the many farmers' markets in Sonoma County. We can talk about how the hens are laying, whether the early lettuce got nipped by the late frost, or how the wild turkeys scratch up the broccoli seedlings. Many of the wine grape growers I respect the most are either organic or biodynamic. Robert Sinskey makes his own compost fertilizer by the tens of tons, and so does Mike Benziger, John Williams at Frogs Leap, and the folks at Fetzer, Frey, Lolonis, and on and on.

CHAPTER

2

Vegetables

The admonition "eat your vegetables" is a good one, but many people are stuck in a rut when it comes to preparing vegetables at home. They think only of the same small group of tried-and-trues, night after night: broccoli, spinach, potatoes, coleslaw. Yet today's farmers' markets, supermarkets, and even big-box stores, carry sections of organic vegetables that range far beyond the ordinary.

Nutritionists encourage us to eat as wide a variety of vegetables and fruits as possible. This chapter takes you on an excursion into the enormous panoply of organically grown vegetables available to us these days. Here's a chance to get creative and add some new flavors to your meals. You've had mashed potatoes, but have you ever tried mashed rutabagas? They are scrumptious.

Vegetables are never of higher quality or better flavor than when they're in season, and organically and locally grown. This chapter gives you the information you need to determine when vegetables are at their peak, which varieties are tops for flavor, what to look for to ensure their freshness and wholesomeness, and how to use them in ways that enhance the quality of the food at your table.

VEGETABLES BY SEASON

Because most vegetables are annuals, their season is defined by the length of the growing season where they are grown. In Minnesota or Maine, only one crop of corn is achievable. But in Florida or California, multiple sowings are possible during a season that extends over many months. The following chart lists vegetables by their season throughout USDA Zones 5-7: roughly from New England to North Carolina, and west to Wisconsin and Oklahoma. At their peak of season, vegetables are at their very best.

SPRING	SUMMER	FALL	WINTER
Artichoke	Avocado	Asian greens	Artichoke
Arugula	Beet	Avocado	Asian greens
Asian greens	Carrot	Beet	Avocado
Avocado	Celery	Broccoli	Broccoli
Broccoli	Chard	Brussels sprouts	Brussels sprouts
Celery	Corn	Carrot	Cauliflower
Chard	Cucumber	Cauliflower	Celery
Kale	Eggplant	Celery	Celery root
Lettuce	Fennel	Celery root	Chard
Onion	Garlic	Chard	Chicory
Pea	Leek	Chicory and endive	Endive
Radish	Lettuce	Fennel	Kale
Shallot	Okra	Kale	Leek
Spinach	Onion	Leek	Lettuce
	Potato	Lettuce	Onion
	Radish	Mushroom	Sweet potato
	Shallot	Onion	Tomatillo
	Spinach	Potato	Winter squash
	Summer squash and zucchini	Radish	
	Sweet pepper	Shallot	
	Sweet potato	Spinach	
	Tomatillo	Summer squash and zucchini	
		Sweet pepper	
		Sweet potato	
		Tomatillo	
		Winter squash	

ARTICHOKE

SEASON: winter through spring

GOOD VARIETIES: European purple, Imperial Star, Kiss of Burgundy, Green Globe

WHAT TO LOOK FOR: Heads should be tightly closed. Once they start to open up, they're over the hill. Brownish or blackish areas on the outside are OK; it's frost damage and doesn't affect quality, although such chokes may be marked down.

STORAGE AND PREPARATION TIPS: To trim artichokes, cut off most of the stem, leaving about 1/2 inch (peel this). Cut off the top (just till you read the feathery center), remove the remaining leaves, and scoop out the feathery filaments with a paring knife or tablespoon. You'll be left with the heart. Unless you're using it immediately, rub the heart with olive oil or lemon juice to it keep from oxidizing and turning brown.

NUTRITIONAL HIGHLIGHTS: antioxidants, fiber, folate, magnesium, potassium, vitamin C

GOES WELL WITH: anchovies, chicken, fish, garlic, lemon, Moroccan spices, olive oil, onions, potatoes, vinaigrette, white wine

Artichokes are most likely a selected form of cardoon, a large thistle found wild in Italy and North Africa that has been eaten since the first person hungry enough to try one discovered they tasted pretty good.

Artichokes arrived in America with the Italian immigrants who settled California's Monterey County coast in the late 1800s; they found the thistle eminently suited to the climate. Their popularity got a boost when Marilyn Monroe was crowned Artichoke Queen in Castroville, California, in 1948.

Almost all the artichokes sold coast to coast are standard marketplace varieties (such as the Green Globe), suited to the California climate and similar in flavor. Don't let that convince you that all artichokes taste the same: artichokes come in many different varieties and have a wonderful range of flavors. The more exotic ones are grown primarily in Europe, but more and more California farmers are turning to these European purplish-green varieties, and they're appearing more frequently at the market.

Organic Advantage

Conventional artichokes are usually sprayed with both pesticides and fungicides. That's why they're blemish free, and you never see an earwig crawl out from the bracts (earwigs love to set up housekeeping in artichoke heads). If you buy organic artichokes, tap them upside down in the sink to dislodge any hitchhikers. Or soak them in a large bowl of water to which you've added two tablespoons of salt and two of vinegar to chase away any earwigs or aphids.

Uses

In Italy and parts of France, artichoke hearts are eaten raw in salads. They're shaved or sliced ultra-fine and tossed with vinaigrette and shavings of good Parmesan.

BABY ARTICHOKES

Baby artichokes, which grow to a much smaller size toward the base of the plant (they get less sunlight), are wonderful treasures. You normally see them in the form of canned artichoke hearts, but they also appear fresh in some markets. Trim the tip of the bud's leaves before steaming or boiling them. Italians cut them in half and bake or grill them, then finish them in a pan with another pan set on top of them to press them down. *Carciofini alla giudia* ("little artichokes Jewish style") dates from ancient Rome, when Jews fried the small chokes in olive oil, which pops open their leaves attractively.

Artichoke hearts can also be baked, braised, marinated, roasted, steamed, grilled, or broiled, but please don't boil them; that leaches out their flavor and nutrients. I like to marinate raw chokes in oil, vinegar, and herbs, then grill them. Or steam them until soft, flavor with lemon, anchovies, garlic, and olive oil. You can dice cooked chokes and mix them with bread crumbs to stuff a fish or a chicken breast.

In Greece they make whole artichoke hearts au gratin with *kefalotiri* cheese. Polish cooks will braise artichoke hearts in white wine and garlic. I've had artichoke hearts cooked with onions, potatoes, lamb, and Moroccan spices in a tagine. Artichokes have a reputation for being difficult to pair with wine—it's said that some wine tends to intensify the artichoke's astringent quality. I personally don't find that to be true.

Artichokes Siciliano

SERVES 4

Most people cook artichokes with the bract tips still attached. The Sicilians, though, have a unique way to serve them that's worth the effort and makes scraping the flesh off the bracts with your front teeth pleasurable indeed.

4 Green Globe artichokes
1/2 cup olive oil
7 cloves garlic, minced
1/2 cup freshly grated hard Italian cheese, such as pecorino or Parmesan
1 cup bread crumbs
2 anchovy fillets, mashed

1. Preheat the oven to 350°F. Prepare the chokes by using scissors or poultry shears to snip away the spiny tips of the bracts.

2. In a bowl, combine the olive oil, garlic, cheese, bread crumbs, and anchovy fillets, mashing and mixing the ingredients together. If it seems a little dry, add 1 to 2 tablespoons of water until the consistency is that of a paste. Pull the bracts open slightly with the tip of a butter knife, and insert a bit of the paste. Do this around each of the chokes for the inner 3 series of bracts.

3. Bake the chokes in an ovenproof glass baking dish for 45 minutes to an hour, or until a toothpick easily penetrates the stem end.

ARUGULA

SEASON: mid- to late spring

GOOD VARIETIES: Astro, Greek arugula, Rocket, Turkish arugula, wild arugula

WHAT TO LOOK FOR: Leaves at their peak of freshness will be about four inches long.

STORAGE AND PREPARATION TIPS: To store, wash if needed, then pat dry with paper towels. Moisten a paper towel and wrap arugula in it, then place in a plastic bag and store in the crisper for up to a week. Trim off any thick stems before using.

NUTRITIONAL HIGHLIGHTS: vitamin A, vitamin C

GOES WELL WITH: avocado, beans, blue cheese, chicken, onions, pears, pecans, pine nuts, radicchio, shrimp, sun-dried tomatoes

Arugula refers to a set of bitter leafy greens that have gone in and out of fashion over the centuries since colonists brought the first plants to North America from England. Popular in Colonial days, arugula went out of fashion in the nineteenth and much of the twentieth centuries. It's wildly popular again now.

Organic Advantage

Much of the arugula that's grown commercially in the western United States is organic because it's not a plant that attracts many insects. (This defense isn't perfect. In the eastern states, the common flea beetle may bite some tiny holes in the leaves.) So if you see a few round holes the size of a pinhead in the leaves, it indicates that the plants weren't sprayed.

Uses

Young arugula (leaves of 4 to 7 inches), which arrives in springtime, has a mild peppery flavor and adds zing and snap to mixed green salads. It also makes a fine bed for cooked meat like grilled chicken or steak.

But it's as a player in mesclun that arugula really shines, balancing the mild and bitter flavors of the other greens with its sharp bite. Toss arugula and mesclun mix with some chopped, pickled artichoke hearts and the pickling solution from the jar, sprinkle on a few pitted oil-cured olives, then top with shavings of Parmesan.

Arugula adds a kick to other foods as well—try it instead of lettuce to add a fresh, peppery quality to everything from sandwiches to potato salad to creamed spinach (add it just before you steam the spinach).

As hot weather arrives, arugula leaves become larger (7 inches and longer) more peppery, and tougher in texture. At that stage, arugula is best cooked, which reduces its pepperiness but increases a pleasant bitterness that works well against savory and sweet foods like beans and onions.

If you find slender, finely toothed wild or Turkish arugulas (usually at farmers' markets), these varieties are quite peppery and are usually cooked, often with beans.

Arugula and Mesclun Salad with Grapefruit and Avocado

A good salad is a balancing act of contrasting flavors and textures. Here, the acidic grapefruit lends brightness to the earthy, peppery arugula. Avocados provide buttery texture, and mangoes add sweetness.

FOR THE SALAD

1 bunch young arugula
1/2 cup pine nuts
1 white grapefruit
2 cups mesclun mix
2 avocados, pitted, peeled, and sliced
1 mango, peeled, pitted, and sliced thin

FOR THE DRESSING

1/4 cup olive oil
2 tablespoons balsamic vinegar
1 clove garlic, minced
Pinch ground cayenne
Salt and freshly ground black pepper, to taste

1. Trim off and discard the thick stems from the arugula. Wash the leaves in cold water until all grit is removed and drain thoroughly.

2. Toss the pine nuts in a small dry skillet over medium heat until toasted light brown. Set aside to cool.

3. Cut off the top and bottom of the grapefruit, then cut down along the sides to remove the peel and bitter white pith. Section the grapefruit into a bowl. Squeeze the juice out of the membrane and peel trimmings into a small cup, and add any juice that collects in the bowl. If you don't have 3 tablespoons of juice, squeeze a section or two. Reserve this juice for the dressing.

4. Toss the arugula with the mesclun and the toasted pine nuts. Divide onto 4 plates. Lay grapefruit segments, avocado slices, and mango slices alternately in a circle on the salad.

5. Blend the dressing ingredients with the reserved grapefruit juice in a blender for a few seconds until creamy, and immediately drizzle over the salads.

ASIAN GREENS

SEASON: fall through spring

GOOD VARIETIES:

Bok choy: Chinese flat cabbage, *mei qing choy*, Ming Choi, *tsoi sum*, Vitamin Green

Chinese cabbage: Burpee's Two Seasons, Nerva, Orange Queen, Green Rocket, *michihli*

Chinese kale: Asparation, Blue Star, Green Delight

Chinese spinach: Perfecta, Red Stripe

Mustard greens: Florida Broadleaf, Magma, Red Broadleaf, Red Giant, Southern Giant Curled

WHAT TO LOOK FOR: The fresher the better is the rule in much Asian cooking. Check the stems of Asian vegetables. Stalks should be turgid and snap. Leaves should look bright, with no signs of yellowing. Avoid plants on which small flowers have begun to form—these are old. Chinese cabbages should have a clean, fresh appearance where they were cut from their roots.

STORAGE AND PREPARATION TIPS: Store wrapped in a moist paper towel in a plastic bag in the crisper for up to two weeks.

NUTRITIONAL HIGHLIGHTS: Folate, beta-carotene, calcium, vitamin C

GO WELL WITH: apples, bacon, caraway, chestnuts, chiles, garlic, lemongrass, olive oil, onions, oyster sauce, scallions, vinegar

Dozens and dozens of varieties of Asian vegetables are available in the United States, and there are hundreds more around the world. They're grouped together here in part because most are members of the mustard and cabbage families, and because they appear in so many Asian dishes—Southeast Asian, Chinese, Korean, and Japanese. Asian vegetables fall into several large groups. You'll notice the word *choi* or *choy* popping up in many of the names, which is the Chinese word for "vegetable." It's almost onomatopoeic when you think of chewing into a crunchy white stem of bok choy.

Bok choy: Bok choy includes leafy plants of varying sizes, shapes, and textures. Their leaves range from small to very large; some form heads; others have loose leaves. A small, flat variety called tatsoi, or Chinese flat cabbage, forms thick, puckered, dark green leaves that make excellent additions to mixed green salads.

Chinese broccoli: Unlike Western broccoli, the plant, which is also called Chinese kale, has tender stems and strongly flavored leaves, with small clusters of buds and a few white flowers at the top. It is increasingly found in mainstream markets. Look for tender, young shoots, not more than 1/2 inch in diameter, with flowers still in the bud stage and stems and leaves that are firm, not limp, with no brown at the cut end.

Broccolini: Also called Asparation, broccolini is a cross between Chinese broccoli and Western broccoli with loose, flowering stalks. Besides being sweet and delicious, its dark green leaves are more nutritious than either broccoli or Chinese broccoli.

Chinese cabbage: There are two main types of this plant: napa cabbage and *michihli* cabbage. Most napa cabbage is found as barrel-shaped cylinders whose leaves curl into a tight head at the top. There's a pleasing savoy-like (crinkly) texture to the leaves, which vary in color from medium green to misty celadon to white. The second type, *michihli* cabbage, forms tight, elongated heads 16 to 18 inches long and 4 to 5 inches thick.

Chinese spinach: Also known as *hinn choy*, Chinese spinach is actually a type of amaranth, a grain. It is a marvelous summer-season spinach substitute.

Mustard greens: Also known as *gai choi*, its leaves vary in shape from curly edged to flat, in surface texture from smooth to crinkled, in color from green to purple to red, and in pungency from mild to hot.

Organic Advantage

Many organic farms around the country grow Asian vegetables. You'll find them in large organic supermarkets as well as roadside stands.

Uses

Bok choy: The succulent, green-to-white stalks exude a mildly cabbagey redolence that instantly says "Chinese cooking." Bok choy leaves make a great cole slaw, and if you like spicy dishes, make them into kimchi. They also are useful in stir fries. The crunchy stalks can be cut from the leaves and used separately in soups and hot pots for texture and bulk, or braised and stir-fried.

Baby bok choy: These days I use a lot of *mei qing choy*, commonly called baby bok choy. It's not really a baby but a smaller variety that matures at 6 to 8 inches tall. It is more flavorful and more tender than larger bok choy. For a delicious, quick sauté, place several in a covered pan with hot olive oil and some finely chopped scallions. Turn them several times until they wilt and sweat and the onions caramelize a little, 5 to 8 minutes. Toward the end of this cooking, toss in a minced garlic clove and some chicken stock, reduce the heat to simmer, cover, and cook 5 minutes more. For variation, add a squirt of fish sauce or soy sauce or a few drops of toasted sesame oil during the final cooking.

Chinese broccoli: The aggressive, bitter flavor of the leaves softens somewhat when cooked. Stalks, leaves, and flower buds can be steamed or blanched to partially cook and then stir-fried, or the flower buds can be dipped in batter and fried as tempura. Served by itself, Chinese broccoli needs a sauce of some kind to bring it to life: a simple splash of oyster sauce works. For something more subtle, mince the tender heart of a stalk of lemongrass and mix it with a little canola oil, minced garlic, scallions, and lime juice, and pour this over the greens.

Chinese cabbage: Use napa cabbage raw in salads and slaw, or lightly stir-fry or braise until just tender, as it loses its flavor with long cooking. *Michihli* cabbage, on the other hand, is specifically suited to long cooking. As it cooks it will take on the characteristics of other foods, absorb pot liquors, and thicken soups and stews.

Chinese spinach: Its leaves can be eaten raw, or they can be boiled, steamed, stir-fried, or used in egg foo yong. If you find plants at the market with large leaves, blanch them and use them for wrapping up other ingredients.

Mustard greens: Young leaves can be included in a springtime mixture of salad greens. When mature, separate the stems with a knife and use them in stir-fries. Tear up the leaves and boil them. The Chinese also pickle the mature stems and use varieties with swollen stems as a preserved vegetable.

Kimchi

MAKES 2 QUARTS

Kimchi is a kind of Korean sauerkraut flavored with chile peppers. It ranges from spicy to hot as hell and is absolutely delicious. You can buy it in jars in good grocery stores and Korean markets, but the homemade kind is more traditional, easy to make, and very tasty. It is served as a side dish at most Korean main meals.

1 head Chinese cabbage, cored and shredded
1 bunch scallions (white and green parts), chopped
1 cup grated carrots
1/2 cup grated peeled daikon radish
3 garlic cloves, minced
2 tablespoons kosher salt
1 tablespoon grated peeled fresh ginger
1 teaspoon ground cayenne
Unseasoned rice vinegar, as needed

1. Place everything except the vinegar in a strong bowl (I used a wooden bowl but a strong stoneware bowl will work). Using a wooden mallet, meat tenderizer, or the blunt handle of a large cleaver, pound everything together until the cabbage is mashed and its juices are flowing.

2. Place the mixture in 1-quart mason jars—you'll probably need two. Use the mallet to press the mixture firmly into the jars until the juices cover the mixture and the top of the kimchi is about 3/4 inch below the lid. If you don't have enough liquid, either add more pressed-out cabbage juice or top with rice vinegar or water. Lightly screw down the lids just until they resist. Allow the jars to sit on the counter at room temperature for 3 days, then refrigerate. Use within 2 weeks.

AVOCADO

SEASON: available year-round

GOOD VARIETIES: Fuchs-20, Fuerte, Gottfried, Hass, Russell (for gardens), Sharpless, Trapp

WHAT TO LOOK FOR: Most avocados are sold still hard; they will ripen quite easily on your kitchen counter. To determine ripeness, squeeze gently: a slight give indicates they're ripe. Avoid avocados with torn skin.

STORAGE AND PREPARATION TIPS: To remove the flesh, cut the avocado in half lengthwise. When the knife blade hits the pit, rotate the avocado along the blade, then twist the two avocado halves to separate them. Whack the pit lightly with the blade of the knife and twist to dislodge it. If the avocado is properly ripe, you can peel off the skin by hand. Otherwise, scoop out the flesh in one piece by running a large soup spoon just under the skin.

If you're only using half of the avocado, spritz the cut side of the remaining piece with citrus juice and tightly wrap with plastic wrap to prevent discoloration.

NUTRITIONAL HIGHLIGHTS: fiber, magnesium, monounsaturated fat, niacin, potassium, riboflavin, thiamin, vitamin A, vitamin B_6, vitamin C, vitamin E

GOES WELL WITH: balsamic vinegar, bananas, chile peppers, citrus, dates, grapefruits, guavas, limes, mangoes, onions, pineapples, salt, sugar, tomatoes

---

The avocado is one-of-a-kind. Unlike most fruits (which avocados are, though we treat them as vegetables in the kitchen), it ripens after it's picked. And instead of sweetening like most fruits as it ripens, it fattens up, filling itself with precious avocado oil. Avocados have been cultivated in the Americas as far back as 5000 BCE. The Aztecs used to make a dish called *ahuacamulli*, what we call guacamole (you can see the similarity between the names).

The two dominant varieties in the Americas are the Hass and the Fuerte. The Hass has a pebbly, greenish black skin when ripe, and a rich, buttery texture owing to its 25 percent oil content—unsaturated, healthy oil (see Are Avocados Good for You?).

From January to June, markets display the leaf-green, pear-shaped Fuerte. Once the leading California avocado, it continues to be the most popular variety in Europe and parts of South America. Its oil content ranges between 12 and 17 percent.

Organic Advantage

Thanks to national outlets like Whole Foods, organic avocados are available around the country now—a good thing, because over one hundred different chemicals are used in conventional avocado farming.

Uses

Avocados' buttery texture and mild flavor contrast nicely with a wide range of flavors—sweet, spicy, sour, salty, and even savory. Grapefruit, with its sweet acidity, makes perhaps the best match of any citrus fruit, although limes aren't far behind.

Pureed ripe avocado gives salad dressing a smooth, creamy texture and can be used to thicken soups—but add it just before serving, as the avocados' tannins turn it bitter when cooked.

Around the world, avocados figure largely into everyday cooking. A salted avocado, tortillas, and a cup of coffee might make an entire meal for Native Americans in tropical Central America. In Guatemala, a ripe avocado is set on the table along with a hot soup or entrée, and the diner scoops out the flesh and adds it just before eating. Breakfast might be half an avocado topped with scrambled eggs and anchovies. Brazilians use avocados in sorbets, ice cream, and milk shakes. Hawaiians go local when they mix avocados with sugar and pineapple. In Java, avocado is sweetened and mixed with strong black coffee as a dessert.

Guacamole

MAKES ABOUT 2 CUPS

This recipe comes from quite a few years of fooling around with guacamole. Organically grown ingredients really make it sing.

2 ripe avocados, halved, pits removed, and peeled
1 medium onion, chopped
1 serrano chile, minced
Leaves of 3 sprigs cilantro
1/4 teaspoon salt
2 small tomatillos, husks removed, diced
Juice of 1 lime

1. Mash one avocado and dice the other. Place 1/2 the onion, 1/2 the chile, the cilantro leaves, and the salt in a mortar and grind together.

2. Mix the mashed avocado with the tomatillos, lime juice, and the contents of the mortar, then gently fold in the diced avocado and the remaining onion and chile. Serve immediately.

ARE AVOCADOS GOOD FOR YOU?

While avocados have a high fat content, it's good-for-you fat: avocado oil has a greater percentage than olive oil of heart-healthy monounsaturated fat (primarily oleic acid), which lowers LDL (bad) cholesterol levels. In one study, subjects were given between one and three avocado halves per day. Their total blood cholesterol began to fall in one week, and their body weight didn't increase. Although they can contain up to 30 percent fat, they average only about 300 calories. They are also higher in potassium than bananas, and have four and a half times more soluble fiber than apples! They're also rich in lipase, which reduces cardiovascular no-nos like blood fats and triglycerides to benign fatty acids and glycerol.

BEET

SEASON: summer through early winter

GOOD VARIETIES: Chioggia, Formanova, Golden, Lutz Greenleaf

WHAT TO LOOK FOR: The skin should be smooth, without rough spots. If you're buying the beet roots only, they should be very firm, with no softness, and have the stub of the stem still attached. If that's been trimmed off, it's a sign the beets are old. Avoid very large beets (unless they're the

Lutz Greenleaf variety, which can grow to the size of footballs without getting tough).

STORAGE AND PREPARATION TIPS: Cut off the green tops (save the greens to use separately), leaving 1 inch of stem attached, and cut off the thin, tapering tail. Wash and scrub with a vegetable brush under running water to remove loose soil.

NUTRITIONAL HIGHLIGHTS: Folate

GOES WELL WITH: anchovies, anise, arugula, chives, cinnamon, citrus, cloves, dill, goat cheese, horseradish, meat, nutmeg, olives, sour cream, spring greens, tarragon, toasted walnuts, vinegar

---

Our modern beet is descended from *Beta maritima*, a wild seashore plant that grew along the edges of tidal marshes and salty water inlets around the Mediterranean Sea and the Atlantic coast of southern Europe. Its descendants include modern cooking beets, the sugar beet—a source of refined sugar—and Swiss chard. A more distant relative is spinach.

Even among cooking beets there is considerable variety. Red beets have a dark, sensual, earthy sweetness. Golden beets have a brighter flavor. White beets have their decorative uses but aren't very flavorful; Chioggia beets, which slice open to reveal pretty, alternating red and white rings, acquire a delicate, almost candy-like flavor when roasted.

Organic Advantage

Root crops like beets, because they grow underground, are especially responsive to nutrient-rich soil full of decaying organic matter, such as compost. In fact, beets are so sensitive to their soil environment that the taste of beets actually reflects different elements in the soil—similar to the way a grape's *terroir* affects the taste of wine. Good, compost-amended soil gives beets a clean, woodsy, "forest floor" note, far more appealing than the slightly dirty taste they can acquire when grown in worn-out soil lacking in organic matter.

Because organic soils harbor a diverse array of soil life, harmful organisms are less likely to survive, so there is less need to use chemicals in the first place. And the actively decaying organic matter bathes the roots in the nutrients they need, when they need them, and in the forms they can best use.

Uses

If you haven't already discovered the glories of roasted beets, I'll bet that roasting becomes your favorite way of preparing them: it concentrates their flavor, enhances their sweetness, and gives them a nutty, smoky caramel flavor no other form of cooking can impart (see at right for instructions). Roasted beets are a perfect foil for intensely flavored meats such as duck, goose, guinea hen, and beef (use both red and yellow baby beets for a special touch). Cold roasted beets can be sliced thin and laid over a salad of fresh goat cheese, toasted walnuts, and spring greens tossed in a mild vinaigrette. Sure, their color prettifies the salad, but it's their deep flavor that gives the dish drama and verve.

When buying beets sold by the bunch, you also get their tender greens. These can be cooked as you would Swiss chard (a close relative). I braise them if they're large or steam them if they're young and tender, then give them a squirt of lemon juice and serve them alongside the beets. When the beet roots are earthy and deeply sweet, the greens are meaty and have a slightly mineral flavor that contrasts beautifully with the roots.

Finally, if you've got a surplus of beets on hand, pickle them! My mom always had a jar in the fridge full of spicy-vinegary beets and raw onion rings that had been pickled along with them. (Her recipe for pickled beets follows below.) And don't think that pickled beets are old-fashioned. I recently had pickled beets, goat cheese, walnuts, and organic greens tossed together at a fancy San Francisco restaurant: the dish was superb.

To roast beets: Figure one medium to medium-large beet (the size of a tennis ball) or two smaller beets (the size of golf balls) per person. Heat the oven to 425°F. Lay a sheet of aluminum foil on a baking pan and set the beets on the foil, then put it in the oven. (Don't place beets directly on your oven racks; they will ooze some juice during baking.)

Larger beets will take at least 1½ hours to cook; smaller ones, proportionately less time. But it's their feel that tells you when beets are done. When beets become soft to the touch, they're still not done. When you gently squeeze the skins and they collapse—revealing that they've shrunk away from the skins—then they're done. The beets will be scalding hot, so let them cool 15 minutes before removing the skins. Peel away a little of the flesh off the stem end; this opens up the skin so you can easily peel the rest away. Make sure you remove all the bits of skin.

I like to finish roasted beets by caramelizing them on the stovetop. Heat a skillet over low heat, then add a pat of butter. Transfer the whole beets to the skillet and shake the skillet periodically so the beets roll in the butter and become covered. They'll acquire a beautiful dark red shine. You can even cook down a little orange juice in the pan, or a tablespoon of balsamic vinegar, ½ teaspoon of maple syrup, or even Cointreau or Grand Marnier.

Pickled Beets

MAKES 1 QUART

This recipe could hardly be simpler—or the results more delicious. Let them sit for just a day and they're ready to eat. Beets' natural sweetness complements the pickling solution's natural tartness.

4 or 5 young red beets (2 to 3 pounds), washed and trimmed
1 medium onion, sliced thin and separated into rings
1/2 cinnamon stick
3 whole cloves
1 cup apple cider vinegar
1/4 cup sugar

1. In a large pot, place a steamer basket and an inch or two of water, and add the whole beets. Steam the beets for 40 to 60 minutes, adding more water as it evaporates. When the beets are tender but not mushy, remove them from the heat and let them cool so they can be handled, then peel. Strain and reserve the liquor from the bottom of the steamer. Slice the beets into 1/4-inch-thick rounds.

2. Place the beets, onion, cinnamon, and cloves in a 1-quart mason jar. In a saucepan, combine the vinegar, sugar, and 1 cup of the beet-steaming liquor (add water to make 1 cup if you don't have enough). Heat over medium heat just until the sugar dissolves, then pour the liquid over the beets and onion rings. If it doesn't quite cover the vegetables, add more vinegar.

3. Screw down the jar lid until the ring just begins to become tight but there's still the tiniest bit of play, and process in a bath of boiling water for 30 minutes, according to standard directions for canning acidic foods. Or, if you plan to use them quickly, place the covered jar in the fridge for a day before serving. These pickled beets will keep that way for 2 weeks.

BROCCOLI

SEASON: late fall through the spring

GOOD VARIETIES: DeCicco, Early Purple Cape (Purple Sicilian), Green Comet, Green Valiant, Premium Crop, Purple Sprouting, Small Miracle, Umpqua

WHAT TO LOOK FOR: The buds of the florets should be tight, a lively dark green, unseparated, and without open yellow flowers, which indicate the broccoli is old and tough. The cut stem end should look fresh and not dried out. The plant should be turgid, with no limpness.

STORAGE AND PREPARATION TIPS: Broccoli's thick stems are full of nutrients, so don't throw those away. Peel their tough outer skin using a vegetable peeler, then slice them lengthwise into 1/4- or 1/2-inch strips and cook them along with the heads.

NUTRITIONAL HIGHLIGHTS: antioxidants, carotenoids, chromium, fiber, folate, phytochemicals, potassium, vitamin C

GOES WELL WITH: anchovies, fleur de sel, garlic, hollandaise sauce, lemon juice, olive oil, Parmesan, pasta, pizza

Although broccoli was introduced to America in the late eighteenth century, it wasn't until the early twentieth that Italian immigrants to the West Coast started growing the plant we recognize as broccoli and universalizing it. In recent years, its popularity has soared

BEYOND BASIC BROCCOLI

While the green varieties are standard, there are purple varieties. They tend to turn green during cooking and generally have a milder flavor than the green types. They add color to a plate of crudités.

Romanesco: A variant, Romanesco or broccoletti is probably closer to cauliflower than broccoli (see Cauliflower, page 52). It has a gorgeous lime green head with many spiral lumps in geometric patterns.
Broccoli raab: Named after the Italian word for turnip, *rapa*, and in fact the Italians call broccoli raab *cime di rapa* (top of the turnip). This strongly flavored, even bitter, plant has a flowering stem and large leaves. It's probably more closely related to a turnip than actual broccoli, but the name broccoli raab has stuck. It's often used wilted and sautéed on pizza and in pastas. If you find the taste strong, blanch it before using it in other dishes. Watch it closely, though, because it overcooks easily.
Asparation: In the spring, you may find broccolini, also called by its cultivar name, Asparation. It's a hybrid between Chinese kale and broccoli and is an excellent potherb. I blanch it for a couple of minutes in boiling water, drain it, then stir-fry it in a wok over very high heat with olive oil, fleur de sel, and a little garlic. It emerges with tender, crunchy stems and wonderfully flavorful flowering heads.

because it not only tastes good, but people realize how good it is for them.

Organic Advantage

Broccoli is a crucifier (along with cabbages, cauliflower, Brussels sprouts, and radishes), and therefore a heavy feeder. It takes lots of nutrients from the soil, especially nitrogen compounds, but also elements like calcium, chromium, magnesium, and iron. There is evidence that organic food, grown in soil that's well supplied with all the major and minor elements it needs, is able to build more of the compounds that make broccoli taste good.

By contrast, soil maintained using conventional agriculture is stripped of many of its nutrients. Only three—nitrogen, potassium, and phosphorus—are added back. This practice yields generic, bland-tasting crops.

Uses

Broccoli is almost always steamed, which helps it retain its juiciness and nutrition. It can also be boiled. Broccoli has a sweet flavor all its own that doesn't really require much fiddling with. However, its flavor can be enhanced by any of the foods mentioned on page 46.

Broccoli with Garlic, Lemon, and Anchovies

SERVES 4

This treatment really exalts the flavor of broccoli. If someone in your family doesn't like broccoli, this recipe will change his or her mind.

4 anchovy fillets
2 tablespoons olive oil
3 cloves garlic, sliced thin
Juice of 1 lemon
1 head broccoli, reduced to florets

1. Place the anchovy fillets in a small, cold skillet and slowly heat over low heat. As the pan warms, you'll be able to mash the anchovies with a fork—they'll actually dissolve. Don't let them sizzle or cook; just delicately melt them. As soon as they've melted, set the pan aside.

2. In a separate pan, heat the olive oil to just shy of the smoking point and add the garlic. Stir until the slices turn light brown. Remove the pan from the heat and, using a fork, take the garlic slices out of the pan and drain them on paper towels.

3. Transfer the melted anchovies to a small bowl and add 1 tablespoon of the garlic oil and the lemon juice. Stir until mixed.

4. Steam the broccoli over boiling water until just tender—no more than 5 minutes—and turn into a warmed bowl. Sprinkle with the fried garlic slices, then spoon over the anchovy-oil-lemon juice.

BRUSSELS SPROUTS

SEASON: fall and winter

GOOD VARIETIES: Energy, Falstaff, Igor (for gardening), Jade Cross, Long Island Improved, Peer Gynt, Prince Marvel, Rubine Red, Valiant

WHAT TO LOOK FOR: Brussels sprouts acquire an unpleasant cabbagey smell if too old or overcooked. The solution? Buy young, small sprouts (2/3 to 1 inch in diameter) that are tightly formed and are a lively blue green, light green, or dark green, with no yellowing. The end should look freshly cut, with no yellowing or drying.

STORAGE AND PREPARATION TIPS: Sprouts lose their sweetness and tenderness within a few days of being picked, so use them as soon as you buy them.

NUTRITIONAL HIGHLIGHTS: antioxidants, fiber, folate, phytochemicals, potassium, vitamin C

GO WELL WITH: bacon, butter, chestnuts, garlic, lemon juice, nutmeg, onion, parsley, thyme

Although there are references in the thirteenth and fifteenth centuries to plants that may have been brussels sprouts, it's more likely they were actually developed from cabbage in the eighteenth century. Gardeners knew that if you remove the main head of a cabbage or broccoli, smaller heads will develop around the cut stem as long as the root stays intact. This feature of cabbage plants was selected for and bred until the brussels sprout was born. The plant forms a group of large leaves at the top of the stalk but develops small heads in each of the leaf axils that stud the elongated stalk.

They didn't really become a farmed crop until the early twentieth century—before that, brussels sprouts were edible oddities of home gardens. Thomas Jefferson grew them at Monticello in 1812, according to his notebook.

Organic Advantage

Like all members of the cabbage family, brussels sprouts are attacked by cabbage moths and European cabbage worms. Conventional growers use pesticides. Organic growers use caterpillar diseases or physical barriers to ward off pests.

Uses

Sprouts can be cooked whole, halved, quartered, or even as individual leaves—a nice way to prepare larger sprouts. To keep their flavor fresh and texture pleasant, brussels sprouts should be cooked quickly.

Boiling is the most common way to cook sprouts: small sprouts will take 5 minutes, medium sprouts 8 minutes, and large sprouts 12 minutes, or until the core is just tender. Steaming takes 5 to 10 minutes, depending on their size. They can be also baked whole, which intensifies their flavor. You can sauté the sprouts if you first halve or quarter them, or slice them lengthwise.

Individual leaves can be quickly sautéed in a hot pan with a little olive oil, a diced shallot or clove of garlic, maybe a shake of crushed red pepper, a couple of tablespoons of stock added at the end, and a squeeze of lemon juice. I've noticed brussels sprout leaves appearing in rice, pasta, and noodle dishes at restaurants these days.

In Belgium and into northern France, chestnuts are often roasted or boiled and added whole or sliced to freshly cooked sprouts to make a delicious dead-of-winter pairing. (See page 175 for information on cooking chestnuts.)

Brussels Sprouts and Sherry Shrimp

SERVES 4

Chinese cooking inspired this light, nutritious dish. The nutty flavor of good sprouts works well with sherry or even a tawny port.

1 pound brussels sprouts (about 3 cups), soaked and trimmed (see Uses, above)
3 tablespoons peanut oil
1 tablespoon butter
2 tablespoons diced scallions
1 pound medium shrimp, peeled and deveined (see Tip, page 50)
1/2 cup peeled, sliced water chestnuts
Juice of 1/2 lemon
Salt and freshly ground black pepper
1/2 cup dry sherry

1. Bring a large pot with salted water to a boil. Add the sprouts and boil for 5 to 12 minutes, depending on their size, or until just tender. Drain and place them on paper towels to absorb excess moisture.

2. Warm a serving dish in a 200°F oven. In a large skillet, heat the oil and butter over medium-low heat until a bit of scallion sizzles when added, then add the scallions and sauté for about 1 minute. Add the shrimp and cook for about 4 minutes, flipping them often so both sides cook. Add the water chestnuts and brussels sprouts, drizzle the lemon juice over them, and add salt and pepper to taste. Stir until everything is heated through. Turn the contents of the skillet into the warm serving dish. Deglaze the skillet with the sherry and turn up the heat so it boils and reduces by half, then pour it over the shrimp and sprouts and serve immediately.

TIP: There is a plastic kitchen gadget called a shrimp deveiner that peels and deveins shrimp in one swift motion; it is sold in most kitchen supply stores and worth having in your kitchen.

CARROT

SEASON: midsummer through fall

GOOD VARIETIES: A-Plus, Beta-Sweet Danvers, Gold Pak 28, Imperator, Kundulus, Nantes Half Long, Rothild, Scarlet Nantes, Yellowstone

WHAT TO LOOK FOR: If you find carrots with their tops on, lively green foliage indicates the carrots are fresh. If the carrots are topless, check the place where the foliage was attached; there should be no mold. The root itself should be firm and not bend easily. If you see fine, white, hair-like rootlets growing from the carrots, avoid them; they're really old

STORAGE AND PREPARATION TIPS: Carrots will keep in the fridge for weeks, but their ephemeral flavor and freshness disappears a few days after being picked. Organic carrots don't need to be peeled; just give them a quick washing.

NUTRITIONAL HIGHLIGHTS: beta-carotene, fiber, vitamin C

GOES WELL WITH: anise, celery, chervil, cinnamon, cole slaw, cumin, dill, garlic, maple syrup, onions, orange juice, parsley, pilaf, pot roast, potatoes, tarragon, thyme

Although the wild carrot called Queen Anne's lace grows just about everywhere in America, the vegetable we know as the carrot probably originated in Afghanistan, where the wild carrots are purple and small. In fact, until the seventeenth century, carrots were all yellow or purple and had slender roots. It was the Dutch who, in the seventeenth century, bred carrots for size and for a rich, orange color. Today botanists are breeding other colors back into carrots, and you can find carrots in maroon, purple, red, white, and yellow.

Organic Advantage

When carrots are organic, you don't have to peel away their thin, flavorsome skins. Conventional agriculture uses pesticides, so it's best to peel the carrots and wash them before eating.

Uses

Carrots can be cooked using just about any technique: boiling, steaming, broiling, and sautéing. You can even bake them in a cake. Personally, I like to roast them: it deepens their flavor, and browning turns some of their starches into sugars, intensifying their sweetness. Try roasting carrots along with onions and potatoes. I grate raw carrots into my cole slaw. In Iran, cooks grate them into pilaf. And in China carrots are preserved in sugar as well as pickled. Carrot juice can be made into a sweet reduction sauce to enhance other vegetables.

If you have organic carrots, you can use their green tops as well. Steam the foliage lightly and use it as a base for fish, as you would dill (a close relative of carrots), or use it uncooked as a bed for freshly shucked oysters.

Unconventional Carrots

We're used to eating long, tapered orange carrots, but good carrots come in all shapes and sizes, from long to short to stubby little golf balls. And be on the lookout for baby carrots—not the stubs sold in bags but miniature whole carrots bred to develop full color and flavor while still small. Farmers have also been breeding certain varieties of carrots with elevated levels of vitamin A so they can be grown in parts of the world suffering vitamin deficiencies

Carrot Soup with Rice (Potage Crécy)

SERVES 4

Potage Crécy is an old recipe from northern France for a delicious carrot soup with rice. Because of its sweetness and creamy texture, kids love it.

1/3 cup diced onion
1 strip of bacon, diced
5 cups chicken stock
3 cups thinly sliced very fresh carrots
1/4 cup uncooked rice
4 tablespoons low-fat buttermilk
1 tablespoon butter
Salt and freshly ground black pepper
4 tablespoons cooked rice, optional

1. In a 2-quart saucepan over medium heat, fry the onion together with the bacon until the onion is translucent and tender, about 5 minutes. Add the chicken stock, carrots, and raw rice. Cover and cook over medium heat for 20 minutes.

2. Pour the mixture into a blender and puree, making sure it still has some texture, then return it to the pot. Bring it to a low boil and add the buttermilk, butter, and season with salt and pepper. Mix thoroughly and ladle into serving bowls. Top each bowl with a tablespoon of cooked rice, if desired.

CAULIFLOWER

SEASON: fall through the dead of winter (and spring in cold regions)

GOOD VARIETIES: Marmalade, Orange Bouquet, Romanesco, Snow King

WHAT TO LOOK FOR: Fresh heads will have a creamy-white or slightly pink surface. Avoid those heads with browned areas or those on which small green leaves or flower buds have begun to form. At the farmers' market, look for heads still wrapped in their inner leaves (if the leaves are fresh, that's a sure sign the head is, too). Check the cut stem for drying or discoloration.

STORAGE AND PREPARATION TIPS: Cauliflower wrapped in plastic will keep for two weeks in the crisper. To prepare, wash and pat dry. Turn the head over and cut out the thick stem in the center. Use whole or reduced to florets.

NUTRITIONAL HIGHLIGHTS: fiber, phytochemicals, vitamin C

GOES WELL WITH: anchovies, bacon, black pepper, cheese, cumin, garlic, mustard, nutmeg.

The first time I tasted a fresh, organic head of cauliflower right from the garden, my estimation of this vegetable changed entirely. It was one of those cabbagey vegetables that I'd eaten cooked to the point of mushiness since childhood. Fresh cauliflower, by contrast, served raw or lightly cooked, is a treat. It has a delicate creamy, nutty flavor, and a pleasant crumbly texture.

Organic Advantage

Organic cauliflower that gets a gentle feeding of nitrogen from the decay of organic matter in the soil develops at a healthy, natural rate and as a result is not as prone to rush toward flowering. One of the problems with conventional cauliflower is that the application of heavy doses of soluble nitrogen fertilizer causes the heads to quickly lose their firmness and begin to form flower buds, which results in a loss of texture and quality.

Uses

Cauliflower is versatile. It's an excellent addition to a tray of raw vegetables, but it also can be baked, boiled, steamed, roasted, stir-fried or sautéed, and pureed after cooking to make a creamy sauce for grilled fish. I only avoid boiling it, for that turns it to mush too quickly and brings out its cabbagey flavor. At its simplest, cauliflower cooked with steam or dry oven heat—even microwaved—also produces good results.

Because of its delicate flavor, cauliflower pairs well with more sharply flavored ingredients. Butter, cream, and bread crumbs are old-fashioned toppings.

Cauliflower fritters: One popular way to handle this delicate vegetable is to batter-fry the florets to create tasty fritters. For a Greek version, steam a head's worth of florets until just tender. Whisk 1/2 cup dry white wine with

1/2 cup all-purpose flour in large bowl. Beat 2 large egg whites in another bowl until stiff, then fold them into the batter. Dip the florets into the batter and fry in a pan of hot olive oil until golden brown.

Spicy Roast Cauliflower

SERVES 4

Cauliflower is a favorite vegetable in Indian cooking. This spring recipe uses Indian spices and spring vegetables guaranteed to wake your taste buds from their winter dormancy.

1 head fresh cauliflower, reduced to florets
1 cup diced onion
1/4 cup olive oil
1 tablespoon grated peeled fresh ginger
1/2 tablespoon curry powder
1/2 tablespoon garam masala (see Tip)
1/2 tablespoon grated lemon zest
1/2 tablespoon fennel seeds
1 teaspoon freshly ground black pepper
1 teaspoon minced garlic
1/4 teaspoon crushed red pepper flakes
1/4 teaspoon salt
1/2 cup shelled fresh garden peas
2 tablespoons chopped fresh parsley

1. Preheat the oven to 400°F. Place all the ingredients except the peas and parsley in a bowl and toss until the florets are coated. Place in a roasting pan and roast for 25 to 30 minutes, turning the cauliflower every 10 minutes so it browns evenly.

2. Just as the vegetables are finishing, lightly steam the peas for 3 to 5 minutes, or until just tender—don't overcook. Place the contents of the roasting pan in a serving bowl and add the peas and parsley. Toss to mix and serve.

TIP: Garam masala can be found in stores, or you can make your own: grind as fine as possible, either with a mortar and pestle or in a spice grinder, the seeds from 2 cardamom pods, 1 teaspoon whole cloves, 30 whole black peppercorns, 2 teaspoons whole cumin seeds, and one 2-inch piece of cinnamon. Store in a tightly closed container in a cool, dark cabinet.

COLORFUL CAULIFLOWER

In addition to white, cauliflower comes in green, purple, and even orange. Romanesco (lime green) and Broccoflower (pale green), intermediaries between broccoli and cauliflower, have beautiful patterns to their structure. These colored varieties are stronger in flavor but also sweeter than either broccoli or cauliflower. Orange Bouquet and Marmalade produce creamy orange curds rich in beta-carotene. Note that purple cauliflower turns green with cooking.

CELERY AND CELERY ROOT

SEASON: year-round for celery; late fall through winter for celery root

GOOD VARIETIES:

Celery: Giant Pascal, Golden Self-Blanching, Matador, Tall Utah 52-70, Tendercrisp, Victoria

Celery root: Alabaster, Diamant, Dolvi, Large Smooth Prague, Marble Ball, Mentor, President, Snow White

WHAT TO LOOK FOR:

Celery: Look for fat, massive stalks—the more massive they are, the more tender they'll be. They should be rigid, never flaccid. And look for a pale green rather than a darker green color.

Celery root: Larger celery roots are best. Look for firm ones the size of a softball or larger, that feel heavy in the hand, that don't give when squeezed. They should be especially firm at the top, where the stalks emerge.

STORAGE AND PREPARATION TIPS:

Celery: Check the area where the stalks attach to the base and wash it well. Sometimes soil splashes up from rains or irrigation flooding of celery trenches and lodges there.

Celery root: Set the celery root on a cutting board and go at it with a serrated knife, slicing deep enough into the flesh to cut out all the pockets and depressions in the root's surface. I work around the root, slicing off the surfaces of the top third piece by piece, then cut off a band of the surfaces around the middle. Then I turn the root upside down and slice off the surfaces of the bottom third so I'm left with a snowy white, vaguely ball-shaped root with many flat surfaces.

NUTRITIONAL HIGHLIGHTS: vitamin C

GO WELL WITH: anchovies, braised meats, capers, caraway seed, carrots, Dijon mustard, dill, fennel, gherkins, herbs, lemon, mayonnaise, onions, parsley, potatoes, risotto, salads, soups, stews, stuffings, winter squash

Celery is grown around the world, and grows wild near the oceans of Europe and Asia. However, commercial British gardeners have a whole class called trench celeries, usually with names that include the words *pink* or *red*: their blanched stalks have a pinkish hue. These are seldom seen in the United States, but keep an eye out for them in farmers' markets or specialty stores.

Celery root, or celeriac as it's sometimes called, is celery that has been bred to grow an enlarged root—usually about the size of a softball—with a rough, brownish surface pitted, pocked, and studded with rootlets. Its leafy stems that form the edible portion of ordinary celery are small and unusually bitter in celery root, and not the prized portion here, although they can be used to flavor soups.

Celery root is a relatively modern innovation, first developed as a separate vegetable in the sixteenth century. The wild progenitor of both stalk celery and celery root is a marsh plant used in rituals and as a flavoring in ancient times.

In the Middle Ages, wild celery was known as smallage; its root was eaten, and it was a delicacy in the Arab world. Because the enlarged roots store water, celery root does not require the soggy conditions necessary for growing stalk celery. Although celery root became very popular in continental Europe, it was never popular in Britain and America until recently.

Organic Advantage

It's especially important to find organic celery, either at the farmers' market or a store. The list of agricultural chemicals used on celery is quite extensive.

Uses

Celery: Celery doesn't star in many recipes. It's an indispensable supporting actor, though. What would Thanksgiving turkey stuffing be without celery and sage? Soups without celery would be bland affairs indeed.

When it does star, it's usually eaten alone, cold and raw. It's the vegetable that refreshes the palate when a tray of crudités is served. I like to remove the outer stalks from a head of celery, cut off the tough base, and devour the heart refrigerator-cold—it's crunchy and herbaceous, with a sort of spiciness in the leaves.

In the kitchen, celery has a hundred uses as an ingredient in savory dishes and salads. It has a liking for its fellow umbelliferous plants: parsley, fennel, and dill. It also blends well with lemon and sharp cheeses. I find lots of uses for celery leaves and always buy celery that still has leaves attached if I can. Chopped fine, they make a fine addition to soups, salads, stews, stuffings, and even rice dishes like risottos.

Celery root: You can do a number of things with celery root, including boil, steam, bake, grate, pickle, shred, julienne, braise, sauté, roast, and microwave it. Its flavor and aroma combine those of parsley, parsnip, and celery.

CHINESE CELERY

In addition to stalk celery, there is also Chinese celery. The same species, it was never selected for size like European varieties. It's closer to wild celery, with slim stalks and a strong flavor. It's invariably cooked with other vegetables as a steamed or stir-fried mixture and is sometimes sold in Asian markets.

In some markets, you can also find wild celery. The progenitor of both our stalk celery and celery root, it has thin stalks and very leafy tops and was used in ancient times as a medicine and flavoring. It's still occasionally sold in France as *céleri à couper* where it is used for flavoring soups and stews; in Italy, it is used to flavor *ragù* or meat sauce. It's very strongly flavored, and not to be used as a raw salad vegetable.

Celery root's real charm is as an adjunct to soups, stews, braised meats, and purees, and as a partner with mashed potatoes—especially garlic mashed potatoes.

Garlic Mashed Potatoes with Celery Root

SERVES 4

Garlic mashed potatoes are great, but when celery root joins the party, they're exquisite!

1 pound red potatoes, peeled and quartered
5 cloves garlic, peeled
1 whole celery root (about 1 1/2 pounds), trimmed and quartered
1/2 cup warm whole milk
2 tablespoons unsalted butter
1/2 teaspoon kosher salt
4 grinds of black pepper
Paprika

1. Bring a large pot of water to a boil. Add the potatoes, garlic, and celery root. Reduce heat to medium and cook until the potatoes and celery root are very soft, about 30 minutes.

2. Pour off the water, returning the ingredients to the pot. Add the milk, butter, salt, and pepper and mash together with a potato masher. If too thick, add a splash more milk and mash again. Transfer to a serving bowl and lightly dust the top with paprika. Serve immediately.

CHARD

SEASON: late spring through early winter

GOOD VARIETIES: Argentata, Bright Lights, Charlotte, Fordhood Giant, Lucullus, Monstruoso, Paros, Virgo

WHAT TO LOOK FOR: Stems should be crisp, not limp. Cut ends should look freshly cut, not dried or shriveled. Leaves should be fresh and glossy, with no signs of decay.

STORAGE AND PREPARATION TIPS: Chard leaves cook more quickly than the ribs, so for perfectly cooked chard I cook them separately. To separate the ribs from the leaves, place whole leaves on a cutting board and make two long cuts along either side of the rib; remove. Mature chard stems may need to be peeled to remove the fibers that run up their backs (similar to celery). Use a paring knife to peel the fibers from base to tip. Fresh chard stems—even big ones—may not require this; give them a tooth test to see how chewy they are.

NUTRITIONAL HIGHLIGHTS: copper, fiber, iron, magnesium, manganese, potassium, vitamin A, vitamin C, vitamin E, vitamin K

GOES WELL WITH: grains, ground meat, nuts, stock

Chard is a subspecies of ordinary garden beets. Bred for its leaves rather than its root, it packs the same kind of nutritional punch as beets do. Although it also goes by the name Swiss chard, it's the French and Italians who have done the most with the vegetable. But the Greeks and Spanish are running a close second: in southern Spain and out on the Balearic Islands, it's cooked much as the Arabs of North Africa prepare it, with spices and hot chiles or sweetmeats. In fact, chard's history goes back to ancient Babylon.

Organic Advantage

Make sure your chard is organic. The high-nitrogen chemical fertilizers used in conventional agriculture can cause the plants to take up too much nitrate, which can change within the human digestive system to cancer-causing nitrites.

Uses

Chard is a versatile vegetable. The leaves have a delicious earthy tang and the stems are succulent, bittersweet, and have a hint of salsify and cardoon in their flavor. Functionally, the leaves and stems are two kinds of vegetables from the same plant.

Chard leaves: Steam them and serve them like spinach, or make them into a quiche. The substantial leaves also make excellent wrappers, dolma-style, for ground meats, grains, or nuts to be baked en casserole.

Chard stems: These take a little more work, but they're worth it. The white midribs of the Lucullus and Argentata varieties are my favorites. They can be braised or parboiled and then simmered in stock or deep-fried. To parboil, cut the stems into 2- to 3-inch pieces and boil in lightly salted water acidulated with a tablespoon of lemon juice for about 5 to 7 minutes. Then rinse them in cold water. To fry chard stems, squeeze parboiled stems dry, dip in a batter of 2 eggs beaten with 3 tablespoons milk, dredge in spiced bread crumbs, and fry in olive oil until golden brown on both sides.

EATING RAW CHARD While you sometimes see chard recommended as a salad ingredient, use it sparingly, because raw chard contains oxalic acid, enough of which can cause gastrointestinal upsets and block the body's ability to absorb iron and calcium. Cooking the chard disarms the oxalic acid.

Winter Green Slaw with Warm Bacon Dressing

SERVES 4

The folks at Planet Organics (www.planetorganics.com) came up with this low-fat, nutritional powerhouse. Use small and tender Lacinato kale leaves (see page 76), fresh, tender beet greens, and tender chard leaves to avoid producing a chewing marathon.

1 teaspoon olive oil
1/2 cup sliced onion
1/4 cup cream cheese, softened
1/4 cup fat-free milk
2 teaspoons white wine vinegar
1 teaspoon Dijon mustard
1/2 teaspoon dried dill
1/2 teaspoon honey
1/8 teaspoon freshly ground black pepper

2 cups thinly sliced (1/4-inch) kale
2 cups thinly sliced beet greens
2 cups thinly sliced chard leaves
2 strips of turkey bacon, cooked and chopped

1. Heat the oil in a pan over medium heat. Add the onion and sauté until tender and browned. Reduce heat to low, add the cream cheese, milk, vinegar, mustard, dill, honey, and black pepper. Stir until well blended. Remove from heat.

2. Place sliced greens in a bowl, pour on the cream cheese mixture, and toss until the greens are evenly covered. Divide on plates and top with chopped turkey bacon.

CHICORY AND ENDIVE

SEASON: fall through winter

GOOD VARIETIES:

Belgian endive: Monroe, Red, Witloof Improved

Chicory: Biondissima di Trieste, Crystal Hat, Dentarella, Italico Rosso, Sugarloaf

Escarole: Batavian Full Heart, Galia, Grosse Bouclee, Pancalieri, Ruffec

Radicchio: Early Treviso, Indigo, Rosso di Verona, Variegata di Castelfranco, Variegata di Chioggia

WHAT TO LOOK FOR: Leaves should be crisp and fresh, with no browning at the cut ends or the tips. Belgian endive leaves should be white to pale yellow with no green showing.

STORAGE AND PREPARATION TIPS: Soil can gather at the base of escarole leaves, so trim off the bottom where the leaves come together and rinse the leaves well. The other chicories and endives simply need a quick rinse. Belgian endive doesn't even need that. Use Belgian endive the day you buy it if possible, for its crisp freshness is its best feature.

NUTRITIONAL HIGHLIGHTS: beta-carotene, calcium, fiber, folate, iron, magnesium, potassium, riboflavin, vitamin B_6, vitamin C

GO WELL WITH: chicken stock, ham, pine nuts, raisins

This group of related vegetables includes chicory, Belgian and curly endive (frisée in France), Italian radicchio, and Batavian escarole. In fact, chicories and endives are both members of the genus Chicorium and are so closely related they are often confused—even in name. The botanical distinction is that chicories are head-forming plants with upright habits, while endives are low-growing, with curly leaves. Frisée is therefore an endive, while Belgian endive is a chicory—despite its name.

No matter what they're called, all of them have an edge of icy-sweet bitterness that helps the cook create a contrast to sweet, savory, or salty flavors. Salads of these greens come to life when set off by apples, blue cheese, figs, ham, pears, nutmeats, or citrus wedges.

The edible chicories are related to the wild chicory we see growing along roadsides and in weedy places just about everywhere in America. This is the plant that develops a flower stalk a foot or two tall with pure blue daisy-like flowers. (Don't try making food out of the wild plants, though.)

Chicories and endives have dozens of types that are grown around the world. Those most often grown in Europe and the United States include Belgian endive, Sugarloaf endive, radicchio, escarole, and frisée.

Belgian endive: The *chicon*, as the head of Belgian endive is called, is the shape of a spearpoint—a cone of overlapping leaves tapering to a point. Its flavor is slightly bitter and its texture delightfully crunchy. Belgian endive is excellent used raw in salads. It can also be braised or wrapped in thin slices of ham and cooked.

Escarole: The large green leaves acquire an unpleasant bitterness, so farmers generally mound soil over the plant to keep it white with a pale yellow to cream-colored center that combines sweetness with the little bit of bitterness that aficionados prefer. Escarole is sometimes sliced into ribbons, added to boiling chicken stock, and served in a soup, *escarole in brodo*. It is also sautéed with raisins and pine nuts, much like spinach. Or keep its leaves intact, stuff the plant's knob with bread crumbs and grated Parmesan, tie up the leaves with string, and simmer the head in chicken stock.

Frisée: The finely cut, frizzy leaves of frisée show up in mesclun mixes, as garnishes, and under fish entrées. Use them in salads, or dip in boiling water until they wilt, then drain, pat dry, and drizzle with olive oil and vinegar.

Radicchio: Once just an Italian obsession, radicchio now shows up in salad mixes across America. There are three types. Some have a red-leafed, white-veined, ball-like head, others form a more elongated, cone-shaped head similar to the *chicon* of a Belgian endive, and still others form a loose head resembling a strikingly red romaine lettuce.

Sugarloaf: This chicory, which forms leafy heads, is also called Sugarloaf endive. It has thick, crunchy leaves that make a fine addition to salads and can be used to protect meats and fish during cooking.

Organic Advantage

Organic varieties of chicory and endive are not treated with agricultural chemicals like the conventionally grown varieties. Belgian endive, however, is never treated with any pesticides, so it doesn't even need to be washed.

Uses

Leafy chicories, endives, and the mild inner leaves of escarole are great raw in salads. They are also commonly braised or used in soups. See individual descriptions for specific uses.

Braised Belgian Endive

SERVES 4

Braising Belgian endive transforms its bittersweet quality into something deliciously savory. It becomes a great accompaniment to roast pork and baked apples.

2 tablespoons olive oil
4 heads Belgian endive
Juice of 1 lemon
1 teaspoon sugar
Generous pinch of salt

1. In a Dutch oven or other heavy lidded pot, heat the olive oil over medium-high heat. When the oil is hot, add the endives and cook for 1½ minutes, or until brown, then turn them over and cook another 1½ minutes to brown the other side. They'll spit and pop in the hot oil.

2. Add the lemon juice, sugar, and salt. Turn the endives to coat. Reduce the heat to low, put on the lid, and simmer for 30 minutes.

Red and White Salad

SERVES 4

The sweet toasted pine nuts contrast remarkably with the bitter red leaves.

FOR THE DRESSING

3 cloves garlic, chopped
Juice of 1 lemon
½ cup olive oil
½ cup freshly grated Parmesan
Salt and freshly ground black pepper

FOR THE SALAD

½ cup pine nuts
1 head frisée (about 6 to 8 ounces)
1 small head radicchio (about 4 to 6 ounces)

1. To make the dressing: puree the garlic and lemon juice in the blender. With the blender running, slowly pour in the olive oil until the dressing is smooth. Add the cheese and blend until thick and smooth. Adjust the seasoning and refrigerate.

2. To make the salad: toast the pine nuts in a dry skillet over medium heat, stirring until they brown and turn aromatic, about 2 to 3 minutes (do not let them burn). Remove the outer green leaves from the frisée and save for another use. Tear up the tender white inner leaves and place in a bowl. Thinly slice the radicchio and toss with the frisée and enough dressing to coat. Sprinkle the pine nuts over the salad and lightly toss again.

CHILE PEPPERS

SEASON: summer and fall

GOOD VARIETIES: Anaheim, ancho, bird, caribe, cascabel, cayenne, Charleston hot, cherry pepper, chilaca, chipotle, Fresno, guajillo, habanero, Hungarian wax, jalapeño, Jamaican hot, mulatto, pasilla, peperoncini, pequin, poblano, Santa Fe grande, scotch bonnet, serrano, Thai, togarashi

WHAT TO LOOK FOR: Fresh chiles should be glossy, firm, and sound, with no soft spots or pitting. The stem end should look freshly cut. Dried chiles should smell good and be free of mold.

PREPARATION TIPS: Wear rubber gloves when cutting chiles to prevent the capsaicin in the peppers from getting onto your fingers and under your nails (see What Makes Chiles So Hot?, page 62). I also wear glasses when cutting fresh chiles to avoid getting a squirt of juice in my eye, especially when working with extremely hot peppers such as Thai chiles, scotch bonnets, and habaneros. Also be aware that cooking really hot peppers like habaneros on the stovetop can release enough capsaicin into the air to cause burning in the throat and even choking.

NUTRITIONAL HIGHLIGHTS: vitamin A, vitamin C

GO WELL WITH: bluefish, butter, cabbage, cider vinegar, crostini, eggs, olive oil, onions, popcorn, salads, salmon, sauces, scallops, shallots, shrimp, soups

---

Among the many gifts from the New World to the Old, fiery chile peppers may be the most valuable. On Columbus's first voyage across the Atlantic, the natives he encountered offered him tiny red wild berries. They looked like the red peppercorns grown in India and even carried a similar spiciness. That led him to believe he'd found India. And so Native Americans became Indians, and those small red berries became peppers. Within a few years of Columbus's first voyage, chiles were being planted in Europe and North Africa, and it wasn't long before they were planted around the world.

The variety of spicy chiles available these days gives you a wide palette of flavors to choose from. Dried poblanos, which are called anchos, have a sweetish flavor; mulattos have a chocolaty taste. Mirasols are fruity; chipotles, which are jalapeños dried over a fire, are smoky. To me, the chile with the best flavor is the habanero; it's sweetly aromatic, fruity, and luscious—but eat too much of it and your mouth feels like its being blasted by a flamethrower.

Chiles' heat is measured in Scoville units of pungency. A typical jalapeño measures about 2,000 Scovilles; a habanero—one of the hottest peppers in the world—measures 200,000 to 300,000. Some argue that pungency ought to join sweet, sour, salty, bitter, and umami (the so-called "savory" taste) as one of the basic tastes, but I think pungency is more a sensation than a flavor.

Organic Advantage

Insects tend to avoid capsaicin, the hot substance in chiles, so most chiles are not sprayed. (In fact, gardeners use hot chiles to make a bug-repelling spray.) But choose organic chiles for their superior culinary quality from being grown in nutrient-rich, compost-amended soil.

WHAT MAKES CHILES SO HOT?

The substance that makes chiles so spicy hot is called capsaicin. Capsaicin is produced in glands on the placenta of the fruits–the whitish substance in the interior of the pod. No other part of the chile produces capsaicin. The burn we experience in our mouths from the capsaicin stimulates our bodies to produce endorphins–natural pain killers that can create a feeling of euphoria. Eating a hot pepper just may be the high point of your day.

If capsaicin causes such pain to the mucous membranes, what does it do to our stomachs? Scientists have looked into the human stomach after the ingestion of chile peppers to see if any damage is done, and it turns out that chile peppers, even very hot chile peppers, cause no trauma at all. In fact, they are beneficial to our systems in many ways. For example, they cause a healthy perspiration–one reason chiles are used so often in hot climates.

Uses

Fresh chiles can be used to add heat to dishes in many ways, from a faint glow to a real burn. Here are some ideas:

Chile-spiced oil and vinegar: Slice a couple of serranos and add them to a cruet of olive oil. Store for a week, then use the oil on salads; for sautéing onions, shallots, shrimp, or scallops; tossed with popcorn; or brushed onto bruschetta or crostini. Similarly, cut up a jalapeño and add it—seeds and all—to a small bottle of cider vinegar. Store this for a week, and then use the vinegar on salads, strong ocean fish like bluefish or salmon, or on cabbage.

Chile butter: Slice open a hot chile, remove the seeds, and scrape out the white inner placental material into a pan of butter. Cook over low heat just until the butter melts, then chill the butter. This produces a deliciously hot butter that's fantastic by itself on bread. A pat of it is also a great way to finish a steak.

Dried chiles: Chiles develop different flavors depending on how they are prepared. Grinding the dried pods in a mortar and pestle or *molcajete* (see recipe at right) produces a strong, assertive pungency when added to salsa or other sauce. Toasting chile pods before grinding them creates a sweeter, richer flavor. (To toast the pods, bake them in a 300°F oven for 10 minutes.) Soaking dried chiles in water for half an hour to soften them before grinding results in a more aromatic taste. Dried peppers can be soaked and stuffed, or pureed and added to soups and sauces; ground dried chiles can be worked into sauces for enchiladas.

Fresh Salsa

MAKES ABOUT 1 PINT

A *molcajete* is a heavy granite mortar in which salsa ingredients are traditionally ground. You can use a food processor pulsed a few times to approximate the chunky texture a molcajete produces.

5 ripe medium Roma or plum tomatoes
3 jalapeño chiles
1 small white onion, chopped
$^1/_2$ cup cilantro leaves
2 cloves garlic, peeled
Salt to taste

1. On a grill or in an iron skillet over high heat, sear the tomatoes and jalapeños, turning them a few times until they are soft and all sides are charred. Remove from heat and allow them to cool.
2. Remove the tomato skins. Remove the stems from the jalapeño chiles and then their skins by rubbing them with a paper towel. Place the peeled tomatoes, chiles, onion, cilantro, garlic, and salt in a molcajete and pound until chunky and blended. If using a food processor, pulse to roughly chop the ingredients.

GREEN SALSA (SALSA VERDE)

Follow the recipe above, replacing the tomatoes with $^1/_2$ pound tomatillos, husks removed, chopped and cooked in a skillet over medium-low heat for 15 minutes. Add $^1/_2$ teaspoon of sugar.

EXTRA-HOT SALSA

To increase the salsa's pungency, add 5 seeded, chopped serrano chiles or 1 habanero.

RAW VS. GRILLED Serranos or habaneros should be used raw; grilling them may release unpleasant fumes.

Moroccan Chicken

SERVES 4

In this traditional Moroccan dish, the chicken is rubbed with a *harissa*, a traditional Tunisian paste made from hot chiles. It is then stewed and finally broiled. Serve it with couscous studded with golden raisins and dried currants.

Two 3-pound chickens, cut in half, backbones removed
2 tablespoons Harissa (recipe follows)
4 tablespoons butter
3 cups diced onions
$^1/_4$ cup chopped fresh cilantro
Salt to taste

1. Wash the chicken halves and dry well with paper towels. Rub the chicken halves with the harissa paste, slipping a little under the skin here and there.
2. Melt the butter in a Dutch oven or heavy lidded pot over medium heat and add the onions. Sauté until the onions are translucent, about 8 minutes.
3. Add the chicken halves to the pot and almost cover with water, about 4 or 5 cups. Bring to a boil, then reduce to a simmer. Cover and simmer 45 minutes, turning the chicken once, or until tender.
4. Transfer the chicken from the pot to a baking sheet. Add the cilantro to the liquid in the pot and boil about 20

minutes, or until the liquid is reduced to about 2 or 3 cups.

5. While the liquid is reducing, preheat the broiler and broil the chicken skin side up until golden brown, about 5 minutes. Transfer the chicken to a platter. Correct the seasoning in the reduced juices if necessary and pour the juices over the chicken. You can strain the liquor for aesthetics, but it's traditionally served unstrained.

Harissa

MAKES ABOUT 1 CUP

This hot sauce originated in Tunisia but has become the staple flavoring agent for many North African dishes. You can buy it canned or in tubes at many Middle Eastern markets, but it tastes best when homemade and will last in the fridge up to six months. Vary the level of pungency by choosing different varieties of chiles. For a good, hot harissa—the way the Moroccans like it—use dried pasillas or chipotles; if you want to maximize the burn, include a dried habanero or two.

12 dried chiles, sliced in half, seeds removed, and roughly chopped
1/2 cup extra-virgin olive oil, plus extra for storage
1 teaspoon ground cumin
4 cloves garlic, coarsely chopped
Salt to taste

1. Soak the chile pieces in warm water for 30 minutes, or until they soften. Drain and place the chiles in a blender with olive oil, cumin, garlic, and salt.

2. Blend until a smooth paste is formed. Put the paste into a small jar and float 1/4 inch of olive oil on top. Cap and refrigerate.

CORN

SEASON: August and September

GOOD VARIETIES:

Standard sugary: Golden Cross Bantam, Honey and Cream, Silver Queen

Sugary enhanced: Ambrosia, How Sweet It Is, Incredible, Silverado, Sugar Buns

Sweet: Early Xtra Sweet, Honey and Pearl, Honey Select, Indian Summer, Supersweet Jubilee

Heirloom: Country Gentleman, Golden Bantam, Luther Hill, Stowell's Evergreen, True Gold

WHAT TO LOOK FOR: There's no need to strip the husks open and inspect each ear to see if it's full. (This will only ruin the ear for the next buyer if you reject it.) You can feel *through* the husks when an ear is full and fat and when it's not. Or pull open only the very top and give it the fingernail test: ripe corn kernels will exude a milky fluid when pressed with a thumbnail.

STORAGE AND PREPARATION TIPS: To husk corn, peel the husks back toward the stem as if peeling a banana, then grasp all the husks with one hand and the ear with the other and twist the husks off with a breaking motion. Remove corn silk. When grilling corn in the husks, remove the tough outer husks and soak the partially husked corn in cold water for a half hour before grilling; this will prevent the husks from burning on the grill.

NUTRITIONAL HIGHLIGHTS: fiber, folate, lutein, thiamin, vitamin C

GOES WELL WITH: bacon, black pepper, butter, cayenne, cheese, lemon, lime, lobsters, onions, salt, seaweed, soft-shell clams

---

Corn was first cultivated by Native Americans in the Tehuacan Valley of Puebla, Mexico, in 5500 BCE. By the time Columbus arrived 6,992 years later, the corn plant had evolved into its modern form—dependent for its survival on human hands to pull the seeds off the cobs and plant them individually a foot or so apart.

Sweet corn is a natural mutation of Indian or field corn, the starchy corn used mainly for cattle fodder in the United States. The corn stays sweet, but only until the ear is picked. Soon after, its sugar begins turning into starch. For maximum sweetness, then, you have to get the corn to the pot of boiling water immediately.

Organic Advantage

As of this writing, over 60 percent of the corn planted in the United States has been genetically modified. Some can grow well in an herbicide-drenched environment; some can actually generate its own pesticides: its been given a gene from a bacterium that expresses a caterpillar toxin. Organic corn is not only free of pesticides, but also of such unnatural genetic alterations.

Uses

Sweet, tender, creamy corn is so luscious simply boiled on the cob that it's hard to believe it could be better. But it's as versatile and delicious a vegetable and grain as we have. Think of all the things that corn gives us. Bourbon! (My folks were from Kentucky, "where the corn is full of kernels, and the colonels are full of corn.") Corn also gives us tortillas, tamales, popcorn, hominy grits, polenta, hush puppies, corn pone, corn bread, hoecakes, johnnycakes, spoon bread, and—hallelujah!—corn smut. This gray and blackish purple fungus invades corn, but it's treated as a delicacy in Mexico, where it's known as *huitlacoche*, and is served steamed or fried.

Indian Corn Pudding

SERVES 6

One taste of this sweet and spicy pudding and you're back with the pilgrims eating wild turkey and oyster pie on the shores of Cape Cod. It's a delight when the weather turns cold and there's a fire in the fireplace.

1/2 cup stone-ground cornmeal
4 cups whole milk
1/2 cup blackstrap molasses

BABY CORN

When I first started growing corn, I found spindly little stalks about 18 inches tall growing among weeds. They had 2-inch ears, which I dutifully harvested. I thought they looked like the baby corn that was showing up in Szechuan dishes in Chinese restaurants, so I tasted one—it was sweet and tender. So I harvested the bunch of them—I got maybe two handfuls from the whole darn patch—and worked them into a stir-fry. That's how I discovered that Chinese baby corn is just that—immature corn picked very young, and not a separate kind of corn.

4 tablespoons unsalted butter plus extra for the casserole
1 large egg, well beaten
2 tablespoons sugar
1 teaspoon ground cinnamon
1 teaspoon ground ginger
1/2 teaspoon salt

1. Preheat the oven to 275°F. Place the cornmeal in a 1 1/2- to 2-quart saucepan, stir in 1 cup of the milk, turn the heat to medium, and add another cup of milk, stirring to avoid lumps. As the milk comes to a boil, slowly add the remaining milk, stirring as you do so. Cook for 3 minutes, then reduce the heat to low and simmer for 15 minutes.

2. Add the molasses and stir until entirely dissolved. Remove the saucepan from the heat and grease a 2-quart casserole while you let it cool.

3. Stir the 4 tablespoons of butter, egg, sugar, cinnamon, ginger, and salt into the batter. When it's well incorporated, pour the batter into the casserole. Bake uncovered for 2 1/2 to 3 hours.

Cheesy Corn Soufflé

SERVES 4

When corn is in season, I can't get enough of it. Here its savory flavor merges beautifully with Fontina cheese in a light and fluffy simple soufflé.

2 ears corn, or enough to make 2 cups kernels
2 tablespoons unsalted butter
1/2 cup shredded Fontina cheese (about 2 ounces)
6 large eggs, separated, plus 2 extra egg whites
4 tablespoons finely chopped chives
Salt and freshly ground black pepper
1/4 teaspoon cream of tartar

1. Cut corn kernels off the cobs. Squeeze remaining corn milk out of cobs with the back of a knife. Place corn and liquid in a blender and blend to a grainy consistency, not a fine puree.

2. Preheat the oven to 425°F. Grease an ovenproof 2-quart soufflé dish with the butter.

3. In a mixing bowl, blend together the corn, cheese, 6 egg yolks, chives, salt, and pepper. Place all 8 egg whites in a separate bowl; add the cream of tartar, and beat them to soft peaks. Using a rubber spatula, fold the whites into the corn mixture until they're well incorporated. Pour the mixture into the soufflé dish, and bake uncovered for 10 minutes. Reduce the heat to 375°F and bake for 30 minutes more.

CUCUMBER

SEASON: summer

GOOD VARIETIES:

Slicing: Burpless, Marketmore 70, Sweet Slice, Sweet Success Pickling: Anka, County Fair 83, Liberty Hybrid Picklebush

Cornichons: Cool Breeze

Middle Eastern: Amira, Kidma

Asian: Orient Express, Palace King

European greenhouse: Holland, Petita

WHAT TO LOOK FOR: Avoid cucumbers that are waxed, a sign of low quality. Cucumbers should be firm, with no give when squeezed, and green all around, without any yellow patches. Seek out cucumbers with bumps or prickly spines (the spines are easily rubbed off with a dish towel).

STORAGE AND PREPARATION TIPS: Cucumbers store for a week in the refrigerator in an open plastic bag. Thin-skinned cucumbers don't require peeling.

NUTRITIONAL HIGHLIGHTS: small amounts of vitamin C

GOES WELL WITH: chiles, cumin, lemon juice, lemongrass, mint, salmon, yogurt

When we Americans think of cucumbers, we usually think of those smooth, dark green supermarket oblongs with thick, tough skins covered by a waxy film. These are American slicers. But there are many types of cucumbers out there other than American slicers. In order of availability:

Pickling: Ideal not only for pickling but also for eating, they have thin skins, little bitterness, and a firmer, crisper, sweeter flesh than American slicers.

Hothouse: Also called European greenhouse, they are long and slender. Their crisp flesh tastes mild but cooly refreshing. They lack any bitterness, have no seeds, are easy to digest, and their ribbed skins are so thin they don't need peeling. They usually come tightly wrapped in plastic.

Cornichons: These miniature cucumbers are ordinarily pickled, but they can be eaten raw as well.

Middle Eastern: Similar to European greenhouse cucumbers, these also have ribbed skins and thin skins. They are my preferred sort for Greek salad.

Asian: Used to make sushi, they are quite flavorful and crisp.

Organic Advantage

Two main beetles feed on cucumber plants, attracted by the chemical cucurbitacin in the vegetable's skin. Rather than use pesticides, organic growers install fine-mesh row covers and interplant their cucumbers with other crops to avoid the monoculture of cucumbers that floods the fields with the cucurbitacin that attracts the beetles.

Uses

I'm so enthralled by their cool, fresh flavors that I almost always use them raw, although they can be cooked. I like them in Thai salad, where they combine well with chiles and lemongrass. On hot days, I may make an Indian *raita*—a refreshing relish made with yogurt and chopped or pureed cucumbers, flavored with mint, cumin, lemon juice, and a bit of spicy chiles. Or I'll just buy some cold, precooked salmon and serve it topped with finely diced cucumbers. At tea time, serve those precious little tea sandwiches made of cucumber slices on buttered crustless bread.

Making pickles: Slice pickling cucumbers lengthwise in quarters and put them in a jar with a small handful of dill seeds, a few coriander seeds, and a tablespoon of kosher salt. Fill the jar with white vinegar. Let it stand on the kitchen counter uncovered for two or three days, then screw the lid on and put it in the fridge. Shake the jar every few days. In about two weeks, you'll have your own pickles.

Greek Salad

SERVES 4

This is real Greek salad, as encountered by my wife and son on a five-week tour of Greece. Greek salad shows off the flavor of fresh summer vegetables, so no lettuce, please. In a perfect salad, the tomatoes will be warm from the garden and the cucumbers firm and juicy. This is actually a great gardener's salad, as its main ingredients are easy to grow in a basic vegetables garden. At the very least, try to make this the same day as you buy the ingredients.

3 ripe tomatoes, cut into 1/2-inch slivers
1 top-quality cucumber, peeled and cut into 1/4-inch slices
1 cup cubed feta cheese (1/2-inch cubes)
3 tablespoons olive oil

GARNISHES (OPTIONAL)

1/2 green bell pepper, seeded and cut lengthwise into thin strips
1 small red onion, cut in half lengthwise, sliced 1/4-inch thick, and separated
1/2 cup pitted kalamata olives
1 tablespoon capers
1 tablespoon red wine vinegar
1 anchovy fillet, mashed and tossed with the oil
1/2 teaspoon dried oregano
Salt to taste

Lay out the tomatoes and cucumbers on a platter, sprinkle with the feta, and drizzle olive oil on top. These ingredients alone form a basic Greek salad. However, even in Greece cooks will add a little something else for flavor. Add any combination of garnishes that you like. I suggest you use either the vinegar or the capers but not both, and reserve the right to use neither.

Tzatziki

SERVES 6

In Greece, this thick cucumber-yogurt dip is served with almost everything. It is great as a spread with pita bread, as a sauce for seafood, chicken, roast lamb, and goat, or as a dip for grilled slices of summer vegetables. Greeks drain excess liquid from their yogurt to thicken it; otherwise, the *tzatziki* will be too watery.

1 quart plain yogurt
1 medium pickling cucumber, peeled and grated
2 tablespoons extra-virgin olive oil
1 tablespoon chopped fresh mint
1 tablespoon red wine vinegar
3 cloves garlic, minced
Salt and freshly ground black pepper

1. Place the yogurt in a double layer of cheesecloth, tie it up like a sack and let it hang 2 hours, until well drained and thickened. Press the grated cucumber between paper towels to remove as much liquid as possible.

2. In a bowl, mix together the drained yogurt, cucumber, olive oil, mint, vinegar, and garlic, and season with salt and pepper to taste. Place in a serving dish, cover with plastic wrap, and refrigerate for several hours to give the ingredients time to integrate.

EGGPLANT

SEASON: August and September

GOOD VARIETIES:

Black-purple: Baby Bell, Dusky, Kurume Long, Pingtung Long Improved

Green: Louisiana Long Green, Thai Long Green

Pink-lavender (Italian): Rosa Bianco, Violetta di Firenze

White: Casper, Italian White, Snowy

WHAT TO LOOK FOR: Look for eggplants two-thirds of their full size or smaller; full-size eggplants tend to turn overly bitter, and their seeds ripen and become hard. When perfect, eggplants have skins with a high gloss; when pressed with a thumb, they have a little give that rebounds when the pressure is lifted. Their green cap and stem are bright and fresh looking. The best eggplants will feel heavy in the hand.

STORAGE AND PREPARATION TIPS: Set them on a cool counter space and use within a day or two after buying. Because of their tropical nature and short shelf life, don't store eggplants in the fridge.

NUTRITIONAL HIGHLIGHTS: antioxidants

GOES WELL WITH: anchovies, capers, garlic, hummus, olives, olive oil, onions, pepper, pine nuts, salt, tomatoes, vinegar

Besides the familiar raven-dark, purple-black eggplant seen in supermarkets, there are eggplant varieties that vary in size from ping-pong balls to two-foot ropes, and in color from orange-red to pinkish lavender to celadon to ivory.

WHY IS IT CALLED EGGPLANT?

Scientists believe the eggplant originated in either India or Burma and was carried east to China and west to Arabia. It was brought to Spain by the Moors, and from there to the rest of Europe in the eighth century.

Eggplant was as much a staple crop in southern Europe as the potato later became. In Italy, it was originally thought to be poisonous and was called *mela insana*, or "insane apple." Today the Italian word for eggplant, *melanzana*, is a corruption of that phrase. In the rest of Europe, it's name is a variant of the word *aubergine*, a term that has come down a convoluted path from its original Sanskrit. Americans know it as eggplant, and if you have ever seen the variety called Osterei, which means "Easter egg" in German, you'd know why: it looks just like a white chicken egg.

If you are already familiar with the common purple eggplant, I suggest looking for pale green types that are exceptional in quality; smaller Japanese and Chinese eggplants with thinner skins and very delicate flavor; white ones with tough skins but an earthy, mushroomy flavor; and the violet or pink-and-white Italian types, especially Rosa Bianco, which is very meaty, with a fine texture and a delicate flavor.

Organic Advantage

Instead of pesticides, organic growers control insects with physical barriers like row covers, sticky traps and, for potato beetles, a strain of *Bacillus thuringiensis* that's harmless to other forms of life.

Uses

Eggplant adds texture and bulk to dishes along with its sappy flavors. It's used around the world in a variety of regional and ethnic dishes. In the Middle East, baba ghanoush joins hummus as a preferred dip for pita bread. In Sicily, caponata relish is made by cooking eggplant, onions, tomatoes, anchovies, olives, pine nuts, capers, and vinegar in olive oil. In Spain, tiny white eggplants are pickled. In Greece, moussaka is a national dish. In France, ratatouille and aubergine au gratin are standard fare. In Russia, they make eggplant caviar from a cooked, peeled, and finely chopped eggplant mixed with grated onion, garlic, minced peeled and seeded tomato, a little olive oil, and salt and pepper.

No matter what color eggplant you start with, cooking is going to turn the skin a shade of gray-brown.

Indian Eggplant with Potatoes (*Salna*)

SERVES 6 TO 8

Spicy Indian flavors transform eggplant and potatoes (two related foods) into an exotic stew with a bright yellow color. It's a fabulous side dish with curried lamb.

2 pounds Japanese or Italian eggplants, quartered
1 pound red potatoes, peeled and quartered
1/4 cup olive oil
2 serrano chiles, halved lengthwise and seeded
1 tablespoon garam masala (see Tip, page 53)
1 tablespoon minced fresh ginger
2 teaspoons minced garlic
1 teaspoon mustard seeds
1/2 teaspoon ground turmeric
2 tablespoons chopped cilantro
2 tablespoons chopped scallions

1. Preheat the oven to 400°F. Place the eggplants, potatoes, olive oil, chiles, garam masala, ginger, mustard seeds, and turmeric in a large bowl and toss the vegetables to thoroughly coat with the oil and spices.

2. Place in a baking pan large enough to hold everything in a single layer. Bake for 45 minutes, stirring the vegetables every 15 minutes. The stew is done when the potatoes are cooked through and golden brown on the outside, and the eggplant is soft. Serve garnished with the cilantro and scallions.

FENNEL

SEASON: Florence fennel is available summer through fall; fennel seed is available year-round.

GOOD VARIETIES: Zefa Fino

WHAT TO LOOK FOR: Look for fennel with the fronds still attached, as they have any number of culinary uses (see below).

STORAGE AND PREPARATION TIPS: When separating the fronds from the bulbs, leave about an inch of the stalks at the top of the bulb.

NUTRITIONAL HIGHLIGHTS: small amounts of calcium, potassium, and vitamin C

GOES WELL WITH: bourbon, cucumbers, eggs, fennel seeds, lemon juice, Niçoise olives, Parmesan, pastis, salmon, sausages

You'll sometimes see this vegetable called anise due to its light anise-like aroma and flavor, but true anise is another plant altogether. And although I've seen it called sweet fennel, that name is reserved for the wild fennel that's a familiar sight (and smell) along roadsides and pathways in the countryside. The same wilding is also found in southern France and in Italy, where its feathery fronds, smelling (and tasting) strongly of anise, are used in soups and sauces and for stuffing fish, poultry, and rabbit.

The bulbous fennel we see in most markets is Florence fennel—or *finocchio*, as it's called in Italian markets. The bulb of Florence fennel isn't an enlarged root; it is formed from enlarged petioles—leaf stems where they attach to the crown.

Organic Advantage

Fennel's distinctive aroma seems to discourage most insects. That means that the fresh fennel you get at the store is most likely free from harmful chemicals—but of course, that's not the same as a certified organic crop with all the benefits that accrue to the environment, the farm, and the vegetable's flavor and nutritive value.

Uses

Fennel's celery-like crunch and light anise (almost dill-like) flavor are irresistible. Its anise character, already mild, is lessened by cooking, so some chefs looking to maintain its flavor will add fennel seeds or pastis, as the French call their anise-flavored liqueurs such as Pernod. Fennel definitely has an affinity for fish, especially salmon, and its flavor merges beautifully with lemon juice, cucumbers, Niçoise olives, bourbon, and good Parmesan. I buy a half pound of fresh bulk sausage at the market, mix it with a heaping tablespoon of fennel seeds and an ounce or two of bourbon, and fry it as patties for a Sunday breakfast of eggs and sausage.

Cooking with fennel stalks: This is the part between the bulb and the fronds in cultivated fennel. Wild fennel has no bulb, just stalks and fronds. Tougher than the bulb, the stalks can be used in braised fennel dishes. Or peel the stalks down to the juicy centers, roughly chop and pan-fry them in garlic and olive oil, then finish by braising in stock until tender. In Provence, cooks grill fish over a fire of dried sweet fennel stalks.

Cooking with fennel fronds: Fennel fronds are often blanched in boiling water for 30 seconds before being used. Try using blanched fennel fronds instead of basil to make pesto, mashing in a few anchovies instead of the cheese.

Whole roast fish stuffed with fennel fronds: Whole roast fish stuffed with fennel fronds is aromatic bliss. For a fish weighing 3 pounds or less, heat the oven to 500°F; for a heavier fish, to 450°F. Wash the fish, pat it dry, and make three or four diagonal slashes on each side. Separate the feathery fronds from the fennel bulb. (If you are using wild fennel, blanch them for 30 seconds.) Coarsely chop the fronds and stuff them into the whole fish. Place the fish in a roasting pan lined with aluminum foil. Roast fish under 3 pounds 25 to 35 minutes, depending on size, and heavier fish 45 minutes or more. To check doneness, use two forks to pull apart one of the slashes: when the flesh is opaque right down to the bone, the fish is done. Serve with a sauce made by processing the coarsely chopped fennel bulb with a peeled and seeded cucumber and a bit of salt.

Fennel and Tomato Salad

SERVES 4 TO 6

In high summer or early fall, when tomatoes are at their garden-fresh finest, use the best you can find—heirloom or good old Beefsteaks, whatever is perfectly ripe—to make this luscious salad.

2 or 3 medium perfectly ripe tomatoes
1 fennel bulb, fronds attached
2 tablespoons freshly squeezed Meyer lemon or orange juice
Grated zest of 1 Meyer lemon or small orange (well scrubbed if not organic)
2 tablespoons olive oil
1 tablespoon apple cider vinegar
Salt and freshly ground black pepper

1. Slice each tomato into 8 wedges. Cut off the stalks and fronds from the fennel bulb, reserving the fronds. Slice the fennel bulb very thin.

2. Toss the tomatoes and fennel bulb with the citrus juice and zest, oil, vinegar, and salt and pepper to taste.

3. Chop the fennel fronds very fine and garnish the salad with a generous tablespoon of them. Toss the salad and serve.

GARLIC

SEASON: summer

GOOD VARIETIES:

Hard-neck: Carpathian, Italian purple, Spanish roja

Soft-neck: California Early, California Late, Creole, Susanville

WHAT TO LOOK FOR: Avoid garlic with green sprouts showing from the tips of the cloves. The heads should feel firm when given a gentle squeeze.

STORAGE AND PREPARATION TIPS: Store garlic in a perforated container (to keep it dry) at room temperature. Its papery husks will keep it fresh for a couple of weeks or longer. Garlic looses its pungency when peeled, so those jars of peeled garlic cloves will have much less flavor than fresh, unpeeled garlic.

NUTRITIONAL HIGHLIGHTS: allicin, phytochemicals

GOES WELL WITH: basil, cheese, chiles, cilantro, cumin, fish, ginger, lemongrass, lime juice, marinades, mayonnaise, meat, olive oil, parsley, pine nuts, potatoes, soy sauce, stock, vinegar

The ancient Egyptians imbued garlic and onions with divinity and took their oaths on them. Among the other treasures in Tutankhamen's tomb were heads of garlic. The wild progenitors of garlic were native to south-central Asia and the central Asian steppes. It's likely the plant made its way west to the Middle East and the Mediterranean on the caravans that plied the Silk Road in deep antiquity. Certainly garlic seems to have remained unchanged since the days of ancient Egypt.

The white-skinned garlic you find at most supermarkets, and sometimes see braided into long strands, is usually soft-neck garlic, which generally has white or silver skins. Hard-neck garlic, which tends to have darker red- or purple-striped skins, is generally more pungent. But the hard-neck varieties are hardier and their flavors are more varied than the soft-neck varieties.

Organic Advantage

Despite its pungent smell and antibacterial properties, heavy applications of agricultural chemicals are used to fumigate the soil in which it grows against root-destroying worms known as nematodes. Because it's easy to grow, many organic farmers grow it, and finding organic garlic is not that difficult. You can also find it fresh from online suppliers (see Sources, page 287).

Uses

Cultures all over the world use garlic to enhance savory dishes. Many of the traditional sauces, marinades, and rubs for meat and fish contain garlic. In Cuba, garlic is combined with lime juice and cumin to make *mojo*, a marinade for grilled chicken, pork, or firm-fleshed fish. In Russia, garlic is pickled. In Southeast Asia it's combined with lemongrass, ginger, soy sauce, cilantro, and hot chiles.

Garlic is also a base ingredient in many sauces and dips. Garlic turns mayonnaise into aioli. Italians pound garlic with basil and pine nuts to make pesto. And *gremolata*, a simple mix of minced garlic, parsley, and lemon peel, is traditionally sprinkled on osso buco. Greeks make the sauce and dip called *skordalia* from pureed baked potatoes, garlic, lemon juice, olive oil, vinegar, parsley, and bread crumbs or ground nuts. Rouille, a hot paste made of chiles, garlic, bread crumbs, and olive oil is the classic garnish for bouillabaisse, the seafood stew of Marseille. *Persillade*, or finely minced parsley and garlic, flavors everything from steamed clams to ricotta filling for ravioli.

Pasta with garlic: An old Italian way to dress pasta involves breaking a dozen whole heads of garlic with the flat blade of a knife, shucking and coarsely chopping the cloves, and heating them in 1/4 inch of olive oil in a large skillet over medium heat until the garlic turns a light golden color, then pouring it all over cooked pasta. (Start the water when you start peeling the garlic). You can use less garlic, but peeling lots of garlic can be a meditative pleasure.

DON'T BURN IT Garlic burns easily at high heat, so add chopped or minced garlic to fried or sautéed dishes during the last minute or so of cooking.

Roasted garlic: Garlic can also be roasted. Indeed, roasted garlic is a precious ingredient to have on hand. Mix it into mashed potatoes. Combined it with olive oil and salt and brush it on toasted bread to make classic bruschetta. Drop a dollop into soups and stews, spread some on an omelet just before folding it, whisk some into soft polenta—it flavors almost anything under the sun.

To roast garlic, heat the oven to 375°F. Put 1/2 inch of water in a lidded casserole and set several heads of garlic upright in the casserole. Cover and roast about 30 minutes, then test a clove: if it's soft, the garlic's done. If it's still firm, uncover and roast 5 to 10 more minutes. Remove the finished garlic from the pan and let cool until you can handle it, then cut off the tops with poultry shears and squeeze the garlicky paste into a bowl.

ALLICIN: THE SOURCE OF GARLIC'S AROMA

Garlic is odorless until you peel the skin from the cloves. Then enzymes start working to produce a compound called allicin, which gives garlic its familiar pungency. The more finely you chop or mash garlic, the more allicin is created, and the stronger the pungency will be (a garlic press, therefore, yields the most intense flavor, whereas whole cloves or coarsely chopped cloves yield proportionately less).

If chopped garlic sits out, however, in less than an hour further enzymatic action degrades the allicin, reducing its punch but increasing garlic's healthful properties. If you will be using garlic raw (in salad dressing, for instance) you may want to prep it 15 minutes ahead of time for that reason. Cooking also reduces the pungency of allicin. When cooking, use freshly peeled cloves for the best flavor.

Greek Garlic Sauce

MAKES 1 CUP

There's evidence in the archaeological records that the ancient Greeks used some version of this sauce on their esteemed fish slices (considered then to be the pinnacle of gastronomy). I use it as a dip for pita bread along with hummus, accompanied by oil-cured olives.

1 slice whole-wheat bread, crust removed

1 head garlic

1/2 cup blanched almonds

Salt to taste

1/4 cup olive oil

1/4 cup red wine vinegar

Soak the bread in a bowl of water. Separate and peel the garlic cloves, and mash them in a mortar with the almonds and salt until a thick paste forms. Squeeze the excess water from the bread and add it to the paste, along with the olive oil and vinegar. Mash and mix thoroughly. Season to taste with more salt if necessary. Refrigerate for up to 1 week.

Garlic Rub for Meat

MAKES ABOUT 1/2 CUP, ENOUGH TO RUB ONE RACK OR ROAST

Rub this on a rack, shoulder, or leg of lamb; on a rolled boneless pork roast; or on a beef roast before cooking.

4 cloves garlic, peeled

1 tablespoon each minced fresh parsley, sage, rosemary, and thyme

2 teaspoons freshly ground black pepper

1/2 teaspoon kosher salt

Mash everything together in a mortar with a pestle or pulse briefly in a food processor, and rub over the surface of the meat before roasting.

KALE

SEASON: fall to early spring

GOOD VARIETIES: Konserva, Lacinato, Red Russian, Redbor, Vates Dwarf Blue Curled, Winterbor

WHAT TO LOOK FOR: Kale should have a rich green color, with no wilting, brown spots, or yellowing leaves.

STORAGE AND PREPARATION TIPS: Keep kale away from any fruit that gives off ethylene gas as it continues to ripen—apples, stone fruits, bananas, and the like. Kale has a tough central midrib that takes longer to cook then the leaves. To remove it, lay a leaf flat on a cutting board and run a sharp knife down either side of the midrib. Cook the midrib and the leaves separately.

NUTRITIONAL HIGHLIGHTS: calcium, carotenoids, copper, fiber, folate, iron, manganese, potassium, vitamin A, vitamin B_6, vitamin C, vitamin K

GOES WELL WITH: bacon, barley, carrots, celery, chicken, clams, garlic, lemon juice, olive oil, onions, parsley, peppercorns, potatoes, sage, salt, sausage, shellfish, smoked ham, white wine

Kale is a member of the cabbage family (along with broccoli, cauliflower, and collard greens). A sturdy, leafy green, when cooked it acquires a pleasant, sweet flavor and a chewy texture. It's also one of the most nutritious vegetables available. Kale is usually categorized by leaf shape and color. There are red kales, green kales, and even black kales, such as Lacinato. Some kales have extra curly leaves, while others have wavy edges.

Kale was the staple green for many of the peasant farmers of the Middle Ages, and probably kept the peasants in better health than their lords and masters, who dined principally on meat. Simple meals of kale, potatoes, and black bread sustained the poor farmers of northern Europe and Russia through long, harsh winters, as kale would grow when no other fresh greens were available. Kale persists quite nicely through most European winters—if things get really frosty, you can just mound snow over it and it will keep fine. Kale actually becomes sweeter and more tender when hit by hard frosts.

Organic Advantage

Like most dark green, leafy vegetables, kale will take in and concentrate nitrogen from the soil in its tissues. In excess (as you find in chemical fertilizers), certain of these compounds can form carcinogenic nitrosamines in the intestines. That's why it's important to find a source of organic kale. Under organic cultivation, the soil is fertilized with compost rather than flooded with chemical nitrogen. Compost is buffered by the action of microorganisms and delivers to plants only the amount of nitrogen they need for their health—and ours.

Uses

I like to separate kale's tough midrib and cook it separately from the leafy greens (see Storage and Preparation Tips, at left). The greens can be sautéed in olive oil with a pinch of salt over medium heat. Or, if I'm frying fatty meat like sausage or bacon, the kale greens cook nicely in some of the rendered fat. Kale greens become especially tender with long, slow cooking. I toss a few leaves into the slow cooker along with an onion, a couple of potatoes, a carrot, a stalk of celery, three or four chicken thighs, a few peppercorns, maybe a handful of barley, a tied-up bundle of parsley and sage, and a bottle of white wine. I cover the pot, turn it on low, and when I get home dinner will be waiting.

Black Tuscan kale (Lacinato) can be steamed and used in place of grape leaves for dolmas, or stuffed grape leaves. Colored varieties of kale make pretty beds for whole baked fish or roast meats.

As for the midribs, I will tie them in a bundle and use them to flavor soup or stew. Or sometimes I'll simmer them in a little water—the longer the better, to retrieve as many nutrients as possible—then reduce the mineral-laden water to use as kale stock for making soup or stews, cooking rice and other grains (or risotto), or for poaching fish.

Caldo Verde (Portuguese Kale Soup)

SERVES 8

I first had this Portuguese staple in New Bedford, Massachusetts, when my fraternity brother Armand Fernandes Jr. took me to a Portuguese restaurant. I never forgot it, and I still make it today. It has a wonderful smoky, earthy, and rich flavor that makes you think of Portuguese fishermen spooning down quantities of this hot soup to bolster themselves against the penetrating cold of the north Atlantic. This is just one version of the soup, but a good one. Serve it with corn bread. Note that you should start this soup a day before you plan to serve it.

2/3 cup dry white cannellini beans
1 smoked ham hock
1/2 pound *chouriço*, or Spanish chorizo sausage, removed from its casing
6 cups deribbed and finely shredded kale leaves
2/3 cup dried split peas
1 teaspoon salt
2 cups finely chopped green cabbage
2 cups peeled and chopped potatoes (red or fingerling)

1. Place the beans in a 3-quart saucepan and add water to cover them by 1/2 inch. Bring to a boil, cook uncovered for 3 minutes, then cover, turn off the heat, and let stand overnight.

2. The next day, brown the ham hock and the sausage in a skillet, then add them to the beans and water along with the kale, peas, and salt. Bring to a boil, reduce the heat to low and simmer, covered, for 2 hours, adding more water if the soup gets too thick. Pull the meat from the ham hock bone and return the meat to the pot. Add the cabbage and potatoes and simmer covered for 30 minutes or more, or until the potatoes and cabbage are tender.

LEEK

SEASON: summer (for young leeks); late September through March (for full-grown leeks)

GOOD VARIETIES: Bleu de Solaise, Electra, Giant Musselburgh, King Alfred, Kurrat, Large American Flag, Titan, Varna

WHAT TO LOOK FOR: Leeks with a long length of usable white to light green stem, fresh-looking leaves, and white, plump, fresh-looking roots. The stem should be slightly limber, not stiff or unyielding, which would indicate toughness.

STORAGE AND PREPARATION TIPS: Trim leeks by cutting off the root and dark green leaves. Leeks must be carefully washed to remove any grit within the stems. To wash leeks, slit its outer layer lengthwise and check for grit. If you see any, slit leeks in half, place under running water, and gently rifle through the layers, making sure each layer is washed.

NUTRITIONAL HIGHLIGHTS: small amounts of calcium, folate, vitamin C

GOES WELL WITH: bacon, mustard, olive oil, parsley, potatoes, thyme. Try in roux and stews.

Leeks have a more delicate flavor than regular onions, with a mineral aftertaste that adds a perfect touch to savory soups.

The progenitor of leeks is a wild onion found all over Europe, around the Mediterranean, and even out on the Cape Verde islands in the Atlantic. The ancient Egyptians and Romans loved them. Nero thought leeks improved his singing voice, which earned him the popular name Porrophagus, or leek eater. In about 640, the Welsh fought and won a battle with invading Saxons by wearing leeks in their hats to identify friend from foe, and the leek has been a symbol of Wales ever since. The word *leek* dates to Anglo-Saxon times, when *leac* in Old English meant any member of the onion clan, including *garleac* (garlic), which meant "spear-onion."

Organic Advantage

As members of the onion family, leeks are prone to many of the diseases that attack onions. Growing them in rich, compost-amended soil, as organic gardeners and farmers do, makes for healthy leeks that resist most of the diseases without the need for toxic sprays.

Uses

Leeks can be steamed and also grilled. Baby leeks can be brushed with olive oil and grilled, which makes a delicious finger food. Leeks especially like a liquid environment when being cooked, and they are excellent braised in stock or used in soups (including the famous vichyssoise) and stews. Making 1/4-inch slices crosswise produces lots of fluffy ringlets that can be tossed into a soup pot. They will add more body than shallots or onions, but a milder flavor. Or use them as an aromatic seasoning when making vegetable stock.

Leeks Simmered Greek Style

SERVES 6

Vegetables prepared *à la grecque* in France are usually served cold or room temperature. Use fat leeks as the French do for a substantial dish. If you use skinny leeks, portion size and cooking time may decrease.

Salt to taste
10 fat leeks, white parts only
3/4 cup vegetable stock
3/4 cup dry white wine
1/4 cup olive oil
2 tablespoons freshly squeezed lemon juice
6 whole black peppercorns
1 bay leaf
1 sprig parsley
1/4 teaspoon dried chervil
1/4 teaspoon dried tarragon

1. Bring a large stainless-steel saucepan of water to a boil and add salt. Cut the leeks into 2-inch pieces and place them in the boiling water. Cover the saucepan, boil over medium heat for 3 minutes, and drain.

2. Return the leeks to the saucepan, and add the remaining ingredients. Cover the saucepan, reduce the heat, and simmer about 20 minutes, or until the leeks are just tender. Set the covered

pan aside with the leeks still in it and let cool to room temperature. Leaving the liquid and herbs in the pan, fish out the leek pieces and serve them with a few tablespoons of the cooled liquid spooned over them.

LETTUCE

SEASON: year-round

GOOD VARIETIES:

Batavian: Nevada, Sierra

Butterhead: Bibb, Butter King, Buttercrunch, Limestone, Merveille des Quatre Saisons, Red Perella, Tom Thumb

Crisphead: Great Lakes

Loose-leaf: Black-Seeded Simpson, Red Oak Leaf, Red Sails, Royal Oak Leaf, Ruby, Salad Bowl

Romaine: Parris Island, Rouge d'Hiver, Verte Maraîchère

WHAT TO LOOK FOR: A fresh lettuce leaf should snap into two crisp pieces rather than bend limply. Outer leaves should be as crisp as inner leaves and not beat up by wear and tear. The growing point (where the leaves emerge) should be moist and white. If you're buying a mix of leaves, they should be crisp and not flabby.

STORAGE AND PREPARATION TIPS: Most lettuces need nothing more than a rinse. Loose lettuce heads should be thoroughly rinsed to remove any earth caught between their leaves.

NUTRITIONAL HIGHLIGHTS: folate, vitamin A, vitamin C

GOES WELL WITH: anchovies, avocados, bacon, blue cheese, cucumbers, fish, garlic, ginger, hummus, lemon juice, lime juice, nut oils, olive oil, peanuts, shrimp, tomatoes, vinegar

It hasn't been very long since the fine loose-leaf lettuces now commonplace began showing up in our markets and stores. Time was, a salad meant a wedge of iceberg lettuce, a slice of tomato, and maybe a little raw onion, all given a plop of Russian dressing. Three factors have wrought major changes in the lettuces we see in today's salads.

The first is that the culinary customs of Europeans have jumped the Atlantic and completely changed our thinking about salads. Second, organic gardeners and farmers, searching for ever-higher quality and different tastes, have grown and popularized the many different European and Asian varieties of salad greens—especially lettuces—and brought them to markets and stores nationwide. The third reason is the work of very talented and pioneering people like Alice Waters at Chez Panisse in Berkeley, California; Sibella Kraus of San Francisco, whose organizational skills brought organic produce to the public's attention; and Renee Shepherd, who founded a seed company devoted to great-tasting varieties of lettuce.

More than anyone, it was Alice Waters who popularized the French people's love affair with mesclun. A mixture of wild greens, mesclun was traditionally gathered in the spring when new shoots and leaves were emerging and country folks needed something fresh and green after a winter of pickles and stored foods.

There are five basic types of lettuce that have been cultivated since the sixteenth century (earlier varieties of cultivated lettuce date back to ancient Egypt). The types are classified here according to their leaf shape and texture.

Batavian: A sturdy type of lettuce that forms shaggy heads with cream-colored centers of fine, sweet flavor and crispy texture.

Butterhead: Also called Boston or Bibb lettuce, it has loose rosettes of leaves, with a creamy, yellow-green center and a soft, buttery texture.

Crisphead: The cabbage-like ball heads often called iceberg, they don't have much flavor or nutrition, but they do provide a very refreshing crunchiness.

Loose-Leaf: These lettuces don't form heads but make a loose collection of leaves from a central growing point instead. They come in dozens of varieties—green, reddish, and speckled; smooth edged, wavy edged, and pointy edged; lobed, ruffled, slender, wide, and everything in between.

Romaine: This lettuce is familiar to everyone as the crunchy tall heads used to make Caesar salad.

Organic Advantage

Although lettuce is cooked in many places around the world, it's almost always eaten raw in the United States. This makes it doubly important to seek out organic lettuce that's free from harmful agricultural chemical residues.

Uses

Because of its mildness, lettuce makes a great foil for stronger flavors, such as

MÂCHE

Mâche (pronounced *mahsh*) is also known as lamb's lettuce or corn salad. This plant has been gathered wild across Eurasia since time immemorial, but has been cultivated only since the 1500s.

The small, spoon-shaped leaves of this plant are crisp and succulent, with a slightly bitter, mildly herbal flavor reminiscent of arugula and radicchio. Mâche is chiefly used fresh in salads or as part of a mesclun mix.

You may find it year-round in farmers' markets or organic supermarkets, but it's most tender and fine flavored from late fall through early spring. Look for leaves that are crisp, turgid, and bright green, without blemish. Look underneath the little head where it was cut from the root. The cut should look fresh, not dried out.

anchovies, blue cheese, garlic, vinegar, and bacon (what would a BLT be without lettuce?). Tomatoes, lemon juice, nut oils, and avocados also enjoy the company of lettuce.

I use lettuce leaves to protect fish such as halibut from drying out during slow cooking. Blanch the leaves in boiling water until flexible, then wrap them around the fish. Blanched lettuce leaves can be used in place of grape leaves to make dolmas. The raw leaves of butterhead varieties are usually flexible enough to be filled with a tablespoon of hummus and rolled up, or stuffed, as Thai cooks do, with dried shrimp, lime, crushed peanuts, cucumber, sweet sauce, and a little grated ginger. Italians sauté lettuce in olive oil and garlic—this method works best with the sturdy Batavians and romaines—until the leaves are tender and wilted.

Loose-Leaf Lettuce and Roasted Beet Salad

SERVES 6

This simple salad is extraordinarily delicious. A mixture of loose-leaf varieties along with the beets makes a nice presentation. A small amount of creamy blue cheese dressing is the perfect topping. It's a favorite salad in Italy.

3 medium red beets
3 medium yellow beets
1/2 cup walnut pieces
1/4 cup pine nuts
1/2 pound mixed loose-leaf lettuce
1 small red onion, sliced thin
Leaves from 4 sprigs watercress
Blue cheese dressing (recipe follows)

1. Roast the beets, let cool, and remove their skins according to the instructions on page 45. Cut into quarters.

2. While the beets are roasting, spread the walnuts on a baking sheet and toast in the oven until lightly browned and fragrant. Toss the pine nuts in a small dry skillet over medium heat until toasted light brown. Set both nuts aside to cool.

3. Place mixed lettuces on 6 serving plates. Place 2 red and 2 yellow beet quarters on each plate. Add some onion rings and sprinkle on watercress leaves, walnuts, and pine nuts. Drizzle equal portions of the dressing across the top of each salad.

Blue Cheese Dressing

MAKES ABOUT 1 CUP

1/2 cup crumbled blue cheese (about 2 ounces)
1/2 cup mayonnaise
1 shallot, minced
1 clove garlic, minced
1 tablespoon red wine vinegar
1 teaspoon Dijon mustard
Splash whole milk
Freshly ground black pepper

Place all ingredients in a bowl and mix well to combine.

MUSHROOM

SEASON: year-round; fall for wild mushrooms

GOOD VARIETIES: black trumpet, button, candy caps, chanterelle, corn smut, cremini, enoki, field mushroom, giant puffball, hedgehog or sweet polypore, hen-of-the-woods, king bolete, matsutake or pine mushroom, milk cap, Oregon white truffle, oyster, shiitake, yellow morel

WHAT TO LOOK FOR: Mushrooms should not be bruised or broken. The end of the stem should look fresh and moist, not dried out or woody.

STORAGE AND PREPARATION TIPS: Fresh mushrooms usually need only a brushing with a soft-bristled brush to remove any dirt clinging to them; washing makes them soggy. Dried mushrooms should be soaked in warm-to-boiling water or other liquid to soften them before use. This soaking liquid can then be added to a dish to flavor it, but should be strained thoroughly to remove any sand.

NUTRITIONAL HIGHLIGHTS: fiber, potassium, niacin, riboflavin, selenium

GOES WELL WITH: beef, chicken, cream, eggplant, Italian hard cheeses, garlic, oregano, onions, parsley, veal

Mushrooms have been held in high culinary esteem since classical times. The ancient Romans called them *cibum diorum*, "the food of the gods." The word *mushroom* comes from the archaic French *mousseron*, usually held to be a derivative of *mousse*, or "moss"—I suppose because, like moss, mushrooms are found on the forest floor.

Most organic markets carry common white button mushrooms, and because of their reasonable cost I still use them in my everyday cooking. They may also carry an array of "wild" mushrooms—which are called wild but are oftentimes cultivated. Depending on the season, I can find cultivated "wild" morels, chanterelles, black trumpets, shiitakes, matsutakes, creminis, oyster mushrooms, enokis, and portobellos (really common button mushrooms that have grown to their mature size). Mushrooms that are actually gathered from the wild are called wild-harvested or wild-crafted mushrooms. Ask your market whether its mushrooms are wild harvested; if you have a local farmers' market, it may have a table run by a mushroom forager. You can also find dried wild-harvested mushrooms in some organic and specialty markets.

Organic Advantage

The best way to ensure the purity of your mushrooms is to buy mushrooms that have organic certification or have been harvested from the wild. To prevent other fungi and molds from growing, conventional growers often sterilize the compost and use sterilizing chemicals on the shed walls and floors. Organic mushrooms have been grown on organic substrates and treated with compost that has been sterilized by heat, not with chemicals.

Uses

All mushrooms impart an essential earthiness to dishes, as well as a luscious, meaty texture. But flavors vary greatly from species to species, so it is best to get a sense of each variety's textures and uses. For instance, porcinis and shiitakes are rich, savory, and meaty; chanterelles, hen-of-the-woods, and oyster mushrooms tend toward earthy. If you are looking for sweet, mild mushrooms, try black trumpets, enokis, or common buttons.

Beef Stew with Porcinis

SERVES 4 TO 6

This stew is a fall favorite at our house, but since dried mushrooms can be used, it can be made any time of the year. It's definitely comfort food. Serve it over noodles.

2 ounces fresh or 1 ounce dried porcini mushrooms
2 pounds lean beef, cut into 2-inch cubes
Kosher salt and freshly ground black pepper
1 tablespoon butter
1 tablespoon extra-virgin olive oil
1 medium onion, diced
2 medium carrots, diced
2 large plum tomatoes, peeled, seeded, and coarsely chopped
1 stalk celery, diced
2 cloves garlic, chopped
1 bay leaf
1 sprig flat-leaf parsley
1 sprig thyme
1 tablespoon all-purpose flour
2 cups dry red wine

1. If using fresh mushrooms, halve or quarter them, depending on their size. If using dried, reconstitute the mushrooms by placing them in a bowl and pouring boiling water over them just to cover. Set the bowl aside for 20 minutes.
2. Place the beef in a bowl and sprinkle with just a little salt and pepper.
3. Heat the butter and olive oil in a large Dutch oven over medium-high heat. Add the meat in small batches (the cubes should not touch one another) and sear so they are evenly browned on all sides, 5 to 7 minutes per batch. Remove each batch to a dish before adding the next.
4. When all the meat is browned, reduce the heat to medium-low and add the onion, carrots, tomatoes, celery, and garlic. Stir, scraping any browned bits off the bottom of the pot. Cook, stirring frequently so vegetables are coated with fat, for about 5 minutes.
5. Return the meat to the pot. Tie the bay leaf, parsley, and thyme sprigs together with a bit of kitchen string and add to the pot. In a little bowl, mix the flour with a couple of tablespoons of the wine, stirring so there are no lumps. Add this along with the rest of the wine to the pot. Stir and cover, and simmer over low heat for 2 hours.

6. After 2 hours, add the fresh mushrooms. If using dried mushrooms, carefully lift them out of their soaking liquor. If they still feel gritty, rinse them lightly under running water and pat dry. Chop the mushrooms and add them to the pot. Slowly pour in the liquor, making sure you don't add any sediment that may have settled at the bottom. Cover and simmer another hour. Remove the bundle of herbs, correct the seasoning, and serve immediately.

OKRA

SEASON: high to late summer

GOOD VARIETIES:

Green: Annie Oakley, Cajun Delight, Clemson Spineless

Pale: Blondy

Red: Burgundy

WHAT TO LOOK FOR: Pods between 2 and 3 inches long are best. Although some pods stay tender at longer lengths, many do not. The surface should have no bruises or discolorations and have a velvety feel.

STORAGE AND PREPARATION TIPS: Trim off the tough stem ends and rinse the pods.

NUTRITIONAL HIGHLIGHTS: fiber, folate, vitamin B_6, vitamin C

GOES WELL WITH: chicken, coriander, cumin, garlic, lemon, onions, parsley, rice, sausage, stews, sweet peppers, tomatoes

Okra is native to Ethiopia and today appears in many of the cuisines of West Africa. Besides the young pods, the seeds are eaten as a sweetmeat and roasted and ground as a coffee substitute. It came to North America with African slaves, and so gained its toehold in the American South. Today one can hardly imagine Southern regional cooking—especially the Creole and Cajun cooking of Louisiana—without okra-thickened gumbos and stews.

Okra pods come in three shades: green, pale green, and red. I find red okra has the best flavor and texture.

Organic Advantage

The organic cook should make an effort to find organically grown okra. A member of the mallow family, okra is related to cotton and is afflicted by many of the same pests. When grown in commercial agriculture, the two crops are often treated with the same pesticides.

Uses

Okra has an herbaceous flavor that recalls asparagus, artichoke, and even sweet pepper. Its salient culinary feature is the sticky liquid it exudes when cut, which enriches and adds body to stews. This gummy liquid makes plain boiled okra a bit off-putting, but turns pan-fried okra delicious: the mucilage sizzles and becomes crunchy, intensifying the okra's flavor. This treatment can be as simple as pan-frying rounds of sliced okra in olive oil over medium heat. Or try the following recipe for okra North African style, which incorporates cumin, tomato, and lemon.

Okra makes a good partner with other high- to late-summer crops such as garlic, onions, tomatoes, and sweet peppers; with spices like cumin and coriander; and with flavorings like lemon and parsley. In fact, that's pretty much a listing of the ingredients that would go into a good gumbo, along with rice, andouille sausage, and a few pieces of chicken.

Okra North African Style

SERVES 2 TO 3

A quick, flavorful side dish.

1/2 teaspoon cumin seeds
1 tablespoon olive oil
7 to 9 okra pods, sliced into 1/2-inch rounds, stem ends discarded
1 teaspoon tomato paste
1 teaspoon freshly squeezed lemon juice
Salt and freshly ground black pepper

1. Heat the cumin seeds in a dry skillet over medium heat for about 30 seconds, or until they become fragrant. Then transfer them to a mortar and, when they're cool, grind them with a pestle.

2. Heat a medium skillet over medium-high heat, add the olive oil, and when hot add the okra. It only takes a few minutes for the okra to tighten up and acquire a little crunchy browning. Once this happens, add the tomato paste and lemon juice, the ground cumin, and salt and pepper to taste. Reduce the heat to medium-low and continue cooking for another minute or so, stirring occasionally, until the okra is fully tender and coated with the tomato mixture.

ONION

SEASON: year-round

GOOD VARIETIES:

Bunching: Beltsville, Evergreen white, Kincho, Red Welsh, Tokyo Negi

Mild: Burgermaster, Copra, Maui, Red Granex, Red Torpedo, Super Star, Texas 1015Y, Vidalia, Walla Walla sweet, White Granex, White Lisbon, Yellow Granex

Pearl: Borettana, Pacific Pearl, Purplette, White Portugal, Yellow Borettana

Pungent: Blanco Duro, New York Early, Northern Oak, Prince, Southport Red Globe, Southport White Globe, Yellow Globe Danvers

WHAT TO LOOK FOR: Hard, pungent onions with thin necks store best, and that's something to look for when selecting onions from a bin. Make sure there are no soft or moldy spots.

STORAGE AND PREPARATION TIPS: Pungent onions store for 2 to 3 months or longer, but mild ones don't last long and should be used fairly quickly. Scallions keep in the crisper for 4 weeks.

To peel pearl or other small onions, pour boiling water over them and let sit 5 minutes, then drain and cover with cold water. Knick the skin at the root end; it will peel off easily.

NUTRITIONAL HIGHLIGHTS: antioxidants, phytochemicals, vitamin C

GOES WELL WITH: bacon, garlic, oregano, peppers, sage, salt, sharp cheeses, thyme, tomatoes, vinegar

---

A wise cook once said that every good meal begins by chopping an onion. And onions do lend a sweet flavor and add texture to all kinds of dishes, from risottos to stews to burritos. But this also means that every good meal begins with a good cry.

Onions are members of the *Allium* genus, which includes leeks, chives, garlic, shallots, ramps, and many other species and cultivars grown all over the world. Normally when we say "onion," we're referring to large bulb onions. Of these, there are two main types: pungent and mild. Pungent types include basic yellow onions. Mild onions, which include Vidalia, Walla Walla, and red onions, sometimes go by the name sweet onions, although they are generally no sweeter—and sometimes even less sweet—than pungent types. They seem sweeter because their mildness allows their sugar content to register on the palate, whereas the bite of pungent onions obliterates the sensation of sweetness.

Besides large bulb onions, there are a few other major types available:

Scallions: These are the slender onions without bulbs. They are sometimes called green onions or green bunching onions.

Spring onions: If scallions are allowed to grow past the slender stage, they become known as spring onions. If you see what appear to be oversized scallions with slight bulges at the base, they are spring onions: snap them up. Brushed with a little oil and laid on the grill to cook until soft, they make a succulent side dish to grilled meats.

Pearl onions: Pearl onions are small red-, white-, or yellowish brown–skinned onions; they are also called boilers, creamers, or baby onions. The Italian *cipollini* are a flat form of pearl onions that have been selected for their tiny size; they are grown in tightly packed groups to keep them small and firm.

Red torpedoes and Egyptian topsets: You may find these in the summertime. The former are medium-pungent onions with an elongated shape. The latter are unique, forming several small bulbs at the base and a cluster of small squiggly tailed, edible bulbils (tadpole-shaped reproductive structures) at the top of their green stems. The bulbils can be used raw in salads or pickled.

Organic Advantage

Slicing any onion may make you cry, but an organically grown onion may bring about a greater stream of tears than a conventional one due to the abundance of sulfur and other minerals the onion will have taken in from the compost-enriched soil (see Crying Onion Tears, at right). The organic advantage arrives when these sulfur-rich compounds are stabilized through cooking into flavorful compounds.

Because conventional onions are so heavily sprayed, many cooks throw the papery skins away. But with organic onions, you can use those papery skins to give color to broths. The onion-skin hue looks especially nice in clear soups.

Uses

Pungent onions are generally best used cooked, while mild onions are generally best used raw, as on salads. The one characteristic all onions share is their sweetness. The sugar in onions and its ability to caramelize is what makes onions so useful in all forms of cooking. Onions can be baked, broiled, boiled, roasted, braised, fried, grilled, sautéed, steamed, or eaten raw.

Their sugar also makes onions a good match for almost any savory food (see Goes Well with, page 87). Onions pair with a number of herbs, including oregano, sage, and thyme. It's as if onions and its partners are the bass and drums for the melody and harmonies played by a dish's main ingredients.

Roasted onions: Roasting small onions is a great way to release their sweet flavor and caramelize their sugar. Use whole unpeeled pearl onions or *cipollini* (about 6 to 8 per person). Roast in a 450°F oven for 15 to 20 minutes, or until they become tender to a knife point. When they cool, they'll peel easily. Then sauté them in a skillet with a tablespoon of olive oil over medium heat until they're hot and slightly browned. Season with salt and pepper to make a fine side dish.

Scallion Frittata

SERVES 4

A frittata is a type of Italian omelet that's easy to make and a tasty way to start a weekend morning. Here scallions play a major role in the flavoring along with their friends, the tomatoes.

CRYING ONION TEARS

Onions concentrate sulfur in their tissues as pyruvate, which is the negative ion of pyruvic acid, a naturally occurring acid found in foods. When an onion is cut, enzymes at the cut area immediately go to work on the pyruvate to produce allicin, a sulfur-containing compound. The more cutting, the more allicin is produced and released. Allicin-bearing fumes meet the film of moisture on our eyes and dissolve into it, producing—sulfuric acid! No wonder our eyes burn and our tear ducts start washing the irritant away. That's why a simple splash of cool tap water on your eyes will stop the burning and tears: it hastens and intensifies what your body is already doing.

8 large eggs

1/2 cup freshly grated pecorino

Leaves from 1 sprig fresh sage, finely chopped

1/2 teaspoon salt

1/2 teaspoon freshly ground black pepper

1 tablespoon extra-virgin olive oil

6 scallions, trimmed, sliced thin, white and green parts separated

18 grape tomatoes, halved

1. Whisk the eggs in a large bowl until well mixed. Stir in the cheese, sage, salt, and pepper.

2. Place the oil in a medium to large nonstick skillet over medium heat. When hot, add the scallions, reserving 1 tablespoon of the sliced green parts. Stir until the scallions wilt, about 2 minutes.

3. Preheat the broiler. Add the egg mixture to the skillet and reduce the heat to medium-low. Cook for 2 to 3 minutes, pulling the cooked eggs toward the center with a spatula and allowing the uncooked portion to run underneath. Sprinkle the tomatoes evenly over the top and continue cooking another 2 to 3 minutes, or until the eggs are almost set through but the top is still runny.

4. Sprinkle the top with the reserved scallions and pass it under the broiler for about 1 minute, or until the top sets and is lightly brown. Loosen the frittata and carefully slide it onto a warm serving plate. Cut into wedges and serve.

PEAS

SEASON: late May or early June

GOOD VARIETIES:

English: Laxton's Progress, Little Marvel, Mr. Big

Snap peas: Sugar Ann, Sugar Snap, Sugar Spring, Super Sugar Mel

Snow peas: Carouby de Mausanne, Mammoth Melting Sugar

WHAT TO LOOK FOR: The best peas have vivid green pods with a glossy surface, no yellowing, and juicy stems that are still attached rather than dried stem ends.

STORAGE AND PREPARATION TIPS: Snow peas have a string running down one side that must be pulled off before use. English peas simply need to be popped out of the pods, and sugar snaps need no prep at all.

NUTRITIONAL HIGHLIGHTS: copper, fiber, folate, iron, magnesium, manganese, phosphorus, niacin, protein, riboflavin, thiamine, vitamin A, vitamin B_6, vitamin C, vitamin K, zinc

GO WELL WITH: butter, ham, mint, mushrooms, nutmeg, onions, powdered sugar, pancetta, squash

The moment peas are picked, they begin to lose their sweetness and their herbaceous, garden-fresh flavor. For that reason alone, I encourage lovers of organic foods to grow their own, just to experience the joyful pleasure of eating the new growing season's first main crop fresh from the vine. Wherever you can find them, fresh-picked peas still in the pod carry a taste of the springtime that's incomparable.

When buying fresh peas in the pod, you want to make sure the peas are fully developed, but not overdeveloped. Open up the pod and examine the peas: they should be plump but not touching each other; that's perfect. Squeeze a pea between your thumb and forefinger. If it mashes rather than splits in half, you've got the peas at their peak.

English or garden peas: These are the familiar peas we find fresh in their inedible shells. They have a firm texture and a delightfully rich flavor.

Snow peas: These flat-podded peas are favored by Chinese cooks. They can be eaten whole and are very useful in vegetable medleys or with rice or meat stir-fries.

Sugar snap peas: Bred fairly recently—they were first released to the public in 1976—their edible pods are fat, sweet, and succulent (like the peas inside). In fact, sugar snap peas are best when the peas inside are still juveniles—and barely noticeable. The pods should be very thin or translucent. They're tender and sweet, so cook them gently.

Pea shoots: These look like little packets of folded leaves, flower buds, and tendrils; they grow at the tips of pea vines. They are common ingredients in Chinese cooking and can be found in Asian markets during pea season.

Organic Advantage

While conventional pea farmers use chemicals on their vines, organic farmers find alternative methods of dealing with diseases and pests. For example, organic growers will spray pea vines with a baking soda solution whose alkaline properties discourage mildews.

FREEZING FRESH PEAS FOR WINTER

Off-season, you can find frozen-fresh organic peas in the freezer section of organic markets, but you can also preserve your own fresh spring peas by freezing a crop at the peak of the season.

To put up fresh peas, blanch them in boiling water, in their pods, for about 1 minute, then drain them and run them under cold water to stop the cooking. Spread the pea pods out on cookie sheets and freeze them solid, then store them in freezer bags.

To use, float the freezer bags in a bowl of hot water for 1 hour. Remove and shell the peas, discarding the pods, and heat through in a little water over low heat. I guarantee they will be the best peas you'll have ever eaten in January.

Uses

Peas are wonderfully versatile. Sugar snaps' and snow peas' edible pods are great in stir-fries and vegetable medleys with other early summer vegetables, such as squash. Mushrooms, nutmeg, onions, and rice—especially risotto—pair beautifully with peas. The French boil garden peas, drain them, add a pinch of powdered sugar, and toss them with butter.

Pea shoots can be stir-fried or steamed. One satisfying way to dress pea shoots is with a few drops of sesame oil, a pinch of salt, and a dash of mirin (Japanese sweet cooking wine); another is with a touch of butter and some fresh chervil.

Baked Sugar Snap Peas

SERVES 4

Garden-fresh snap peas are perhaps best eaten raw from the vine, but lacking a garden source, here's a way to highlight the flavor of peas fresh from the market.

1 pound sugar snap peas
2 tablespoons olive oil
2 tablespoons minced shallots
2 teaspoons chopped fresh thyme
Salt to taste

Preheat the oven to 450°F. Mix peas and oil in a bowl until peas are coated, then turn onto a medium baking sheet in a single layer. Sprinkle them with the shallots, thyme, and salt. Bake 7 minutes, or until tender but still firm.

POTATO

SEASON: summer through fall (and into winter in mild climates)

GOOD VARIETIES:

Waxy: All Red, Anna Cheeka's Ozette, Bintje, Chieftain, Desiree, German fingerling, Red Cloud, Red LaSoda, Rose Finn Apple, Ruby Crescent

Starchy: Butte, Island Sunshine, Kennebec, Norgold russet, Russet Nugget, White Rose, Yellow Finn, Yukon Gold

WHAT TO LOOK FOR: Potatoes should have no soft, discolored, or rough black spots, no cuts, no moldy pits, and should feel firm, even hard. Make sure no green shows through the skin. (It's a poisonous alkaloid and should never be eaten; if you do find green areas in your potatoes, peel them away.) On the other hand, the presence of dried soil is a good sign: soil protects potatoes from mold and bacteria.

STORAGE AND PREPARATION TIPS: Store potatoes in the dark at room temperature. If you put them in the fridge, the cold will cause the starches to change into sugars, giving them a sweet, off flavor.

NUTRITIONAL HIGHLIGHTS: niacin, potassium, thiamine, vitamin B_6, vitamin C

GOES WELL WITH: bacon, butter, celery root and other root vegetables, cream, garlic, leeks, onions, salt

Potatoes have kept whole cultures alive. Not only the Incas, who first cultivated the tuber, but (after potatoes reached Europe in the sixteenth century) also many countries in the northern parts of Europe. Potatoes were a staple of the Irish, at least until a blight decimated the potato crops in the mid- to late-1840s, causing starvation and necessitating emigration.

It used to be that potatoes were generic, and either brown or red skinned. Nowadays you can find many other kinds of potatoes (two hundred varieties total in the United States) in all kinds of shapes and in colors from red to pink to yellow to purple and violet. I love the French or German fingerlings, with their dense, waxy, rich flesh and luscious flavor.

Organic Advantage

A potato's flavor and texture can change dramatically depending on the soil and climate where it's grown. Potatoes grown in rich, dark organic soil have an earthy, comforting flavor that disappears during storage, and that you won't find in conventional potatoes grown in chemically fertilized soil.

Because we get the full benefit of potato nutrients only when we leave the skins on, it's extremely important to eat only organic potatoes, which don't have to be peeled. Anyone who cooks with conventional potatoes would be wise to peel them to remove the bulk of the chemical residue.

Uses

Red potatoes have a flesh that's classified as waxy, while the big Idaho baking potatoes are starchy. As a rule of thumb, waxy potatoes take to boiling better than starchy potatoes, which tend to become too soft and watery; the starchy ones are best for baking. For that reason, I prefer red potatoes for mashed potatoes. Yukon Golds and Yellow Finns are halfway between waxy and starchy, and can be used any way. Yukon Golds have a sweet flavor and sap that caramelizes easily when pan-fried. Either type makes good french fries.

All potatoes are champions at enhancing and holding the flavors of other foods. Cooked with celery root or turnips or garlic, and mashed with cream, butter, and salt, they are fantastic. Potatoes with bacon or with onions or leeks are irresistible combinations.

For fingerling potatoes, cut them on the diagonal into thirds, then sauté them in a heavy skillet over medium heat in a little olive oil, just until they start to brown, about 8 minutes. Add a chopped onion, salt, and pepper to taste, and finish them for 20 minutes in a 350°F oven. I also like to boil them with their skins on and slice them cold into salads, especially the tangy German-style potato salad.

NEW POTATOES

New potatoes are potatoes that have been harvested from the plant's trailing underground roots while the plant is still growing. They tend to be small and their skins are thin and flaky. They are prized for their fine, delicate flavor, so if you find them—usually in early summer and again in September when the crops are still weeks from harvest—make good use of them.

Potato Soufflé

SERVES 4

Don't be swayed by the word *soufflé*. This is a simple old German recipe that shows off the flavor of good potatoes. Freshness really makes a difference here, so start with young, starchy potatoes and farm-fresh eggs, and grate your nutmeg just before using it.

1 pound russet potatoes, peeled
4 large eggs, separated
2 tablespoons butter
1/2 teaspoon freshly grated nutmeg
Salt and freshly ground black pepper
1/3 cup grated Gruyère cheese

1. Fill a large pot with water and add the potatoes. Bring to a boil, salt lightly, reduce to a simmer, and cook for 20 to 30 minutes, or until the potatoes are tender. Drain well.

2. Preheat the oven to 375°F. Mash the potatoes in a large bowl with the egg yolks, butter, nutmeg, and salt and pepper to taste.

3. Beat the egg whites in another large bowl until soft peaks form. Fold into the potato mixture. Pour into a buttered shallow 9 × 9–inch baking dish and sprinkle the top with cheese. Bake for 12 minutes until it puffs a little and turns golden brown on top.

RADISH

SEASON: mid-spring through fall

GOOD VARIETIES:

Asian: April Cross, Misato Rose

Black: Long Black Spanish, Round Black Spanish

Western: Champion, Cherry Belle, D'Avignon, Easter Egg, French Breakfast, Plum Purple, Sparkler

WHAT TO LOOK FOR: Radishes should be firm to the touch, not soft. Reject any with splits or cracks. The leaves should look fresh, not yellowed or dried out.

STORAGE AND PREPARATION TIPS: Use radishes soon after buying them. They can be pickled or grated into salads and served as crudites.

NUTRITIONAL HIGHLIGHTS: phytochemicals, vitamin C

GOES WELL WITH: bread, caviar, chervil, daikons, *fromage blanc*, pickled herring, quark, sashimi, sauces, sea salt, smoked salmon, soups, sushi, thyme

The source of our modern radishes is thought to be central Asia, although the actual wild progenitor plant can no longer be found. Modern radishes, though, have been known since ancient times. In the fifth century BCE, Greek historian Herodotus described an inscription on the great pyramid of Egypt that told of the slaves who built the monument eating great quantities of radishes, along with onions and garlic.

Here are some of the most familiar radishes available today:

Asian radishes: Some, like the daikon, are white cylinders up to 18 inches long, with myriad uses. Others may be green skinned or have green shoulders or flesh. These can be sweet rather than pungent.

Black radishes: These large radishes are favored in eastern Europe and Russia. The skin is a dark black and the flavor carries a heavy kick of earthy, rooty pungency.

European radishes: The familiar variety found in supermarkets. They can be red, white, or a mix. Some of my favorite varieties are Cherry Belle and Scarlet Globe among reds; White Icicle, Burpee white, and Snow Belle among whites; and French Breakfast among bicolored types. All have a succulent crunch and a mild to strong bite, depending on how fast they grew and whether they matured in cool or hot weather.

Rat-tailed radishes: Grown in Asian countries, they produce long seed pods—up to a foot in length—that are eaten raw, cooked, or pickled.

Organic Advantage

When buying small radishes, inspect the leaves. If they have an abundance of tiny holes in them, it's a good bet they were made by flea beetles—a difficult-to-control pest. If flea beetles are making holes, that signifies that the crop is most likely organic, or at least not sprayed.

Uses

Whichever of the bulbous-rooted radishes you find, they all are versatile. Take a slice of black bread or pumpernickel—or if you can find it, a slice of German *Landbrot*—spoon on some quark cheese or yogurt, add a layer of minced pungent radishes, garnish with chopped chervil or thyme, then grind a pinch of coarse sea salt on top.

All radishes are delicious raw, but they can also be stir-fried, braised, steamed, or boiled in stews and soups. Cooked, they'll lose their pungency and function more like turnips—to which they're closely related—in texture and taste. Slice daikon radishes into rounds and use them as a canapé base instead of a cracker for smoked salmon, pickled herring, caviar, or *fromage blanc*. Grate or shred them to accompany sashimi. Julienne them for inclusion in sushi. Add chopped daikons to soups and sauces or cook them with meat—they soften, absorb juices, and add texture. Pickle daikon or other Asian radishes as the Koreans do, in their kimchi (add some to the recipe on page 41).

Radish Salsa

MAKES ABOUT 1 1/2 CUPS

The radish adds a different kind of pungency to the peppery heat of a typical salsa. It also adds a nice crunch and color when the red radishes are young and crisp. Use as a topping for chicken, pork, or fish tacos; as an addition to meat, rice, and beans in burritos; or eat with chips.

1/2 cup finely diced small red radishes
1/2 cup seeded and diced ripe plum tomato (1 large tomato)
1/4 cup finely chopped scallions (white parts only)
2 tablespoons freshly squeezed lime juice
2 tablespoons olive oil
2 tablespoons roughly chopped cilantro
1 teaspoon minced garlic
1 teaspoon minced jalapeño or serrano chiles
Salt and freshly ground black pepper, to taste

Toss all ingredients together in a serving bowl, seasoning with salt and pepper.

SEAWEED

SEASON: year-round

GOOD VARIETIES: arame, bladder wrack, dulse, grapestone, hijiki, kelp, nori, sea lettuce, sea palm fronds, wakame

WHAT TO LOOK FOR: Make sure the seaweed has been kept dry, with no soft or moldy spots.

STORAGE AND PREPARATION TIPS: Store it in a closed container in a dark, dry cupboard. Seaweed is reconstituted by soaking in water or covering with boiling water.

NUTRITIONAL HIGHLIGHTS: chondroitin, glucosamine

GOES WELL WITH: eggs, lemon, lime, olive oil, smoked meats, spicy chiles

Seaweed is marine algae that grows in the tidal zones or shallow ocean water where sunlight can penetrate. It's collected for food in parts of the world where the water is pure, including the bays of northern Japan, the Pacific coast from northern California to Washington, and the Atlantic coast from Maine to the Canadian Maritimes.

Scientists say our blood has the same mineral content as seawater, so consuming seaweed provides us with the minerals we need for optimal health. It may also help protect us against one of the newest dangers on earth—radioactivity. Kelp, for instance, contains iodine-127. This beneficial isotope of iodine helps prevent the body from absorbing radioactive iodine-131, which is released into the atmosphere during so-called normal operations of nuclear power plants and weapons facilities. Kelp also contains sodium alginate, which can bind with radioactive strontium-90 and cesium-137, as well as heavy metals, and aid the body in excreting them.

People who eat a lot of processed foods unknowingly eat seaweed all the time, in the form of fillers, extenders, and texturizers such as agars, carrageenans, and alginates—all seaweed extracts. But many varieties of whole seaweed—either fresh or dried—form a staple of a healthy organic diet and can be used in endless ways, from a seasoning to a main ingredient.

Arame: A mild seaweed, it cooks in about half the time of hijiki (below). Both hijiki and arame are Japanese imports and fairly easy to find at natural food stores.

Bladder wrack: Known as rockweed on the East Coast, bladder wrack is used as a healing tea and also in soups. At Maine clambakes, it's used to steam lobsters and clams.

Dulse: A common seaweed, it is shaped like the palm of a hand. the best is a red algae variety called Grand Manan. It's frequently dried and used raw, as a condiment in place of salt, or to accent eggs, vegetables, rice, casseroles, chowders and—especially—potatoes. When cooked in a soup, it acts as a thickening agent, disintegrating and imparting a reddish color.

Grapestone: This seaweed resembles a deep red, exotic mushroom; it's excellent in stir-fries.

Hijiki: Famous for being exceptionally nutritious, it is full of trace minerals and known as a blood strengthener. It has a strong flavor and sturdy texture, and it takes about 10 minutes to cook.

Kelp: Also commonly known as *kombu*, its Japanese name, kelp is probably the seaweed most familiar to most people. Roasted, dried, and ground into flakes, it's used as a seasoning and salt substitute. But it can also be purchased as a dried whole vegetable to add to soups and other vegetable dishes.

Nori: This black seaweed, which is used to wrap sushi, is often bought in sheets, but the best nori is dried in leaf form. It can be used as is, lightly roasted, or even fried as tempura. Roasted nori can be crumbled over grains and vegetables as a condiment. (To roast nori, place it on a dry skillet over medium heat for 15 seconds per side.) It's nutritious: about one-third pure protein.

Sea lettuce: Called *ao nori* by the Japanese, this bright green seaweed is used as a condiment.

Sea palm fronds: Unique to the Pacific Northwest, from San Francisco to Vancouver, British Columbia, they're used raw, sautéed, and in soups and salads.

Wakame: This sweet, relatively tender seaweed is a standard addition to miso soup. It has an appealingly clean, salt-air aroma. Use it in soups, stir fries, or in salads (see recipe).

Organic Advantage

In addition to its healthy culinary uses, seaweed provides a range of agricultural benefits to the organic gardener. Those who live near the ocean can use salt hay—the marsh grasses that grow in tidal swamps—as easy-to-harvest mulch, or mix it with seaweed to make a mineral-rich compost.

Seaweed can be used to make a nutritious extract that's sprayed onto and absorbed through the leaves of fruit trees and vegetable plants. When seaweed is applied to the soil, it returns elements to the soil that may have been leached out by acid rain or abuse from years of conventional farming. Everything finally returns to the sea, and the use of seaweed in organic culture is a way of recycling scarce nutrients back to crops so they can grow healthy tissues.

Uses

Seaweed is an important part of the diet in Japan, in maritime Ireland and Scotland, and in Iceland, Norway, France, and eastern Canada. But it's been slow to make inroads in the American kitchen. Once you start to use seaweed, however, you begin to wonder how you got along without it. It imparts a true flavor of the sea to food.

Wakame Orange Salad

SERVES 3 TO 4

This recipe is from Simone Parris, a private chef who cooks for celebrities in the Los Angeles area. The celebs like to stay slim and healthy, and her dishes help them achieve both goals. This salad combines the sweet flavor of cucumbers and oranges with a salty matrix of seaweed and soy sauce and adds a spicy kick from the ginger and cayenne.

1 medium slicing cucumber
1/2 teaspoon sea salt
1 tablespoon wakame flakes (purchased precut)
2 medium oranges
1/4 cup raw sesame seeds
1 piece fresh ginger, about the size of your thumb, peeled
2 teaspoons soy sauce
2 teaspoons unseasoned rice vinegar
1 teaspoon mirin (Japanese sweet rice wine) or pure maple syrup
1 teaspoon toasted sesame oil
Dash of ground cayenne
Pinch of freshly ground black pepper
2 scallions, finely chopped

1. Peel stripes down the length of the cucumber, slice it in half lengthwise, then cut in 1/8-inch-thick half rounds. Toss the cucumbers in a bowl with the sea salt. Place a plate on top of the cucumbers and place a weight, such as a gallon jug of water, on the plate, and let sit for 20 minutes. This procedure removes some of the water from the cucumbers and breaks down cell walls, making them easier to digest.

2. Soak the wakame flakes in enough water to cover until they're soft, about 10 minutes, then squeeze out and discard the water.

3. With a sharp knife, cut the tops and bottoms from the oranges deeply enough to remove the white pith, then do the same all around the sides of the oranges. When all the pith is removed, slice the orange lengthwise into quarters, remove any seeds and the white core, and cut the quarters crosswise into 1/2-inch pieces.

4. Wash the sesame seeds in a fine mesh strainer and let drain. Heat a small skillet over medium heat, add the sesame seeds, and toast, stirring continuously with a wooden spoon. If they start jumping around, the heat is too high. When you can easily crush a seed between your thumb and ring finger, the seeds are done. (Be careful not to overcook.) As soon as they're done, transfer them to a small bowl.

5. Grate the ginger until you have 1 heaping tablespoon; press the gratings by placing them in a soup spoon and pressing out the juice into a small dish with the back of a second spoon. Extract about 1 teaspoon of juice.

6. Prepare the dressing by whisking together the ginger juice, mirin, soy sauce, vinegar, oil, cayenne, and black pepper.

7. Rinse and gently squeeze the liquid out of the cucumbers and combine them with the oranges and wakame in a medium bowl. Toss with the dressing and garnish the top with a sprinkling of toasted sesame seeds and scallions.

Braised Hijiki with Vegetables

SERVES 3 TO 4

Here's another recipe from Simone Parris. The savory flavor of toasted sesame oil envelops the vegetables in a very elegant way.

1 cup dry hijiki
2 medium carrots
1 large or 2 small onions
1/2 cup sugar snap peas
1 tablespoon toasted sesame oil
1/2 teaspoon sea salt
2/3 cup fresh or frozen sweet corn kernels (from 1 large ear)
1 tablespoon soy sauce
1 tablespoon mirin (Japanese sweet rice wine) or pure maple syrup
2 tablespoons chopped scallions

1. Soak the hijiki in 3 cups of water until soft, about 10 minutes; strain and discard the water. Slice the carrots 1/2 inch thick on the diagonal, then cut into matchsticks. Peel the onion, cut it in half from top to bottom, then slice into thin half rounds. De-string the snap peas and slice in half on the diagonal.

2. Heat a deep skillet over medium-high heat. Add the sesame oil. When the oil is hot, add the onions and sauté until translucent, 5 to 7 minutes. Add the hijiki and sauté 5 minutes.

3. Layer the carrots on top and add 2/3 cup of water. Sprinkle on the sea salt, cover, and reduce the heat to medium-low. Cook for 45 minutes, checking occasionally and adding more water if necessary to prevent burning.

4. Add the corn and the soy sauce and cook 5 more minutes. Remove the lid, add the mirin, and turn the heat to medium-high. Cook off the liquid, and just before the liquid is gone, add the peas, replace the lid, and cook for 2 minutes. Taste and add more soy sauce if necessary. Garnish with the scallions.

Dashi

Kelp's most common and important use is in the preparation of dashi, the basic stock for Japanese soups, stews, and sauces.

Soak a 6-inch piece of kombu in 4 cups of water for 2 hours, then slowly bring to a boil. Just before the water boils, remove the kelp from the water, turn off the heat, and let the broth cool. The dashi can be used as a delicious vegetarian broth in Japanese and other dishes.

SHALLOT

SEASON: spring through fall

GOOD VARIETIES: Drittler white, Dutch yellow, French gray, French red

WHAT TO LOOK FOR: Mature shallots are firm and unbruised, with intact skins, no soft spots, and no mold. They should feel heavy for their size.

STORAGE AND PREPARATION TIPS: Shallots keep up to two weeks in a dark, airy place. Don't remove their papery skins until just before using.

NUTRITIONAL HIGHLIGHTS: antioxidants, phytochemicals, vitamin A, vitamin B_6, vitamin C

GOES WELL WITH: black pepper, butter, chicken, garlic, leeks, meat, olive oil, onions, vermouth, wine

Why not just use onions? They may look similar, but shallots are different from other onions, and certainly from garlic. They have a unique flavor that's more delicate, with a pungency specifically their own, and a lovely tenderness that allows them to soften quickly and easily during cooking.

Organic Advantage

Shallots are very hardy in the garden, resistant to pests and diseases, so even conventionally grown shallots will mostly be free from chemicals.

Uses

Shallots are a great addition to soups and stews, as they flavor and thicken them. Combine them in an all-onion medley with onions, garlic, and leeks, then roast or sauté them to use around meats. Or braise them along with veal or lamb shanks. They can also be creamed as you would pearl onions. Whole shallot cloves can be tossed with a little oil and baked at 350°F for about 30 minutes, or until they caramelize, then served with grilled or roasted meats. Shallots also make fine pickles.

Shallots are part of many classic rich French sauces. But shallot sauces do not have to be heavy and can be made quickly during the process of deglazing a pan that has been used for roasting or sautéing meats (recipe follows).

Deglazing Sauce

MAKES ABOUT 1 CUP

For a deglazing liquid, I use a mix of beef stock and red wine for red meat, chicken stock and white wine for white meats. The shallots thicken the sauce and add sweetness to it. You can beat in a tablespoon of butter or two to enrich the sauce, but I find it needs nothing more than a grind or two of black pepper.

3 shallots, minced
1/4 cup wine or dry vermouth
3/4 cup chicken or beef stock
Black pepper

1. When the meat is done, remove it from the pan to a platter to rest. Pour off all but a teaspoon of fat from the pan and place it on a burner at medium heat.

2. Add the shallots, and sauté them for about 1 minute. Add the wine and the stock.

3. Turn up the heat until the mixture boils and stir, scraping up any pan drippings or congealed bits. As the liquid reduces to the consistency of a thick sauce, lower the heat to prevent scorching.

4. When the mixture is thick enough to coat the back of a spoon, add a grind or two of black pepper, pour it over the meat, and serve.

SPINACH

SEASON: early spring through mid-fall

GOOD VARIETIES:

Full size: America, Bloomsdale Long-Standing, Indian Summer, Whale

Baby: Correnta, Melody hybrid, Monnopa, Teton, Wolter

WHAT TO LOOK FOR: Spinach should have leaves that are glossy and crisp, with no limpness or yellowing. The cut end of the stem should look freshly cut, not blackened. If you see some small holes in organic spinach leaves (where a bug got dibs on the first bite), take that as a good sign that the plant has indeed been grown organically.

STORAGE AND PREPARATION TIPS: Strip off and discard the stems. Then plunge the leaves into cold water and wash thoroughly: spinach can be sandy.

NUTRITIONAL HIGHLIGHTS: calcium, carotenoids, fiber, folate, iron, magnesium, potassium, riboflavin, vitamin A, vitamin B_6, vitamin C

GOES WELL WITH: anchovies, cheese, curry spices, eggs, garlic, lemon zest, mushrooms, nutmeg, olive oil, onions, parsley, tomatoes, vinegar, yogurt

Eat spinach on a regular basis—if it's organic, that is. Spinach is what growers call a heavy feeder—it pulls a lot of nutrients from the soil to stoke its quick growth, and when that soil is organic and full of all necessary minerals, spinach can be one of the most nutritious foods on earth.

Spinach is native to Iran, where the species still grows wild. It made its way east to China in the first millennium, probably along the Silk Road, and west to Arabia and then to Spain with the Moorish invasions and on to the rest of Europe. The name comes from the Old Persian *aspanakh*, and the linguistic root *span-* has entered Greek in the names of spinach-based dishes such as spanakopita.

There are two types of common spinach. The old-fashioned savoy types have large crinkled leaves and thick stems. They're best when cooked. Asian types (sometimes labeled baby spinach) have smaller oval-shaped leaves, and are thinner, more tender, and sweeter. They're best eaten raw in salads.

Organic Advantage

Because spinach is a heavy feeder, it will absorb an excessive amount of whatever is present in the soil—that means nutrients as well as pesticides, fungicides, and chemical fertilizers. The sheer number of chemicals that go into cultivated spinach reminds us once again why we might want to choose organic produce.

Uses

Besides its significant nutritional benefits, spinach has an amazing ability to blend well with a wide range of ingredients, especially the flavors mentioned above.

Spinach is also a joy to cook with. When I'm in a hurry, I simply toss the leaves in a steamer, steam them until they collapse, turn them into a warm bowl, give them a squeeze of half a lemon and maybe a pinch of salt, and voilà. But sometimes it's fun to gussy them up a little, too. Then I'll toss spinach with a few tablespoons of *gremolata* (a mixture of finely minced garlic, lemon zest, and finely chopped parsley). In India, hot, spicy foods are served with a salad of chopped spinach, cucumbers, potatoes, and eggplant topped with raita and seasoned with garam masala (see Tip, page 53).

Here's a simple vegetarian use for spinach: in a Dutch oven, sauté a diced small onion in a tablespoon of canola oil over medium heat until the onion turns clear, then add a bunch of clean, stemmed spinach and stir in 1/2 cup of rice. Add 1/2 cup of diced tomato, 1 finely chopped garlic clove, and salt and pepper to taste. Finally, add 1 cup of hot water, cover, and simmer for 1 hour.

Creamed Spinach

SERVES 4 TO 6

As a child, I loved spinach, especially my mom's creamed spinach. But I wondered if something was wrong with me, because in cartoons, comic books, movies, and on radio programs, spinach was the butt of jokes about how terrible it tasted. Popeye was a role model because spinach gave him super powers, but I knew this was just a way to convince kids to eat their spinach. I didn't understand the revulsion that spinach was supposed to cause—until one day I tasted canned spinach.

Creamed spinach made from fresh savoy-type leaves stripped of their stems is ambrosial. Here's the recipe Mom used.

2 pounds (about 2 bunches) large savoy-type spinach
1 teaspoon freshly squeezed lemon juice
1 clove garlic, smashed
3 tablespoons butter
2 tablespoons minced shallot
2½ tablespoons all-purpose flour
Salt to taste
1 cup half-and-half
½ teaspoon freshly grated nutmeg

1. Strip the leaves from the stems and wash them well, then steam in a basket until collapsed, 3 to 5 minutes.

2. Placed the spinach in a bowl (so as to catch the liquid) with lemon juice and chop it into tiny pieces with two knives. (Some people force it through a coarse strainer, but using two knives seems more honest to me.)

3. Rub a skillet with the garlic. Heat the skillet over medium-low heat, add the butter, and let it melt.

4. Add the shallots and stir in the flour. Add salt to taste. Cook for about a minute. Slowly stir in the half-and-half and cook until the sauce has become smooth, 3 to 4 minutes.

5. Add the spinach, stir to blend it in well, and cook for 3 minutes. If it seems too thick, add a little milk or water. It should have a thick consistency, neither pasty nor soupy. Add the nutmeg, stir well, and serve.

SUMMER SQUASH AND ZUCCHINI

SEASON: summer to late fall

GOOD VARIETIES:

Middle Eastern: Grise de Algiers

Round: Eight Ball, Elite, Ronde de Nice

Scalloped: Early White Bush, Peter Pan Hybrid, Starship, Sunburst, Tromboncino

Yellow crookneck: Dixie, Early Golden Summer Crookneck, Early Prolific Straightneck, Sundance, Sundrop, Zephyr

Zucchini: Ambassador, Aristocrat, Black Beauty, Burpee Fordhook, Caserta, Gold Rush, Greyzini, Italian Largo, Tatuma

WHAT TO LOOK FOR: Choose small, brightly colored, shiny squash with fresh-looking cut ends. Straight, crookneck, and yellow squash should be 6 to 8 inches long; tromboncinis 8 to 10 inches; and round and pattypan types the size of golf balls. Scrape the skin with your thumbnail. It should nick easily, with little resistance.

STORAGE AND PREPARATION TIPS: Summer squash are perishable: the freshest ones will last only up to a week.

NUTRITIONAL HIGHLIGHTS: magnesium, potassium, vitamin C

GO WELL WITH: almonds, béchamel, butter, olive oil, Parmesan

Tender summer squash—zucchini being the most familiar—are mildly flavored, slightly nutty, slightly sweet, and great combined with other foods, as they won't interfere with the flavors of meats and vegetables. Delicate, perishable, and soft skinned, they are so different from their more robustly flavored, hard-shelled, and hard-fleshed winter cousins.

Summer squash occur in an appealing variety of shapes. The simplest may be the zucchini—a long, cylindrical squash that can be green or yellow and begs to be sliced into coins or split lengthwise and grilled. Others include golf ball–sized pattypan squash, which are round, with a wavy, scalloped edge, and crookneck squash, which are usually yellow, with a bulbous bottom and an elongated neck that curves gently toward the stem. There are even summer squash shaped like eggs.

One thing to keep in mind: for summer squash (as well as many other vegetables), bigger is not better. There is a fixed amount of flavor in each squash, so increasing size dilutes their flavor. Buying smaller squash will result in tastier, less watery vegetables.

Organic Advantage

Because summer squash is subject to leaf mildew and insect attack from striped and spotted cucumber beetles, squash bugs, stem borers, and other pests, conventional growers spray them with fungicides and pesticides. Organic growers have nontoxic ways of controlling both mildews and pests. You then avoid these toxic agricultural chemicals by choosing organics.

Uses

To me the best way to prepare summer squash is to grill it. In the summer, I cut small squash into halves, brush them with olive oil, and grill them on both sides so they acquire some delicious charring and a tender interior. They really don't need anything else.

The Greeks layer slices of fresh summer squash in an oiled baking pan with béchamel sauce, finish the top with *kefalotiri* cheese and bread crumbs mixed with a little melted butter, then bake at 325°F for 30 minutes. If you have a mandoline, you can make ultra-thin slices of long squash and layer them in vegetable casseroles. Or roll them up with a filling made of Parmesan and ground almonds, set the little cylinders in a baking dish, top them with bread crumbs, and bake at 350°F for 20 minutes.

Squash blossoms (often called zucchini blossoms)—big, satiny, deep golden, and evanescently luscious—add to the fun of summer cookery. They can be stuffed and baked, stuffed and served raw, battered and fried, used as wrappers, and cut into thin strips to garnish soups.

Angel Hair Pasta with Summer Squash

SERVES 6

This recipe is from Jesse Cool, one of the country's finest organic chefs. She suggests making this in the summer, when just-harvested summer squash has wonderful flavor and an almost creamy texture.

1/4 cup olive oil
1 small red onion, thinly sliced
1 pound summer squash (pattypan, yellow or green zucchini, or crookneck), cut into bite-size pieces
1/4 cup dry white wine
One 2-ounce can anchovies, drained and chopped fine
2 cloves garlic, minced
1 tablespoon capers
1 tablespoon chopped green or red chiles
1 pound angel hair pasta (capellini)
1 cup coarsely chopped fresh basil
Freshly ground black pepper, to taste
Freshly shaved or grated Parmesan

1. Bring a large pot of salted water to a boil.
2. Meanwhile, in a large sauté pan over medium heat, warm the olive oil. Add the onion and cook until translucent, about 4 minutes.
3. Add the squash and cook until it is just al dente, about 5 minutes. Add the wine, anchovies, garlic, capers, and chiles. Set aside.
4. Add the pasta to the boiling water and cook until al dente. Drain the pasta and toss with the zucchini mixture, basil, and pepper to taste. Put on a large platter or on six individual plates and top with the cheese.

SWEET PEPPER

SEASON: summer into fall

GOOD VARIETIES: Blushing Beauty, Chervena Chujski, Chocolate Beauty, Giant Marconi, Golden Summer, Lipstick, Nardello, Quadrato d'Oro, Red Heart, Vidi

WHAT TO LOOK FOR: Peppers with a deep color that are shiny and wrinkle free, firm but not stiff (which would indicate immaturity), that have bright green stems, and—most importantly—that seem heavy for their size are the ones you want. This indicates maturity and means they'll be extra sweet.

STORAGE AND PREPARATION TIPS: Refrigerate in plastic bags in the vegetable crisper for up to 10 days.

NUTRITIONAL HIGHLIGHTS: beta-carotene (red pepper), vitamin B_6, vitamin C

GOES WELL WITH: olive oil, onions, tomatoes

If you think you don't like peppers, it might be because you're thinking of green bell peppers, which have a vegetative, almost metallic edge to their taste. Red, yellow, and other colorful peppers, by contrast, are wonderfully sweet. Most sweet peppers are green when immature and turn color only as they ripen.

Not all sweet peppers are the blocky bell type. Some are tapered, some look like horns, some have a conical shape, and some have irregular twisty shapes. These curvesome peppers are choice because you can bet they are grown to ripen fully—you seldom see these other types sold green. A rich red color indicates the best flavor. Orange or yellow varieties are sweeter than other colors and have a smooth taste. The rule of thumb is that unripe peppers are sharper and less sweet than ripe peppers, no matter their color.

PEPPER MATURITY BY COLOR

IMMATURE COLOR	RIPE COLOR
Brown	Dark red
Green	Red, yellow, orange, or brown
Purple	Dark red
White	Ivory turning lilac turning red

Organic Advantage

Organically grown colorful, ripe sweet peppers at the farmers' market in the summer and fall are usually priced well below what the big markets—even the organic ones—charge. And organically grown sweet peppers set the standard for flavor. Because organic farmers have less interest in high-volume turnaround, they are more likely to choose varieties of peppers that are meant to color up and ripen to their full flavor potential, rather than typical conventional peppers more often bred to be picked green and immature. Conventional growers, by contrast, flood the soil with soluble nutrients, causing the peppers to grow extra large and the plants to produce more fruits. But each pepper contains a fixed amount of flavor compounds, so larger fruits tend to be mostly water and lack flavor.

Uses

Ripe peppers are sweet and succulent raw. I always add ripe sweet pepper to my crudités and salads. They have a real affinity for tomatoes, onions, and olive oil—staples of Italian cooking—and can be added to risottos.

Roasted peppers (see page 106) can be cut into thin strips, marinated in olive oil flavored with salt and pepper for 30 minutes, and eaten. Or dredge the marinated peppers in flour, dip them into well-beaten eggs, and fry them in hot olive oil until they're golden brown. I make a savory, salty paste by squashing and melting several anchovy fillets in olive oil over medium heat, then adding peeled and seeded fire-roasted red sweet peppers. I cook them until they soften and can be mashed with the back of a fork, then I mash everything together. I add 2 or 3 minced garlic cloves and 1 very ripe chopped tomato then reduce the heat and simmer until the tomato is softened. Spoon this over pasta for a simple, quick, easy lunch or dinner.

Roasting peppers: Roasting red sweet peppers is one of the best ways to prepare them for optimum flavor. I have a gas grill that does it beautifully, but you can use a charcoal grill, the broiler, the gas flame of the stove top, or even a stove-top electric element turned to high. The goal is to blacken and blister all sides of a pepper. Place the pepper 3 inches above the heat source and turn every minute or two. The process should take about 20 minutes total. You want the skin to blister without cooking the flesh underneath any more than necessary.

When the peppers are properly blackened and blistered, immediately place them in a paper bag tied shut or covered bowl. Let them sit for 10 minutes (the steam will loosen their skins), and then peel off the skin, removing any bits that cling with a paring knife. Don't rinse the peeled peppers or you'll rinse away flavor. Cut the peppers open and remove the seeds.

Pasta with Hunter's Sauce

SERVES 6

Claire Criscuolo, chef and owner of Claire's Corner Copia in New Haven, Connecticut, prepares this sauce using plump red, yellow, and green organic bell peppers. She says it's one of the most popular selections at her vegetarian restaurant, which has been keeping Yalies and townies happy and healthy for three decades.

1/4 cup extra-virgin olive oil
8 large cloves garlic, coarsely chopped
5 large bell peppers, assorted colors, seeded and coarsely chopped
1 pound mixed mushrooms, sliced
1 large red onion, coarsely chopped
1 tablespoon fresh rosemary leaves, chopped
2 teaspoons fennel seeds
1/2 teaspoon crushed red pepper flakes
Salt and freshly ground black pepper
Two 28-ounce cans Italian whole peeled tomatoes, crushed with your hands
1 pound rigatoni, penne, or other pasta

1. Put a large pot of salted water on to boil.

2. Heat the olive oil in a heavy pot over medium-low heat. Add the garlic and cook for 2 minutes, stirring frequently, until softened. Add the peppers, mushrooms, onion, rosemary, fennel seeds, red pepper flakes, and salt and pepper to taste.

3. Cover, raise the heat to medium and cook for 15 minutes, stirring frequently,

or until the peppers are softened. Add the tomatoes. Bring to a boil, reduce the heat, and simmer for 30 minutes, uncovered, stirring frequently, or until the sauce reduces by about one quarter. Taste and adjust seasonings. Keep the sauce warm.

4. About 10 minutes before the sauce is done, add the pasta to the boiling water, and cook according to the package directions. Drain and turn into a warm serving bowl. Spoon one quarter of the sauce over the top and toss to coat the pasta. Spoon the remaining sauce over the top. Grind additional black pepper over the top if desired.

Sweet Pepper and Sausage Frittata

SERVES 6

This delicious dish is quintessentially Italian. It's perfect for an outdoor lunch on a fall weekend.

1/2 pound sweet Italian sausages, casings removed
2 ripe sweet peppers, red or yellow, cut into very thin 2-inch strips
1 large red onion, cut in half, sliced thin, and separated
8 large eggs
1/4 cup chopped Italian flat-leaf parsley
1/4 teaspoon salt
1/2 teaspoon freshly ground black pepper
1 cup shredded mozzarella cheese (about 4 ounces)

1. Preheat the oven to 350°F. Crumble and cook the sausage in an ovenproof, nonstick skillet over medium heat until cooked through, about 5 minutes. Remove and drain on paper towels.

2. Add the peppers, onion, and 1/2 cup of water to the skillet and cook over medium heat for about 12 minutes, stirring every couple of minutes, or until the peppers are tender and the water has evaporated.

3. In a bowl, beat the eggs, parsley, salt, and pepper. Stir in the mozzarella and sausage, then pour this mixture over the vegetables in the skillet. Cook over medium heat about 3 minutes, or until the egg mixture begins to set around the edges. Place the skillet in the oven for about 12 minutes, or until the frittata is set. Loosen the frittata and slide it onto a warm serving plate. Cut into wedges.

SWEET POTATO

SEASON: late summer through early winter

GOOD VARIETIES:

Orange: Garnet, Jewel, Vardaman, Yellow Yam

White: Boniato, White Triumph

WHAT TO LOOK FOR: Sweet potatoes should be firm, fat, unblemished, heavy roots.

STORAGE AND PREPARATION TIPS: Although sweet potatoes look sturdy, they are very perishable and should be used within a few days of purchase. Store them at room temperature, not in the fridge, as cold hastens their deterioration. When peeled raw, they discolor rapidly, so either cover them with water immediately or cook them whole and remove the skins later.

NUTRITIONAL HIGHLIGHTS: beta-carotene, fiber, manganese, potassium, vitamin B_6, vitamin C

GOES WELL WITH: acorn squash, apples, butter, cinnamon, dried apricots, duck, ginger, maple syrup, nutmeg, orange juice, pork, salt, sherry

The root we know as the sweet potato is, in fact, not related to the common white potato at all. As far as names go, sweet potatoes are actually the original potato. When Columbus reached the New World, the Native Americans he encountered showed him the sweet potato and called it *batata*. When Spanish adventurers later discovered the white potato, it bore a resemblance to the *batata*, or *patata*, as they sometimes called it, and the name was transferred by the Spanish to white potatoes. The word *sweet* was bestowed upon them by the English as a way to tell them apart from white potatoes. A more contemporary naming confusion relates to the difference between a sweet potato and a yam. Many Americans think they are the same thing. In fact, the sweet potato bears no relation to any of the yam species grown in Africa and Asia.

Depending on the variety, sweet potato skins can be white, yellow, red, tan, brown, or purplish red. The flesh varies from white to orange. The orange ones are moist and creamy; the white ones, dry and starchy (these are popular in Japan).

Organic Advantage

Scientists are hurriedly trying to develop disease resistance in and otherwise "improve" the sweet potato through genetic engineering. These scientists don't say what foreign genes will be inserted into sweet potatoes. Nor do we know how the additions might affect sweet potato agriculture or the potato consumers. All the more reason to locate and eat organic sweet potatoes.

Uses

I like sweet potatoes with meats such as pork and duck. They pair nicely with winter flavors: try enhancing sweet potato puree with any of the ingredients mentioned above. Mix baked sweet potatoes with baked acorn squash, then accent the combination with a little butter and maple syrup.

Baked sweet potatoes: Bake in a 400°F oven for an hour or until the very center of the root is soft and creamy (as disclosed by the point of an inserted knife). Sweet potatoes will often exude a syrupy-sweet liquid during baking that will fall to the bottom of your oven and burn. To prevent this, wrap the roots in aluminum foil before baking.

Candied sweet potatoes: To make these sweet treats, parboil three whole roots for 10 to 15 minutes. Remove the skins, cut the sweet potatoes into 1-inch-thick rounds, and lay them in a greased baking dish. Pour on about 1 cup of orange juice and sprinkle on 1 cup of brown sugar, a little salt, and a pinch or two of ground ginger. Dot the top with smidgens of butter and bake at 375°F for 45 minutes.

Sweet Potato and Spinach Flan

SERVES 6

I got the idea for this recipe from Rhonda Carano of Ferrari-Carano Vineyards and Winery in Sonoma County, California. When I tried it, I was amazed at its silky texture and the rich and tangy taste. Aromatics like marsala, orange zest, and nutmeg lift the dish out of the realm of the ordinary.

2 large sweet potatoes
3 tablespoons olive oil
1/4 cup bread crumbs
1 tablespoon butter
1 clove garlic, minced
1 tablespoon marsala
1 cup chicken stock
1 bunch fresh spinach, washed, dried, and stemmed
1/2 cup freshly grated Parmesan
4 large eggs
2 teaspoons freshly grated orange zest (well scrubbed if not organic)
1/2 teaspoon freshly grated nutmeg

1. Bring a pot of water to a boil. Add the sweet potatoes and parboil for 5 minutes. Drain, peel, and cut into 1/2-inch slices, then into 1/2-inch-wide strips.

2. Preheat the oven to 350°F. Lightly grease a 6-cup muffin pan or 6 ramekins with 2 tablespoons of the olive oil. Coat each with bread crumbs.

3. Heat the remaining olive oil and the butter in a sauté pan, add the sweet potato, cover, and cook, turning often, until tender, 15 to 20 minutes. Add the garlic during the last few minutes.

4. Uncover, add the marsala, and cook until it evaporates, then add the chicken stock and spinach and cook until the liquid has almost evaporated and the ingredients are soft, 8 to 10 minutes. Let the mixture cool slightly, then blend or process in a food processor until smooth.

5. Empty into a bowl and add the cheese, eggs, orange zest, and nutmeg. Stir until well blended, then pour into the muffin pan or ramekins. Place these in a roasting pan with 1 inch of warm water. Bake for 35 to 40 minutes. Cool for 10 minutes. Run a knife around the edges of each flan, then invert on a plate and serve warm.

TOMATILLO

SEASON: late summer through winter

GOOD VARIETIES: Giant, Indian, Large green, Purple, Rendidora, Toma Verde

WHAT TO LOOK FOR: Buy tomatillos with the husks intact. The fruits should be firm, not soft and squishy.

STORAGE AND PREPARATION TIPS: These fruits have thin skins but store well for many weeks if their husks aren't removed. When you are ready to use them, remove the husks and rinse the tomatillos well; they tend to be sticky on the outside.

NUTRITIONAL HIGHLIGHTS: lutein, vitamin C

GOES WELL WITH: chicken, corn, fish, tomatoes

Although the tomatillo is just now coming into widespread distribution and use in the United States, it has been known for ages in Mexico, where it was a staple part of the diet in Aztec and Mayan times, was cultivated even before the tomato, and remains an important food to this day.

There are over a hundred varieties of tomatillos in Mexico, with a wide range of flavors, colors, and sizes, but only seven varieties are sold in the United States

Organic Advantage

Many tomatillos sold in the United States are grown in Mexico or simply harvested from wild plants, so it's hard to tell how much, if any, pesticide is used in their production. I have not found organic certification on any tomatillos so far, but their increasing popularity may help bring organic tomatillos to your local stores soon.

Uses

Tomatillos are usually used somewhat underripe to make salsa verde and mole verde, and to add an acid snap to sauces and Mexican dishes. If allowed to ripen fully, they acquire a yellow cast and become milder and sweeter, with a light, citrusy flavor that's good for chutneys and preserves. A few razor-thin slices add a mouth-watering essence to salads. Cooked by boiling for 3 to 5 minutes, depending on their size, they soften in both texture and flavor. Roasted in a 450°F oven for 10 to 15 minutes, they gain concentration of flavor, but be conservative in cooking time; if they go too long, they can burst. Cool them before pureeing.

Salsa Verde

MAKES ABOUT 1 1/2 CUPS

This spicy green sauce is a specialty of Michoacan on Mexico's west coast. It's particularly good as an accompaniment to chicken, and the tomatillos' tanginess adds zing to ocean fish like seared ahi and black grouper. I spoon it on soft tacos, burritos, enchiladas, tamales, and sometimes on grilled steak.

5 fresh serrano chiles
8 to 10 tomatillos (about 2/3 pound), husks removed
1 pickled serrano chile, seeds and stem removed, pickling juice reserved

1 clove garlic, peeled
1/2 teaspoon salt
1/2 cup coarsely chopped cilantro
1 avocado, pitted, peeled, and cubed
1/3 cup minced onion

1. Bring a large saucepan of water to a boil. Add the fresh chiles and boil for 5 minutes. Add the tomatillos and cook 3 minutes more. Remove and drain the chiles and tomatillos. Stem the chiles.

2. In a blender, combine the fresh chiles, tomatillos, pickled chile, 1 tablespoon of the pickling juice, the garlic, and salt, and puree well. When pureed, add the cilantro and blend with two or three 2-second bursts.

3. Transfer to a serving bowl, add the avocado and onion, and mix. Serve immediately. If you plan to serve it later, refrigerate the puree and add the onion and avocado just before serving.

TOMATO

SEASON: late summer

GOOD VARIETIES:

Large: Aunt Ginny's purple, Beefsteak, Big Beef, Black from Tula, Brandywine, Carmello, Caro-Rich, Caspian pink, Cherokee purple, Costoluto Fiorentino, Doublerich, Dr. Wyche's yellow, Early Girl, Garden Peach, Golden Queen, Green Jubilee, Marvel Striped, Oregon Spring, Oxheart, Persimmon, Siberia

Cherry: Juliet, MS-5, Sun Gold, Sweet 100

For sauce and canning: Roma, San Marzano Lampadina

WHAT TO LOOK FOR: Tomatoes should be smooth and free of dark, depressed spots, punctures, mold at the stem end, or scarred indentations at the blossom end.

STORAGE AND PREPARATION TIPS: Store in the pantry, not the refrigerator, or tomatoes will quickly lose quality. To peel tomatoes, cut out the small core, score a shallow X at the other end, blanch in boiling water for 15 to 30 seconds, then dunk in ice water until the skins loosen.

NUTRITIONAL HIGHLIGHTS: beta-carotene, lycopene, potassium, vitamin A, vitamin C

GOES WELL WITH: basil, black pepper, cheese, eggs, garlic, meats, olives, olive oil, onion, oregano, parsley, peppers, thyme

Our modern tomatoes are the result of many generations of selection, starting with pea-sized cherry tomatoes that still grow wild in Peru, Ecuador, and other places in South America. This wild species was domesticated in Mexico, where the Aztecs called them *xitomatl* (the root *-tomatl* means "plump fruit"). The Spanish dropped the prefix and the final l, and the name became *tomate*. It was taken over into English as *tomato*, its vowels pronounced as in the existing word *potato*. Sixteenth-century Europeans thought tomatoes were poisonous and grew them as ornamental plants. Later they were thought to be an aphrodisiac and became known as love apples, or *pommes d'amour* in French and *pomodori* in Italian.

There are three main types of tomato: cherry or grape cluster tomatoes, which are either round or pear-shaped and grow up to the size of golf balls; regular tomatoes that can grow up to 8 or 9 inches in diameter but are usually half that size; and Italian plum tomatoes, which are meatier than the others and used for tomato sauce. Tomatoes can also be categorized by skin color: white, red, green, purple, multicolored, black, orange, and yellow. Tomatoes can be on the mild and sweet side, like the yellow pear-shaped varieties, acidic like Beefsteaks, or a balance of the two, like Brandywines.

Your best chance of finding perfect tomatoes is in peak season: mid- to late August. Buy them vine ripened from a roadside stand or farmers' market (or grow them yourself), or seek out vine-ripened tomatoes at the market.

Organic Advantage

Conventional tomatoes are treated with agricultural chemicals, and genetic engineers have been able to reduce the amount of cell wall–softening enzymes in certain tomato strains so they stay harder longer, giving them a longer supermarket shelf life. You get none of that when you buy organic.

Uses

Tomatoes can be grilled or griddled, fried, broiled, baked, roasted, stewed, sautéed, or eaten raw. You can stuff them, turn them into a condiment (ketchup), make them into juice or sauce, add them to main dishes like ratatouille, smear them on pizza, eat them raw in salads, or top a burger with a slice. Roasting intensifies the tomato's flavor. If you choose to seed your tomatoes, do so over a sieve placed over a bowl; the liquid is flavorful and a good addition to whatever you're cooking.

Tomato sauce: The perfect time to buy a ton of tomatoes and make sauce is just past the peak of tomato season, when supply outstrips demand and prices start to drop. You can halve or quarter this recipe. Start by peeling about 20 pounds of tomatoes (see Storage and Preparation Tips, page 111), and place them in a large, nonreactive pot that will easily hold them. Add 3 peeled and diced onions, 6 heads of peeled, roughly chopped garlic cloves, the leaves of 2 bunches of basil, 1 bunch of Italian flat-leaf parsley, a handful of chopped fresh oregano, half that amount of thyme, and 1 cup of olive oil. Place on low heat and let sit, uncovered, for several days (turn off and cover at night), stirring once in a while, until reduced in volume by at least a third, even better by one half. (Total cooking time to reduce by a third will be 12 hours; if you need to leave the house before the sauce is done, cover the pot and turn off the stove, then turn it back on when you come home.) Be careful not to let the sauce scorch on the bottom. When it has reduced, pack it into canning jars and pressure-cook five jars at a time for 20 to 30 minutes (follow canning directions carefully). An opened jar of sauce will keep 10 to 12 days in the refrigerator.

Untraditional Gazpacho

SERVES 4

Chef Greg Hallihan of Stella's Café in Sebastopol, California, tweaks classic gazpacho into something refreshingly new and delicious—a sort of Spain-meets-Thailand cold vegetable soup.

4 large ripe tomatoes
1 medium slicing cucumber
1 stalk lemongrass
1 piece fresh ginger, about the size of your thumb
Juice of 4 limes
1 teaspoon superfine sugar
Salt to taste
1 small white onion, peeled
1 ripe avocado, halved and pitted
1 lemon

1. Bring a saucepan of water to a boil, add 3 of the tomatoes, and blanch for 1 minute. Remove and rinse under running water until the skins slip off easily. Wrap in plastic wrap and place in the refrigerator for 1 hour, or until thoroughly chilled.

2. Quarter and seed the 3 peeled tomatoes over a bowl; strain and reserve any juice. Peel, seed, and coarsely chop the cucumber. Remove the woody outer layers of the lemongrass until you reach the whitish heart; mince the tender heart very fine. Peel and coarsely chop the ginger.

3. In a blender, combine the quartered tomatoes and strained tomato juice, cucumber, lemongrass, ginger, lime juice, the sugar, and a pinch of salt, and blend until smooth. Refrigerate.

4. Seed and finely dice the remaining tomato, the onion, and 1/2 teaspoon of the avocado, and combine. Set aside. Remove the peel of the lemon with a vegetable peeler, but leave on the white pith under the peel. Cut the lemon into 1/4-inch-thick rounds, removing any seeds.

5. Pour the chilled gazpacho into four bowls. Add a tablespoon-size scoop of avocado to each bowl and set a tablespoon of the tomato-onion-avocado salsa on the avocado scoop. Float a lemon slice on the surface of the soup. Serve at once or chill until ready to serve.

WINTER SQUASH

SEASON: mid-fall through the end of winter (peaking between October and January)

GOOD VARIETIES: Blue Ballet, Blue Hubbard, Bush Delicata, Carnival, Delicata, Gold Nugget, Golden Hubbard, Red Kuri, Rouge Vif d'Étampes, spaghetti squash, Sunshine, Sweet Dumpling, Sweet Meat,

Table Ace, Turk's Turban, Waltham butternut

WHAT TO LOOK FOR: Unless you intend to use it right away, make sure that each squash is firm and sound, with its tough, dried stem intact and its skin totally free of cuts.

STORAGE AND PREPARATION TIPS: Winter squash free of cuts or bruises will last in a cool room for 2 to 3 months and will actually sweeten over time. Don't refrigerate it. If you are roasting squash whole, make sure to pierce it through in a few places so it doesn't explode. If you are going to cut the squash into chunks before cooking, peel it first.

NUTRITIONAL HIGHLIGHTS: fiber, folate, potassium, vitamin A, vitamin C

GOES WELL WITH: cheese, curry powder, ginger, leeks, maple syrup, oranges, sage, sherry, thyme

---

The New World contained many unexpected treasures: squash was one. The name *squash* is an abbreviation of the Narragansett word *asquutasquash*; the prefix *asq-* means "uncooked" or "raw." Along with corn and beans, squash is one of the Native Americans' "three sisters": three crops that were often grown together, and which together formed a staple diet complete in all necessary proteins.

The types of winter squash seem endless. There are acorns, buttercups, butternuts, Hubbards, *kabochas*, spaghettis, pumpkins, and more. Butternut, buttercup, and Hubbard squash all have fine, nutty flavors and smooth textures. *Kabocha*, a Japanese squash, has silky flesh and a flavor like a sweet potato. Spaghetti squash yields masses of stringy (but tasty) fibers that look like spaghetti—in fact, you can serve it like spaghetti. Acorn squash has milder flavor than the others. Big jack o' lantern pumpkins are great for carving, but not so good for eating.

Organic Advantage

Squash are heavy feeders that ingest large amounts of nutrients from the soil. If the soil isn't rich in organic matter, the stressed plants produce substances that attract pests that must then be combated with pesticides. Organic growers get off this destructive treadmill by giving the plants all the nutrients they need by adding compost.

Uses

Even the richest-flavored winter squash is still fairly mild, which means it can successfully absorb a wide range of other flavors. Think of squash flavored with cheeses like cheddar and Fontina, or with ginger, or with leeks, oranges, sage and thyme, maple syrup, sherry, curry powder—the list can go on and on; squash's forgiving flavors can work so many different ways.

Roasting squash: The classic way to treat winter squash is to roast it. Cut the squash in half. Scoop out the seeds and

DELICATA AND SWEET DUMPLING

If any winter squash can challenge butternut for top quality honors, it's Delicata, a pretty, loaf-shaped squash 7 to 9 inches long and 3 to 4 inches wide, with dark green stripes running down a ribbed surface and a creamy white to yellowish background. The flesh is finely textured, light orange, and nutty sweet, with a hint of caramel when roasted until the surface has browned a bit.

Also look for the Sweet Dumpling, a tasty morsel of a squash only 3 to 4 inches wide and about 3 inches high. Very pretty, with the same color pattern as the Delicata, it can be roasted and used as a serving container. After roasting, cut the top off like a lid (as you would a Halloween pumpkin), scrape out the seeds and flesh, fill (try hot squash soup, or baked squash chunks with diced ham and potatoes), then fit the top snugly back on.

pulp and place each half cut side up in a shallow pan of water. For a less sweet variety such as acorn squash, plop a bit of butter and some maple syrup in the cavities, but sweeter squash like butternut doesn't need a thing. Then bake at 400°F for roughly 1 hour (small squash will take less time, big ones, longer). That's it.

"Pumpkin" Pie Made with Butternut Squash

MAKES ONE 9-INCH PIE

Ever since I first tried substituting butternut squash for pumpkin in a pie, I've used them ever since. I love the rich color, silky texture, and excellent flavor of the squash. Because pumpkin pie filling is so wet, it's a good idea to prebake the piecrust before filling it.

1 large or 2 small butternut squash (about 4 pounds)
Single crust for a 9-inch pie (recipe follows)
1½ cups heavy cream
½ cup dark corn syrup
3 large eggs, separated
6 tablespoons brown sugar
2 tablespoons white sugar
2 tablespoons blackstrap molasses
1 teaspoon vanilla extract
½ teaspoon salt
1 teaspoon ground cinnamon
½ teaspoon ground ginger
¼ teaspoon freshly grated nutmeg
¼ teaspoon ground allspice
¼ teaspoon ground cloves

1. Preheat the oven to 350°F. Cut the squash lengthwise in half. Remove the seeds. Place the halves cut side up in a baking pan with 1 inch of water in the bottom, and lightly place aluminum foil over the squash. Bake for 1½ hours, or until the squash is soft and falling apart. While the squash is baking, prepare the

dough for the pie crust and refrigerate for 1 hour.

2. Remove the squash from the oven and raise the temperature to 425°F. When the squash is cool enough to handle, remove any tough browned or burnt skin that may have formed on the surface, spoon out 2 cups of the soft meat, and reserve (save the rest for another use).

3. Roll the dough into a circle about 1/8 inch thick and 12 inches in diameter. Transfer to a 9-inch pie pan. Trim the edges 1/2 inch larger than the edge of the pan and crimp with the back of a fork. Poke holes here and there with a fork. Line the dough with wax paper, then fill with pie weights or dry beans to weigh down the dough. Bake for 10 minutes. Remove the weights and wax paper, return the crust to the oven, and bake for 3 to 4 minutes, or until the crust is a golden brown.

4. While the crust is baking, prepare the filling. In a large bowl, combine the 2 cups squash, cream, egg yolks, corn syrup, brown and white sugars, molasses, vanilla, salt, and spices, and mix well with a whisk.

5. Using an electric mixer, beat the egg whites in another large bowl until they form soft peaks. Fold them into the squash mixture. Fill the prebaked crust to within 1/2 inch of the top of the crust. If any pie filling is left over, pour it into a ramekin and bake it alongside the pie.

6. Bake the pie for 45 minutes to 1 hour, or until a butter knife inserted in the center of the pie comes out clean. Remove from the oven and let cool.

Single Crust for a 9-Inch Pie

MAKES 1 CRUST FOR A 9-INCH PIE

1 cup all-purpose or pastry flour
1/4 teaspoon salt
4 tablespoons butter, chilled
2 tablespoons canola oil, chilled
1/4 cup cold water

1. Mix the flour and salt together in a bowl. Cut the butter into 4 pieces and add them to the flour along with the canola oil. Using 2 knives or a pastry cutter, cut the butter into the flour until the pieces of butter are smaller than peas and the mixture resembles a coarse meal.

2. Add 3 tablespoons of water and toss the mixture lightly using two forks. Add more water, if needed, until you can press the mixture together into a ball that retains its shape. Cover and refrigerate for at least a half hour before rolling.

Spaghetti Squash with Tomato and Basil

SERVES 4

Few dishes could be simpler, healthier, or tastier than this one. The fresher the ingredients, the better the dish. When prepared, spaghetti squash looks like glistening rice noodles. It has a mild squash flavor and slick texture that needs the enhancement of the tomatoes and basil.

1 spaghetti squash, about 2 pounds
1/4 pound fresh plum tomatoes
4 cloves garlic
1/4 cup extra-virgin olive oil
1/2 teaspoon salt
3 or 4 basil leaves, finely shredded
Crushed red pepper flakes

1. Place a rack in the middle of the oven and preheat the oven to 375°F.

2. Stab the spaghetti squash in 5 or 6 places with the point of a knife to allow the steam to escape, then set the squash in a baking dish or on a piece of aluminum foil placed on the middle rack of the oven. Bake for about 1 hour, until the squash is tender when pierced with a skewer or thin knife.

3. While the squash is cooking, bring a small saucepan of water to a boil. Add the tomatoes, blanch for 1 minute, then run under cold water. Slip off the skins. Cut the tomatoes in half, remove the seeds, and finely dice the tomatoes.

4. Roughly chop the garlic cloves. Heat the olive oil over medium heat. Add the garlic and cook for 1 minute, stirring in the salt toward the end; remove from the heat.

5. When the squash is finished, let set until cool enough to handle, cut it in half lengthwise, remove the seeds, and separate the strands of the "spaghetti" (actually the tender but fibrous inner flesh of the squash) with a fork. Place the strands in a bowl. Add the tomatoes and shredded basil leaves. Sprinkle on the crushed red pepper and pour on the garlic and oil mixture. Toss well with two forks and serve.

CHAPTER 3

Fruits

Did you know that there is no such thing as cherries or apples or strawberries?

Every kind of fruit is a specific, named variety of the abstract idea of cherries, apples, strawberries—or any fruit. Some varieties are better than others for certain sought-after qualities. You might look for Bing cherries, Braeburn apples, or Sparkle strawberries because these varieties are known for their great flavor. With any fruit, it's very important to know the names of the top-rated varieties, because it's varieties that you're buying and the top-rated ones that you want.

This book tells you the varieties to look for. Many markets don't name the varieties of fruits they display. You should ask the management to do so, for only then can you know you're getting the best. Organic fruit growers, especially when selling at farmers' markets, will know the varieties they've grown, even if the names aren't displayed.

Fruits are among the foods most highly dosed with toxic agricultural chemicals. Farm workers in California call strawberries the devil's fruit because the fields are so toxic. But organic growers use nontoxic techniques for controlling pests and diseases. That means better conditions for workers and cleaner fruit for you.

FRUITS BY SEASON

Whether you want local, organic fruits to eat or to put up, they are never less expensive or better than when they are in season. Most fruits are available year-round, but they have either been kept in climate-controlled storage, trucked in from far away, or shipped in from other countries that have their summers during our winter, like Chile and Australia. In all of those cases, the fruit loses quality. It may not be organic. And it is sure to be expensive compared with its price in season. That's why canning or freezing organic fruit in season makes economic as well as gustatory sense.

SPRING	SUMMER	FALL	WINTER
Cherimoya	Apple (early varieties)	Apple	Citrus
Cherry	Apricot	Cranberry	
Loquat	Blackberry	Date	
Papaya	Blueberry	Fig	
Pineapple	Currant	Grape	
Strawberry	Fig	Kiwifruit	
	Gooseberry	Pear	
	Huckleberry	Persimmon	
	Mango	Pomegranate	
	Mulberry	Quince	
	Melon	Raspberry	
	Nectarine	Strawberry	
	Papaya		
	Passion fruit		
	Pineapple		
	Peach		
	Plum		
	Raspberry		
	Strawberry		
	Watermelon		

APPLE

SEASON: late summer through early winter

GOOD VARIETIES:

For eating: Braeburn, Cox's Orange Pippin, Fuji, Gala, Gravenstein, Honey Crisp, Jazz, Jonagold, Stayman Winesap

For cooking: Jonathan, Northern Spy, Granny Smith, Pound Sweet

WHAT TO LOOK FOR: Apples should look plump and shiny, firm when pressed on the shoulder by the stem, without any give. Avoid apples with bruises, cuts, or blackened scabs. Check the blossom end for black spots called frass (a sign of insect larvae): it should be blemish free.

STORAGE AND PREPARATION TIPS: Apples keep very well in the fruit crisper of the refrigerator. Apples that are harvested late in the season—in October and November—keep the best, and they will often last the winter in a cold fridge.

NUTRITIONAL HIGHLIGHTS: fiber, vitamin C (Many of the nutrients are found in the skin.)

GOES WELL WITH: butter, cinnamon, cloves, currants, lemons, nutmeg

For all their goodness, apples have figured in some deep-rooted and nefarious stories, from Adam and Eve in the Garden of Eden to the poisoned apple in "Snow White and the Seven Dwarfs." All those dark associations were dispelled for me when I grew my own apples in Pennsylvania: varieties like Northern Spy, Rhode Island Greening, Smokehouse, and Cox's Orange Pippin. My homegrown apples were the fruits of my soil, my sunshine, my rain, and my work—totally salutary and absolutely delicious.

I've seen figures that there are anywhere from 1,400 to 7,000 named apple varieties being sold. Yet only a handful make it into major marketplaces. The best varieties you'll probably find at a supermarket are Galas, Fujis and, if you're lucky, some really good Braeburns and Honey Crisps (avoid the Red Delicious, grown more for its color than its bland taste).

Your best chance of finding other delicious apple varieties is at farmers' markets and roadside stands, especially from organic growers.

Organic Advantage

All apples are prone to attack by certain pests, but instead of coating the orchard with insecticides, organic producers use natural methods of protecting the fruit: Tanglefoot, a proprietary tar-like goo smeared on paper round the trunk of trees to catch insects; tillage under the trees to disrupt the life cycle of insects; and red balls coated with stickum to lure and capture apple fruit flies. They'll also plant cover crops in the orchard—crops that attract and host beneficial insects, which then attack the apple pests. Organic growers are more likely to choose apple varieties with great taste and natural resistance to orchard pests and disease. Conventional growers are more likely to choose apple varieties that travel well and look pretty, although even conventional growers are turning to new apple varieties.

Uses

Apples are excellent for eating just as they are, but the cooking varieties are superb as applesauce, charming as chutney, and of course, perfect in pies, crisps, Betties, and other kinds of pastries. Diced apple makes a nice addition to morning dry or cooked cereals. Apples are at their best when firm and crisp, before they soften and lose their bracing acidity.

Apple Pie

MAKES ONE 9-INCH PIE; SERVES 6 TO 8

Pastry for double-crust 9-inch pie (double the recipe on page 116)
6 medium apples, such as Jonagold, Cortlandt, or Rhode Island Greening
1/2 cup brown sugar
1 tablespoon cornstarch
1/8 teaspoon freshly grated nutmeg
1/8 teaspoon salt
1 3/4 teaspoons ground cinnamon
1 tablespoon freshly squeezed lemon juice
1 1/2 tablespoons butter
1 1/2 teaspoons white sugar

1. Prepare the pie dough, divide in half, then cover and chill 1 hour.

2. Peel, quarter, and core the apples, and thinly slice pieces lengthwise. Place the apples in a bowl. Combine the brown sugar, cornstarch, nutmeg, salt, and 1/4 teaspoon of the cinnamon, and add them to the apples. Toss the apple slices gently until they are evenly coated.

3. Preheat the oven to 450°F. Place a sheet of aluminum foil on the oven rack to catch any drips.

4. Roll out one of the balls of pie dough and line a 9-inch pie pan. Place the apple mixture in the shell and sprinkle it with the lemon juice, then dot the top with the butter. Roll out the second ball of dough, place on top and trim off the excess. Crimp the top and bottom crusts together along the rim of the pie pan with the back of a fork. Mix the remaining 1 1/2 teaspoons of cinnamon with the white sugar. Very lightly sprinkle the top of the pie with the cinnamon sugar mixture. Prick the dough in 5 places with a fork.

5. Bake for 10 minutes, then turn the heat down to 350°F and bake for 45 to 60 minutes, or until the crust is golden brown and the juices are bubbling. Remove from the oven and cool on a wire rack.

APRICOT

SEASON: summer

GOOD VARIETIES: Goldbar, Moorpark, Patterson, Rival, Royal Blenheim

WHAT TO LOOK FOR: Look for ripe apricots that are beginning to soften but are not yet mushy. They should be fragrant, with aromas of citrus and even cinnamon.

If you can taste one, the flesh should be juicy and sweet, fine textured, with a flavor that matches the fragrance. An unripe apricot will get softer but not sweeter. Outside of the prime season, consider buying organic dried apricots. These have been picked at peak ripeness and often taste better than fresh apricots picked out of peak season.

STORAGE AND PREPARATION TIPS: Apricots are ready to eat as soon as they feel soft to the touch; they will keep for just a few days. If you have too many to eat, halve and pit them, store halves in freezer bags with just enough orange juice to cover them, and freeze.

NUTRITIONAL HIGHLIGHTS: fiber, potassium, vitamin A, vitamin C

GOES WELL WITH: almonds, citrus, citrusy liqueurs such as Grand Marnier and Cointreau, lamb, pork, poultry, veal

---

Apricots, like peaches, originated in China. Today there are over two thousand varieties of apricots in that country. Like so many fruits and vegetables from that region, apricots were carried west along the ancient Silk Road, reaching Persia and the Middle East, then Europe, being finally brought across the Atlantic to the Americas.

Apricots are summer fruits and taste best when the season is hot and dry and farmers can let them ripen on the tree without fear of rot. The window of opportunity with this fruit is narrow. Don't jump the season by buying early apricots in May or early June. The early varieties have been bred for a market hungry for summer's fresh fruits, but they usually lack the flavor and character of fruits of July and August.

Organic Advantage

Apricots attract a wide range of diseases and pests. Organic growers are faced with the same challenges as conventional farmers but use nontoxic controls such as planting disease-resistant fruit varieties, using wasps and sex pheromones to interrupt the mating of the oriental fruit moth (a major pest), and spraying the developing fruit with elemental sulfur and other natural products to control rot.

Uses

Apricots have an amazing ability to enhance and blend with other flavors, including other fruits—citrus fruits in particular. Apricots and almonds are a natural match. Sauces made with their juice or puree have countless uses, from vanilla ice cream to roast pork. The apricot's tangy richness can add zest to fruit salads and desserts. But don't leave out savory dishes. Apricots' acidity enlivens veal and lamb, chicken and duck. Dried apricots can be chopped and added to couscous or rice, plumped by reconstituting them in simmering water, or stewed with meats like lamb shanks.

Apricot Preserves

MAKES 8 HALF-PINT JARS

When a surplus of good apricots are in season, make apricot preserves to

MY FAVORITE APRICOTS

One summer day, walking down a quiet back street in Emmaus, Pennsylvania, I saw a 30-foot-tall apricot tree practically weighed down with ripe fruit. A low branch hung within easy reach, so I climbed a little way up into the tree and spent an unforgettable fifteen minutes eating one perfectly ripe apricot after another. Their flesh was orange and full of sweet juice. They had a rich perfume and a luscious flavor that became my standard of apricot quality ever since.

Some years later, I grew two apricot trees on my own property—a Moongold and a Sungold. Each year they flowered and each year brown rot took all the fruit before it ripened. But that same apricot in Emmaus (about 10 miles away) would be full of spotless ripe fruit! Why hadn't the brown rot infected it? Then one year, my two apricots unexpectedly bore crops of healthy fruit. Hooray! But why?

After some sleuthing, I discovered that the conditions in Emmaus—with yards of grass and asphalt streets—gave the brown rot fungus no place to build up, whereas my country property was a cleared meadow surrounded by woods where the fungus was plentiful. I also found out that apricots must ripen on the tree. If wet weather settles in when that fruit is ripening and beginning to soften, the rot will be able to proliferate. If it stays hot and dry—midsummer conditions—the fruit may avoid the rot. Some years are apricot years and some aren't; my trees were just having a good year.

brighten meals the rest of the year. Homemade apricot preserves are an out-of-this-world confection. Spread them on muffins, use them to glaze a ham or a fruit tart, or add their sweet tang to a pork tenderloin.

4 pounds fresh apricots
5 cups sugar
Juice of 2 lemons, strained

1. Pit the apricots and slice them into coarse pieces. Mix them with the sugar in a large bowl and let the mixture stand on the counter, covered, for at least 1 hour but preferably overnight. This allows the apricots to exude their juices and dissolve the sugar.

2. Chill a dinner plate in the fridge. Transfer the apricot mixture to a large nonreactive saucepan and bring to a boil over high heat. Stir frequently to prevent sticking, and be careful not to let it foam up and over the sides. Reduce the heat to medium and cook, skimming the light, foamy material that will rise, until it looks like preserves (about 15 to 20 minutes).

3. While the preserves are cooking, boil the jars, lids, and bands in a

separate large pot with enough water to cover them for 5 to 10 minutes. Keep them in the hot water until you're ready to fill them.

4. Test the consistency of the preserves by spooning a bit onto the chilled plate. When the preserves reach the right consistency (as thick or as thin as you like), remove from the heat, and stir in the lemon juice.

5. Spoon the preserves into the jars, leaving ½-inch headroom, put on the lids and bands, and process according to the jar manufacturer's instructions, or refrigerate 4 to 6 weeks.

ASIAN PEAR

SEASON: late summer through early fall

GOOD VARIETIES: Hamase, Hosui, Kosui, Shinko

WHAT TO LOOK FOR: Unlike many European pears like the Bartlett, which must ripen after picking, Asian pears ripen on the tree, so look for fully ripe Asian pears. A ripe Asian pear is juicy, lightly sweet, and crisp, but not hard.

STORAGE AND PREPARATION TIPS: Asian pears will keep for a couple of weeks at room temperature.

NUTRITIONAL HIGHLIGHTS: fiber, vitamin C

GOES WELL WITH: chocolate, lime juice, mild cheeses, other fruits

Some people find Asian pears confounding, since we're trained to associate sweetness in fruits with a soft texture. But Asian pears, even at peak ripeness, have a crisp, even crunchy, texture. Inside these russeted, round bronze fruits, the crisp, white flesh is mild and very juicy. Where you might expect a luscious sweetness like a ripe Bartlett pear, you get only a light sweetness, and where you might expect an acid tang like an apple, you get only a subdued acidity.

Organic Advantage

Asian pear trees are fairly delicate and prone to a terrible bacterial disease called fire blight as well as insect infestation, so organic orchardists do spray their trees, but not with toxic chemicals. Instead, they use one of a number of organic sprays. Sulfur, for example, is allowed in organic agriculture to ward off fungus and mildews. Dormant oil sprays, made from mineral or vegetable oils, are used during the trees' dormant season to kill insects wintering in bark crevices. Bacillus thuringiensis is a sprayable disease that affects only caterpillars, which emerge in late spring; liquid seaweed can be sprayed on leaves as a natural plant food. And the list of harmless sprays goes on and on.

Uses

The crisp texture of Asian pears makes them great additions to salads. Slices of fresh Asian pear are excellent splashed with a little lime juice, and a fine accompaniment to a selection of cheeses, especially mild ones such as fresh goat cheese, taleggio, and Swiss. They pair up beautifully with chocolate. Because crispness is their most salient feature, Asian pears are generally not cooked.

Asian Pear Granita

SERVES 4 TO 6

Asian pears make very delicate and refreshing granita.

1 pound ripe Asian pears (3 or 4 pears), peeled, cored, and roughly chopped
1 cup superfine sugar

In a blender, combine pears and sugar. Puree well, and pour the mixture into a bowl or tray. Place it in the freezer and give it a stir every 10 minutes or so, until it's frozen and grainy.

BANANA AND PLANTAIN

SEASON: year-round

GOOD VARIETIES: Ice Cream, Lady Finger (4-inches long), red banana

WHAT TO LOOK FOR: Check bananas for bruises or tears in the skin. Buy them when there's still a little green showing at the stem ends and eat them when the skins develop light freckling.

STORAGE AND PREPARATION TIPS: Urban legends to the contrary, bananas can be stored in the refrigerator—but it's not necessary. They ripen slowly on the kitchen counter.

NUTRITIONAL HIGHLIGHTS: fiber, potassium, vitamin B_6, vitamin C; prevents stomach ulcers, stimulates calcium absorption

GO WELL WITH: blackberries, caramel, chocolate, coffee, cream, lime juice, raspberries, other fruits

Strangely enough, although bananas are mostly grown far away in tropical regions of the world, they are one of the most ubiquitous organic fruits available. The reason is that while many other organic fruits tend to be locally grown by small farms, and therefore of spotty (and seasonal) availability, organic bananas often grow on a huge network of large corporate plantations and reach us through international delivery systems. We may believe our organic bananas come from dedicated, small-scale, organic family farmers, but that's almost never the case.

Besides the standard banana variety (the Cavendish), red bananas are increasingly available. Greenish maroon when unripe, they ripen to a bronze-red, with black flecks and ends when fully ripe. Their flesh is very aromatic, yellow-orange, and dense. I love their flavor and firm, creamy texture.

Organic Advantage

Organic bananas are well worth seeking out because their production avoids a host of toxic chemicals used on conventional plantations that affect everything from the health of the plantation soils and surrounding ecosystems to the health of the workers who must grow and handle them, the health of the bananas, and ultimately, the health of those of us who eat them.

Uses

Bananas: Fresh bananas can be tossed into fruit salads or sliced over breakfast cereal. They make a delicious base under vanilla ice cream covered with chocolate (or chocolate–peanut butter) sauce. For a special treat, dust bananas with sugar, douse with warmed brandy, and flambé.

If your bananas are ripening too quickly for you to eat them all, peel them and freeze some in plastic freezer bags. Frozen bananas can be pureed with other, usually fresh, fruits and a splash of milk (or use vanilla soy milk) to make a thick milkshake-like smoothie.

Plantains: In Latino markets, especially those in Puerto Rican neighborhoods, you will find 10-inch-long, green banana-like fruits called plantains, which taste like a cross between potatoes and squash. They're very starchy when green and unripe. They are usually peeled, sliced on the bias, and added to soups, or fried. They become yellow and brown when semiripe, when they're normally boiled or sautéed and served as a side dish. When they turn black and slightly sweet, they're often baked in their skins and served as dessert. Plantains are almost always cooked.

Tostones: One popular treatment for plantains is tostones, a dish of fried plantains made when their skins are still green. Peel the plantains, slice them on the bias about 3/4-inch thick, and fry the slices in enough oil to cover until they are light golden and partially cooked. Remove the plantains from the oil, drain, cool, then place between sheets of wax paper and smash them with the bottom of a glass to flatten. Return the plantains to the hot oil and fry until they are golden brown and fully cooked.

Bananas with Coconut Cream

SERVES 3

This is a wonderful way to make an unusual and delicious dessert of those ripe bananas that you know will never get eaten before they become overripe. I guarantee they'll be eaten when served like this.

3 ripe bananas, peeled
1/2 cup light brown sugar, mixed with 1 teaspoon ground cinnamon
1 tablespoon melted butter
1/4 cup lime juice
3 tablespoons coconut cream

Preheat the oven to 350°F. Place the bananas in a small baking dish, and sprinkle on the cinnamon sugar. Drizzle with the butter and lime juice, and bake until the bananas are tender, 10 to 15 minutes. Serve each banana on a warmed plate with a tablespoon of coconut cream alongside.

BLUEBERRY

SEASON: early summer through midsummer

GOOD VARIETIES: Blueray, Brigitta, Northland, Patriot, Sierra, Spartan, wild blueberries

WHAT TO LOOK FOR: Check containers of berries for mold, squashed fruit, or overly soft berries. The bluish bloom on their surface is natural and should be there. If at all possible, seek out the nonhybridized, old-fashioned varieties (such as the ones mentioned above), which are closest to wild blueberries.

STORAGE AND PREPARATION TIPS: Fresh blueberries store well in the fridge for up to two weeks. No fruit freezes better than blueberries—their waxy bloom protects them—so you can have in-season summer fruit year-round. Freeze them in one layer on cookie sheets, then store in freezer bags. When thawed, they're good for winter fruit compotes or baked in muffins rather than eaten out of hand, because freezing renders them soft.

NUTRITIONAL HIGHLIGHTS: antioxidants, fiber, vitamin C

GOES WELL WITH: butter, chocolate, cream, hazelnuts, lemon, pork, strawberries

Blueberries, of which several hundred species exist, are one of the most common plants in the woodlands, growing in millions upon millions of acres. As a child, I lay in my bed at night and looked at the glowing mountaintops

THE SMALLER THE BERRY, THE SWEETER THE FRUIT

Cultivated varieties of blueberries from blueberry farms tend to be bigger than wild blueberries because they have been chemically fertilized, while the wildings are suited to nutrient-poor soils and the berries stay small. However, any single blueberry has a set amount of flavor compounds, so the smaller the berry, the more intense the flavor. Really big blueberries tend to be watery and lack that intensity.

There's a blueberry farm not far from me in California where farmer Bruce Goetz has made the transition from conventional to organic blueberry culture. His story is typical of organic blueberry growers. Blueberries like an acid soil rich in decaying organic matter, and so organic compost, with its acidic pH, is perfect for them. The cool nights and sunny days of summertime allow Goetz to grow small but highly flavored berries. While most hybrid blueberries are big and watery, with a 10 percent sugar content, his smaller, more flavorful berries are about 15 percent sugar because of the climate and the low pH, organic soil.

of Pennsylvania's Pocono Mountains to the south. They were on fire. The fires were nothing exceptional. Everyone knew they were purposely set to burn off the forest canopy so that native blueberries would regrow. The harvesters would then pick the blueberries and sell them in the big Northeastern markets.

Until 1916, when Elizabeth White of the New Jersey Pine Barrens marketed the first cultivated blueberries, they were an entirely wild-harvested crop. Thanks to her, cultivated varieties began to appear, and blueberry farms sprang up. But the harvesting of wild blueberries continues to this day, and you can find them at markets, roadside stands and—most fun of all—at pick-your-own farms, where folks with land on which wild blueberry bushes grow thick set out signs, sit down on lawn chairs, and admit the public for a small fee.

Organic Advantage

Since blueberries tend to be free of pests and diseases, even conventional cultivation often includes only chemical fertilizer and herbicides. Organic growers use organic means to control weeds and fertilize their crops.

Uses

Blueberries are a choice ingredient in muffins, scones, pies, and other pastries. Pour them over your morning cereal. Eat them out of hand. When they're in season and at a reasonable price, keep them on hand daily. Soon they'll be out of season, prohibitively priced, and lower in quality.

Freeze summer-fresh blueberries for muffins, compotes, and blueberry pancakes year round.

Vegan Blueberry Muffins

MAKES 12 MUFFINS

Here's a recipe for blueberry muffins that goes easy on the saturated fat but heavy on the nutrition (and it's vegan, too). Make lots of these and freeze them. Take them out of the freezer before you go to bed so they'll be ready to go in the morning.

3/4 cup whole-wheat pastry flour
3/4 cup unbleached all-purpose white flour
1/2 cup cornmeal
1 tablespoon baking powder
1/4 teaspoon sea salt
1 cup soy or rice milk
2 ounces soft tofu
1 cup fresh or frozen blueberries
6 tablespoons canola oil
1/3 cup maple syrup

1. Preheat the oven to 375°F. Oil 12 muffin tin cups or line them with cupcake papers.
2. In a medium bowl, sift together all the dry ingredients.

3. Puree the soy milk and the tofu together in a blender.

4. In a separate bowl, mix the tofu puree, bluberries, oil, and maple syrup.

5. Stir the wet ingredients into the dry ingredients, just enough to mix.

6. Spoon the batter into the muffin cups, filling each 2/3 full. Bake for 20 to 25 minutes, or until golden brown.

CHERRY

SEASON: early summer through midsummer

GOOD VARIETIES: Bing, Montmorency (sour), Black Tartarian, Rainier, Yellow Spanish

WHAT TO LOOK FOR: Purchase whole, fresh cherries with bright (rather than dull) skins, without splits or blemishes. The fruit should be firm rather than soft. Cherries grow in pairs; look for pairs with their stems still joined together.

STORAGE AND PREPARATION TIPS: To preserve in-season cherries for year-round use, pit and freeze cherries in one layer on a cookie sheet, then store them in a freezer bag in the freezer.

NUTRITIONAL HIGHLIGHTS: antioxidants and phytochemicals (in dark-colored cherries), fiber, vitamin A, vitamin C

GOES WELL WITH:

Sweet cherries: basil, chocolate, lemon, mint, tarragon, vanilla

Sour cherries: Cointreau, cream, duck, pork, vanilla

There comes a time in late June when the cherries are at their peak of quality, and that alone makes it one of my favorite times of the year. Although cherry season runs from May to July, the earliest cherries lack the rich flavor of the midseason ones, and tend to split into disfigured twins. After the early cherries come the so-called white or yellow cherries, usually Rainier or Royal Ann. The luscious Bings arrive in mid-June and by month's end are at their peak.

Over one thousand varieties of cherries are sold around the world, but they can all be classified as either sweet or sour. Sweet cherries (Prunus avium) are the ones we most often find fresh at our markets. Containing up to 20 percent sugar, they're perfect for eating out of hand. Organic sweet cherries are also available frozen.

Sour cherries, also called pie cherries, contain an abundance of acid, but when mixed with sugar and used in pies and cobblers, their tartness is one of their features. Sour cherries are almost always sold canned. If you want to buy fresh sour cherries, you'll most likely find them at farmers' markets. You may also find them dried, usually in bulk, at organic markets.

Organic Advantage

When buying sweet cherries, it's very important to find an organic source because conventional sweet cherries are one of the most heavily sprayed crops.

Organic farmers have plenty of options (including a solution of baking soda used as a fungicide) that do not wreak havoc on the orchard ecosystem.

Sour cherries, by contrast, are virtually disease resistant, and so they are rarely sprayed with chemicals. I have seen sour cherry trees laden with bright red fruit sitting happily through the late spring rains, unsprayed, while a nearby sweet cherry crop was nearly entirely taken by brown rot.

Uses

Sweet cherries are mostly eaten out of hand, but they are also made into ice cream, used in pastries, or dried. If you have a food dehydrator, try drying fresh pitted sweet cherry halves to use like raisins in ice cream, muffins, or granola.

Sour cherries are typically sweetened and cooked into pies and pastries, but some are also made into cherry soup, and some are dried. These dried sour cherries can add some zing to a wide range of dishes but especially to sweet meats such as pork and duck.

BING CHERRIES

Many people's choice for the best-tasting cherry is the Bing, a purple-skinned variety of sweet cherry with a rich, sweet, wine-like flavor. Bings originated in Milwaukie, Oregon, in 1875 through the work of an orchardist named Seth Lewelling; he gave the fruit the name of a Chinese laborer who worked for him.

One day back in 1973, I visited a friend who had three mature Bing cherry trees on his property, each a good 35 feet tall, with thick trunks and widespread limbs laden with fruit. I climbed up to where a limb forked into two smaller branches. All around me, burnished burgundy-black cherries hung within reach, and I perched there happy as a bird, gobbling my fill.

It was one of those moments in life that seem so natural and usual when it's happening—just me in a tree with some cherries—but in retrospect becomes an extraordinary pleasure when I realize it is never to be repeated.

Brandied Cherries

YIELDS ABOUT 8 CUPS OF CHERRIES (1/2 GALLON)

For me, cherry season always means that it's time to get out the old crock and make brandied cherries. My crock is ceramic with a lid that snaps closed, but any glass container with a tight-fitting lid will do; use at least a half-gallon crock to make the endeavor worthwhile. If your crock's glass is clear, store it in a dark closet while it ages.

1. Fill the container with ripe but firm, unblemished cherries—I'll use

either sweet or sour, depending on which look the best. You can pit them, but I think the pits' slight almond flavor adds a grace note to the cherries, so I don't. For sweet cherries, add 1 cup of sugar to the crock for every 2 pounds of fruit; for sour cherries, use 1½ cups of sugar.

2. Fill the crock with a decent brandy to within 1 inch of the top, cover with 2 layers of wax paper, and snap down the lid. Because my ceramic crock is light proof, I store the cherries on the kitchen counter: room temperature allows the cherries to macerate better than in the fridge. Once the cherries have steeped for a month or two, I move them to the fridge to keep them from becoming overly soft and falling apart, and they stay there until the holiday season.

TIP: Brandied cherries over homemade organic vanilla ice cream (using a real vanilla bean) make a fine finish to the Thanksgiving turkey or any special meal. Or make cherry-vanilla ice cream with them, adding a few tablespoons of the brandy liquid from the crock (don't use too much brandy or the ice cream won't harden).

Cherry Pie

MAKES ONE 9-INCH PIE; SERVES 6 TO 8

Pies are best made with fresh, midsummer sour cherries.

Pastry for double-crust 9-inch pie (double the recipe on page 116)
4 cups pitted fresh sour cherries
1 cup sugar
¼ cup all-purpose flour
2 tablespoons kirsch, or ¼ teaspoon almond extract
1½ tablespoons freshly squeezed lemon juice
2 teaspoons quick-cooking tapioca
1 tablespoon butter, diced
Milk, or 1 egg mixed with 1 tablespoon water

1. Cut the dough in half and roll out one half about ¼ inch thick to line a 9-inch pie pan, keeping the other half refrigerated. Put the cherries in a large bowl. Combine the sugar, flour, kirsch, lemon juice, and tapioca, and gently mix into the cherries. Fill the pie crust with this mixture. Dot the top with the bits of butter.

2. Preheat the oven to 450°F. Roll out the remaining dough ¼ inch thick and cut it into ½-inch strips. Weave the strips into a lattice top for the pie, trimming off all but ½ inch of the overlap and moistening the ends of the strips where they meet the bottom crust along the edge of the pie plate, squishing them together with the back of a fork. Brush the lattice with the milk. This makes the lattice glossy.

3. Bake for 10 minutes, then reduce heat to 350°F and bake for another 30 minutes, or until the lattice is golden brown.

CITRUS

SEASON: year-round; high season is late fall and winter

GOOD VARIETIES:

Grapefruit: Marsh (white), Shambar (pink)

Lemon: Meyer

Lime: Key

Mandarin orange and tangerine: Clementine, Owari, Satsuma

Orange: Blood orange, Cadenera, Pineapple, Republic of Texas, Valencia (for juicing)

WHAT TO LOOK FOR: Citrus fruit should be without nicks or cuts, and feel heavy in the hand.

STORAGE AND PREPARATION TIPS: Citrus stores well in the vegetable crisper for a week, after which it tends to dry out. When making zest (grated rind), always use organic citrus, as it will not have been sprayed.

NUTRITIONAL HIGHLIGHTS: antioxidants, fiber, folate (oranges), vitamin C. Citrus lowers cholesterol and protects against certain cancers.

GOES WELL WITH:

Grapefruit: goat cheese

Lemon: black currant, honey, lime, olives

Lime: corn, raw fish

Mandarin orange and tangerine: strawberries, vanilla, coconut,

Orange: chocolate, strawberries

Citrus fruits are the most widely grown, diverse, and useful fruits in the world. The joy of citrus fruits is their delicious taste and sharp acidity, which stimulates the appetite and slakes the thirst. Citrus's sweet-sour spectrum ranges from sharp and biting in lemons to toothsome and honey-like in tangerines and oranges.

While a few citrus fruits in commerce are the original wild species, most are hybrids, crosses, and further crosses of species and other hybrids. For instance, Minneola tangelos are a cross between Dancy tangerines and Bowen grapefruits. The limequat is a cross between a lime and a kumquat. The oversized pomelo looks like a cross between a grapefruit and a soccer ball, but it is actually its own species and a probable parent of the grapefruit.

Organic Advantage

Buying organic citrus is especially important if you're cooking with citrus peel or zest, because that's where most chemicals end up. But even if you're just eating the inside it's worth buying organic, because the amount of chemicals used to treat citrus fruits is appalling. In 2001, California growers alone used over 3,000 tons (6 million pounds!) of agricultural chemicals on their oranges. Now add more tons of chemicals used on grapefruit, lemons, and other citrus: you can see the importance of buying organic whenever possible.

Uses

The wide range of citrus fruits have innumerable uses. Who could predict that oranges would be the perfect match for chocolate and strawberries, that lime juice would focus the taste of corn and meld with raw fish, that grapefruit's acidic sweetness and goat cheese would be a natural match? Grapefruit, in fact, may be the most useful of all the citrus. It pairs well in a mâche salad with red wine or balsamic vinegar and mild cheeses. It's perfect with honey and rum. Splash grapefruit segments with a bit of liqueurs like Grand Marnier, curaçao, Cointreau and Chambord. Use it in compotes with pomegranates, pineapples, bananas, melons, and strawberries.

A delicious citrus salad can be made by spooning out the contents of cold grapefruit and mixing them with orange segments. (Use a grapefruit spoon to coax the pieces out of each grapefruit half, or use a sharp knife to slice the rind off a whole fruit, then make inward cuts to free each section). Fresh lemon and lime juices are the traditional marinade for raw fish used for seviche. Orange juice and butter make a good coating for roasted beets. Lemon or orange sauce enhances fish and chicken.

Asian-Style Orange Chicken

SERVES 8

Lemon chicken is the traditional kids' favorite in Chinese restaurants, but I think orange chicken is even better. This version of the Chinese restaurant classic harmonizes sweet citrus with Asian flavors. This is a great dish to make in a large batch to serve to company—or enjoy leftovers yourself the next day!

2 oranges, such as Valencia or Pineapple
4 scallions, sliced 1/4 inch thick
1/2 cup freshly squeezed orange juice (1 to 2 oranges)
1/3 cup soy sauce
1/4 cup sugar
Canola oil for deep frying, plus 2 tablespoons
3 pounds chicken breasts and thighs, boned, cut into bite-size pieces, and thoroughly dried on paper towels
1 tablespoon shredded peeled fresh ginger
1/4 teaspoon hot pepper sauce, or to taste

1. Score the peel of 1 orange into quarters. Pull off the peel and reserve. Remove the white pith from the peel by scraping with the edge of a sharp knife. Cut the peel into long 1/4-inch-thick strips. Repeat with the second orange. Section both oranges, and set aside the sections and orange peel strips.

2. In a small bowl, combine the scallions, orange juice, soy sauce, and sugar; set aside. Pour the oil into large, heavy saucepan or deep skillet to the depth of 2 inches. Heat to 375°F on a deep-fry thermometer. Fry the chicken pieces, a large handful at a time, about 4 minutes, or until the pieces lose their pinkness and

are done through. Remove with a slotted spoon and drain on paper towels.

3. Heat 2 tablespoons of oil in a large skillet or wok. Add the ginger, hot pepper sauce, and strips of orange peel. Stir-fry over high heat for 90 seconds. Add the chicken pieces. Stir-fry 3 minutes. Add the orange juice mixture. Stir-fry 3 minutes more. Transfer to a heated serving dish. Garnish with the orange sections.

Key Lime Tart

MAKES ONE 9-INCH PIE; SERVES 6 TO 8

This sumptuous little tart is from Kimberly Sklar, who served the dish when she was the pastry chef at the restaurant Lucques in West Hollywood. If you can't find Key limes you can substitute regular limes. But Key limes are better because the juice is sweeter and the color is a wonderful yellow.

Key limes are grown year-round in warmer climates all over the world. Indigenous to Malaysia, they were brought to North Africa by Arab traders, to Europe by the crusaders, and to the Caribbean by the Spanish. Around 1835, the first grove was planted in the Florida Keys. Organic Key limes are becoming increasingly common.

FOR THE CRUST

15 graham cracker squares
5 tablespoons sugar
10 tablespoons unsalted butter (1 1/4 sticks)
Nonstick cooking spray

FOR THE FILLING

1 cup plus 2 tablespoons crème fraîche or sour cream
1/2 cup plus 1 tablespoon sugar
7 tablespoons freshly squeezed Key lime juice (2 to 4 limes), strained
3 extra-large eggs, at room temperature
3 tablespoons all-purpose flour
Whipped heavy cream

1. In a food processor or in a plastic bag using a rolling pin, grind the graham crackers to fine crumbs. (You need 2 cups of crumbs). Mix in the sugar. Melt the butter, add to the graham cracker crumbs, and mix to form a crumbly dough the consistency of damp sand. Spray a 9-inch pie pan with nonstick spray and pour in the mixture, pressing it evenly up the sides and across the bottom. Refrigerate for 1 hour.

2. Preheat the oven to 350°F. Bake the shell on the middle rack until golden, 18 to 20 minutes. Cool completely on a rack before adding the filling.

3. In a medium bowl, whisk together the crème fraîche, sugar, lime juice, eggs, and flour. Set aside until the pie shell is cool. Whisk one more time before pouring into the prebaked shell. Bake until almost set—the center will jiggle slightly when gently shaken—20 to 24 minutes. Chill until ready to serve.

4. Serve with a dollop of whipped cream.

Grapefruit Cooler

SERVES 2

A very simple yet enormously refreshing drink. Use Marsh white grapefruit if you can find it.

4 mint sprigs, plus more for garnish
2/3 cup freshly squeezed white grapefruit juice
1 tablespoon freshly squeezed lime juice
1 tablespoon superfine sugar
3 ounces light rum
Ice cubes
Chilled club soda
Dash Angostura bitters
White grapefruit segments for garnish

In a cocktail shaker, crush the mint sprigs with the back of a tablespoon against the inside of the shaker. Add the fruit juices and sugar and stir until the sugar dissolves. Add the rum and about 1 cup of ice cubes, cap the shaker, and shake for 30 seconds. Strain the mixture into two collins glasses filled with ice cubes. Top each glass with club soda and top with a dash of bitters. Stir and garnish with a small mint sprig and a segment of grapefruit.

DATE

SEASON: fall through early winter

GOOD VARIETIES: Barhi, Khadrawi, Khastawi, Medjool

WHAT TO LOOK FOR: Dates often come packaged in boxes. Check to make sure there's no mold, which would indicate they were exposed to moisture.

STORAGE AND PREPARATION TIPS: Dates store perfectly well on the kitchen counter or in the refrigerator. They can also be frozen almost indefinitely.

NUTRITIONAL HIGHLIGHTS: fiber, potassium

GOES WELL WITH: bacon, cinnamon, cream cheese, ginger, nuts, rum, seeds, vanilla

The ancient Sumerians began the cultivation of dates over four thousand years ago between the Tigris and Euphrates rivers. Their caravans, which wended their way from oasis to oasis across this region, planted date palms, which flourished with their heads in the furnace-like heat of the desert and their feet rooted in the high water tables of the oases and brackish marshes. Because they still grow best in this kind of environment, certain deserts in Arizona, and especially California's Coachella Valley, are the center of date production in the United States.

There are six hundred varieties of cultivated dates in the world, most of them limited to areas of North Africa and the Middle East, with an especially strong presence around the southern Iraqi town of Basra. (California has about 250,000 acres of cultivated dates; Iraq has more than 20 million acres.)

Organic Advantage

Organic growers often say that they use organic methods as much for the quality of the product they reap as for its purity and its light environmental footprint. One example is the Oasis Date

Gardens in Thermal, California, in the Coachella Valley (see Sources, page 287). This relatively small date garden (as date farms are called) has about 9,500 trees on 175 acres and ships just under one million pounds of organic dates a year. The folks at Oasis believe dates obtain the best flavor and fullest sweetness under organic conditions, such as feeding the date palms rich organic compost.

Uses

For those who haven't cooked with dates all their lives, it may not be readily apparent what to do with these chewy, candy-like, dried fruits besides eat them plain. They make easy appetizers when stuffed, either with cream cheese or, as I prefer, with pistachios, pine nuts, or toasted, ground sesame seeds bound with a little almond butter.

Dates can be chopped and used in breakfast cereals, puddings, breads, cakes, cookies, ice creams, and candy bars. They work in savory dishes like couscous and stews as well.

SOFT, SEMISOFT, AND DRY DATES

Dates are classified as either soft, semisoft, or dry, which refers to their moisture content.

Soft dates have been harvested while still moist and fresh. Medjool and Barhi dates are high-quality soft dates and have a juicy, melting quality.

Semisoft dates have drier, thicker skins and a sticky, chewy texture. These are the dates most people are used to seeing packed into small boxes. Deget Noor is a semi-soft date.

Dry dates, also called bread dates, are dry like pastry and crumble when chewed. They were a staple of Middle Eastern desert nomads because they kept so well. Thoory is a dry date variety.

Medjool Date Nut Loaf

MAKES ONE 9-INCH LOAF

Soft Medjool dates are best for this recipe, as they have the smoothest texture when incorporated into the loaf. The finer you chop the nuts and the dates for this loaf, the nicer the texture and the richer the flavor will be. Dates and nuts have an affinity for each other, as this sweet, nutty loaf reveals. I like a slice toasted and slathered with butter for breakfast or as a snack with a small glass of port or sherry.

The recipe comes from the folks at the organic Oasis Date Gardens.

3/4 cup brown sugar
2 tablespoons canola oil
1 large egg
1 1/2 cups whole milk
3 cups sifted all-purpose flour
3 1/2 teaspoons baking powder
1/2 teaspoon salt

1 cup pitted and finely chopped Medjool, Barhi, or other soft dates
1/2 cup chopped walnuts

1. Preheat the oven to 350°F. Grease a 9 × 5 × 3–inch loaf pan.

2. In a large bowl, combine the sugar, canola oil, and egg, and mix thoroughly. Stir in the milk.

3. In a separate bowl, sift together the flour, baking powder, and salt. Add the dry ingredients to the liquid mixture and stir thoroughly to combine. Add the dates and nuts.

4. Pour the mixture into the pan and let stand for 20 minutes, then bake for 50 to 70 minutes, or until a wooden toothpick inserted into the center comes out clean.

FIG

SEASON: late summer and early fall

GOOD VARIETIES:

- **Black:** Black Mission
- **Bronze:** Hunt
- **Green:** Kadota
- **Violet:** Hardy Chicago
- **Yellow:** Calimyrna, LSU gold

WHAT TO LOOK FOR: Figs whose stems are browned and flaccid will be the ripest and sweetest. The fig itself should be soft.

STORAGE AND PREPARATION TIPS: Fresh, ripe figs should be eaten as soon as possible. Dried figs store well in a kitchen cabinet for up to four months.

NUTRITIONAL HIGHLIGHTS: calcium, fiber, potassium, vitamin B_6

GOES WELL WITH: caramel, cinnamon, duck, honey, lavender, lemons, oranges, peaches, pears, pork, port wine, prosciutto, raspberries, rosemary

The fig is native to the eastern Mediterranean, where its cultivation has been traced back 4,500 years, almost to the dawn of agriculture. Figs are so rich and delicious, and they dry so well and keep in dried form for such long periods, that the first farmers would have been crazy not to plant a fig in their dooryard, just as so many who live in Mediterranean climates around the world do today.

Figs can be blackish purple, green, brownish bronze, violet, or yellow. However, unlike grapes, whose flavor is concentrated in their skins, fig skin is relatively tasteless. It's the pulp inside that contributes the taste. The flavor of fresh, tree-ripened figs is sweet, rich, and fruity—very different from the concentrated caramel-nuttiness that dried figs acquire.

Only those who have spent time in fig-growing regions know the luscious texture and flavor of a fresh tree-ripened fig. That's because tree-ripened figs are supremely perishable and will quickly break down if bruised. Therefore, most fresh figs are picked unripe and they never reach their sweet potential. (If you happen to have access to a fig tree, you can spot a tree-ripe fig because the fruit hangs limply from the branch.)

Luckily, most dried figs are picked tree-ripe and carry something of a tree-ripe fig's flavor. Black Mission and Calimyrna figs are especially good dried.

Organic Advantage

While California figs aren't a heavily sprayed crop, agricultural chemicals are nevertheless used annually by conventional farmers. Large-scale fig producers may spray ethephon growth regulator on the crop to speed up ripening if rain threatens or it's known that an insect will shortly make its appearance, which doesn't help the fruit's flavor profile. Organic figs ripen in natural course.

Uses

If you can find fresh figs, by far the best way to eat them is right out of hand. (Some people peel them, but there's really no need.) Figs are excellent with a little cream and sugar. Figs go with salty foods such as prosciutto and pancetta—an Italian tradition that may hearken back to ancient Rome, when figs were used in savory dishes. In addition to the flavor combinations mentioned above, use fresh figs in fruit salads with raspberries, blueberries, melon cubes, and bananas, all with a splash of orange juice. Fresh figs can be preserved in sugar syrup, perhaps with cinnamon to add a spicy note.

With dried figs, poaching softens them and, depending on how they're poached, can form a chord of harmonious flavors. Try poaching them in red wine sweetened with honey and orange juice, a dash of vanilla, and a pinch of cinnamon, and serving them over vanilla ice cream or a fruit sorbet (boil down the poaching liquid to make a sauce). Dried figs can be stuffed with goat cheese. Or they can be mashed with a fresh juicy fruit such as plums or fresh apricots to make a paste that can be smeared on a butterflied pork roast before it's rolled and tied (see page 245).

Oatmeal Fig Cookies

MAKES ABOUT 24 COOKIES

Make these kid-friendly but nutritious cookies with organic ingredients (especially the citrus zests, because the skins of conventionally farmed citrus may have unacceptable levels of agricultural chemicals) and get none of the chemicals and hydrogenated vegetable oils that food processors feel compelled to put in their cookies—and into our children.

2 tablespoons vegetable oil or nonstick cooking spray
1 cup dried figs
1/2 cup unsalted butter
3/4 cup honey
2 large eggs
4 tablespoons milk
1 1/2 cups whole-wheat pastry flour
3 teaspoons baking powder
1/4 teaspoon salt
1/2 cup 1-minute rolled oats

1 teaspoon freshly squeezed lemon juice
1 teaspoon freshly grated lemon zest (well scrubbed if not organic)
3 tablespoons freshly grated orange zest (well scrubbed if not organic)

1. Preheat the oven to 350°F. Line 2 cookie sheets with wax paper and coat the paper with vegetable oil or nonstick spray, or simply grease the sheets. Put the figs in a small saucepan, cover with cold water, cover the saucepan, and bring to a boil. Turn down the heat and simmer for 10 minutes. Drain the figs and chop into a small dice.

2. In a medium bowl, heat the butter just until it melts—several 20-second visits to the microwave will do it. Set aside. In another bowl, beat the honey and eggs until well mixed and thick. Combine this with the butter and beat again, then add the milk and beat again until the mixture is smooth.

3. Sift together the flour, baking powder, and salt, and add this to the batter, mixing until fully incorporated. Add the figs, oats, lemon juice, and zests, and mix well. If the batter seems a little stiff, add a splash more milk.

4. Drop heaping tablespoonfuls of batter onto the sheets, about 12 drops to each cookie sheet. Bake 20 minutes or more, depending on the size of the cookies, or until golden brown. Check the bottoms of several cookies. Do not bake too long or the honey will scorch.

GRAPE

SEASON: late summer and early fall

GOOD VARIETIES:

American table grapes: Alden, Canadice, Catawba, Delaware, Einset, Himrod, Interlaken

Wine grapes: Crimson seedless, Flame seedless, Gold, Muscat Hamburg, Muscat of Alexandria

Wild varieties: Concord, Muscadine

WHAT TO LOOK FOR: As grapes age, they begin to shrivel. Feel the grapes; they should be plump and turgid, not soft. Hold a bunch up and give it a gentle shake: no grapes should fall off.

STORAGE AND PREPARATION TIPS: Grapes will keep in the refrigerator for a week or more, but it's best to eat them before they begin to soften. Freeze in-season grapes in a single layer on cookie sheets, and store them in freezer bags in the freezer to add to winter compotes.

NUTRITIONAL HIGHLIGHTS: antioxidants and phytochemicals (red grapes only), vitamin C

GOES WELL WITH: honey, yogurt, in salads or savory meat dishes

Grapes are the flavor chameleons of the fruit world. Some grapes taste of strawberries, others of black currants, still others of apples, or lemons, or plums. Very few of the top-quality organic table grape varieties show up in supermarkets.

You will find some of them at farmers' markets and roadside stands in various parts of the country, however.

Most of the table grapes you'll see for sale will be American, European, or a cross of the two. Cultivated American grapes have a foxy flavor that reduces their value as wine grapes. (Welch's grape juice defines the Concord grape taste, which is called foxy in the wine industry.) Cultivated European grapes—both for wine or eating out of hand—have a pleasantly sweet flavor, almost like candy. Crosses combine the fine flavors of European wine grapes with the foxiness of the American parent.

In addition to American and European grapes and their hybrids, there are Muscadines and Concord grapes, both derived from wild American grapes, with a flavor all their own.

RAISINS

Homemade raisins from organic grapes are to ordinary store-bought raisins what a good mattress is to sleeping on the hard ground. They are soft and chewy, sweet and tangy, plump and delicious. Any grape can be dried for homemade raisins. I dry mine in a dehydrator, but you can sun-dry them if you live in a hot, dry climate.

Probably the best white grapes for homemade raisins are the Interlaken, Himrod, and Lakemont seedless varieties: these green-skinned grapes ripen to a light amber or gold color, then dry to a deep amber. The best seedless red grapes for raisins are Vitis vinifera types such as Flame and Ruby seedless, and among blue-skinned grapes, Black Emerald and Black Monukka.

Organic Advantage

Most conventional table grapes are subjected to applications of fungicides, pesticides, herbicides, and chemical fertilizers—as well as gibberellic acid, a plant growth hormone that stimulates grapes to grow much larger than their natural size. Unsprayed, they would be about the size of your little fingernail.

Today there are many sources of organic grapes. California alone has 66,000 acres of grapes in organic culture—many of them used to make wine. Grapes can be grown organically in all the climates of the United States (there are even grapes grown on Mount Haleakala, on the tropical island of Maui). If you're interested in growing some vines organically, perhaps on an arbor over a picnic table, you might look for my book, *From Vines to Wines* (1999), which, although it focuses on growing wine grapes, details all the techniques and materials you'll need to handle table grapes organically.

Uses

Grapes are elemental in fruit compotes, pies, jams and jellies, and salads; on open-faced fruit tarts; for making sherbets; and mixed simply in a tall glass with yogurt and honey. But grapes can also be used in savory cooking. They combine well with soft-ripened cheeses or with cream cheese (see recipe), make a delicious topping for savory crêpes, and pair well with roast or grilled pork tenderloin.

Grape and Almond Gazpacho

MAKES ABOUT 1 QUART; SERVES 4

This recipe is from Cindy Pawlcyn, a legendary chef and restaurateur of San Francisco and the wine country to the north. The first time I met Cindy, she was serving this gazpacho at a wine event in Napa Valley. It was so good and so unusual—creamy, herby, spicy, and sweet-tart—that I begged her for the recipe.

3 cups seedless green grapes (about 1 1/2 pounds)
2 medium cucumbers, peeled and chopped (seeded if the seeds are maturing and firmer than the flesh)
One 8-ounce package cream cheese
3/4 cup plain yogurt
2/3 cup heavy cream
1/3 cup unseasoned rice vinegar
1/3 bunch fresh dill
2 1/2 tablespoons olive oil
1/2 teaspoon ground cayenne
1/4 teaspoon ground white pepper
1/4 teaspoon salt

FOR THE GARNISH

2/3 cup almonds
2 bunches scallions, sliced thin

Blend the soup ingredients thoroughly in a blender until smooth. Refrigerate until cold.

In the meantime, toast the almonds in a dry skillet over medium heat, stirring constantly, until they are fragrant and golden. Let them cool, then finely chop them. Serve the soup garnished with the scallions and almonds.

MANGO

SEASON: midsummer through early fall

GOOD VARIETIES: Ataulfo, Carrie, Edward, Julie, Kent

WHAT TO LOOK FOR: Some mangoes turn yellowish or acquire a red blush as they ripen, while others stay green, so don't go by skin color alone when choosing them; a ripe mango will feel soft at the stem end. Don't pass up mangoes with a few black spots—that can indicate a high sugar content. But don't buy any that are squishy, shriveling, or showing signs of decay.

STORAGE AND PREPARATION TIPS: Most mangoes you'll find in stores are not ripe, and will need to ripen on the countertop until soft to the touch. Do not store unripe mangoes in the fridge, as it stops them from ripening, though they can be refrigerated once ripe, and their pulp can be frozen.

The simplest way to cut up a mango, given that its yellow flesh clings to the very large but flat fibrous seed inside, is to stand the fruit upright on its stem end with the narrow side facing you. With a sharp knife, slice off the left and right sides of the fruit, getting as close to the sides of the pit as possible without including the fibers. Score each piece vertically and horizontally, being careful not to cut into the skin. Now turn it inside out; the fruity chunks will stick out and can be easily sliced away with a knife. Trim the remaining flesh from the pit.

NUTRITIONAL HIGHLIGHTS: beta-carotene, fiber, vitamin C, vitamin E

GOES WELL WITH: fish, other tropical and semitropical fruits

Take a guess as to the most-consumed fruit in the world. We in the United States might guess banana or apple, but the answer is mango. The mango is a native of Southeast Asia. It's a tropical fruit grown only in Hawaii, southern Florida, and southern California in the United States, but these plantings are not large. Most of our organic mangoes come from Mexico, with some also coming from Haiti, Jamaica, and Trinidad and Tobago.

The mangoes we get here in the United States tend to be picked unripe and hard, and they must be allowed to ripen. You can speed this up by placing mangoes in a bag with an apple, which gives off ethylene gas, a natural ripening agent. A ripe mango will have softened and will yield to gentle pressure when pressed with the thumb. I find that a mango ripened at home is a fair approximation of the tree-ripened fruit.

FAIR TRADE MANGOES

Many organic mangoes are certified as fair trade products by TransFair USA, which ensures that the workers and growers involved in producing the food have the right to organize and bargain collectively. It's important that the farmers we support with our organic food dollars are not exploited but rather are able to sell their environmentally sound fruit at a price that ensures them dignity and a decent standard of living.

People wonder why organic produce costs more than conventional when they imagine that organic simply means using fewer agricultural inputs. The answer, of course, is that organics is not about farming cheaply and maximizing profits for corporations. The organic bottom line supports a system of producing food that's healthy for the environment, fair to the farm workers, profitable for the businesspeople, and safe, wholesome, and tasty for consumers.

Organic Advantage

Conventionally grown mangoes from other countries, especially Mexico, may have been heavily sprayed with toxic chemicals, so it's important to look for organic mangoes. I always avoid conventional mangoes because they often come from countries that do not have the same kind of pesticide controls the United States has.

Uses

Ripe mangoes mix beautifully with other tropical and semitropical fruits like citrus and bananas. Puree ripe mango flesh to make sorbet or to use as a sauce with white-fleshed tropical fish like grouper and escolar. Unripe mangoes are useful, too. They are the main ingredient in mango chutney and make a tangy pickle. Unripe mangoes are firm to the touch, even on the shoulder of the fruit near the stem.

Melon and Mango

SERVES 4

This simple but oh-so-delicious combination makes a fine snack or dessert.

3 pounds bite-size muskmelon or watermelon chunks (about 6 cups)
2 mangoes, peeled, seeded, cut into 1-inch chunks (see Storage and Preparation Tips, page 142)
Juice of 1 lime
1 teaspoon freshly grated lime zest (well scrubbed if not organic)
1/2 teaspoon superfine sugar

Toss all the ingredients in a bowl, then cover and refrigerate for at least 30 minutes before serving.

MELON

SEASON: midsummer through winter

GOOD VARIETIES:

Cantaloupes: Charentais

Honeydews: Earli-Dew, Orange Blossom

Melons: Amy, Canary, Crenshaw

Muskmelons: Ambrosia, Iroquois, Angel

Watermelons: Black Diamond, Sugar Baby, Yellow Doll

WHAT TO LOOK FOR: Most melons are ripe when their blossom ends have a distinctly fruity aroma. Watermelons are ripe when the light spot where they rested as they grew turns a yellowish color and they sound hollow when thumped.

STORAGE AND PREPARATION TIPS: Melons store well on the kitchen counter or in the fridge for up to three weeks. For year-round consumption, remove the seeds and rinds and cut the flesh into bite-sized chunks when the melons are at their peak. Then either freeze in one layer on a cookie sheet and pack them in freezer bags, or pack fresh melon pieces in sugar syrup (1 cup of water per 1/3 cup of superfine sugar) in freezer bags, leaving a little head space, and freeze. Thaw gently in a bowl of warm water, and serve when they still have a little ice in them but have come free of the sugar syrup.

NUTRITIONAL HIGHLIGHTS: beta-carotene (in darker-fleshed melons), vitamin C

GOES WELL WITH: berries, cucumber, citrus, grapefruit, ginger, mint, port wine, prosciutto, sparkling wine

It took me years to figure out how to grow really sweet melons. The secret is to keep the vines up off the ground, in full sun, and give them a gentle sulfur spray after each rain—all organic methods designed to keep the leaves free of mildew.

The leaves of melons are their sugar factories, and keeping them clean, healthy, and free of mildew allows them to pump more sugar to the developing fruits. After taking the better part of the summer to ripen, melons reach their peak quality in late August.

Organic Advantage

Sulfur spray is the chief way melon farmers—both conventional and organic—prevent mildew. However, conventional farmers also employ more questionable chemical treatments, including 1,3-dichloropropene (used to combat nematodes), which the U.S. Department of Health and Human Services has identified as a possible carcinogen and which can adversely affect the health of farm workers.

In addition to avoiding possibly harmful chemicals, organic growers serving local markets are more likely to plant the best-tasting types of melons because they don't have to worry about their shipping ability, like big conventional growers, who must ship across the country. Their proximity to their markets means organic growers can let those melons ripen on the vines. Finally, a rich, nutrient-filled organic soil does a much better job of holding water like a sponge than chemically fertilized soil, and so keeps wilt-prone melons hydrated. All these factors contribute to the luscious flavor of well-grown organic melons.

Uses

Melon slices are good all by themselves, but they do brighten up when squirted with a little fresh lime juice. Melon balls or chunks make a fine addition to salads and pair especially well with pineapple.

Charentais Melon Cockaigne

SERVES 4

If you can lay your hands on vine-ripened Charentais cantaloupes, make this. The Charantais melon is sweet on its own; when assisted by a mélange of fresh berries and a soupçon of white, nutty dessert wine, it defines lusciousness.

2 vine-ripened Charentais cantaloupes
Juice of 1 lemon
1/2 pint fresh strawberries
1 banana
1/2 pint fresh red raspberries
1/2 cup sweet white dessert wine, such as Sauternes, Barsac, or Beaumes de Venise
1/2 teaspoon vanilla extract

MANY MELONS

We usually lump cantaloupes, muskmelons, honeydews, Canaries, Crenshaws, and watermelons under the heading of melon, but if you love the fruit, you'll enjoy exploring the different types.

Cantaloupes (named after the town of Cantalupo near Rome) are generally considered to be the best-tasting melons. Most of the melons you'll see labelled as cantaloupes at the supermarket, however, are actually muskmelons. A true cantaloupe is about the size of a baseball, with a hard, buff- or gray-green rind with some bumps or scales, but no netting. A French variety called Charentais is one of the best known. As a cantaloupe ripens, its grey-green rind changes to a buff color and the blossom end gives off a faint aroma.

Muskmelons, often mislabeled cantaloupes in supermarkets, are named for the pleasant, musky smell they develop when ripe. A whiff of the blossom end will strongly tell you that a muskmelon is ready to eat. (Their blossom ends will also yield to moderate thumb pressure.) You can keep the ripe melons a few days on the kitchen counter; they'll eventually become meltingly delicious, but don't let them go past the point of perfection or they'll only be good for sorbet. A muskmelon's flesh can be green, salmon, orange, or white.

Honeydews have cream-colored rinds and green or orange flesh. As with muskmelons, they are ripe when the blossom end softens and yields to moderate thumb pressure. They carry a lovely fragrance.

Crenshaws are a unique sort of melon with a fine flavor all their own. Their salmon-pink flesh is spicy-sweet and refreshing.

Canary melons are a type of winter melon, which means they keep well into the winter months. Their rinds are bright yellow and their white flesh has an orange lining by the seed cavity. They develop a softening at the blossom end when ripe.

Watermelons are a different genus from other melons. They range in flesh color from yellow to orange to bright red, and in size from 6-inch Sugar Babies to the full-size Charleston Grays.

1. Scrape out the seeds from the cantaloupes, coat the exposed flesh with lemon juice, and reserve.

2. Stem and dice the strawberries; dice the banana. Peel and gently toss them in a bowl with the raspberries, dessert wine, and vanilla. Fill the melon halves with the fruit mixture. Snuggle each half into a bed of crushed ice so it stands upright, and serve.

PAPAYA

SEASON: spring through mid-fall

GOOD VARIETIES: Solo, Sunrise, Washington

WHAT TO LOOK FOR: Most papayas are sold unripe. When papayas ripen, they turn from green or yellow-green to bright yellow all over, and soften to the touch. Grab ripe papayas if you see them at the store, but reject any that have an off aroma or are bruised and moldy. (A few black spots are usually no problem.)

STORAGE AND PREPARATION TIPS: If you want to hasten the ripening of a green papaya, place it in a closed paper bag: it won't get any sweeter, but it will get softer. Once ripe, papayas quickly go past their prime in a warm kitchen; you can slow this process a couple of days by keeping them in the refrigerator.

NUTRITIONAL HIGHLIGHTS: fiber, folate, vitamin C

GOES WELL WITH: lime juice, other tropical fruits, seafood

Organic Advantage

In the early 1990s, the Hawaiian papaya industry was near collapse because ring-spot virus was attacking the plants. Genetic engineers inserted a foreign gene into two varieties of papaya—Rainbow and SunUp—that conferred resistance to the virus. Organic growers there have since been complaining that pollen from genetically modified papayas may pollinate their crops—which would contaminate their new papayas and no longer qualify them as organic. To prevent this, organic growers have had to bag their flowers or get organic seeds from elsewhere.

Uses

This soft, sweet fruit just begs to be drizzled with lime juice; this is the perfect way to eat a papaya. I don't care what else you do to papayas, you won't beat this treatment: while this fruit's texture is luscious and creamy, its flavor is mild, lacking acidity. Lime juice, with its distinct flavor and sharp acidity, complement's papaya's flavor profile precisely.

Of course, there are plenty of other ways to use them. Papayas—either the Hawaiian kind or the larger Mexican type—are one of the bases for a tropical fruit salad. Scooped out papaya halves make edible serving containers for tropical fruit salad, sorbets, and seafood salads. Make a dreamy smoothie by blending 2 ripe, peeled, seeded papayas (about 8 ounces each), then adding and blending 1/2 cup of orange juice and 1/2 cup of vanilla frozen yogurt.

Papaya contains the meat tenderizing enzyme papain, so the next time you're marinating meat, add mashed ripe papaya to the marinade to impart a subtle flavor and tenderize the meat. In fact, the enzyme is so strong that you can't use raw papaya in gelatin dishes, as the papain will prevent the gelatin from setting. And if you do add papaya to a fruit salad, add it at the last moment, because papain will tenderize fruit as well.

Papaya seeds: The seeds of the papaya are edible: they have a peppery quality. Try a few out of hand the next time you cut open a papaya. You can make a salad dressing with them by processing 1/2 cup sugar, 1/2 teaspoon dry mustard, 1/2 cup rice vinegar, and a little salt to taste in a blender or food processor until smooth, then slowly pouring in 1/2 cup olive oil while the blender is running, adding 1 minced small onion and blending again until smooth. Add 2 or 3 teaspoons of papaya seeds and pulse a few times to incorporate the seeds and release their peppery quality.

Thai Green Papaya Salad

MAKES 4 SALADS

My friend Wai-Ching Lee of the San Francisco Professional Food Society introduced me to this salad in one of the city's Thai restaurants many years ago, and it's been a favorite of mine ever since.

1 green (unripe) papaya (about 1 pound)
1 cup Chinese cabbage, sliced crosswise 1/2 inch thick, then cut into 1/2-inch squares
1/2 pound sugar snap peas, strings removed, julienned
3 tablespoons freshly squeezed lime juice
3 tablespoons soy sauce
1 red jalapeño chile, seeded and chopped
1 tablespoon sugar
3 cloves garlic, minced
3 small tomatoes, cut into wedges
5 tablespoons peanuts, lightly roasted and coarsely chopped
1/4 cup chopped cilantro leaves

1. Peel, halve, and seed the papaya. Grate it with a coarse grater. You should have about 2 cups. Place the cabbage pieces on a serving plate. Layer on the grated papaya, then the snap peas.

2. In a small bowl, make a dressing by whisking together the lime juice, soy sauce, jalapeño, sugar, and garlic. When ready to serve, drizzle the dressing over the salad and garnish with the tomatoes, peanuts, and cilantro.

PEACH AND NECTARINE

SEASON: summer through early fall

GOOD VARIETIES:

Peach: Babcock, Elberta, Flavorcrest, Halehaven, O'Henry, Red Haven, Springcrest, White Lady

Nectarine: Flavortop, Heavenly White, Mericrest, Red Gold, Snow Queen

WHAT TO LOOK FOR: Buy peaches that are fully colored and have at least a slight give at the stem end. Yellow varieties should be yellow to yellow-orange, with a rosy blush. White varieties should show a creamy white color with a pronounced blush. Avoid fruits that are green and hard: they will not ripen properly. Ask whether the fruits are freestone or cling. Freestone pits are easy to remove, while cling pits attach to the flesh, which must be carved off. Freestone fruit is usually of higher quality. Because it can be halved (and then sliced) easily, it is also the better choice for canning.

STORAGE AND PREPARATION TIPS: Store on the counter out of direct sun if they need to ripen. If ripe, use them right away.

NUTRITIONAL HIGHLIGHTS: fiber, potassium, vitamin A, vitamin C

GO WELL WITH: blackberries, blueberries, figs, fresh mint, plums

---

Nectarines are actually fuzzless peaches—or peaches are fuzzy nectarines. They are both the same species, Prunus persica, although as breeding carries nectarines farther and farther from peaches, they are starting to be classified separately. The fact remains that peach trees may occasionally produce nectarines and vice versa: the two fruits are that close botanically.

There are thousands of cultivated varieties of peaches and nectarines today, in addition to the wild peaches of Tibet and western China, where both fruits originated and were grown as early as 2000 BCE. They arrived in Greece by 300 BCE. From there they traveled to Rome and went on to take their place among the world's best fruits.

When ripened on the tree, the texture, flavor, scent, and lusciousness of peaches and nectarines are incomparably sensuous. But finding them tree ripened is not easy; tree-ripened fruits are soft and easily bruised and don't ship well at all. The best time to find them is at the peak of the season—around mid July. You can also order tree-ripened peaches and nectarines online (see Sources, page 287).

Organic Advantage

Insects and diseases seem to love these fruits as much as we do, which means conventional peaches and nectarines are heavily sprayed with pesticides, fungicides, and herbicides. Organic growers, however, have good nontoxic remedies for the common problems, of which there are many.

Chemical use, combined with the fact that the best varieties of peach and nectarine do not ship well, or are shipped unripe, means it's wise to seek out organic fruit in season, sold as close to the source as possible: at roadside stands or farm stands.

Uses

Peaches and nectarines can be used interchangeably, and they have so many uses, it's hard to know where to begin: cobblers, compotes, pies, tarts, pastries. Slice them over breakfast cereal or dice them and add to pancake batter. Mix nectarine slices with slices of fresh figs tossed with a little orange juice; dust lightly with cinnamon and garnish with a sprig of mint. And if you have white peaches, you can make one of Papa Hemingway's favorite drinks: the Bellini (recipe follows).

WHITE PEACHES AND NECTARINES

White peaches and white nectarines have white rather than yellow flesh. Their flavor is less robust than yellow varieties, but sweeter. Until the mid-1980s, breeders discarded most white peaches in favor of yellow ones because the market demanded yellow, and because white ones are more prone to bruising during shipping. It was the Asian markets that were first willing to pay for extra sweet white varieties. Today you'll find both kinds in most markets.

While white peaches and nectarines are delicious for eating, when pureed they yield an incomparably sweet nectar. To make it, peel the peaches (or nectarines) by first submerging them a minute or so in boiling water to loosen their skins. Slice them into chunks, then puree them in a blender or food processor with 1 tablespoon of fresh lemon juice for every 4 peaches. Squeeze the puree through the double fold of a cheesecloth. Freeze the puree in an ice cube tray, then store the cubes in freezer bags and freeze for year-round use.

Peach Melba

SERVES 4

None other than the great chef Auguste Escoffier invented this dessert in 1893 to honor Dame Nellie Melba, the famous Australian opera singer. Escoffier poached his peaches in wine and honey, but if you have good tree-ripened peaches, they'll be just perfect raw, as long as they're juicy and soft enough to eat with a spoon. Make sure to use freestone rather than cling peaches, because they need to maintain their shape.

2 cups red raspberries
1/4 cup sugar
Freshly squeezed lemon juice
2 tree-ripened freestone peaches
1 pint high-quality vanilla ice cream

1. Start by making a sauce from the raspberries. Place the berries and sugar in a medium nonreactive saucepan and heat on low until the raspberries release their juice and the sugar dissolves. Mash the berries and turn the mixture into a fine sieve set over a bowl. With the edge of a spoon, scrape the mixture back and forth against the mesh to express the syrupy juice into the bowl, leaving the dry pulp and seeds behind. Add a little lemon juice to give it just a slight tang.

2. Blanch the peaches in boiling water for a minute, then plunge them into ice water. Before you remove the skins, cut along the suture (the slightly raised line that runs the circumference of the peach) to the pit, all the way around

the peach. Twist the halves in opposite directions and remove the pit, and then remove the skins from the halves.

3. Place each peach half in a small bowl, cut side up. Place a scoop of vanilla ice cream in the hollow of the peach half, and drizzle raspberry syrup all over the ice cream and peach.

Nectarine-Blackberry Cobbler

SERVES 4

Nectarines have an affinity for blackberries that makes this summer cobbler a real treat.

5 tablespoons cold unsalted butter, plus extra for the baking dish
1 cup white sugar
2 teaspoons cornstarch
2 large nectarines, pitted and coarsely chopped
2 cups ripe blackberries
1 cup all-purpose flour
1 teaspoon baking powder
1/4 teaspoon salt
1/2 cup whole milk
1/2 cup brown sugar
1/4 cup crushed almonds

1. Preheat the oven to 350°F. Butter an 8-inch round or square baking dish. In a medium bowl, mix 2/3 cup of the white sugar and the cornstarch. Add the nectarines and blackberries and gently toss to coat evenly.

2. In a separate bowl, mix the flour, the remaining 1/3 cup white sugar, baking powder, and salt. When well combined, cut in 5 tablespoons of butter with 2 knives until the mixture looks like coarse meal. Add the milk and stir just until well combined. If it seems too stiff, add a tablespoon or two of milk or water, but not enough to make the mixture loose and runny.

3. Spread the fruit mixture in the bottom of the baking dish. Drop the dough by spoonfuls onto the fruit to cover. Mix together the brown sugar and crushed almonds and sprinkle evenly over the top. Loosely cover with a piece of aluminum foil and bake for 1 hour, removing the foil during the last 5 minutes of baking so the top is melted and golden.

Bellini

MAKES 1 COCKTAIL

White peach nectar is used to make a classic Bellini, one of the world's great cocktails.

1 ounce white peach nectar
1 teaspoon simple syrup (see Tip)
3 to 4 ounces ice-cold Prosecco (Italian sparkling wine)

Pour the peach nectar and simple syrup into a champagne flute. Fill the flute with the Prosecco.

TIP: To make simple syrup, combine equal parts water and superfine or regular sugar, heat to dissolve the sugar, then cool.

PEAR

SEASON: late summer through early fall

GOOD VARIETIES: Abate, Anjou, Bartlett, Bosc, Clapp's Favorite, Comice, Duchesse d'Angoulême, Red Bartlett, Seckel

WHAT TO LOOK FOR: A pear's skin should have no breaks, cuts, or scratches.

STORAGE AND PREPARATION TIPS: European-style pears don't ripen on the tree (an enzyme causes them to go mushy), so it's fine to buy them green and let them ripen at home. Pears need air circulation to ripen, so don't store unripe pears in a bowl. I place them on a table in a cool, shady room, arranged so none touch each other, or on the windowsill if it's not too sunny. You can tell they're ripe when you feel some give when you gently press the stem end.

NUTRITIONAL HIGHLIGHTS: fiber, potassium, vitamin C

GOES WELL WITH: almonds, anise, brandy, chocolate, cloves, cinnamon, figs, honey, ginger, Parmesan, quince, red wine (especially Pinot Noir and Beaujolais), vanilla

Pears originated in the same region as apples—the great swath of land in central Asia that runs from the Caucasus Mountains in the west to the Chinese border in the east. There are twenty known wild species, but thousands of cultivated varieties.

Most of our modern pear varieties came into being due to a great deal of breeding work done in France in the sixteenth through the eighteenth centuries, especially in the area around Angers. Anjou and Duchesse d'Angoulême are two popular varieties developed in those years. In the nineteenth century, Belgium became the center of pear breeding; the so-called butter pears (for their buttery flavor, not their texture), including Bosc, were bred there. The Bartlett originated in England around 1770, the Comice was bred in Angers in the nineteenth century, and Clapp's Favorite was bred in Massachusetts in the mid-nineteenth century.

Organic Advantage

Organic fresh pears may have some surfaces blemishes, but that's a small price to pay for the knowledge that the pears have been spared toxic sprays. In addition, tree fruits like pears that are fertilized by rich composts instead of factory-made chemicals allow Mother Nature to do what she does best—nurture her children through better quality.

In addition to fresh pears, these days one can find canned and dried organic pears in the markets. Make sure that dried organic pears are unsulfured. Sulfuring helps prevent darkening, so if the dried pears are light in color, they've most likely been sulfured. This sulfur compound can cause severe allergic reactions in some people. You give up something in appearance but gain in purity with unsulfured organic dried fruit.

Uses

Pears have a sweet spiciness all their own and are best eaten out of hand. Softer varieties such as Anjou and Comice also bake well in galettes and tarts, while firmer Seckel and Bosc pears are best for poaching and for putting up as spiced pears.

SECKEL AND COMICE PEARS

I've lived in a number of old Pennsylvania Dutch farmhouses, and each invariably had a Seckel pear tree growing somewhere near the front of the house. These small green or yellow-brown pears stay firm even when ripe, and their intense, spicy-sweet flavor is alluring. Discovered by a man named Dutch Jacob growing in a parcel of northern Delaware woodland he bought in 1765, the Seckel helped feed the "pearmania" that broke out in New England in the nineteenth century, when enthusiasm for pears reached a fever pitch. Given the novelty and quality of the Seckel, pearmania must have quickly extended its range all over the Northeast.

One of my favorite soft pear varieties is the Comice. These plump, squat, lopsided pears are delightfully aromatic, very sweet, and juicy, with a silkier, more melting texture than that of other pears.

Bartlett Pear Salad

SERVES 4

Stephanie Pearl Kimmel of Restaurant Marché in Eugene, Oregon, kindly shared this recipe.

FOR THE VINAIGRETTE

2 teaspoons sherry vinegar
1 teaspoon minced shallots
Pinch of salt
1 tablespoon extra-virgin olive oil
1 tablespoon walnut or hazelnut oil
Freshly ground black pepper

FOR THE SALAD:

1/2 pound mixed greens (3 to 4 cups)
3 ounces hazelnuts (just over 1/2 cup)
1 large ripe Bartlett pear
4 ounces blue cheese, crumbled (1 cup)

1. Make the vinaigrette. Place the vinegar, shallot, and salt in a small bowl and let marinate for up to 1 hour. Whisk in the olive oil and walnut oil until emulsified. Season with pepper.

2. Preheat the oven to 325°F. Wash the greens and dry them well. Place the hazelnuts on a cookie sheet and toast them in the oven for 3 to 4 minutes. When the hazelnuts are golden and aromatic, remove them and allow to cool before chopping them coarsely. Peel, core, and slice the pear.

3. To assemble the salad, toss the greens with half of the vinaigrette. Divide the greens among 4 salad plates, piling them high in the center. Divide the pear

slices among the four plates, arranging them around the greens. Sprinkle each salad with the blue cheese and then the chopped hazelnuts, then drizzle with the remaining vinaigrette as needed.

PERSIMMON

SEASON: fall through early winter

GOOD VARIETIES: Early Golden, Eureka, Fuyu, Tanenashi, Yates

WHAT TO LOOK FOR: Persimmons should be sound, with no cuts or bruises, so that they will soften evenly. Black spots on the surface of Hachiya persimmons are not signs of decay.

STORAGE AND PREPARATION TIPS: Ripen Hachiyas on the kitchen counter. Once they soften and their insides are jelly-like, they are not rotting but are ready to eat. If that jelly turns from a clear red-orange color to a muddy reddish brown, then they are actually beginning to rot and should be discarded. Store Fuyus on the kitchen counter. Fuyus have thick skins that are best peeled with a vegetable peeler or paring knife, or blanched in boiling water for a couple of minutes and then peeled. Fuyus are also past their prime when the flesh turns brown.

NUTRITIONAL HIGHLIGHTS: beta-carotene, fiber, vitamin A, vitamin C

GOES WELL WITH: cinnamon, lemon, pecans, pork, quail, yogurt

Persimmons are delicious but underutilized. Once people discover them, they can quickly become their favorite fruit. Because they have few pests of leaves, stems, or fruits, they are favorites with organic growers.

There are dozens of species scattered around the world, including the native American persimmon, which grows wild from Connecticut south to Florida and west to Kansas and Texas. When unripe the wild fruits are bitterly astringent from tannin, which slowly disappears as the fruits blett (turn soft and ripe) and become candy sweet as they dry still attached to the branches. A native persimmon tree with possums and raccoons feasting on the ripe fruits on a cold fall night is a classic American sight.

The persimmons found in markets originated in China and Japan. There are two main types. The Hachiya, an orange-red, heart-shaped fruit, must blett until its insides turn jelly-like and the bitter tannins yield to a candy-like sweetness. The Fuyu, a smaller, round, slightly flattened fruit, is not astringent, and can be sliced and eaten as a crunchy treat before it fully ripens and softens. You'll also find black persimmons in Texas and Mexico, known as chapotes.

Organic Advantage

Although it may be hard to find organically certified persimmons, it's usually not hard to find unsprayed persimmons, because this tree crop is not beset by many pests. Few agricultural chemicals are used on persimmons and most are herbicides used to keep down weeds between the trees. Still, if you can find an organic grower who sells persimmons, snap them up.

Uses

I like to slice open ripe Hachiya persimmons, spoon the jelly-like fruit into a cup, spoon on a few tablespoons of yogurt, and then stir: it's a fabulous breakfast. A dollop of ripe persimmon can be added to the batters of cakes, coffee cakes, loaves, and home-made energy bars to impart a subtle flavor. Fuyu persimmons can be peeled and sliced when firm for use in salads. They will eventually become soft and squishy, but are still usable then.

Persimmon Sundae

SERVES 3

Sometimes simpler is better, as this recipe proves.

3 jelly-soft ripe persimmons
Vanilla ice cream

Place each persimmon in a cup, stem end down. Slice down from the top in an X shape. Remove the cores and fill the centers with vanilla ice cream.

PINEAPPLE

SEASON: spring and summer

GOOD VARIETIES: Abacaxi, Extra Sweet, Sugarloaf

WHAT TO LOOK FOR: A rich golden yellow color—not of the segment scales, but rather between the scales—signals a pineapple's ripeness: a ripe pineapple glows yellow-gold as though lit from within. A ripe pineapple also yields slightly when it's gently squeezed, and gives off a rich fragrance.

STORAGE AND PREPARATION TIPS: Pineapples acquire the bulk of their sugar content right at the end of their development and, once picked, they sweeten no further. A pineapple that isn't ripe when you buy it isn't going to get any better sitting on your kitchen counter.

NUTRITIONAL HIGHLIGHTS: vitamin C

GOES WELL WITH: apricots, Cointreau, kirsch, other tropical fruits, raspberries, strawberries

Imagine Columbus's delight and astonishment when he landed in Guadeloupe in 1493 and found the natives cultivating pineapples! Here was a new food worthy of the trans-Atlantic exploration. After a couple of months of salt cod and hardtack, a pineapple must have seemed like a gift from heaven.

The pineapple originated in the lowlands of Brazil, where the Tupi Indian word for it was nana or anana, which meant "excellent fruit." It became pineapple in English because of the fruit's resemblance to a pine cone, and the general use of the term apple for any fruit. (Although Spanish speakers call them piñas, their Italian, Portuguese, and French cousins continue to call them ananas.) Although cultivated in pre-Columbian times in South America, the pineapple didn't make it to Hawaii until Captain Cook brought it in 1777. Conditions were so right for pineapple culture on the islands that it soon became a local favorite and eventually a major crop. Hawaiian pineapples have reddish scales covering their segments, while Caribbean pineapples are greenish or yellow-green when ripe.

Organic Advantage

Conventional pineapple growers typically load their soils and plants with fungicides, herbicides, and pesticides. The nematocide methyl bromide is usually used to kill the root-destroying nematodes in the soil, but which also destroys most other forms of life, rendering the soil an ecological wasteland. This chemical also contributes to the greenhouse effect in the atmosphere.

Now for the good news: organic farmers are growing pineapples in Hawaii, Mexico, and the Caribbean, as well as in Africa, the Philippines, and Southeast Asia. And pineapples respond to rich, compost-amended soils with better flavor. Look for organic pineapples in organically oriented supermarkets such as Whole Foods.

Uses

Undoubtedly the best way to eat a pineapple is plain and fresh, by itself, savoring the delicious flavors. But of course pineapple makes a fine addition to any of the fruits and other foods mentioned above. Some old-fashioned uses are still valid—they do make the perfect garnish for baked ham. Pies, cakes, puddings, sauces, and preserves have all been made with pineapple. In Malaysia, it's used in curries and in meat dishes.

Don't use raw pineapple in gelatin-based dishes because the enzyme bromelain, which it contains, will digest the gelatin's protein and prevent jelling. (Cooking deactivates the enzyme.) Raw pineapple juice used as a marinade will tenderize meat, and eventually cause the meat to fall apart. The bromelain in pineapple juice is thought to be a digestive aid.

Indonesian Chicken in Pineapple Sauce

SERVES 4

Here's a different way to prepare good old chicken breasts. The flavors marry marvelously.

Nonstick cooking spray
4 boneless skinless chicken breasts
4 tablespoons Dijon mustard
1/2 cup crushed gingersnaps
1 tablespoon canola oil
1 medium red onion, chopped
1 clove garlic, minced
1 cup finely chopped fresh pineapple, with juice
1/4 cup unseasoned rice vinegar
1/4 teaspoon crushed red pepper flakes
1/4 teaspoon ground allspice
1/4 cup chopped red bell pepper
2 tablespoons chopped fresh basil

1. Preheat the oven to 350°F. Spray a 9 × 13–inch baking dish with nonstick spray. Place each breast between sheets of wax paper and flatten to an even thickness with a rolling pin or meat mallet. Brush both sides with mustard, reserving 1 tablespoon for the sauce, then dredge the breasts in the gingersnap crumbs. Place in the baking dish and refrigerate 20 minutes to firm the coating.

2. Heat the oil in a medium skillet over medium heat. Add the onion and garlic and sauté them for 2 minutes. Mix in the pineapple (with juice), vinegar, red pepper flakes, allspice, and reserved mustard, and cook, stirring, for 4 minutes or until the mixture bubbles and thickens slightly. Scrape into a blender and puree until smooth. Pour this sauce back into the skillet and keep it warm, but don't overcook.

3. Bake the chicken uncovered about 20 minutes, until it's no longer pink in the center. To serve, mix the bell pepper and basil into the sauce, and put $^{1}/_{4}$ of the sauce on each of four plates. Top the sauce with the chicken.

PLUM

SEASON: summertime

GOOD VARIETIES:

Plums: Coe's Golden Drop, Santa Rosa, Stanley

For plum preserves: Blue Damson, Mirabelle

WHAT TO LOOK FOR: Look for fruits that yield slightly to gentle pressure; these are perfect. Avoid very hard plums—they'll never sweeten. And avoid overripe (very soft) plums, as quality drops off sharply after their peak passes.

STORAGE AND PREPARATION TIPS: Eat plums as soon as possible; they don't keep for very long on the kitchen counter or in the refrigerator.

NUTRITIONAL HIGHLIGHTS: antioxidants, vitamin C

GOES WELL WITH: brown sugar, cinnamon, duck, goose, lemon, oranges, peaches, pork, rhubarb, walnuts

---

Our modern era of succulent, juicy plums really began with an indefatigable plant breeder by the name of Luther Burbank, who lived during the late nineteenth and early twentieth centuries. From his home in Santa Rosa, California, and his nearby 11-acre experimental farm, he introduced over seven hundred varieties of fruits, vegetables, and ornamental plants to the world, including the russet potato, the Shasta daisy, the thornless blackberry, and the Santa Rosa plum.

In 1885, Burbank started crossbreeding Japanese plums with American ones in the hopes of creating new delicious varieties. He made over thirty thousand crosses of plums alone, and by the 1920s had released 113 new varieties of plums, many of which are still with us today. One of the sweetest he named the Santa Rosa, which remains the gold standard for Japanese-type plums. It's an aromatic, very sweet plum of exquisite flavor, with red skin and juicy, yellowish flesh with red overtones.

In addition to these red-skinned Japanese-type plums are several European varieties, such as Italian prune plums, which ripen from late summer into early fall. Their skin varies from yellow to blue-black, usually with a dusty bluish bloom; their greenish yellow flesh is dense and sweet. Similar to these are Gage-type plums, which have green or yellow skin and a less intense flavor.

PLUOTS AND APRIUMS

Along with plums, Luther Burbank had plenty of other stone fruits (including peaches, apricots, and cherries) growing at his farm, which he crossed to make some unusual hybrids. He came up with the plumcot by crossing a plum with an apricot, and even a stoneless and seedless plumcot, which, unfortunately, has been lost to us.

Burbank's work has been carried on in recent years in California's Central Valley by Floyd Zaiger, who has bred a great number of hybrids between plums and apricots, called pluots or apriums, depending on which fruit contributes more genes. Pluots have smooth skins like plums, while apriums more closely resemble apricots in flavor and have their scant fuzz. Both of them taste like a blend of fruit juices and tend to have higher sugar concentrations than their parents.

Organic Advantage

Conventional plum growers use agricultural chemicals to deal with a number of difficult pests and diseases, including plum curculios, brown rot, bacterial cankers, aphids, and scale. Organic remedies exist for all these problems, although the healthier the tree and the more biodiverse the orchard, the less severe the problems tend to be in the first place. I find that organic plums from trees cared for in an environmentally sensitive way taste noticeably superior to most conventional types, with a richer, more concentrated plum flavor.

When buying prunes, which are dried plums, look out for ones that are unsulfured and organic (important for people with certain allergies); they're widely available at organic supermarkets and online (see Sources, page 287).

Uses

Plums, along with pluots and apriums, are juicy and delicious eaten out of hand, but shine just as brightly in desserts such as galettes, tarts, clafoutis, crisps, and my favorite—cobblers (see recipe).

Plums are a versatile ingredient, making natural flavor harmonies with citrus (serve them sliced and flavored with a little Limoncello or Grand Marnier) and the other foods mentioned above. The sharp acidity and sweetness of plums ameliorate the fattiness of pork, goose, and duck.

Plums are also fermented and distilled into brandy, especially in the Balkans, where the fiery drink slivovitz is used to punctuate just about any occasion.

Plum and Peach Cobbler

SERVES 6 TO 8

The way the plum's sweet flesh and tangy skins mix with the lush peaches in this mouthwatering cobbler is sheer heaven. You can bake it in a large casserole or make the cobbler in individual ramekins with little dough tops (see Tip).

1 pound ripe plums, pitted and sliced
1 pound ripe peaches, peeled, pitted, and sliced
1 cup plus 3 tablespoons white sugar, plus more for sprinkling
1 tablespoon Grand Marnier
1 tablespoon ground cinnamon
2 cups all-purpose flour
2 teaspoons baking powder
1/4 teaspoon salt
1 1/2 cups heavy cream, chilled
1/2 cup buttermilk
6 tablespoons unsalted butter, chilled and diced small
Melted butter
2 tablespoons confectioners' sugar
1 teaspoon vanilla extract

1. Preheat the oven to 375°F. Place the fruit in a bowl, toss with 1 cup of the sugar, Grand Marnier, and cinnamon then spoon into a 3- or 4-quart baking dish.

2. In a separate bowl, combine the flour, remaining 3 tablespoons of sugar, baking powder, and salt, and mix well. Add ½ cup of the heavy cream, buttermilk, and cold butter in quick succession. Combine them quickly and coarsely with a spoon or spatula so the mixture is as lumpy as possible.

3. Turn the dough onto a lightly floured board. Use a rolling pin to gently flatten the dough until it's about 1 inch thick and just big enough to cover the fruit in the casserole. Place the dough in the baking dish and pull the edges out so they touch the sides. Brush the dough with melted butter, sprinkle the top with a little sugar, and bake for 20 to 25 minutes, or until the dough is nicely browned and the juices bubble thickly.

4. Whip the remaining 1 cup of heavy cream with the confectioners' sugar and vanilla and serve with the cobbler.

TIP: If baking in ramekins, follow the recipe but use a biscuit cutter the size of the ramekin to cut the dough into rounds. (Or set a ramekin on the dough as a template and cut around it with a knife.) Bake about 20 minutes.

POMEGRANATE

SEASON: fall and early winter

GOOD VARIETIES: Ambrosia, Granada, Sweet, Wonderful

WHAT TO LOOK FOR: Select fruits that feel heavy—they'll have more juice. The leathery skin should not be dried out or wrinkled.

STORAGE AND PREPARATION TIPS: Pomegranates will keep for several weeks on the kitchen counter, but do not improve as they wait.

NUTRITIONAL HIGHLIGHTS: antioxidants, potassium, vitamin B_6, vitamin C

GOES WELL WITH: chicken, duck, lamb, rice, yogurt

For a fruit that's not much used in American cuisine, pomegranates sure figure widely in the fundamental myths and legends of Western culture. They supposedly grew in the Hanging Gardens of Babylon, not only for their fruit but also because they are a beautifully ornamental plant—a small, many-trunked tree with reddish orange flowers on light green leaves.

By the early Bronze Age (ca. 2000 BCE), Canaanites living in what is now Lebanon and Israel were growing pomegranates, although they aren't native to that region. Their true home is what is now Iran, where wild species still grow. Our name pomegranate comes from the Latin for "grainy fruit." The first recorded instance of the word in English comes from Chaucer's time. In 1320, it was written that "A poumgarnet ther she brak," or as we would say now, "She peeled a pomegranate." Our word garnet comes from the color of the seeds in a "poumgarnet."

In the Dahlem Museum in Berlin, hangs Rembrandt's magnificent—and dramatic—painting of Pluto, the god of the underworld, dragging Persephone into the Stygian darkness below. The painting illustrates a Greek myth: Persephone vowed never to eat while held captive by Pluto, but broke her vow by swallowing six pomegranate seeds, thereby condemning her to life in Hades. (Pluto later struck a deal with Ceres, Persephone's mother, that allowed the girl to spend six months aboveground—spring and summer—and six months below—wintertime—when the world would be barren.)

Today, pomegranates flourish wherever the climate is subtropical, including the Mediterranean, South Africa, Australia, parts of South America, California, Florida, Texas, the Caribbean, and the Middle East.

Organic Advantage

In the markets, organic pomegranates will carry the USDA organic seal. You can mail order organic pomegranates from Diamond Organics or by searching the Web site of the Organic Trade Association (www.ota.com), where you can find scads of organic comestibles and products (see Sources, page 287).

Uses

The seeds and juice within them are the usable parts of the fruit. Sprinkle pomegranate seeds on salads, rice dishes, or desserts. In its home territories of Iran,

Azerbaijan, Armenia, northern Iraq, and India, pomegranate juice is boiled into a sweet-and-sour syrup used to color rice and add zest to chicken, duck, and lamb.

You can make your own fresh pomegranate juice or purchase it (make sure to buy unsweetened juice for cooking). Use pomegranate juice in the water when cooking white rice to add a pleasant, light pink color. Marinate a butterflied leg of lamb in the fridge overnight in fresh pomegranate juice with some fresh lemon juice, lemon zest, and an ounce of Cointreau.

Fresh pomegranate juice makes a very refreshing drink if slightly sweetened and splashed with sparkling water and a spritz of lime juice. (A couple of ice cubes and a shot of vodka don't hurt, either.) Sweeten the juice further and mix into yogurt or pour over bananas, or make a pomegranate-and-honey flavored frozen yogurt.

Fresh pomegranate juice: Place a colander in the kitchen sink. Quarter a pomegranate and run the pieces under cold water, letting the seeds fall into the colander and removing as much of the bitter white membrane as you can. Drain the seeds and pick out any remaining bits of membrane. The best way to extract the juice is to wrap the seeds in a double thickness of cheesecloth and mash with a potato masher, then twist and wring it out. You can speed this up by first breaking up the seeds in a blender, but the juice won't be quite as fine, as some seed bits will make their way in.

Duck Stew with Walnuts and Pomegranates (Fesenjan)

SERVES 4

This version of the classic Persian stew originated in the province of Gilan, where the shores of the Caspian Sea teem with wild ducks. The sweetness of the duck meat harmonizes beautifully with the pomegranates and nuts. Chicken or lamb chunks can be substituted for the duck. Serve this stew with plenty of white steamed rice to soak up all the flavorful juices.

4 tablespoons olive oil
1 large onion, chopped fine
1/2 teaspoon freshly ground black pepper
1/2 teaspoon ground turmeric
1 pound boneless skinless duck breasts, cut into thin strips
1 tablespoon all-purpose flour
1/2 pound walnuts, coarsely chopped (about 1 3/4 cups)
3 cups unsweetened pomegranate juice, fresh pressed or store bought
Salt to taste
Juice of 1 lemon, to taste
White sugar, to taste
1 small eggplant
1 1/2 teaspoons ground cardamom

1. Heat a large skillet with 2 tablespoons of the oil over medium heat, and

add the onion, pepper, and turmeric; sauté until translucent, about 5 minutes. Remove the onion, leaving the oil in the skillet.

2. Add the duck and sauté until browned, about 10 minutes, stirring occasionally. Sprinkle the meat with the flour. Add the walnuts and sauté 3 more minutes, turning once or twice.

3. Add the pomegranate juice and salt to taste. The taste should be a nice balance of sweet and sour. If it needs more sour to balance the sweetness, add lemon juice. If it needs more sweetness, add a little sugar. Cover the skillet and reduce the heat to low. Simmer, stirring occasionally so the nuts don't burn, for 40 minutes.

4. As soon as the juices start to simmer, peel the eggplant and cut it lengthwise into 6 or 8 slices. Sprinkle each slice with salt, stack one on top of the other, and let sit for 5 minutes, then rinse under cold water. Pat dry with paper towels, then sauté in another large skillet over medium heat with the remaining 2 tablespoons of oil until browned on both sides. When the eggplant is browned, arrange the slices on top of the meat in the skillet, replace the cover, and finish simmering.

5. Gently stir the cardamom powder into the stew and serve. The sauce should be the consistency of heavy cream. If it's too thick, dilute it with a little warm water.

RASPBERRY AND BLACKBERRY

SEASON: midsummer to early fall

GOOD VARIETIES:

Red raspberry: Baba, Chief, Heritage, Meeker (good for home gardens), Taylor, wild berries

Black raspberry: Allen (great for jam), Bristol, Haut, Jewel, wild berries

Blackberry: Apache, Arapaho, Black Satin, Navaho, Siskiyou, Triple Crown, wild berries

WHAT TO LOOK FOR: Berries can develop mold within days of being picked. Look into the berry's hollow center—that's usually where mold starts. Make sure the berries aren't squished: they should be plump and sound. Taste one if you can—ripe berries will be sweet and aromatic, not sour. Blackberries that are dead ripe lose some of their shine in favor of a slightly dull finish.

STORAGE AND PREPARATION TIPS: Fresh raspberries and blackberries are soft and very perishable. Use them fast, as they don't last long. If you have a surplus of fresh berries, you can freeze them in a single layer on cookie sheets, then store the frozen berries in freezer bags.

NUTRITIONAL HIGHLIGHTS: antioxidants, fiber, folate, vitamin C

GO WELL WITH:

Raspberry: almonds, blackberries, chocolate, cream, lemon, peaches, red currants, yogurt, vanilla

Blackberry: apple, cinnamon, cream, lemon, peaches, raspberries

Have you ever opened up a package of fresh, plump raspberries or blackberries, popped one in your mouth, and encountered a taste more sour than sweet? That's because many commercial raspberries and blackberries are picked and shipped young and not fully ripe so that they will last longer. Consequently, they don't develop the sweetness and dusky, brambly flavor of the ripe fruit.

Since ripe berries are delicate and don't travel well or last very long, the best way to get them is to find a local source. Both blackberries and raspberries are grown throughout the country, so look for them at farmers' markets and roadside stands. Even markets like Whole Foods sometimes carry locally grown berries.

Off season, frozen organic raspberries and blackberries are widely available and may be an even better choice for use in sauces, smoothies, compotes, and the like.

Organic Advantage

Raspberries don't need a lot of coddling, so even conventionally grown berries are not likely to carry a load of toxic chemicals, although organic raspberries are available, too. Blackberries are subject to rots and mildews in wet weather. Organic growers plant varieties resistant to orange rust, a contagious disease that is otherwise coped with by rooting out infected plants.

Organic berries grown in rich, compost-amended soil will have an exceptionally appealing, bright, sprightly flavor. And if they're locally grown, they're more likely to be recently picked, at their peak of freshness, and free of mold.

Uses

Red raspberries have an affinity for many other flavors, especially chocolate. Raspberry ice cream topped with dark chocolate syrup is perfection. Chocolate and raspberry cake is classic. Try them with almonds, cream, lemon, black or red currants, and with red wine.

Blackberries ripen at the same time as the first apples of the season, and blackberry-apple compote is luscious. Blackberry pie with vanilla ice cream is classic. Fresh blackberries and muesli make a nutritious breakfast. Try a few blackberries with orange segments at breakfast, too.

If either kind of berries are very ripe and losing their shape, mash them up and pour them over ice cream, puree them to make a sauce, or cook with them. Both berries make surpassingly good preserves.

Raspberry Clafoutis

SERVES 6

This dish is about as yummy as raspberries get (unless you just serve them plain, I suppose). It's a French classic. Serve it alone, or with raspberry sauce, or vanilla ice cream—or both.

OTHER BRAMBLE BERRIES

Black raspberries: An entirely different species than red raspberries, despite their resemblance, these shiny black berries have a luscious taste similar to Chambord liqueur. Around the Fourth of July—the height of black raspberry season—ads for pick-your-own black raspberry patches pop up in local newspapers throughout the Mid-Atlantic and New England regions. Their season is short, ending around July 15, so get them while you can. Frozen black raspberries are also available and make excellent black raspberry ice cream if you strain out the seeds—the perfect summer treat—but they are commercial varieties and don't have the interesting flavor of the black caps that grow wild.

Boysenberries: Named after Ralph Boysen (who discovered them growing on his farm in southern California), they're a cross between a red raspberry, a blackberry, and a loganberry. They have a purplish color and flavor components of all three. The berry was first cultivated by Walter Knott, and became the basis for the initial development of the Knott's Berry Farm fruit and entertainment complex near Los Angeles.

Loganberries: A cross between a red raspberry and blackberry, these berries have a distinctive tart flavor. Loganberries once were planted on thousands of acres in the West but have fallen out of favor with growers. They make superb jams, jellies, preserves, and pies.

Wineberries: A wild relative of the red raspberry, it grows in meadows in the northeastern United States. When they ripen, they change from orange-red to a deep, jewel-like translucent ruby-red, and become sticky and very fragile—and indescribably delicious. Look for them in mid-July growing along east-facing edges of woods and dappled, shady roadsides, or at the odd farmers' market.

2 pints fresh red raspberries
4 1/2 ounces (3/4 to 1 cup) whole raw almonds
1 1/4 cups sugar
3/4 cup all-purpose flour
7 large egg whites
Juice and freshly grated zest of 1 orange (well scrubbed if not organic)
2 1/4 sticks unslated butter

1. Puree 1 pint of the raspberries in a blender. Grind the almonds fine in a food processor. In a bowl, combine the raspberry puree, ground almonds, sugar, flour, egg whites, orange juice and zest. Whisk together until well blended.

2. Preheat the oven to 350°F. In a saucepan, gently heat the butter until it

browns lightly—what the French call *noisette,* or a nut-like color. Pour the butter through a very fine strainer into the raspberry mixture, stirring as you pour.

3. When the ingredients are thoroughly mixed, pour the batter into 6 round, fluted ramekins. Drop 6 to 8 raspberries from the remaining pint on top of each ramekin. Bake for 35 minutes, or until golden brown.

Nora's Superb Blackberry Cobbler

SERVES 4

I received this recipe from Nora Pouillon, one of America's finest organic chefs. She owns two acclaimed restaurants in Washington, DC, Nora and Asia Nora.

FOR THE BERRY MIXTURE

4 cups blackberries
1 tablespoon Grand Marnier
1/2 cup sugar
1 tablespoon arrowroot
2 pinches ground cardamom

FOR THE COBBLER DOUGH

1 cup unbleached all-purpose flour
5 tablespoons sugar
1 teaspoon baking powder
1/2 teaspoon baking soda
1/2 teaspoon sea salt
3 tablespoons unsalted butter, chilled and cut into 1/4-inch dice
1/3 cup buttermilk, or 1/3 cup whole milk with 1 tablespoon fresh lemon juice
1 egg yolk
Mint sprigs

1. Preheat the oven to 400°F. Grease a 4- to 6-cup baking dish or ceramic pie plate. Toss the berry mixture ingredients together in a large bowl, then transfer the mixture to the dish.

2. Combine the flour, sugar, baking powder, baking soda, and salt in a medium bowl. Add the butter and work the mixture quickly between your fingertips, until it is crumbly and has the consistency of cornmeal. Or use a food processor, pulse it on and off to mix the flour and butter. Add the buttermilk and egg yolk and stir to combine. The dough should be soft.

3. With a large spoon, drop the dough onto the berry mixture. Bake for 30 to 40 minutes, or until the topping is browned and cooked through and the juices bubble. The berry mixture should be quite saucey. Garnish with mint.

STRAWBERRY

SEASON: early summer

GOOD VARIETIES: Delmarvel, Fairfax, Ruegen, Sequoia, Sparkle, Suwannee, wild strawberries

WHAT TO LOOK FOR: Buy strawberries that are bright and fresh, not dull, softening, or molding.

STORAGE AND PREPARATION TIPS: Strawberries are best eaten as soon as possible. They can, however, be frozen: slice them into "chips" and freeze in one layer on a baking sheet, then store in freezer bags. Freezing breaks down their structure, so they will have to be cooked or used in smoothies or sauces.

NUTRITIONAL HIGHLIGHTS: fiber, vitamin C

GOES WELL WITH: balsamic vinegar, Champagne, chocolate, cream, crème fraîche, mascarpone, oranges, tangerines, pineapple, red wine, rhubarb, sugar

---

Referring to the strawberry, Izaak Walton, the seventeenth-century English writer, famously said, "Doubtless God could have made a better berry, but doubtless God never did." One of my earliest memories is the jingle of the Good Humor truck coming up my street, selling vanilla ice cream with frozen strawberry syrup intermingled in it for a nickel a cup. I don't think you need any convincing that strawberries are as heavenly a fruit as there is.

Strawberries are delicate things—quick to lose their evanescent esters and other fragrance and flavor compounds, easily crushed in transit, and prone to rapid mold growth. Big, conventional, commercial growers plant hardy but bland berry varieties designed to keep their shape during shipping. The most flavorful berries are going to be locally grown—the nearer your house the better—so that they can ripen fully on the plant.

For the best of all strawberries, look for locally grown June-bearing varieties, which produce a big crop in June and then are finished for the season. June-bearers are usually better flavored than ever-bearing types, which produce a sprinkling of berries throughout the summer. (Something about the intensity of the June sun brings out the sugars and flavors of strawberries, and also their nutritional quality.) These are the ones to buy by the flat for eating, making preserves, and freezing.

Organic Advantage

No berry is more loaded with agricultural chemicals than a conventionally grown strawberry. Pickers who have to enter the poison-drenched fields call strawberries the devil's fruit, not just because of the backbreaking labor it takes to harvest them, but also because of the toxic environment of the fields. Millions of pounds of agricultural chemicals have been used on strawberries in recent years in California alone. In a study of forty-two fruits and vegetables by the Environmental Working Group, strawberries were found to have one of the highest concentrations of chemical contaminants. That's the chief reason to buy organic strawberries. But in addition, the best-tasting strawberry varieties (such as the June-bearing crops) are most likely to be grown by organic farmers, so by seeking out organic strawberries you'll also increase your chances of getting the most flavorful varieties out there.

Uses

When making stewed rhubarb, throw some strawberries in the pot—the combination of the two flavors is wonderful. For a super treat, dip fresh strawberries in melted chocolate, which hardens at room temperature. Make a cooked strawberry puree, cool it in the fridge, then swirl it into your homemade vanilla ice cream just before it's finished. Add frozen strawberries directly to winter fruit compotes or pair them with bananas and other fruits to make smoothies in a blender.

Strawberry and Peach Succulence

SERVES 4

This recipe is easy to make, but the results are heavenly. I wait for the perfect day each summer when I can make this with tree-ripened peaches and fragrant, sweet strawberries.

1 pint fresh ripe strawberries
2 ripe peaches
1 cup Italian Moscato or other late-harvest dessert wine (such as a Beaumes de Venise)
2 tablespoons sugar
Freshly grated zest of 1 lemon (well scrubbed if not organic)

1. Stem and slice the strawberries. Peel the peaches by blanching them for 1 minute in boiling water, then run them under cold water until the skins loosen. Halve, pit, and thinly slice the peaches.

2. In a bowl, toss the fruit with the wine, sugar, and zest. Spoon into individual bowls and serve.

Strawberry-Rhubarb Crisp

SERVES 6

A classic marriage of flavors, strawberries and rhubarb melt together in this simple summertime dessert.

1 pound fresh strawberries
3 cups chopped rhubarb stems
1/2 cup white sugar
1 tablespoon cornstarch
2/3 cup ground pecans
2/3 cup brown sugar
1/2 cup all-purpose flour
Freshly grated zest of 1 lemon (well scrubbed if not organic)
1 teaspoon ground cinnamon
8 tablespoons (1 stick) unsalted butter, chilled

1. Preheat the oven to 350°F. Lightly grease a 1½-quart baking dish or casserole.

2. Stem and slice the strawberries. In a large bowl, thoroughly combine the strawberries, rhubarb, white sugar, and cornstarch, and turn this mixture into the baking dish.

3. Combine the pecans, brown sugar, flour, lemon zest, and cinnamon in another large bowl. Cut in the butter using 2 knives or your fingers until the mixture has the consistency of coarse meal. Sprinkle this over the fruit. Bake for 35 to 40 minutes, or until the top is lightly browned.

CHAPTER

4

Nuts, Seeds, Beans, and Grains

Around the world, it's the seeds of plants that support human life. Rice is king throughout most of Asia. In Europe, it's wheat, rye, and oats. In Africa, many kinds of beans and peanuts play a big role. In the Western Hemisphere, native populations lived mostly on corn and beans. And just about everywhere except the New World, barley was grown for its life-giving stores of minerals like bone-building calcium, and its high amount of health-giving fiber.

In this chapter, you will be introduced to some grains, beans, and nuts—all of them seeds of plants—that you probably don't use very often. But you should try as wide a variety of them as you can, because they are among nature's richest and most concentrated sources of energy. Wheat, rye, oats, barley, and corn (maize) are the seeds of grasses. Beans, peas, lentils, chickpeas, and peanuts are the seeds of legumes. Nuts like pecans, hazelnuts (filberts), walnuts, and many others, are the seeds of trees. And then there are seeds from a variety of other plants, like pumpkin, quinoa, amaranth, sesame, poppy, caraway, cumin, and cardamom. All are rich storehouses of nutrition, and all can be found as organic. Organic soil is rich soil, full of life. That imparts health to the plants that grow in it, and to their seeds. And those seeds can impart that health to us.

TYPES OF FATS IN NUTS AND SEEDS

It's not just the amount of fat in your diet that affects your health, but also the type of fat. Certain fats trigger deleterious responses in your cholesterol and triglyceride levels. Nuts and seeds, for example, are particularly rich in fats, but much of the fat is monounsaturated, or "good" fat. Here's a breakdown of the three major types of fats, followed by a chart of the percentage of each type in various nuts and seeds.

Saturated fats: Found primarily in animal products, but also in some vegetable oils. They tend to raise LDL ("bad" cholesterol) and triglyceride levels. Check out the amount in raw coconut meat (below).

Polyunsaturated fats: Found in plants and seafood, they consist of omega-6 and omega-3 polyunsaturated fatty acids. Omega-6 fatty acids can negatively impact your HDL ("good" cholesterol) by lowering it. Omega-3 fatty acids may help to beneficially increase your HDL levels. (See page 277 for further discussion of this.)

Monounsaturated fats: Found in plant foods such as seeds and nuts, they lower LDL cholesterol and triglycerides in the blood. If you replace most saturated, trans, and polyunsaturated fats in your diet with monounsaturated fats, they can raise HDL levels. They are the all-around good fats, and they are found in abundance in olive, canola, peanut, hazelnut, and grape seed oils, as well as in the seeds and nuts in the chart below. The oleic acid in monounsaturated fats can lower bad cholesterol (LDL) while not affecting levels of good cholesterol (HDL).

The values below are percentages of each type in the seed or nut.

Type of Seed or Nut	Saturated Fat	Polyunsaturated Fat	Monounsaturated Fat	Other Fat
Almond	6.4	21.1	68.0	4.5
Brazil nut	24.3	36.4	34.8	4.5
Cashew	19.8	16.9	58.8	4.5
Coconut	88.7	1.1	4.3	5.9
Hazelnut	7.3	9.6	78.4	4.0
Macadamia	15.0	1.7	78.9	4.4
Peanut	13.9	31.6	49.6	4.9
Pecan	8.0	24.8	62.3	4.9
Pine nut	15.4	42.1	37.6	4.9
Pistachio	12.7	15.1	67.5	4.7
Pumpkin seed	18.9	45.6	31.1	4.4
Sesame seed	14.0	43.8	37.8	4.4
Sunflower seed	10.5	66.0	19.1	4.4
Walnut	9.0	63.0	23.0	5.0

NUTS

ALMOND

SEASON: late summer

GOOD VARIETY: Nonpareil, Marcona

WHAT TO LOOK FOR: Purchase whole almonds still in their brown shells.

STORAGE AND PREPARATION TIPS: Store almonds in an airtight jar in a dark cupboard.

NUTRITIONAL HIGHLIGHTS: calcium, copper, fiber, iron, magnesium, manganese, monounsaturated fat, phosphorus, potassium, protein, riboflavin, vitamin E, zinc

GOES WELL WITH: chocolate, most fruits, pastries, sautéed green beans

The almond is actually a stone fruit, similar to the cherry, peach, plum, and apricot. In this case, though, it's not sweet, juicy flesh we're after, but rather the seed inside the pulpy husk that covers it.

Almonds were one of the first plants to be cultivated. Almond farming began some time before 3000 BCE. The wild progenitors of almond trees are from central and western Asia, although today 80 percent of the world's almonds come from California.

Organic Advantage

In California, millions of pounds of agricultural pesticides, herbicides, and fungicides are used on conventionally farmed almonds. Much of the chemicals eventually find their way into the tributaries that lead into San Francisco Bay, raising pesticide levels above what the Environmental Protection Agency considers safe. Yet an organic almond market is steadily growing, at between 18 and 20 percent a year. To locate organic almond producers, see Sources, page 287.

Uses

Almonds are a multipurpose nut. Add chopped almonds to salads. Sprinkle them on a soup or pasta dish to add flavor and crunch. Top muffins and other baked goods with almonds.

Toasting almonds right before you use them releases their flavors and aromas. To toast almonds, place sliced almonds on a baking sheet in a 350°F oven, stirring occasionally, for 8 minutes, or until golden.

Biscotti

MAKES ABOUT 20 BISCOTTI

Biscotti are twice-baked Italian cookies. First, the sweet dough, usually containing ground almonds, is baked into a loaf and sliced. The slices are then baked again, yielding a hard, crunchy texture. Crisp and dry, biscotti are ideal for dipping into coffee, milk, or vin santo, the Italian dessert wine.

2 tablespoons canola oil or nonstick spray
1/2 cup roughly chopped almonds
2 cups all-purpose flour
2 teaspoons baking powder
1/4 teaspoon salt
1/2 cup brown sugar
1/4 cup well-beaten eggs (1 extra-large or 2 small)
2 tablespoons honey
1/2 teaspoon almond extract
1/4 teaspoon vanilla extract

1. Preheat the oven to 350°F. Lightly oil or spray a large baking sheet and spread the almonds in a single layer. Toast for 5 to 8 minutes, until golden and fragrant. Set the pan aside to cool.

2. Combine the flour, baking powder, and salt in a small bowl and mix well. In a large bowl, beat together the sugar, eggs, honey, and almond and vanilla extracts until thoroughly mixed. Stir in the toasted almonds. Add the flour mixture and mix until well incorporated.

3. Divide the dough into 2 balls. Roll each into a cylinder 10 inches long and 2 inches wide. Lay them on the baking sheet about 6 inches apart. Bake for 20 to 25 minutes, until the top is golden brown and slightly cracked.

4. Remove from the oven and let cool until barely warm.

5. Lay the cookie loaves on a cutting board and cut 3/4-inch-thick slices on the diagonal. Return the slices to the baking sheet and bake 10 to 12 minutes more, until firm and lightly golden. Cool on a wire rack.

BRAZIL NUT

SEASON: late winter

GOOD VARIETIES: Brazil nuts are the wild species; no cultivated varieties exist.

WHAT TO LOOK FOR: Purchase Brazil nuts still in the shell.

STORAGE AND PREPARATION TIPS: Brazil nuts rapidly turn rancid after shelling, so crack them as needed.

NUTRITIONAL HIGHLIGHTS: copper, fiber, magnesium, manganese, monosaturated fat, phosphorus, protein, selenium, thiamin, vitamin E, zinc

GOES WELL WITH: apricots, chocolate, coconuts, raisins, rice, strawberries

Almost all Brazil nuts are gathered from the virgin rain forests of Brazil; small amounts are gathered in Venezuela, Colombia, the Guyanas, Bolivia, and Peru. The trees that bear them are huge—150 feet tall with crowns up to 100 feet in diameter. The fruit, called an *ouriço*, are spherical pods that weigh from one to five pounds and grow in the tree canopy far out of reach of pickers. So the pickers wait for them to fall. But a five-pound weight dropped from 150 feet can kill a person—and has—so pickers wear large protective wooden hats and avoid gathering the ouriço on rainy or windy days.

When hacked open by a machete, each ouriço reveals ten to twenty-five nuts packed inside like orange segments. Each nut is covered with the very hard shell we're familiar with.

Brazil nuts are related to the sapucaia nut, also called the paradise nut, supposedly one of the best-tasting nuts in the world. That treasure, grown locally by property owners, is available only in Brazil and the Guyanas.

Organic Advantage

Because Brazil nuts are gathered wild, they are unlikely to have encountered any chemicals.

Uses

When fresh, these oily nuts have a sweet, creamy flavor that's very appealing. The flavor is enhanced by lightly toasting them in the oven right before use. They are a familiar addition to mixed nuts, but you can also make Brazil nut milk by pulverizing them with water in the blender, then straining the liquid.

Brazil Nut Bark

MAKES ABOUT 1 POUND

You can get chocolate bark at the chocolate shop, but it's easy to make at home. The chocolate must be melted in a double boiler or it will scorch.

12 ounces semisweet chocolate
1 tablespoon unsalted butter
1 cup chopped Brazil nuts
1/2 cup seedless raisins

Melt the chocolate with the butter in the top of a double boiler, keeping the water beneath at a simmer. When melted, remove from the heat, stir in the Brazil nuts and raisins, and spread in a thin layer on a cookie sheet lined with wax paper. Place in the refrigerator until cold and firm. Break into pieces and store in a tightly covered container in the refrigerator.

CASHEW

SEASON: Traditionally an autumn crop, they are now available year around.

GOOD VARIETIES: Cashews are the wild species; no cultivated varieties exist.

WHAT TO LOOK FOR: In the store, you'll find both organic and conventional cashews sold both salted and unsalted, and also either roasted or "raw." Raw nuts aren't really raw, but have not been roasted beyond the initial processing (see below).

STORAGE AND PREPARATION TIPS: Store cashews in an airtight jar in a dark cupboard.

NUTRITIONAL HIGHLIGHTS: copper, fiber, magnesium, manganese, monounsaturated fat (see chart, page 170), phosphorus, protein, selenium, thiamin, vitamin E, zinc

GOES WELL WITH: coconut, cream, raisins

The cashew is a medium-size, handsome tree native to northeastern Brazil.

It produces pear-shaped fruits called apples; the cashew nut forms inside a hard shell at the end of the apple. The outer surface of the shell contains urushiol, the same substance found in poison ivy and poison oak that causes dermatitis. There is a layer of toxic resin inside the shell but outside of the nutmeat as well, so people who handle the shells have to wear protective gloves. To process cashews for eating, most purveyors steam the shells until they burst open, or roast them until the shells become brittle and crack. In either case the toxic elements cook away and the cashews come out safe and clean. To get truly raw cashews, however, the shells have to be removed by hand very carefully, a slow and expensive process. To find a source, visit Sunfood Nutrition's Web site (www.rawfood.com).

Organic Advantage

While much cashew production is conventional, there are organic suppliers in places like Sri Lanka and Indonesia.

Uses

Cashews have a wonderful, softly crunchy texture and a light nutty flavor. They are great as a snack all by themselves. Use them lightly toasted and crushed in stir-fries with chicken strips and vegetables, and in curries in place of peanuts. They're essential in high-quality trail mixes. Cashew butter is rich and usually made from toasted cashews to increase its nutty flavor. It makes a great topping for veggie burgers.

To toast cashews, place them on a cookie sheet in a 350°F oven for 5 to 7 minutes; be careful to remove them from the oven when they're just turning a light brown, as they scorch easily.

Cashew Sauce

MAKES 1 1/2 CUPS

This easy-to-make sauce is perfect for enhancing stir-fried tofu or grains such as rice or barley.

1/2 cup raw cashews
1/4 medium onion, chopped coarsely
2 cloves garlic
1 tablespoon arrowroot powder
1 tablespoon tamari

Place the cashews, onion, garlic, arrowroot, and 1 cup of water in a blender and blend until smooth. Pour into a small saucepan and add the tamari. Place the pan over medium heat and stir until it thickens, about 5 minutes. Be careful not to overcook, as it thickens further as it cools.

CHESTNUT

SEASON: fall through early winter

GOOD VARIETIES: Appalachia, Carolina, Revival, Colossal, Nevada, Silverleaf

WHAT TO LOOK FOR: Fresh chestnuts should be plump, with tight, uncracked shells. (Their condition reflects how carefully and quickly they were harvested after falling from the trees.) Chestnuts that are already peeled will have lost quality. Be wary of dried chestnuts, which can turn rancid if stored too long.

STORAGE AND PREPARATION TIPS: Store chestnuts in their shells in the freezer.

NUTRITIONAL HIGHLIGHTS: copper, fiber, folate, magnesium, manganese, phosphorus, potassium, riboflavin, thiamin, vitamin B_6, vitamin C

GOES WELL WITH: chicken, game, pork, sausage, turkey

Organic Advantage

Almost all chestnuts sold in American markets, whether European, Asian, or American, are grown without pesticides. They may not be certified organic, but they are likely to be clean.

Uses

Good chestnuts are sweet and flavorful. Given their starchiness, they function culinarily more like potatoes or grains than like nuts. As such, they are quite versatile in the kitchen. Shelled chestnuts are excellent as a meat garnish or in stuffing for the Thanksgiving bird. Try adding whole shelled chestnuts to a chicken and vegetable stir-fry. Whole peeled chestnuts can be candied (see recipe, page 176) or preserved in syrup for *marrons glacés*.

Chestnuts can be roasted in their shells, but are more commonly shelled and boiled. Chestnut shells must be removed before eating them, and their bitter inner skin should be peeled away, too.

To shell and peel chestnuts: Use a paring knife to cut an X in the flat side of each nut, then drop them in a saucepan of cold water. Bring to a boil. Boil for 1 minute, then remove from the heat. Lift them out one by one from the hot water, and peel away the shell and inner skin while they're warm. If the inner skin refuses to come loose, set those chestnuts aside and reboil them for 30 seconds, then try peeling them again.

To roast whole chestnuts: Make a slit in the shell (to prevent bursting), then roast them in a 375°F oven for 30 minutes, until the inside is tender. When our woodstove is going, I just set them on the top of the stove until they're tender (but don't forget the slit).

Unsweetened chestnut puree can be served as a savory side dish. It can be added to sauces, or used in poultry and meat stuffings, and is the base for croquettes and chestnut soufflés. Sweetened chestnut puree—*purée de marron*—is fantastic with yogurt or ricotta cheese, and used in ice creams, candies, cookies, and pastries.

To make chestnut puree: Boil 2 cups of shelled fresh chestnuts for 10 to 20

KING OF THE FOREST

Chestnuts were once the kings of the forest in the eastern United States, but by 1910 were virtually wiped out due to chestnut blight, a fungus that crossed the ocean from China. Before the chestnut blight hit the forests of the eastern United States, an estimated four billion American chestnut trees dominated the woodlands of Appalachia. The beautiful trees could reach 100 feet, with trunks 6 feet in diameter. The wood was straight-grained, visually beautiful, and exceptionally rot resistant. The annual drop of nutrient-rich chestnuts supported many forms of domestic and wild animals—as well as Native Americans and newly arrived settlers. But by 1950, only fifty to one hundred American chestnut trees remained in all of North America.

However, European and Asian chestnut varieties that had traveled to North America were resistant to the blight. The remaining American chestnuts were crossbred with these types in order to develop blight resistance, then rebred with American chestnuts again and again in order to yield trees that were almost purely American but resistant to blight. Today, thousands of these resistant American chestnut trees have been planted throughout their old range and the lovely American chestnut is making a comeback. Real American chestnuts can again be found in specialty markets. (See Sources, page 287, for suppliers.)

When I lived in Berks County, Pennsylvania, I occasionally used to find American chestnut trees along country back roads. The giant trees had died, but their roots continued to send up sprouts that reached about 8 to 10 feet in height, whereupon they were taken by the chestnut blight. But sometimes that was tall enough for the sprouts to flower and form a few nuts. I have eaten American chestnuts both raw out of hand and roasted. They are delicious—a delicacy that only underscores what a tragedy befell the king of the forest.

Chestnut blight continues to be a problem, and people all over America are working to grow blight-resistant chestnut trees. For more information, visit the American Chestnut Foundation (www.acf.org).

minutes, until tender. Peel them and puree in the blender with a little water.

Glazed Chestnuts

MAKES 30

These little sweetmeats are just right for the holidays.

2 cups sugar
Pinch of salt
1 pound shelled fresh chestnuts (see To Shell and Peel Chestnuts, page 175)

1. In a 2-quart saucepan, combine 2 cups of water with the sugar and salt.

Bring to a boil over medium-high heat, then reduce the heat to low and cook for 25 minutes, allowing the syrup to thicken.

2. Meanwhile, place the chestnuts in a separate 2-quart saucepan, cover with water and bring to a boil over high heat. Reduce the heat to low and cook for 10 minutes, then drain the chestnuts and run under cold water to stop the cooking. Add the drained chestnuts to the sugar syrup, cover, and simmer over low heat for 20 minutes. Remove from the heat, let cool to room temperature, then refrigerate overnight.

3. The next day, bring the chestnuts and syrup to a simmer over low heat and cook for 15 minutes. Cool again to room temperature, then cover and refrigerate overnight for a second time. Remove the chestnuts from the syrup and place in a jar. Cover and store in the refrigerator for up to four weeks.

HAZELNUT

SEASON: Hazelnuts are picked in August, but reach their peak of flavor from November to December.

GOOD VARIETIES: Barcelona, Red Aveline, Royal

WHAT TO LOOK FOR: The best hazelnuts will feel heavy in the hand.

STORAGE AND PREPARATION TIPS: Hazelnuts store well at room temperature but should be eaten within a month of purchase. They'll store indefinitely in the freezer.

NUTRITIONAL HIGHLIGHTS: copper, fiber, folate, iron, magnesium, manganese, monounsaturated fat (see chart on page 170), protein, thiamin, vitamin B_6, vitamin E

GOES WELL WITH: chocolate, coffee

Hazelnuts are easy to grow, bear heavy crops of nuts in almost every climate in the United States, and have a mild, delicious flavor after they've cured.

Organic Advantage

Organic hazelnuts are widely available and can be purchased by mail order (see Sources, page 287). Some are given a mold-prevention treatment with sulfur dioxide and some are not. I never sulfured my home-grown hazelnuts, and they invariably developed a little mold on the more porous part of the shell. But this never resulted in any quality loss for the nuts inside; the small amount of mold remained on the shells' surface.

Uses

To get the best flavor from hazelnuts, lightly roast the shelled nuts and cool them before crushing or grinding them for breads, pastries, and confections. Their flavor harmonizes well with coffee and chocolate. The nuts' brownish skin contains fiber and minerals, so there's no need to remove it.

One pound of hazelnuts in the shell equals about 1½ cups of shelled nutmeat, and 1 cup of shelled whole nuts is about 5 ounces.

Hazelnut oil is excellent in salad dressing. A little goes a long way. The delicate flavor of the oil is quickly ruined by heat, so it's not an oil for cooking. And it tends to go rancid quickly, so buy the oil in small quantities and use it within a few weeks.

Hazelnut-Crusted Pork Loin

SERVES 4

This recipe turns an ordinary pork loin into something very special. It combines the sweet meat with toasty nuts, fruity peaches, and tangy lemon. Since you'll be cooking the hazelnuts when you cook the pork loin, don't toast them before grinding.

2 pounds hazelnuts in the shell
1/4 cup all-purpose flour
1 large egg
2 tablespoons milk
2 boneless pork tenderloins, each cut in half crosswise
2 tablespoons canola oil
2 or 3 fresh peaches
2 cups chicken stock
1/2 cup half-and-half
Freshly grated zest of 1/2 lemon (well scrubbed if not organic)
Salt and freshly ground black pepper

1. Shell the nuts and pulse in a food processor or blender to grind them fine but not to a pasty meal. You should end up with about 1 1/2 cups of ground nuts.

2. Preheat the oven to 450°F.

3. Set up 3 shallow bowls. Place the flour in one bowl. Beat the egg and milk together, and place the nuts in the third bowl. Coat the pork loin pieces in the flour first, then the egg and milk mixture, then the nuts, making sure they're entirely covered, including the cut ends.

4. Heat the oil in a large skillet over medium heat and sauté the loins on all sides until golden brown, about 5 to 8 minutes. Start a pot of water on high heat to be used for peeling the peaches. Transfer the loins to a clean skillet or baking pan and roast them in the oven for 20 minutes.

5. While the loins are roasting, drop the peaches in the boiling water for a minute or two, then peel and pit them and cut them into thin slices. (You should have 2 cups.) Mash the slices to a pulp using a potato masher, or puree them in the blender. Combine them in a 2-quart saucepan with the chicken stock, half-and-half, lemon zest, and a pinch of salt and pepper. Place the pan over low heat and simmer until heated through, about 5 minutes. Be careful not to overcook or scorch the mixture.

6. When the loins are done, cut each piece into 1/2-inch slices, place on a plate, and spoon some of the peach sauce around the slices.

MACADAMIA NUT

SEASON: late fall to spring

GOOD VARIETIES: Beaumont, Cate

WHAT TO LOOK FOR: Purchase shelled nuts with no blemishes and a light creamy-yellow color. Be aware that conventional macadamia nuts may be dressed in coconut oil and salt.

STORAGE AND PREPARATION TIPS: Store in the fridge or freezer to prevent rancidity. If you find unshelled macadamias (a rare treat), crack them on a flat rock or cement with another flat rock or a brick; a nutcracker won't work.

NUTRITIONAL HIGHLIGHTS: copper, fiber, folate, iron, magnesium, manganese, monounsaturated fat (see page 170), phosphorus, protein, thiamin, vitamin B_6, vitamin E

GOES WELL WITH: chocolate, coconut, coffee

Before 1880, only Australian Aborigines knew of and feasted on macadamia nuts. But that year, a botanist by the name of Dr. Hill "discovered" them in their native range around Brisbane, Queensland, in northeast Australia, and named them for his friend, Dr. John Macadam. Within a few years, they were brought to Hawaii where they flourished, as the climate was perfect for them. Today, about 90 percent of the world's supply is grown in Hawaii, and the nut joins sugar and pineapples as the top three exports from the islands. Large commercial groves have also been established in Australia and New Zealand. The nut has exceptional qualities—delicate flavor, sweetness, and a wonderfully crunchy (but not hard or brittle) texture—and world demand greatly exceeds supply.

Organic Advantage

On Hawaii, a macadamia nut farmer named Tuddie Purdy and his family is the foremost supplier of naturally grown macadamia nuts. Stinkbugs and tropical nut borers can be a problem for macadamias, but the Purdys remain committed to chemical-free, if not organic, production.

Uses

Use macadamias in cookies and as you would any other nut. Freshly shelled, roasted macadamias are probably the premier treat of the nut world.

To toast macadamia nuts: Roast them in a baking pan in a 350°F oven for 10 minutes. Lower the heat to 250°F and let the nuts roast to a golden brown, about another 30 minutes, shaking them occasionally. The flavor of the nuts will be concentrated and enriched.

Trout Macadamia

SERVES 4

Instead of the classic French dish of trout with almonds, substitute unsalted, unprocessed macadamia nuts to create a special dinner.

1¼ cups all-purpose flour
½ teaspoon salt
½ teaspoon freshly ground black pepper
4 small trout, cleaned and gutted
4 tablespoons unsalted butter
2 tablespoons canola oil
1 cup chopped raw macadamia nuts
Juice of 2 lemons
2 tablespoons chopped fresh parsley

1. Preheat the oven to 200°F.

2. Mix the flour, salt, and pepper together on a plate, then dredge the trout in the mixture, shaking off any excess. Heat the butter and oil together in a large skillet over medium heat and cook the trout for about 7 minutes, turning once or twice, until the flesh is white all the way through. Place the trout on a warm platter and set aside in the oven.

3. Add the macadamia nuts to the pan and stir until they are lightly toasted, about 5 minutes. Add the lemon juice and parsley, and cook them for 1 minute, reducing the pan juices slightly to a glaze. Pour this mixture over the trout and serve.

PECAN

SEASON: fall

GOOD VARIETIES: Desirable, Mohawk, Stuart

WHAT TO LOOK FOR: Buy large, plump nuts. Discard any that feel light in the hand.

STORAGE AND PREPARATION TIPS: Once shelled, the nutmeats quickly go rancid and should be frozen if stored.

NUTRITIONAL HIGHLIGHTS: copper, fiber, magnesium, manganese, monounsaturated fat (see chart, page 170), phosphorus, thiamin, zinc

GOES WELL WITH: bourbon, brown sugar, caramel, chocolate, oranges, rum

Pecans grow throughout the South, from the Mid-Atlantic states to the Gulf of Mexico. The trees grow to 100 feet and shower the ground with nuts in the fall. While not as highly flavored as their wild cousin, the hickory nut, pecans have some sterling advantages, especially their thin shells, which let you crack them easily and extract the halves intact.

Organic Advantage

Pecans (and hickory nuts) are native to the regions of the U.S. where they grow and need little protection, and so they are usually grown naturally, if not organically.

Uses

Pecans are a healthy snack, great crushed and used to top breakfast cereals, made into pecan pie, marinated in soy sauce then dried, and candied to add to salads. Hickory nutmeat can be substituted in any recipe calling for pecans and will ratchet the flavor up several notches. Add chopped hickory nuts to your chocolate chip cookies—they are out of this world.

HICKORY NUTS

If you like pecans but have never tasted a hickory nut, wow, do you have a treat coming. Hickory nuts carry something of the same intense hickory flavor as the wood that's used to smoke meats.

I have seen them at farmers' markets in the fall in the East, husks removed but sold in the shell, and a small basket will provide work for several hours because the shells of wild nuts are as hard as bone, and the nutmeat is buried in folds and caverns within. The best way to shell them is to smash them between two bricks, then carefully separate the pieces of nutmeat from the pieces of shell. Rare is the nut that shells out an intact half of a wild hickory nut. Once shelled, they quickly go bad, so eat up!

In addition to regular pecans and hickory nuts, breeders have crossed the hickory with the pecan to create the hiccan. These capture some of the hickory nut's full flavor but have much thinner shells, making it possible to shell each half out in one piece.

Southern Pecan Pie

SERVES 8

If your mama didn't make pecan pie like this, after one taste you'll wish she had. Using hickory nuts or hiccans will make a much more flavorful pie.

1 single crust for a 9-inch pie (see page 116), chilled
1 cup sour cream
1 cup white sugar
4 tablespoons cornstarch
2 large eggs, separated, plus 1 large egg yolk
1/4 teaspoon lemon zest (well scrubbed if not organic)
Pinch of salt
1 cup packed brown sugar
1 cup chopped pecans (or hickory nuts, or hiccans)

1. Preheat the oven to 350°F. Roll out the dough to a circle about 1/8 inch thick and 12 inches in diameter. Transfer to a 9-inch pie pan. Trim the edges 1/2 inch larger than the pan and crimp with the back of a fork. Poke holes here and there with a fork. Chill 20 minutes. Line the shell with wax paper then fill with pie weights, dry beans, or raw rice. Bake for 20 minutes, remove from the oven, remove the weights and wax paper, and let cool.

2. In the top of a double boiler, mix the sour cream, white sugar, cornstarch, egg yolks, lemon zest, and salt. Cook very gently over low heat (the water beneath should not boil) and stir until the mixture thickens enough to coat a spoon. Don't over cook or heat the mixture too quickly or the yolks will

curdle. Pour the thickened mixture into the pie shell.

3. In a large bowl, beat the egg whites until soft peaks form. Add the brown sugar slowly and fold it in. Fold in the pecans. Spread this mixture over the pie filling and bake for about 50 minutes or until lightly browned. Cool before serving.

PEANUT

SEASON: late summer to early fall

GOOD VARIETIES: Red Spanish, Virginia

WHAT TO LOOK FOR: Many imported peanuts are contaminated with cancer-promoting aflatoxin, so look for peanuts grown in the United States. If you can't find a good producer of U.S.-grown organic peanuts, order fresh raw organic peanuts when the new crop comes in (from August to September) from Diamond Organics (www.diamondorganics.com), then freeze them immediately for year-round use.

STORAGE AND PREPARATION TIPS: Peanuts store indefinitely when frozen in a tightly closed container. Thaw and use them raw or roast them.

NUTRITIONAL HIGHLIGHTS: copper, folate, iron, magnesium, monounsaturated fat (see chart, page 170), niacin, phosphorus, zinc

GOES WELL WITH: chicken, chocolate, curries

Peanuts have seized the imagination of cooks (and eaters) around the world since they were discovered in their native Andean lowlands—where the Incas ate them and fashioned gold necklaces and ornaments in their shape.

Like all legumes, peanuts grow colonies of nitrogen-fixing bacteria on their roots, thus enriching the soil they grow in, and so make excellent additions to any garden.

Organic Advantage

Unlike the makers of conventional brands, organic purveyors don't mix their peanut butter with hydrogenated vegetable oils, which include potentially harmful trans fats. They also don't use the kinds of additives and chemicals that make most commercial peanut butters taste like peanut-flavored vegetable shortening. Make sure your peanut butter is from 100 percent organic peanuts and your whole peanuts are certified organic.

Uses

The peanut is a staple ingredient in many cuisines, including West African, Indian, Southeast Asian, and Chinese. Peanuts go beautifully with chicken—in Indian curries, Thai satays with peanut sauce, and Chinese stir-fries with crushed peanuts—and with beef, too. Use crushed roasted peanuts to garnish salads.

Peanuts have reddish-brown skins, which I like to leave on, even when making peanut butter. If you prefer to remove them, freeze the peanuts overnight: the skins will slip off easily.

PEANUT SAFETY

If not stored properly, all peanuts, whether grown organically or conventionally, are prone to develop Aspergillus flavus, a mold that produces a potent carcinogen called aflatoxin. For that reason, bulk peanuts grown and shipped from China—the peanuts often used to make commercial peanut butters—are to be avoided. U.S.-grown peanuts are not as problematic because of the more reliable storage conditions here, but they, too, will develop the mold if stored incorrectly. Organic producers in the United States take great pains to store their crops properly, checking aflatoxin levels to make sure they are below government maximum levels.

Peanuts can be eaten raw, but are delicious roasted and lightly salted.

Peanut oil is mild and used extensively in Chinese stir-frying because it can take high heat without smoking or turning bitter.

To toast peanuts: Place 2 cups of shelled raw peanuts on a baking sheet and roast in a 350°F oven for 15 to 20 minutes. Salt to taste.

To make peanut butter: Place 2 cups roasted peanuts in a blender with 1½ teaspoons of peanut oil, salt to taste, and blend them into a smooth paste. This makes about 1 cup of peanut butter, which you should store in the fridge and use within two to three weeks.

Peanut Salvage Bars

MAKES 8 BARS

They're called salvage bars because they'll save you when you need a burst of energy and nutrition. They're as delicious as they are nutritious.

¼ cup raw or toasted wheat germ
½ cup shelled peanuts
¼ cup shelled sunflower seeds
Salt to taste
2 cups 1-minute rolled oats
2 cups puffed rice cereal
½ cup raisins
½ cup firmly packed brown sugar
½ cup crunchy peanut butter
½ cup pure maple syrup
1 teaspoon vanilla extract
Nonstick cooking spray

1. Preheat the oven to 350°F.
2. If using raw wheat germ, spread it on a baking sheet and toast for a few minutes until fragrant.
3. Spread the peanuts and sunflower seeds in an even layer on separate baking sheets and toast in the oven—the sunflower seeds will take about 6 minutes and the peanuts will take 15 to 20 minutes. Remove and let cool; salt the peanuts lightly.
4. Mix the wheat germ, peanuts, sunflower seeds, oats, puffed rice, and

raisins in a large bowl. In a separate bowl that fits in your microwave, mix the brown sugar, peanut butter, and maple syrup; microwave on high for 2 minutes. Add the vanilla extract and stir until well blended. Pour over the dry ingredients and fold in until everything is evenly coated.

5. Coat an 8-inch square baking pan with nonstick spray and transfer the peanut mixture to the pan. Cover the surface with wax paper and press it down firmly. Let this stand until completely cool, at least an hour. Cut into eight 2 × 4–inch bars.

PINE NUT

SEASON: late summer

GOOD VARIETIES: U.S. pine nuts are from the wild species; no cultivated varieties exist.

WHAT TO LOOK FOR: Check pine nuts carefully, as they rapidly turn rancid. If possible, taste one before buying. Fresh pine nuts will taste clean and sweet; older nuts will have a musty flavor.

STORAGE AND PREPARATION TIPS: Store in a freezer bag in the freezer.

NUTRITIONAL HIGHLIGHTS: copper, folate, magnesium, manganese, monounsaturated fats (see chart, page 170), phosphorus, protein, vitamin E, vitamin K, zinc

GOES WELL WITH: basil, cheese, olive oil

Pine nuts are the edible hard-shelled seeds of certain pine trees. They develop inside pine cones, in the crevasses between the scales. One reason that pine nuts are so expensive is that they defy cultivation, and most are still gathered in the wild.

Pine nuts are very old food, both in Europe and the Americas. They have been harvested around the Mediterranean since biblical times; Roman soldiers brought them north on their forays into northern Europe and the British Isles.

Native Americans relied on pine nuts for millennia as a concentrated source of protein. Then in the 1970s, the U.S. government bulldozed thousands of acres of piñon pines—which produce most of our pine nuts—and ran cattle on the cleared land. The goal was to give the Native American tribes a source of protein. Ironically, the amount of protein that could be obtained per acre from beef cattle didn't approach what could previously have been obtained from harvesting pine nuts.

Organic Advantage

Pine nuts are gathered from the wild, so they are unlikely to have encountered any chemicals.

Uses

Pine nuts are incredibly versatile. Use them ground or whole with meat, fish, and game dishes; in all kinds of desserts, from cakes and pies to puddings;

in stuffings; with vegetables; in sauces; and in soups. (Just don't mix them into polenta or it won't set up firmly.) The classic use for pine nuts is pesto (see recipes, pages 216 and 228).

PISTACHIO

SEASON: mid- to late summer

GOOD VARIETIES: Kerman, Sfax, Sirora

WHAT TO LOOK FOR: Purchase green, undyed pistachios. Domestically grown pistachios are usually sold undyed, while imported kinds are often dyed red.

STORAGE AND PREPARATION TIPS: Store pistachios in an airtight jar in a dark cupboard.

NUTRITIONAL HIGHLIGHTS: calcium, copper, fiber, magnesium, manganese, monounsaturated fat (see chart, page 170), phosphorus, potassium, protein, thiamine, vitamin B_6

GOES WELL WITH: cream, lemon, pork

Pistachios grow wild across the Middle East and central Asia, where they have been eaten since before recorded history and have been cultivated for the last five thousand years. Pistachios from abroad come mostly from Iran, but the more southerly reaches of California's San Joaquin Valley have a prime climate for these trees and produced 346 million pounds of the nuts in 2004 on 104,000 acres. Most of the pistachios you'll find in the United States come from California.

The FDA has named pistachios part of a heart-healthy diet (the nuts are 55 percent unsaturated fat, and only 13 percent saturated fat). This means that eating a regular portion of tree nuts, including pistachios, may lead to the prevention of heart disease. I've been hearing for years what I shouldn't eat, so it's nice to hear that something as crunchy and satisfying as a pistachio is actually good for you. Additionally, pistachios are 18 percent protein, very high in potassium and calcium, and contain the vitamins and minerals mentioned above, among other trace elements. And they're addictive. A single serving (a handful, or about fifty nuts) does contain 200 calories, but you're getting a lot of bang for your buck.

Organic Advantage

Many outlets sell organic pistachios, both grown in California or Nevada and imported. Commercial growers use about a million pounds of pesticides of various kinds on the crop, so luckily organic nuts are widely available.

Uses

Ground pistachios can be used to form a crust on meats and fish and, of course, incorporated into ice cream. But by far the most common way to eat these addictive nuts is out of hand.

Grilled Veggie Burgers

SERVES 6

Yes, you can buy veggie burgers at the store, but how wonderful to make your own—you'll know exactly what's in them. Make a double batch and freeze the patties you won't use right away. Let them thaw through before cooking. The California Pistachio Commission provided this recipe, and the burgers are delish. Serve in buns with burger fixings.

Two 15-ounce cans red kidney beans, rinsed, drained, and mashed
2 cups coarsely grated zucchini
1 cup finely chopped pistachios
1/2 cup dry bread crumbs
1/2 cup freshly grated Romano cheese
1 large egg
1 teaspoon freshly ground black pepper
1/2 teaspoon dried rosemary
1/2 teaspoon dried thyme
1/4 teaspoon salt
1 tablespoon extra-virgin olive oil
1 tablespoon unflavored rice vinegar

Combine the beans, zucchini, pistachios, bread crumbs, cheese, egg, pepper, rosemary, thyme, and salt and mix well. Shape into 6 patties. Whisk together the oil and vinegar, and brush both sides of each patty generously with this dressing. Place the patties in a grill basket with a fine grid. Grill in a covered barbecue for about 5 or 6 minutes, until browned, depending on the heat of the coals. Baste with the dressing and flip the grill basket, then cook another 5 or 6 minutes.

WALNUT

SEASON: fall

GOOD VARIETIES: Franquette, Hansen, Hartley Himalaya, Payne

WHAT TO LOOK FOR: Walnuts rapidly turn rancid, so buy them still in the shell or look for nutmeats sold refrigerated or frozen. A paint-like odor indicates they have turned and should be discarded.

STORAGE AND PREPARATION TIPS: Store shelled nuts in airtight bags in the refrigerator or freezer. Unshelled walnuts will stay fresh from their fall harvest until late winter or early spring if kept in a cool, dry place.

NUTRITIONAL HIGHLIGHTS: antioxidants, copper, fiber, magnesium, manganese, monounsaturated fat (see chart, page 170), omega-3 fatty acid, phosphorus, protein, thiamin, vitamin B_6

GOES WELL WITH: blue cheese, mushrooms, pork, sherry

We call them English walnuts and the English call them Persian walnuts. These are cold-sensitive walnuts—although there is a similar type called Carpathian walnuts that can weather winter temperatures down to 35°F below zero—and so most walnuts grown in the United States are grown in California, especially the Central Valley. There once was a large

BLACK WALNUTS

There's a saying among the Pennsylvania Dutch that the trees of the black walnut will protect a home from lightning. A 75-foot black walnut tree grew beside our 150-year-old stone farmhouse in Pennsylvania. One June night I took the family to the movies, and when we emerged, a huge flickering thunderstorm was moving away toward the east. When we got home, we saw that the tree had been shattered by a bolt of lightning. The limbs had all fallen, missing the house completely, although the trunk grew only 10 feet from the front porch. The tragedy of losing our sheltering tree—tempered by knowing it had done its job—was compounded when there were no black walnuts in the fall.

We used to gather up the nuts in early fall and lay their green, pebbly husks in the tire ruts of our dirt driveway, driving over them for several days. Black walnuts are so hard that the tires never cracked them. But they did squish open the green husks, after which I could pry out the nuts with a knife. We'd place the nuts in a basket, wash them down with a strong jet from the hose, then leave them in the shed to dry and cure until late fall. Then we'd all sit out on a large rock and smash the nuts open with bricks, picking out the nutmeats and eating our fill on the spot. It was hard work for our young ones, but they relished it nevertheless.

Black walnuts have an intense, robust, more volatile flavor that is to regular English walnuts what hickory nuts are to bland pecans. They have no cholesterol, very little saturated fat, lots of polyunsaturated fat, and some monounsaturated fat. They contain iron and other trace minerals. Black walnuts can be used in any recipe calling for English walnuts, and their unique flavor stands up better to cooking. Although some black walnuts have been cultivated to produce thinner shells (allowing complete halves to be picked out) most black walnut nutmeats on the market are from wild trees. This means the nutmeat is natural, unprocessed, and not sprayed, even if not strictly organic.

Look for black walnuts sold by the Hammons Products Company of Stockton, Missouri, (see Sources, page 287), which purchases millions of wild nuts from 250 locations in thirteen Eastern states. They are available for sale on the company's Web site (www.black-walnuts.com).

walnut production in Napa and Sonoma counties during Prohibition, but with the return of legal wine, growers eventually replaced walnut acres with wine grapes.

Organic Advantage

Until recently, organic walnut production was held back by the walnut husk fly. It could destroy a walnut crop, and there were no organic controls available to stop it. Agricultural researchers have come up with a method of spraying walnut trees with kaolin, a natural clay that turns trees white, prevents the husk fly from penetrating the nuts, prevents sunscald, and scatters enough light onto the leaves to hasten ripening. This has allowed the development of an organic walnut supply, giving farmers the chance to increase their income by 50 percent over what they make raising conventional walnuts (organic nuts bring a 50 percent premium over less expensive conventional nuts).

Uses

Thin-shelled English walnuts are indispensable in salads, crushed as part of crusty coatings for anything from meats to cheesecake, broken up over ice cream, and used in all sorts of sweet and savory dishes.

One reason English walnuts are so versatile is that they have a mild taste that seldom interferes with other flavors in a dish. Toasted, they increase in flavor, but not greatly. Candied, they become wonderful additions to salads and desserts (see recipe). And walnut oil is super for dressing salads—and for oil painters: Michelangelo used it to thin his paints when working on the Sistine Chapel.

Serve toasted or raw whole walnuts on top of breakfast cereals, tossed into salads or on pastas, in risottos, sprinkled into stir-fries, and as a healthy between-meal snack. Chopped, they can be applied to a frosted cake or muffin, used on top of pastries, and added to waffles. Ground walnuts make an excellent coating for fried fish and can be added to bread doughs.

One last note: When chopping walnuts in a blender or food processor, don't overdo it, because the oil in the walnuts will soon reduce the pieces to a paste.

Hot Candied Walnuts

MAKES ABOUT 2 DOZEN CANDIED WALNUT HALVES

Candied walnuts are best when they have a little spicy heat to them, which this recipe provides. They're great in salads.

1 cup walnut halves
1/4 cup sugar
1/4 teaspoon ground cayenne
1/8 teaspoon salt

Place a large skillet over medium heat and when it's hot, add the walnuts, sugar, cayenne, and salt. Shake the skillet constantly until the sugar melts and the walnuts are thoroughly coated, 3 to 5 minutes. Pour the mixture onto a greased cookie sheet and set it aside to cool. When the mixture has cooled completely, store in a tightly covered jar.

SEEDS

FLAXSEED

SEASON: summer

WHAT TO LOOK FOR: Check both fresh flaxseed and flaxseed oil for the expiration date.

STORAGE AND PREPARATION TIPS: Store flaxseed in the freezer and flaxseed oil in the refrigerator.

NUTRITIONAL HIGHLIGHTS: fiber, magnesium, manganese, omega-3 fatty acid

Flaxseed is more of a food supplement than a tummy-filling food. A tablespoon of flaxseed daily, either well-chewed or ground in a coffee grinder (to break open the hard seed coat that would otherwise prevent the grains from being digested) provides the daily requirement of alpha-linolenic acid, one of the essential omega-3 fatty acids that help reduce LDL (bad cholesterol). Its soluble fiber levels have been shown to reduce triglyceride levels and blood pressure.

Flaxseed is of special benefit to women. It provides lignan, a plant source of the female hormone estrogen, which is thought to inhibit the onset of estrogen-stimulated breast cancer. Flaxseed oil is used by menopausal women to help balance hormone levels. One teaspoon per day is enough.

Uses

Flaxseed oil should always be used raw, as cooking destroys some of its health benefits. Tasty ways to incorporate flaxseed into your diet include mixing ground flaxseed into fruit smoothies and sprinkling it on cold cereals. Use raw flaxseed oil on salads, in dips, and in homemade mayonnaise—or take it straight up.

PUMPKIN SEED

SEASON: fall

GOOD VARIETIES: Because pumpkin seeds from Trick-or-Treat and Triple Treat pumpkin varieties have no hulls, the entire seed can be eaten.

WHAT TO LOOK FOR: Seeds should be dry, fresh, and olive green.

STORAGE AND PREPARATION TIPS: Store in the freezer.

NUTRITIONAL HIGHLIGHTS: B vitamins, copper, iron, magnesium, manganese, protein, phosphorus, vitamin K, zinc

GOES WELL WITH: brown sugar, cheese, olive oil

Organic pumpkin seeds are easy to find and sold loose at most organic food stores. They can also be purchased raw from organic purveyors. Organic seeds can also be found roasted or fried, sometimes drenched in some kind of salty flavoring, such as tamari. I like to buy raw, hulled, unflavored organic pumpkin seeds and roast them myself.

Besides the seeds, you can find raw organic pumpkin seed oil made in France. It has a lightly nutty taste and is rich in omega-3 and omega-6 essential fatty acids, along with zinc and other vitamins and minerals.

Organic Advantage

Pumpkins, being members of the squash family, are beset with the mildew and insect problems common to other squash. Conventional growers use chemicals to counteract the squash bugs, stem borers, cucumber beetles, and mildews that attack the plants. Organic growers have nontoxic, nonchemical methods of foiling all of the diseases and pests that plague pumpkins.

Uses

Raw pumpkin seeds have a chewy texture and a slightly vegetal flavor. Grind them up and add them to soups or stews as a nutritious thickener and to breads and sweet rolls to boost their nutrition. Roasted, they become rich and nutty, with a crunchier texture that works well in savory dishes and soups, in trail mix, or simply by themselves as a snack. Toasting releases their flavor. If you like peanut butter and jelly sandwiches, vary your routine with fresh, raw organic pumpkin seed butter, available from Rejuvenate Foods (www.rejuvenative.com); see Sources, page 287.

To toast pumpkin seeds: Spread seeds in a single layer on a cookie sheet and cook for 5 to 7 minutes in a 350°F oven until they darken slightly and develop an irresistibly nutty flavor. Salt them to taste, if desired.

Fish fry: Make a great coating for fried fish by placing 2 tablespoons of toasted sesame seeds, 1/2 cup of toasted pumpkin seeds, 1 1/2 cups of fresh bread crumbs made from crustless bread, and salt to taste in a blender or food processor. Blend until the pumpkin seeds are coarsely chopped. Ocean fish such as Pacific halibut or Dover sole and farmed freshwater fish such as catfish and tilapia fillets have mild flavors that won't interfere with the flavor of the coating. Dredge the fish in flour, dip it in beaten eggs, then coat with the pumpkin seed mixture. Fry in canola or olive oil for a few minutes on each side, until the coating is golden and the fish is just done. Serve the fish with lemon wedges.

Salad dressing: Make a nutritious salad dressing by whisking together 4 tablespoons of pumpkin seed oil and 2 tablespoons of freshly squeezed lemon juice, then add 1 teaspoon (or less, to taste) of fleur de sel, 1/2 teaspoon dried basil, 1/2 teaspoon dried oregano, 1 clove garlic

SPROUTING YOUR SEEDS AND BEANS

The chemical changes that occur when seeds and beans sprout change starch to complex sugars and activate powerful enzymes. Sprouting seeds, grains, and legumes (with the exception of soybeans and kidney beans—see Beware of Raw Kidney Beans and Soybeans, page 193) greatly increases their vitamin content. For example, the vitamin A content of sprouted mung beans is two and a half times higher than the dried bean, and some beans have more than eight times as much vitamin A after being sprouted. The vitamin B_{12} in wheat berries quadruples, other B vitamins increase three to twelve times, and the vitamin E content triples.

Dried seeds, grains, and legumes, while rich in protein and complex carbohydrates, contain no vitamin C. But after sprouting, they contain around 20 milligrams per 3.5 ounces. Also, if grown in decent soil or taken from your own garden, seeds, grains, and legumes will be high in minerals—so your sprouts will be an excellent source of minerals as well as vitamins. Adzukis, chickpeas, whole lentils, marrowfat peas, and mung beans can all be sprouted.

mashed through a garlic press, and a few grinds of black pepper. Whisk until everything is well blended. Store in the fridge for up to a week.

BEANS

DRIED BEANS AND OTHER LEGUMES

WHAT TO LOOK FOR: Make sure the beans are dry, hard, and slightly shiny.

STORAGE AND PREPARATION TIPS: Dried beans keep for up to a year in a closed container in a cool, dark place. Before using dried beans, soak them in water to cover for 8 hours or overnight (mung beans can soak for 4 hours; lentils need no soaking). Before using canned beans, which are already cooked, drain them and rinse well to remove the salty liquid they come in.

NUTRITIONAL HIGHLIGHTS: fiber, folate, iron, magnesium, phytochemicals, potassium, protein

GO WELL WITH: bacon, cheese, chiles, garlic, onions, rice, tomatoes

The category of dried beans covers a lot of ground. The common field bean (Phaseolus vulgaris), includes cannellini beans, kidney beans, French beans, navy beans, black beans, pinto beans, and more. And each of these categories carries many different cultivated varieties.

In addition to common field beans there are three other common species of bean, which include the tepary bean, runner bean, and lima (or butter) bean. Another whole group of beans falls into a separate genus (Vigna), which includes adzuki beans, fava beans, mung beans, black-eyed peas, and yard-long beans. Finally, there are ten other genera that include jack beans, chickpeas, soybeans, lentils, velvet beans, and winged beans.

Beans are excellent vegetarian sources of protein. Soybeans (covered more extensively in the next entry) contain the highest, at 35 percent protein by weight, followed by French green lentils (24 percent), but most other dried beans contain nearly that much. Unlike meat, however, legumes do not contain all the necessary amino acids and must be supplemented with other foods, notably cereals, to make them complete and fully nourishing to humans. Mexicans mix corn and beans in their cooking, and many tribes of the pre-Columbian Americas ate a combination of corn, beans, and squash—called the Three Sisters—as their staple food. Many dishes combine beans and rice, such as New Orleans' red beans and rice.

Organic Advantage

Beans are subject to a wide variety of pests and diseases, but organic farmers have nontoxic solutions for them.

A field or patch of beans not only provides good food but also improves the soil. As legumes, beans are colonized by nitrogen-fixing bacteria. After the beans are harvested, organic farmers turn the bean plants into the soil; as they decompose, the plants enrich the soil with organic matter, along with the nitrogen and other nutrients present in their tissues. Bean plants are also choice additions to any compost pile and stimulate the thermophilic bacteria that convert plant matter into valuable fertilizer.

Uses

Different beans are favored in different regions of the world. Lentils are a staple in India, soybeans in China and Japan, black beans and pigeon peas in the Caribbean, kidney beans in North America, and so on.

Add any cooked beans to soups and stews; make chili con (or sin—"without") carne; sprinkle a few in a salad; use chickpeas to make hummus (see recipe, page 194); use white beans for minestrone soup or in cassoulet, or mix them with leftover rice, some minced garlic and tomato paste to make a quick side dish.

While canned beans are convenient, they don't taste as good as beans you soak and cook yourself. And the aroma of a pot of beans simmering on the stove is evocative of home for many. If flatulence is a worry for you, add a pinch of anise, caraway, dill, or fennel seeds to the pot.

To cook dried beans: After soaking beans 8 hours or overnight, discard the soaking water and replace it with fresh water at a ratio of three parts water to one part beans. (Don't salt the water—this toughens the beans; you can add salt after the beans have finished cooking.) Bring the water to a boil and boil for 10 minutes uncovered, then reduce the heat and simmer covered for 1½ to 2 hours, skimming off any foam from the surface. Be careful the beans don't boil dry and scorch. Add more water if necessary.

Exceptions to cooking dried beans in this manner:

- Boil dry soybeans for 1 hour, then simmer for 2 hours.
- Simmer fava beans for 2 to 2½ hours.
- Simmer black beans and lima beans for just 1 to 1½ hours.
- Bring lentils to a boil, then cover, reduce the heat, and simmer for 25 minutes.
- Bring mung beans to a boil, then cover, reduce the heat, and simmer for 1 hour.

BEWARE OF RAW KIDNEY BEANS AND SOYBEANS It's not safe to eat raw or uncooked kidney and soybeans, even in their dried state. Hemagglutinin is a substance in raw beans that causes red blood cells to clump together and prevents the transport of oxygen to the body's tissues. As few as four raw beans have caused serious hemagglutinin poisoning. Hemagglutinin is completely destroyed by high heat cooking—hence the 10 minutes of rapid boiling required before simmering. Slow cookers do not reach high enough temperatures, so kidney and soybeans should be boiled for 10 minutes before being added to these appliances. Kidney and soybeans must never be sprouted.

Mexican Refried Beans

MAKES ABOUT 1 QUART

Refried beans are a tasty way to start putting together a burrito. Smear some of the bean paste on the tortilla. Or serve them as a side dish along with rice and salad with grilled meat.

1 pound dried pinto beans
1 medium onion, minced
2 cloves garlic, minced
¼ teaspoon crushed red pepper flakes
¼ teaspoon salt
3 tablespoons lard
3 tablespoons bacon fat (or substitute 6 tablespoons canola oil for these two fats)
4 ounces grated Jack cheese (about 1 cup)

1. Soak the beans overnight, then place in a large pot along with 2 quarts fresh water, the onion, garlic, and red pepper flakes. Bring to a boil, boil for 10 minutes, reduce the heat, and simmer for 1½ hours. Drain the cooked beans and reserve the cooking liquid.

Add the salt. Mash the beans with a potato masher—do not use a blender or food processor.

2. In a large skillet, heat the lard and bacon fat (or oil) over medium-high heat until the fat just begins to smoke, or the oil sizzles if a small drop of water touches it. Add the mashed beans, being careful not to let any spatter on you. Reduce the heat to medium-low and cook, stirring constantly, until the fat or oil is absorbed. Add the reserved cooking liquid a little at a time to thin the beans just until a moist consistency is reached.

3. Add the cheese and cook 15 minutes longer until the cheese has melted and been incorporated completely.

The Best Hummus You've Ever Tasted

MAKES ABOUT 2 CUPS

Hummus is the thick, addictive spread you scoop up with torn bits of pita bread and eat along with tabbouleh. Organic chickpeas—also called garbanzo beans—are available both as dried beans and canned in water. Several sources also sell organic tahini—raw sesame seeds ground to an oily paste.

Chickpeas contain low glycemic carbohydrates: instead of spiking your body's insulin levels, they slowly release sustained energy to the body and keep insulin levels steady, which keeps your blood sugar levels moderated instead of jumping all over the place.

When soaked chickpeas and tahini get together, a synergy of flavor makes the result irresistible. The following recipe is from chef Mark Stark of Monti's Rotisserie and Bar in Santa Rosa, California. His additions of spices and harissa to the basic recipe give this hummus a flavor surge. Serve it with pita bread.

1 cup dried chickpeas or 2 cups cooked or canned chickpeas, drained
2 teaspoons cumin seeds
5 cloves garlic, chopped coarsely
3 tablespoons freshly squeezed lemon juice
3 tablespoons tahini
1/2 teaspoon Harissa (page 64)
Pinch of salt
3 tablespoons extra-virgin olive oil
1/2 teaspoon minced fresh parsley

1. If you're starting with dried beans, soak them in cold water overnight. Drain, place in a heavy pot, and cover with fresh water to a depth of 3 inches. Bring to a full boil and boil for 10 minutes, then reduce the heat, and simmer, covered, 1 to 2 hours, until they are uniformly tender. Cool and drain. If using canned chickpeas, rinse them in fresh water.

2. Toast the cumin seeds in a small dry skillet over medium heat until fragrant, just a minute or two. Set aside to cool, then grind in a spice or coffee grinder, or with a mortar and pestle.

3. Place the chickpeas, garlic, lemon juice, and 1/4 cup of water in a blender

and puree until smooth. Add the cumin, tahini, harissa, and salt, and blend until incorporated. Place the hummus in an shallow oval bowl and with the back of a tablespoon, make a depression in the center. Fill the depression with the olive oil. Sprinkle the parsley over the top.

SOYBEAN

SEASON: summer

GOOD VARIETIES: black-skinned varieties such as Black Jet and Kuromame

WHAT TO LOOK FOR: Buy hard, dry, blemish-free beans.

STORAGE AND PREPARATION TIPS: Store dry soybeans in an airtight jar in a dark cupboard. Soak beans overnight before cooking.

NUTRITIONAL HIGHLIGHTS: calcium, fiber, folate, iron, magnesium, manganese, phosphorus, potassium, protein, riboflavin, thiamin, vitamin C

GOES WELL WITH: bacon, cheese, ham hocks

Soybeans have been cultivated in China for at least five thousand years, but in America they've been grown in quantity only since World War II, when they were used as a meat extender during wartime rationing. About that time, margarine (which is frequently made with soybean oil) also came on the scene as a supposedly healthy butter substitute.

Nowadays, soybeans are used in all sorts of food products to add nutrition and texture, and as extenders. They're grown across the United States as part of a typical corn-and-beans crop rotation that supports dairy and meat farms in the form of animal feed.

Soybeans are fabulously nutritious, containing 30 to 50 percent protein—more than any other plant product and more than most meat. But because they are legumes, the protein is not complete (that is, it doesn't contain all the essential amino acids). Eating soybeans with rice or whole grain pasta makes a complete protein.

Higher intake of soy foods has been linked with reduced incidence of heart disease and some forms of cancer, particularly breast, lung, and prostate cancers, as well as leukemia. Studies on humans have established that soy consumption is significantly associated with reduced levels of blood cholesterol.

Organic Advantage

Most American soybeans are grown using a wide range of agricultural chemicals, and genetic engineers have been working on them, too. Under organic production, soybeans are usually grown as part of a crop rotation that includes grains such as wheat, oats, or corn, and legumes like alfalfa. By only growing soybeans every third or fourth season, the life cycles of many soybean pests are interrupted.

Uses

While mature yellow soybeans remain tough even after long cooking and have a bitter, beany flavor, you're more likely to encounter whole soybeans in their immature, green form, when they're called edamame. Boil the pods in heavily salted water for a Japanese-style treat.

Of course, we mostly encounter soybeans in one of their processed forms that have developed over centuries to render the beans tasty and digestible. There is soy milk, which can be used as a milk substitute, or processed further into tofu. Cooked soybeans can also be inoculated with a mold that ferments them, producing the compact white cake called tempeh, which is often roasted, grilled, or fried like meat.

Soybeans can also be fermented into soy sauce, Chinese black beans, or miso, a paste which, dissolved in hot broth, is used to make miso soup.

Soybeans are also the world's chief source of cooking oil. Fourteen to 20 percent of the bean is oil, mostly unsaturated, containing good amounts of healthful linoleic and oleic acids.

Boiled and Salted Edamame

Salted edamame are a common Japanese bar snack and a popular appetizer at Japanese restaurants in the United States. You can boil them whole, pod and all, or just boil the frozen shelled beans—they'll cook in the same time either way.

Edamame, fresh or frozen
Salt

Bring a large pot of heavily salted water (it should taste like seawater) to a boil. Add the edamame and boil 7 to 8 minutes, then drain and cool. If using beans in the pod, nick open one end of each pod and squeeze the beans out. Salt the beans to taste and serve hot or cold.

GRAINS

BUCKWHEAT

SEASON: summer

WHAT TO LOOK FOR: Buckwheat kernels should be perfectly dry and hard.

STORAGE AND PREPARATION TIPS: Grind buckwheat into flour, or buy buckwheat flour at the market and store it in the freezer.

NUTRITIONAL HIGHLIGHTS: fiber, magnesium, manganese, protein

GOES WELL WITH: butter, eggs, maple syrup

Unlike most grains, which are grasses (wheat, oats, barley, etc.), buckwheat seeds are the fruits of an annual herbaceous plant related to the silver lace vine and the Japanese knotweed. Buckwheat seeds consist of an outer layer or hull, an inner layer that is the seed coat (or middling), a starchy endosperm, and the germ in the center. Most of the buckwheat sold in the United States is milled and sold as buckwheat flour. (Milling removes the hull and part of the seed.) Buckwheat can also be roasted, in which case it's called kasha or groats.

Organic Advantage

Buckwheat is one of the chief "green manures" used by organic farmers and gardeners. It is sown thickly on a plot of tired ground previously used for a crop that takes up a lot of nutrients from the soil. When it flowers, bees love it and make buckwheat honey. If allowed to go to seed, we get the nutritious buckwheat seeds. But most farmers plow it into the soil just after it flowers for its strong fertilizing and soil-rejuvenating powers.

Uses

Buckwheat kasha is boiled to make porridge. Buckwheat flour can be used to enrich wheat flour in pancake batter to make buckwheat pancakes, as well as in breads and other baked goods. Use 2 tablespoons buckwheat flour per cup of wheat flour. Darker flour contains some of the seed coat (which is high in protein), while lighter flour has had most or all of the seed coat milled away.

OAT

SEASON: summer through fall

WHAT TO LOOK FOR: Oatmeal of any type (steel cut, rolled, or "instant") should smell of fresh, clean oats.

STORAGE AND PREPARATION TIPS: Store oatmeal in a closed container in a dark cupboard.

NUTRITIONAL HIGHLIGHTS: fiber, magnesium, protein, selenium

GOES WELL WITH: brown sugar, chocolate, cream, molasses, peanuts

Oats, like wheat and barley, are a member of the grass family, with very nutritious seed high in fiber.

It's a cliché that a steaming bowl of oatmeal makes a healthy, hearty, stick-to-the-ribs breakfast—and with good reason. Oats have the highest percentage of protein of any grain (12 to 20 percent). Their fat content (5 to 9 percent) is the highest among the cereal grains, and it's almost entirely unsaturated fat. Oats contain the most calories of any grain, and are among the grains highest in soluble fiber (only rye and whole wheat have more). Oat bran, where the fiber is concentrated, is the richest source of soluble dietary fiber.

Oats have always had a split personality, appreciated by some as a useful food staple, and shunned by others. The Greeks made a sweet called plakous from oat flour, honey, and cheese, but the Romans considered oats barbarian food until they conquered Celtic Britain, where they found oats to be an easy-to-grow and nutritious grain. Oats have been identified with the British Isles ever since, but only in Wales, Ireland, and Scotland. The English consider oats to be fodder for horses.

Most oats are grown in northerly climates, like those found in the upper tier of the United States, lower Canada, Scandinavia, Germany, Poland, and especially Russia, because they are a cool-season, moisture-loving crop. Often oats are planted in the fall as a cover crop to hold the soil together during fierce winters, after which they awaken early in the spring to produce a crop before the heat of summer.

Organic Advantage

Like the other cereal grains, oats are part of a good, organic crop rotation, along with corn and a legume. They are a relatively trouble-free crop to grow.

QUAKER OATS

If you are an aficionado of oats, or just curious, travel to Akron, Ohio, and stay at the Crowne Plaza Quaker Square Hotel. The hotel is built into the original grain silos of the Quaker Oats Company, which invented rolled oats in the 1870s. The lobby is full of rolled oat memorabilia. This was an extraordinary advance for the consumption of oats. The folks at Quaker took steel-cut oats—the chunks of the whole oat grains that take 40 minutes to cook—steamed them to stabilize the fats and oils so they wouldn't turn rancid, then sent them through roller mills that flattened them into oat flakes, which cooked up in just five minutes. The company still sells tons of them, and they're still just as good for you now as they were a century ago.

Uses

Besides making fantastic porridge, oats can be used to thicken stews, add texture to cookies and pastries, and enrich bread dough. (By the way, those steel-cut oats from Ireland and Scotland don't have to take 40 minutes to cook. Soak them in water overnight and you'll be able to cook them in 10 minutes after draining them the following morning.)

Oats are also used to make a number of drinks. The Japanese sometimes use oats instead of rice to make a sweet kind of sake called amazake. Oatmeal stout, a dark, viscous beer, is made with 5 to 10 percent oats in the grist, the grains used to brew the stout. It doesn't impart a taste of oats, but does add an appealing, creamy texture.

Oat Smoothie

Here's a fabulously delicious way to get a jump start in the morning—and much of your daily requirement of fiber.

4 cups cold water
2 cups cooked oatmeal
1 ripe banana, peeled
1 tablespoon pure maple syrup
1 teaspoon vanilla extract
Pinch of salt

Place all the ingredients in a blender and blend until entirely smooth. Refrigerate; shake before drinking.

QUINOA AND AMARANTH

SEASON: summer

WHAT TO LOOK FOR: Quinoa and amaranth are available not only in grain form but also as cereal and flour; there's even a butter substitute made with amaranth oil.

STORAGE AND PREPARATION TIPS: Store both grains in airtight containers in a dark cupboard. Rinse quinoa well before using.

NUTRITIONAL HIGHLIGHTS:

Quinoa: copper, fiber, iron, magnesium, manganese, niacin, phosphorus, potassium, protein, riboflavin, vitamin E, zinc

Amaranth: copper, fiber, iron, magnesium, manganese, phosphorus, potassium, protein, riboflavin, vitamin E, zinc

GO WELL WITH: cream, fruits, sugar, maple syrup, cinnamon

Quinoa (pronounced keen-wah) and amaranth are two of the most nutritious foods on the planet. Unlike most grains (such as wheat, corn, and barley), whose protein stores lack the key amino acid lysine, the protein in quinoa and amaranth is a complete protein, with all the amino acids needed for building muscle, tendons, and other tissue. That's why they are grouped together here. The World Health Organization has rated the quality of their proteins as at least equivalent to that of milk, which makes them invaluable for people on vegan and vegetarian diets. Amaranth is also high in calcium (it has twice that of milk) and three times the fiber of wheat.

Both grains are seeds of annual herbaceous plants. Quinoa grows under harsh climatic and soil conditions. It has been cultivated in the Peruvian Andes for over five thousand years. Because of its nutritional value, the Incas called quinoa the mother grain. Today, most quinoa is imported from South America, although some is grown at high altitudes in the Colorado Rockies. Amaranth was originally cultivated farther north in modern-day Mexico by the Aztecs, who called it the food of the gods, because of its high nutrient content—and because it would grow just about anywhere (see The Food of the Gods, page 200).

Organic Advantage

Both grains share vigor and resistance to pests, and so there's little need to use pesticides when growing them. But that's not to say they're necessarily grown organically. Look for grain that is certified organic to ensure that no artificial fertilizers or toxic chemicals are used to grow them.

Uses

Quinoa cooks up to a light, fluffy texture, with a crunchy "tail" formed by the germ. To cook quinoa, bring 2 cups

THE FOOD OF THE GODS

I first heard about amaranth back in the mid-1970s when I was an editor at Organic Gardening magazine. The magazine publisher, Bob Rodale, returned to the office one day from a trip to Mexico and said he discovered a grain called amaranth that the Aztecs called the food of the gods.

Bob thought it could make a dent in world hunger and be useful for farmers in difficult climates. Rodale Press had recently purchased a 300-acre farm in the Pennsylvania Dutch country, and Bob hired scientists to search the world for varieties of amaranth to start a center for the plant's cultivation and dispersal to farmers worldwide. We soon had the world's largest collection of amaranth varieties. The research center staff distributed amaranth seeds to farmers around the globe and published many scientific papers on its cultivation. Today amaranth is considered one of the chief nutritional grains of the world.

of water (salted if desired) to a boil, add 1 cup of quinoa, reduce the heat to low, and simmer, covered, for 15 to 17 minutes, until grains become translucent and tails emerge. A light toasting in a dry skillet over medium heat (about 5 minutes, stirring frequently) gives the grain a rich, toasty flavor.

To cook amaranth, follow the same procedure but use 2 cups of water for every 1 cup of amaranth and simmer, uncovered, for 25 minutes, until most of the liquid has been absorbed; the texture will be slightly crunchy. Both quinoa and amaranth can also be popped like popcorn (see Amaranth Popcakes, at right).

Quinoa and amaranth flour can be combined with all-purpose flour to give a nutritional boost to breads, muffins, pancakes, cookies, and as a thickener in sauces. If making a yeast bread, use 1/2 cup of amaranth flour for every 2 cups of all-purpose flour. You can use up to twice the amount of amaranth flour in pancakes, muffins and cookies.

Quinoa Pilaf

SERVES 4

You'll be surprised at the delicacy of the texture and intensity of flavor that quinoa lends to this Moroccan-style pilaf. Serve it as the side dish for roast chicken—or better yet, cut a whole roast chicken into quarters and serve them on top of the pilaf so some of the chicken juices percolate down.

1 cup quinoa grain

2 tablespoons extra-virgin olive oil, plus extra for the casserole

1/3 cup blanched whole almonds

1 cup minced onion

1/2 cup minced carrot
1/2 teaspoon ground cinnamon
3 cups chicken stock
1/3 cup golden raisins
2 teaspoons freshly grated orange zest (well scrubbed if not organic)
1/4 teaspoon ground cayenne

1. Rinse the quinoa thoroughly until the water runs clear. Preheat the oven to 375°F.

2. Lightly oil a 1½-quart covered casserole. Place the olive oil in a skillet on medium-high heat. When hot, add the almonds and sauté for about 2 minutes, until they become golden and fragrant. Add the onions, carrots, and cinnamon, and cook for about 3 minutes, stirring occasionally. Add the quinoa and stir thoroughly so that all the little grains are coated with oil; cook 1 minute. Add the chicken stock, raisins, orange zest, and cayenne and bring the mixture to a boil.

3. Pour this hot mixture into the casserole, cover, and bake for 45 minutes. When done, turn the pilaf onto a platter.

Amaranth Popcakes

SERVES 4

These pancakes awaken the taste buds and satisfy that craving for a little crunchiness as it boosts the protein power of the pancakes. Let the kids watch you pop the amaranth.

1/2 cup whole amaranth grain
1 cup all-purpose flour
1/2 teaspoon salt
1 tablespoon baking powder
1 large egg
1 cup milk
1/4 cup canola oil

1. To pop the amaranth, heat a large dry skillet over medium-high heat, then pour in the amaranth grain in a single layer. Shake the skillet so the grains don't burn. They'll soon start to pop. When the popping slows and is nearly finished, remove from the heat and pour the popped amaranth into a bowl and reserve.

2. Combine the flour, baking powder, and salt and mix until well blended. In a separate bowl, beat the egg into the milk, then pour this into the dry ingredients and lightly fold them together, drizzling the oil into the batter as you do so. Fold in the popped amaranth. You don't have to beat the batter smooth—a little lumpiness is fine. If it's too thick, add a little more milk or water.

3. Heat a well-oiled skillet over medium heat. When hot, ladle in ½ cupfuls of batter and turn once when the bubbles that arise consistently form holes that retain their shape. There's an old saying, "The first child is like the first pancake," so don't worry if the first one is a "learning experience."

RICE

SEASON: late summer or fall

GOOD VARIETIES: See below.

WHAT TO LOOK FOR: Look for grain that is unbroken and silky looking. It should be dry, with no clumping.

STORAGE AND PREPARATION TIPS: Store rice in a closed container in a dark place. In humid climates, tie a teaspoon of salt in a paper tissue and add it to the rice jar to keep the rice dry.

NUTRITIONAL HIGHLIGHTS:

> **Brown rice:** fiber, magnesium, manganese, phosphorus, selenium
>
> **White rice:** folate, iron, thiamin

GOES WELL WITH: cinnamon, curry powder, nuts, saffron

Rice, a member of the grass family, covers about 10 percent of the world's arable land, an area second in size only to the land used to grow wheat. It grows in semitropical and tropical areas and is the subject of intense research because it is the staple food of so many people. In many countries, especially tropical regions with high rainfall, rice is the chief source of calories, carbohydrates, and protein. Although its protein content is not particularly high (6 to 7 percent), it is almost a complete protein, lacking only the amino acid lysine; its complement of B vitamins (at least in brown rice) is excellent.

Worldwide there are forty thousand different varieties of rice. They include unmilled brown rice in long-, medium-, and short-grain varieties, plus aromatic rices such as basmati and jasmine. Here are some of the most commonly found varieties in the United States, along with cooking instructions for each:

RICE, BROWN AND WHITE

Whole-grain rice is naturally brown; it turns white only after processing. White rice is lighter and many prefer its taste. But when the grain's bran and germ are milled away to produce white rice, much of the fiber and many of the minerals and vitamins are lost.

In places such as India, where huge populations depend on rice for the bulk of their calories, brown rice is parboiled—steeped in hot water, then steamed and dried—before being milled into white rice. During the heating, some of the B vitamins and minerals move into the interior of the rice grains, improving them nutritionally compared with ordinary white rice.

Arborio rice: A plump, medium-grain rice with a characteristic white dot in its center, Arborio rice has an enormous capacity to soak up liquids as it's cooking, making it perfect for risottos. It's also used in paellas. Cook like medium-grain brown rice, page 204, or make risotto.

Basmati rice: Its long, slender grains don't swell much when cooked, but they do elongate. This aromatic rice gives off a beautiful, nutty aroma. It's great for side dishes or as a base for light vegetable stir-fries and medleys. To cook, place rice grains in twice their volume of water, bring to a boil, reduce the heat, cover, and cook for 15 minutes. Brown basmati rice will take about 20 to 25 minutes to finish.

Converted or parboiled rice: Parboiling or steaming rice is a technique, first developed in India, to improve its nutritional content. (Historically it prevented the thiamine or vitamin B_1 deficiency disease called beriberi.) The process gelatinizes the starch, rendering the grains extra fluffy and separate. Do not rinse this rice. To cook, place the rice in twice its volume of water, bring to a boil, reduce the heat, cover, and cook for 15 minutes.

Enriched rice: This is white rice that has had vitamins or minerals added back after they've been milled away with the bran and germ. Do not rinse it for that reason. To cook, add the rice to twice its volume of water, bring to a boil, reduce the heat, cover, and cook for 15 minutes.

Glutinous (sticky) rice: Sticky rice comes in long-, medium-, and short-grain varieties. When cooked, the grains stick together, making the rice easy to eat with chopsticks. It's great for making sushi and for the basic rice that goes under Asian stews and stir-fries. Soak overnight and cook in an equal volume of water for 12 minutes.

Instant rice: Instant rice has been completely precooked, then dehydrated. Don't rinse it, as nutritive elements have usually been added back. Rehydrate according to the package directions.

Jasmine rice: Jasmine rice is the perfect base for Thai food. Its aromatic steam, lovely texture, and fluffiness make it ideal under curries. To cook, place it in twice its volume of water, bring to a boil, reduce the heat, cover, and cook for 15 minutes. Brown jasmine rice takes 30 minutes.

Long-grain brown rice: The rice looks pleasantly golden brown after it's cooked, and the grains are fluffy. It's chewy, with a firm texture and nutty flavor. It can be used in pilafs, fried-rice dishes, salads, as a side dish, and as a base for meat or vegetable stews. To cook, soak it overnight, then cook with an equal volume of water for 20 minutes.

Long-grain white rice: It has the same uses as long-grain brown rice, and it yields a fluffy rice good for fried-rice dishes. To cook, place the rice in twice its volume of water, bring to a boil, reduce the heat, cover, and cook for 15 minutes.

Medium-grain brown rice: These plump grains aren't as dense and sticky as short-grain brown rice, but they have a moist, tender texture. Use this rice in soups and as the starch dish along with meats and vegetables. To cook, place it in twice its volume of water, bring to a

CAROLINA GOLD

Glenn Roberts at Anson Mills, a certified organic rice grower and processor in South Carolina, is reviving an old heirloom variety of American rice called Carolina Golden that dates back to the antebellum South. "It was the most popular rice on earth from 1720 until the Civil War," he says, "so much so that Carolina Golden rice allocations to royals in Asia became the reason for battles there. Until 1930, most rice produced in the United States for retail was labeled 'Carolina Rice'—whether it was grown in the Carolinas or not."

Carolina Golden rice is softer than normal long-grain rice and cooks to independent grains. Roberts says that "this heirloom rice was named Carolina Golden for its beauty at harvest and the fortunes made from it by the antebellum Carolina and Georgia plantation aristocracy. It became the foundation for America's first internationally recognized antebellum cuisine, the Carolina Rice Kitchen, where French, German, Italian, and English colonial cooking merged with Native American and African food ways. It can be argued that the greatest cooks in America before 1800 were south of Virginia, and they were almost all African."

The real cause for the rise of this special rice in bygone days was the Gullah community on the Sea Islands of Georgia and the Carolinas. In the late seventeenth century, Carolina plantation owners tried growing rice by old European methods, but those didn't work well in the South. The African method of rice growing worked fine, though.

Roberts waxes ecstatic as he describes the smell of the cooked Carolina Golden rice. "The aromas are like those you experience out in the rice fields—hay, alfalfa, caramel, lemon blossoms, floral, a nuttiness—from sesame to pecan with walnut in between. Beyond that," he continues, "there are almost herb-like aromas, green, then into lilac, violet, jasmine—seductive, deep, floaty stuff; finally: mushroom. This rice gives a sense of well-being, a sense of comfort. I suspect there's melatonin in this rice."

SPECIALTY RICES

Occasionally, my wife and I used to sneak away to Victorian Gardens, an isolated and beautiful inn on the California coast in Mendocino operated by the late Luciano Zamboni and his wife Pauline. Luciano, an Italian, cooked authentic Italian dinners for his guests, and these sometimes included risotto. He told me that he considered the organic Arborio rice from Lundberg Family Farms in the Sacramento River delta superior to any Italian Arborio he'd tasted.

The Lundbergs have been growing rice since 1937. Over the years, they have sunk a lot of money into their operation to make sure their product is as clean as can be. For example, organic standards require that rice silos be refrigerated, rather than fumigated with chemicals, to suppress insects, so a large capital investment is required. In addition, it costs about $22 per acre more to produce organic rice than conventional, due to added costs for extra tractor and hand work pulling weeds—among other requirements.

That is, unless you follow the method of Japanese rice farmer Masanobu Fukuoka. This man, the author of *The One-Straw Revolution*, a book about his experiences growing rice, told me that he achieved enlightenment when he stopped asking himself, "What can I do next to grow rice better?" and started asking himself, "What can I stop doing to grow rice better?"

After years of wrestling with the question, he decided to scatter rice seed amid the clover that was growing in his paddy. When the rice grew to a foot tall, he would flood his paddy, killing the clover, which would then decay and fertilize the paddy. When the rice was ripe and ready to harvest, he'd scatter clover seed among the rice plants, harvest the rice, and cut the stalks—the stalk clippings would then decay themselves and give the clover plants a good source of fertilizer. When the clover was lush, he'd scatter rice seed, then flood the paddy again, and another yearly cycle would begin. Today he's got it down to three operations a year—most rice farmers are out in the paddies working all year long. And his yields are as good as if not better than his conventional neighbors. His rice is sold only in Japan, but his Zen way of thinking is applicable to our hustle-and-bustle way of doing things.

Here in the United States, Lowell Farms produces organic jasmine rice on a farm in El Campo, Texas. Linda Raun and her husband Lowell operate the business and sell a long-grain jasmine rice called Jasmine 85 (the year it was developed from Thai jasmine rice) retail from coast to coast, and even more via mail order. Their rice is grown under USDA organic rules: the Texas Department of Agriculture oversees the certification. The rice is very aromatic and of very high quality.

Lundberg, Lowell, and Anson Mills (see Carolina Gold, at left) sell their products by mail order as well as through retail outlets. See Sources, page 287, for details.

boil, reduce the heat, cover, and cook for 25 minutes.

Medium-grain white rice: It has the same uses as the medium-grain brown rice but a stickier texture. To cook, soak the grains overnight, then cook with an equal volume of water for 12 minutes.

Short-grain brown rice: This whole grain type becomes somewhat sticky when cooked and is chewy in texture. It's good for rice pudding, croquettes, veggie burgers, and sweet desserts. Soak it overnight and then cook it for 20 minutes in twice its volume of water.

Short-grain white rice: Removing the bran and germ to make white rice results in a stickier and softer grain. Use for sushi, rice balls, and sweet desserts. To cook, soak the rice for 20 minutes, then cook, covered, in $1^1/_8$ times its volume of water for 10 minutes, or until it's done.

Organic Advantage

While organic growers are developing new and better ways to produce high-quality organic rice in efficient, environmentally sound ways, large-scale conventional rice agriculture is plowing ahead with the genetic engineering of rice. Studies are underway to develop new rice varieties with increased tolerance to chemical herbicides through mutation breeding. Syngenta, one of the world's leading genetic engineering companies, has engineered a so-called golden rice, which has about 8 percent more provitamin A than ordinary rice. However, an adult would have to eat 20 pounds a day to satisfy his or her need for vitamin A from golden rice alone.

Uses

Rice is a starch to use as a base for a wide variety of cuisines. Indian tikka masala and vindaloos beg to be served on rice. It soaks up all kinds of sauces. Whole-grain brown rice is the most nutritious.

In addition to its almost endless uses as a grain, rice is also made into beverages, many of them organic. There's Rice Dream, a milk substitute, and the ice creams and other "dairy" foods based on rice milk. There's sake, the Japanese rice wine of significant alcohol content, and many other products.

WHEAT

SEASON: Winter wheat ripens in early summer. Spring-sown wheat ripens in late summer or fall, depending on the variety.

NUTRITIONAL HIGHLIGHTS: fiber, magnesium, manganese

Wheat is a type of grass, as are many common grains, including oats, barley, and even corn. We use its seeds, called wheatberries, to make flour. Wheatberries are composed of a white starchy grain and its germ (the living part of the grain), covered with a fibrous coat of bran. When a wheatberry sprouts, the germ sends out a small root. The starchy part of the grain is food for this growing seedling.

Whole-wheat flour, which is very nutritious, is produced by milling the entire wheatberry—bran, germ, and starch. If the germ and bran are removed, the white starchy part can be ground into unbleached white flour, which is far less nutritious. (Bakeries sometimes make whole-wheat bread from dough made from all-purpose flour to which they've added germ and bran back in.) This flour can then be bleached to make bleached white flour, which is almost entirely devoid of its former nutritional potential.

Whole-wheat baked goods have significantly higher nutritional content than those made with refined flour. Wheat germ is a rich source of vitamin E, iron, folic acid, and thiamine. Bran is a good source of insoluble fiber, which studies show lowers the risk of heart disease. Despite what many people think, insoluble fiber doesn't protect against colon cancer, but it is a healthy addition to every diet.

About 90 percent of the wheat grown in the world is bread wheat. Bread wheat can be divided into various categories, but one of primary use to cooks is hard versus soft.

Hard wheat (also called strong wheat) contains 10 to 16 percent protein and therefore a high amount of gluten, a protein found in wheat. The gluten gives dough made with hard-wheat flour an elastic, gluey quality that allows it to captures the bubbles of carbon dioxide released by yeast fermentation, which causes dough to rise. When baked, the bubbles in the dough cook and stabilize, and bread emerges porous and spongy. All-purpose and bread flours are made from hard wheat.

Soft wheat contains less protein, usually 7 to 9 percent, and thus less gluten. The weak flour (often called pastry flour) made from them is generally used for pie doughs, cakes, cookies, biscuits, and pancakes. Pastries made with soft-wheat flour are usually leavened by baking powder or steam instead of yeast, because the soft-wheat dough won't hold the bubbles produced by the yeast. (Hard wheat would make stiff pastries, but soft wheat makes tender, cake-like treats.)

Hard wheat grows best across the colder northern regions of the world, and so yeast-leavened loaves of high-gluten breads were the staples of cultures in northern Europe, Russia, Canada, and the northern part of the United States. Soft wheats are typically grown in warmer climates, such as the southeastern United States, which gave us biscuits, pancakes, and such.

Most of the other 10 percent of the world's wheat is durum. Durum wheat is well suited to the warm, dry climate

THE NEED FOR VITAMIN B_{12}

Wheat, other grains, seeds, and legumes are all excellent sources of the B vitamins so necessary to our health. But there's one vitamin they lack, and that's vitamin B_{12}. The only reliable, unfortified sources of B_{12} are meat, eggs, and dairy products, such as milk and cheese. Pasteurized milk and yogurt have had their B_{12} destroyed.

Vitamin B_{12} plays an important role in DNA synthesis and neurological function. Deficiency can lead to a wide spectrum of blood, cardiovascular, and neuropsychiatric disorders, such as anemia and atherosclerosis. Bacteria in our digestive tracts can synthesize B_{12}, and indeed they do, but it happens too far down the colon for absorption to occur.

The current view among nutritionists is that no plant food contains a reliable and safe source of B_{12}. Vegetarians, therefore, should make sure that eggs and dairy products are a regular part of their diets, and vegans should absolutely include B_{12}-fortified foods in their diets. Many are available as yeast extracts, breakfast cereals, textured vegetable protein, and veggie-burger mixes.

of the Mediterranean, where it's used to make pasta, couscous, and bulgur. The word semolina refers to the coarse flour made from the starchy part of durum's kernel after the bran and germ are milled away. Semolina is high in protein and is used to make pasta.

There are other wheat-like grains. Spelt was one of the earliest forms of wheat to be cultivated. Spelt is full of protein, has lots of B vitamins, and a tough outer husk that protects the grains from insects, making spelt very suitable for organic farming. It tends to have more flavor than regular bread wheat. Triticale is another wheat-like grain available today—it's a cross between bread wheat and rye.

Organic Advantage

Studies have shown that organic wheat fertilized with green manure or cow manure compost has better baking characteristics than conventional wheat grown with chemical nitrogen fertilizers. The gluten in the organically fertilized wheat has more elasticity and holds carbon dioxide better than that in conventional wheat. Chemical fertilizers are shown to promote quick-growing, lush, but ultimately weak plants.

Uses

Wheat can be mixed with other flours to make more nutritionally diverse and flavorful bread. Quinoa or amaranth flour (see page 199) will improve the amino acid profile of wheat flour. But don't stop there—oat, barley, rice, and other grain flours, ground-up seeds, rye, and crushed nuts, all will enrich homemade breads. Just remember that the dough must be at least three-quarters wheat flour to have enough gluten to rise properly. The rule of thumb is that the more variety, the better the nutrition and flavor, but the denser the final product.

Pita Bread

MAKES 8 PITAS

Fresh, golden pita bread hot from the oven is a revelation. Sauté summer squash and tomatoes in a little olive oil, give the vegetables a sprinkle of fresh oregano and a topping of grated Asiago cheese, and slip the mixture into the pocket for a quick, superb lunch. These pitas puff up beautifully.

3 cups all-purpose flour, or 2 cups all-purpose and 1 cup whole-wheat flour, plus extra for kneading
2 tablespoons extra-virgin olive oil, plus extra for the bowl and baking sheet
2 teaspoons active dry yeast (about 2/3 of a package)
2 teaspoons sugar
1 teaspoon salt

1. Combine all of the ingredients in a warm mixing bowl and mix until they form a loose, somewhat dry dough. Place the dough on a lightly floured board and knead for 10 minutes, until smooth and elastic. Clean and lightly oil the mixing bowl, place the dough in it, cover with a damp kitchen towel, and let rise in a warm place for 1 hour. It will become puffy.

2. Preheat the oven to 500°F. Place one rack on the lowest position and another at the upper-middle position. Punch down the dough and place it onto a lightly oiled, nonporous surface, such as a plastic cutting board or clean countertop. Cut it into 8 equal pieces. Lightly oil a baking sheet. Roll several dough pieces into 6-inch circles, depending on how many fit on your baking sheet (usually 2 to 4 circles). Make sure they don't touch. When the sheet is full, place it on the lower rack and bake for 5 minutes.

3. Roll out the next batch of dough while the first batch bakes. If the first batch hasn't puffed up after 5 minutes, bake another minute. If still not puffed, your oven isn't hot enough—raise the heat to 550°F for the next batch. As soon as the bread is puffed, place the baking sheet with the first batch on the top rack for 2 minutes, or until the pitas have browned. Remove from the oven and cover the baking sheet in a clean dish towel to keep the bread soft.

4. Bake the subsequent batches. Store the cooled pitas in a plastic bag.

WILD RICE

SEASON: late summer

GOOD VARIETIES: There is only one species–the wild one.

STORAGE AND PREPARATION TIPS: Store in a tightly closed jar in a dark cupboard.

NUTRITIONAL HIGHLIGHTS: fiber, magnesium, manganese, protein, zinc

GOES WELL WITH: almonds, green beans, mushrooms, pine nuts

Wild rice is not actually rice. It's an aquatic grass that grows wild in the thousands of lakes and ponds of the upper Midwest region of America. Early French explorers saw it growing in the water and called it riz.

Traditionally, the grain was harvested as a staple food by Native Americans of the Ojibway tribe—who called it manomi—and other nearby tribes of what are now Minnesota, Wisconsin, and Michigan. It sustained them over the long winters.

Harvesting the grain from the wild is traditionally done by two people in a canoe. One guides and propels the canoe through the stand of rice plants. The other uses two sticks: one to sweep the seed heads over the canoe, the other to rap them so the grains fall out. Commercially grown wild rice uses modern harvesting equipment. California is now the world's production leader of the grain, where it's grown in the waters of the Sacramento River delta.

Until the 1970s, wild rice was expensive because it was all harvested wild from the Great Lakes region. Commercial growing made wild rice the only grass grain domesticated in historical (rather than prehistoric) times.

Organic Advantage

Even commercial growers plant wild rice in natural settings, and so—even if wild rice is not certified organic—it's unlikely to have encountered any chemicals.

Uses

Mix wild rice with regular rice to add some pizzazz. Use it in stuffings for fowl as you would regular rice. Its nutty flavor combines especially well with green beans.

Wild Rice and Corn Bread Stuffing

MAKES ABOUT 2 QUARTS, ENOUGH FOR A 14- TO 17-POUND TURKEY

Here's one of the traditional Thanksgiving turkey stuffings we make at our house. My wife and I rotate through several different stuffings because we grew up in different families with different ideas of what constitutes the best stuffing, plus we've added a couple of our own favorites over the years. We both agree that this one is the winner.

6 cups chicken stock

1 cup uncooked wild rice

1/2 pound pork sausage, casing removed

2 medium onions, diced

4 stalks celery, diced

4 cups coarsely crumbled corn bread

3 cups toasted bread cubes

2 teaspoons ground dried sage

1 teaspoon freshly ground black pepper

2 large eggs

Nonstick cooking spray

1. Combine 3 cups of chicken stock and the rice in a heavy medium saucepan and bring to a simmer over medium-high heat. Reduce the heat to medium. Cover and simmer for 40 minutes, until the grains pop open and become soft and the stock is absorbed.

2. In a large skillet over medium heat, cook the sausage, onions, and celery until the sausage is cooked through and the onions are translucent, about 7 to 8 minutes.

3. In a large bowl, combine the corn bread, bread cubes, sage, and pepper. Add the sausage mixture and the wild rice and combine thoroughly.

4. Lightly beat the eggs, whisk them into the remaining chicken stock, and add to the stuffing, a little at a time, until the stuffing is moist but not soggy.

5. Use to stuff the turkey loosely. Cook the remaining stuffing (or all the stuffing, if you prefer) in a covered baking dish oiled with nonstick spray at 350°F for 45 minutes.

CHAPTER

5

Herbs and Spices

All kinds of markets these days have not only a rack with dried herbs, but also sell fresh herbs in the produce department. How wonderful that we have fresh tarragon, cilantro, chervil, and other herbs at hand. But how often do we use them?

In this chapter, you'll find ways to include fresh herbs in everyday cooking, in salads, and in marinades, and to flavor meat and vegetables. Fresh herbs have most of their essential oils—the compounds that give them their unique flavors—intact. The drying process eliminates some of these essential oils as it concentrates other flavor compounds, and so dried herbs impart different characteristics to foods than their fresh equivalents.

The essential oils in herbs and spices are created by nature to repel insects, and so these plants aren't usually heavily sprayed with pesticides. But they may be sprayed with fungicides to keep off molds and mildews, and the soil around them may have been treated with herbicides. It's best to look for fresh herbs that are certified organic. At their best, fresh herbs create a marriage with other foods that is greater than either partner. Tomatoes and basil are one such example. Each is good on its own.

Together they are great. That kind of synergy is what you're looking for whenever you use herbs and spices in your cooking.

Most herbs and spices quickly lose their aromatics when ground or crushed. This means that it's important to get your fresh herbs in particular picked as close to the time you'll use them as possible and to grind or crush your dried herbs and spices just before you use them. Avoid the cabinet full of years-old plastic boxes of dead seasonings. My kitchen equipment includes a peppermill, a nutmeg grater, a mortar and pestle, and an electric spice mill dedicated to reducing whole spices such as cardamom, anise, cumin seed, and caraway—among others—to flavorful bits.

Fresh herbs carry the purest flavors, with all their aromatic essential oils and nuances intact. If you have the outdoor space, put in a little culinary herb garden. A small area (5 by 9 feet) is plenty big enough. Or if you have a sunny deck but no land, most herbs do well in containers. Some of the leafy herbs such as basil, chervil, cilantro, and parsley like a rich soil, but Mediterranean herbs such as thyme and oregano prefer dry, well-drained soils that intensify their essential oils. Some, such as rosemary and lavender, thrive in poor, sandy, dry soil.

Herbs are easy to grow for several reasons. Most of our common culinary herbs come from areas of the world with poor, dry soil and can take a lot of neglect because of it. And their essential oils tend to keep insects at bay (except nectar-gathering honeybees, which just love the flowers of thyme, oregano, and rosemary).

All the herbs and spices listed in this chapter can be found grown organically. Large supermarkets with organic sections will carry many of them. Others can easily be found by searching online. The best solution for many of the herbs, of course, is to grow your own.

BASIL

SEASON: summer through fall

GOOD VARIETIES: See below.

WHAT TO LOOK FOR: Leaves and stems should be fresh and green, not dark or bruised.

STORAGE AND PREPARATION TIPS: If you want to store basil for long-term use, drying the leaves won't work—it drives off the essential oils that give the herb its aroma. See Uses for four better ways to preserve basil's freshness for the winter months.

NUTRITIONAL HIGHLIGHTS: small amounts of manganese and potassium, vitamin A, vitamin C, vitamin K

GOES WELL WITH: cannellini beans, eggplant, fish, lemons, olives, pasta, pizza, salad, summer squash, tomatoes

Basil is an indispensable herb for any cook. Yes, you can find fresh basil at almost any time of year in the supermarket, but off-season, it's usually tired and lacking some of its oomph. Basil has more species and varieties than most other herbs, and they vary by flavor, color, texture, size, and aroma. These types loosely fall into one of five categories: regular (cinnamon or clove-scented), anise-scented, dwarf, lemon-scented, and purple-leafed.

Here is a cook's take on the commonly available top basil varieties:

Cinnamon basil: This variety has a distinct cinnamon scent with a hint of cloves.

Genovese basil: Also called perfume basil because of its intense basil fragrance, it is the best variety for pesto.

Holy basil: Holy basil is very pungent, with the aroma of black walnuts and exotic spices. This is one basil that takes to stir-fries, soups, and curries—but add the leaves toward the end of cooking.

Lemon basil: A new cultivar, Sweet Dani, is an improved variety with an even stronger lemon character.

Lime basil: Enjoy its distinct lime scent.

Purple basil: Also called opal basil, this is the one to use to make infused vinegar because of the pretty pink color it imparts.

Purple ruffles basil: Its ruffled, highly-colored leaves carry an anise scent with a hint of mint.

Sweet basil: A strong clove and anise scent rises from the leaves. It is perfect for pesto, tomato and mozzarella salads, and pizza.

Thai basil: Its small, slender, yet highly aromatic leaves are used in many Thai dishes, soups, and curries. Siam Queen is a prized new variety with a strong licorice character.

Uses

Tear up bits of leaves to add color and aroma to salads. Use whole leaves as a bed for baked or poached fish. All basils marry beautifully with tomatoes (and, therefore, with pizza!), and with Italian dishes made with eggplant, lemons, olives, pastas, cannellini beans, summer squash, and Italian cheeses. Chop it finely and mix with bread crumbs and pine nuts to stuff light meats like pork and veal. Thai basil merges beautifully with Southeast Asian condiments like garlic, ginger, galangal, Kaffir lime leaves, and lemongrass.

To preserve fresh basil: There are four good ways to preserve the delicate flavor of fresh basil.

1. **Make pesto:** See the recipe on page 228, but substitute 2 cups well packed basil leaves for the rosemary and parsley.
2. **Freeze basil puree:** Put fresh basil leaves in a blender along with just enough water to turn them into a thick slurry. Pour the slurry into ice cube trays and freeze until solid. When frozen, transfer the basil cubes to a freezer bag and store in the freezer. One cube will flavor two cups of tomato sauce.
3. **Make basil oil:** Loosely pack fresh basil leaves in a jar with a tight-fitting lid and fill with good-quality olive oil and a tablespoon of red wine vinegar. Shake the jar daily and store it in a dark place. After three or four weeks, fish out the leaves and pour off the oil into a nice-looking jar for storage (discard the vinegar at the bottom). Store in a cool, dark place and use the oil to drizzle on pizzas, salad, or baked fish. Don't use it as cooking oil, as the heat will disrupt some of the flavor.
4. **Make purple basil vinegar:** Take 1 tightly packed cup of purple basil and place it in a 1-quart mason jar. Fill the jar with a mild vinegar, such as unseasoned rice wine vinegar. (Its light acidity allows the spiciness of the basil to come through, and its light color shows off the pretty pink color the basil imparts.) Place wax paper over the top of the jar and then screw on the lid with a ring band. Store on a shelf out of direct sunlight for a month, then pour the vinegar through a strainer and store it in a glass bottle or jar. You'll love the color and the pungency. Combine this vinegar with some of your basil-infused olive oil to make an all-basil salad dressing.

CHIVES

SEASON: spring

GOOD VARIETY: garlic chives

WHAT TO LOOK FOR: The chives should have fresh-cut ends and not be limp.

STORAGE AND PREPARATION TIPS: Although chives can be stored in the refrigerator for a week, it's best to use them within a day or two of buying or picking them.

NUTRITIONAL HIGHLIGHTS: niacin, phytochemicals, vitamin A, vitamin C, vitamin K, zinc. (We don't usually eat enough chives to make them nutritionally significant, however.)

GOES WELL WITH: eggs, potatoes, salad greens

Think of chives as small onions—which they are, as you might guess by their taste: they are members of the same genus (Allium) that includes onions, garlic, ramps, scallions, leeks, and many other vegetables.

RAMPS

While we're talking about chives, this is a good place to mention a much-sought-after relative called ramps, a kind of leek that grows wild in open woodlands and fields from Appalachia across to the Great Lakes states and from eastern Canada to the Carolinas. In Appalachia they're called ramps; in the Midwest, wild leeks. When I was a kid growing up in Pennsylvania, where we bought milk from a local dairy, it was not uncommon to be confronted with onion-flavored milk in the spring. The cows, turned out to early pasture, ate the ramps that grew among the shrubs on a slope near our house. While onion milk doesn't have much to recommend it, the ramps that impart the flavor do.

Ramps are best from March to May, before the flower stalks appear. Their leaves can be used to wrap delicate fish for poaching or braising, and to flavor egg dishes, soups, or sauces. The bulbs can be used like shallots to impart a strong onion flavor to omelets and other dishes. Three tablespoons of minced leaves can be whisked together with 1/2 cup each of mayonnaise and yogurt, 1 tablespoon of fresh lemon juice, and 1 tablespoon of Dijon mustard to make a sauce for spring asparagus.

Chives should be used fresh and raw. Fortunately, they're easy to grow, even for a novice. They will flourish all year round in a pot in a protected place, such as a sunroom or under a skylight. Select a few good-looking leaves from the outside of the clump and snip them off 2 inches above ground level. This encourages new bulblets to form under the soil.

Chives flower in late spring. Tear the light fuchsia blossoms into florets and sprinkle them in salads. Or infuse unseasoned rice vinegar with the flower heads for 3 weeks, then strain off the vinegar into a fancy clear glass container. This will give the vinegar a light, oniony aroma and a pretty pinkish color.

Chive varieties: A subspecies of ordinary, hollow-leafed chives called Siberian chives have a stronger, garlicky flavor. Garlic chives, with flatter green leaves that contain a mild garlic flavor and aroma bloom later in the summer, with white florets that carry a sweet smell.

Uses

Chives are a natural on baked potatoes topped with sour cream or butter. For a healthier alternative, potatoes can be stuffed with soft tofu that's been mashed with a little canola oil and lemon juice, seasoned with salt and pepper, then topped with minced chives.

Garlic chives will add a mild garlic flavor to foods. Toss a few leaves into the soup pot, then remove them when the soup is done. Or chop them into small bits to use in soups, stews, or any time a garlic flavor is called for. The flowers can be torn up and used to garnish a salad, but they won't impart much garlic flavor.

Caponata with Chives

MAKES ABOUT 2 CUPS

Caponata is an intensely flavorful sweet-and-sour Sicilian eggplant relish that benefits from the texture, appearance, and light onion flavor imparted by the chives. Serve this on bruschette or as a side dish to accompany chicken, broiled fish, or veal.

4 cups peeled and chopped eggplant (1 large or 2 smaller eggplants)
Kosher salt
1 medium onion, chopped
2 tablespoons olive oil
2 stalks celery, chopped
2 cloves garlic, chopped
3 tablespoons toasted, crushed pine nuts
2 tablespoons pitted, chopped black oil-cured olives
1/2 teaspoon capers
2 plum tomatoes, chopped
1/2 cup chopped chives
1 tablespoon balsamic vinegar

1. Place the chopped eggplant in a colander, set in the sink, and toss liberally with kosher salt. Let sit 1 hour, then drain, rinse off the salt, and squeeze to extract the excess moisture.

2. In a large skillet over medium-high heat, sauté the onion in the oil until it is translucent and golden, about 5 minutes. Add the celery and garlic and cook 2 minutes longer. Add the chopped eggplant to the skillet. Cook for 5 minutes. Add the pine nuts, olives, and capers and cook 5 more minutes, until the eggplant is tender. Remove the skillet from the heat, turn the mixture into a serving bowl, and let cool to room temperature. Stir in the tomatoes, chives, and vinegar. Serve at room temperature.

CILANTRO AND CORIANDER

SEASON: spring and fall

WHAT TO LOOK FOR: Cilantro leaves should be a fresh-looking green. The stem ends should look freshly cut.

STORAGE AND PREPARATION TIPS: Cilantro will keep for 3 to 4 days in the vegetable crisper of the fridge. Coriander will keep up to a year in a tightly closed jar stored away from sunlight.

NUTRITIONAL HIGHLIGHTS: vitamin A, vitamin K; small amounts of vitamin C

Cilantro: small amounts of vitamin A and vitamin C

Coriander: small amounts of calcium and iron

GO WELL WITH: avocado, chicken, citrus, coconut, corn, fish, lamb, lentils, shellfish, tomatoes

Cilantro refers to the fresh, frilly leaves of the coriander plant, whose seeds are the spice we know as coriander. And while most people, including myself, find coriander seeds' sweet, spicy, lightly lemony flavor very agreeable, opinion is strongly divided on the flavor of cilantro's leaves. Fans use it enthusiastically, but some find the taste off-putting.

Cilantro is a cool-weather crop best suited to spring and fall cultivation. In hot climes, it loses its peculiar aroma and taste. In the garden, it dislikes weed competition, so young plants should be mulched. It likes rich, humusy, constantly moist soil and reaches leaf-harvest stage after a couple of months; it will flower within a month after that.

Uses

Cilantro is a chief flavoring in many Mexican salsas, in guacamole, and appears extensively in South American and Southeast Asian cooking, usually as a garnish or in a raw sauce, as cooking destroys its unique aroma and flavor.

Coriander is a mainstay in chutneys, curries, and garam masala (see Tip, page 53). Many cooks use both the herb and the seed form of the plant to flavor these staples. It makes a natural partnership with cumin and sweet spices such as allspice, cinnamon, clove, and nutmeg. It also enhances ginger, soy, and garlic marinades. In the United States, whole coriander seed is a principal component in pickling spice blends. Coriander is one of the spices whose essential oils dissipate rapidly after grinding, so buy the seeds whole and grind them as needed in a spice mill.

Fresh Hot Salsa

MAKES 4 CUPS

Serve with tacos or burritos, spoon some over roast chicken, or add some to your morning omelet to wake up your taste buds.

10 fresh serrano chiles, stemmed
5 cups chopped ripe tomatoes
1/2 cup chopped white onion
1 cup chopped cilantro leaves (from 1 bunch)
4 cloves garlic, chopped
2 teaspoons fresh oregano leaves, chopped
1 teaspoon salt

1. Preheat the oven to 350°F. Roast the chiles on a baking sheet until tender, about 5 to 7 minutes or until a fork easily penetrates a chile.
2. Transfer them to a blender with 1 cup of tomatoes and blend to a chunky texture. Add the remaining ingredients and blend to a coarse consistency.

DILL

SEASON: summer to fall

WHAT TO LOOK FOR: Dill weed should look fresh and have a sweet smell and taste. Dill seed should have a strong aroma.

STORAGE AND PREPARATION TIPS: Store dill weed in the vegetable crisper for up to a week. Store dill seed in a covered jar in a dark cabinet for a year.

NUTRITIONAL HIGHLIGHTS: vitamin A, vitamin C; small amounts of manganese

GOES WELL WITH:

Dill weed: cabbage, cauliflower, cucumbers, salmon, smoked salmon

Dill seed: beets, cucumbers, vinegar

Even if you only use dill once in a while, it's an organic gardener's blessing, like most umbelliferous plants (fennel, carrots, and caraway are among the others) because it attracts and supports beneficial insects. (I've planted it under my apple trees, where it attracts beneficial insects to control apple pests.)

The ferny, feathery leaves of dill are called dill weed and are widely used in poaching liquids for fish and shellfish. Creamy dill sauce is standard with gravlax. Dill is commonly paired with cole crops—cabbage and cauliflower—across the northern tier of states and in Europe, and with sour cream as a sauce for cucumbers, as folks of Polish descent will know. And Germans like horseradish and dill with their beef.

Dill seed is a chief ingredient of dill pickles—and for most Americans, pickles don't taste like pickles without dill seed in the pickling mix. The seeds can also be infused in vinegar to make an interesting vinaigrette: Simply add 1/2 cup of dill seeds to 1 quart of white vinegar and let it infuse for a month, then pour off the vinegar, discard the spent seeds, and rinse the bottle. Pour the vinegar back into the bottle, and use as you would other vinegars in a vinaigrette recipe.

Dilled Salmon

SERVES 4

This is my favorite way to cook salmon—so much so that I hardly ever cook it any other way. To begin, ask your fishmonger to remove the skin from a salmon fillet of whatever size you prefer.

4 bunches fresh dill weed
1- to 2-pound salmon fillet, skin removed

1. Arrange the oven racks so that the distance between the bottom rack and the one above it will accommodate an uncovered Dutch oven. Preheat the oven to 300°F. Fill a Dutch oven halfway with water and bring to a boil over high heat on the stovetop.
2. Line the bottom of a baking pan with the dill weed in approximately the same shape as the salmon fillet, and then lay the fillet on top of the dill, with what was the skin side down.
3. When the pot is boiling well, set it on the bottom rack of the oven and place the salmon on the rack above. Bake exactly 30 minutes. Lift the salmon off the dill, using two spatulas if necessary, and transfer it to a warmed serving platter. Discard the dill.

MINT

SEASON: mid-spring through early fall

GOOD VARIETIES: See below.

WHAT TO LOOK FOR: Mint should be fresh looking, without discoloration, and strongly aromatic.

STORAGE AND PREPARATION TIPS: Mint stores well in a plastic bag in the fridge for 3 to 5 days.

NUTRITIONAL HIGHLIGHTS: small amounts of manganese, vitamin A, vitamin C

GOES WELL WITH: chocolate, fresh fruit, peas, yogurt

Mint's sweet menthol aroma and flavor, its calming effect, and its digestive properties make it the perfect herb. If you are a lover of mojitos—buy more.

While spearmint is the most useful and prevalent of the culinary mints, there are other mints to be aware of. The entire mint family of many plants has one feature in common: their stems are square.

Apple mint: These big fuzzy leaves carry an apple-like flavor. Apple mint is the best mint for making candied mint leaves, as its tiny leaf hairs trap the sugar very effectively. To make them, whisk 1 egg white with a few drops of water and paint this on leaves of apple mint. Then sprinkle superfine sugar over the leaves from a spoon; set the leaves aside on a sheet of wax paper until completely dry (up to a day or two). When crisp and absolutely dry, store them in a closed jar in a cool, dark cupboard for up to 6 months. A related form of mint, called pineapple mint, is also good for candying.

Peppermint: Peppermint smells like candy canes. It has a pungency and a sharp, biting sensation that can overwhelm, and so should be used judiciously, especially in peppermint tea, as too much of the volatile oil is not good for you. Pour boiling water over a teaspoon of the fresh leaves.

Chocolate mint: A variety of peppermint, this mint has a bit of the aroma of a peppermint patty.

Uses

Spearmint is what's usually meant when a recipe simply calls for mint. It is wonderfully versatile; used fresh and roughly chopped, it merges seamlessly with chocolate desserts, punctuates the sweetness of fruit salads, and blends nicely with yogurt and peeled, sliced cucumbers on a hot summer's evening. Add it during the last minutes of cooking to carrots, black beans, and lentils.

Spearmint is traditionally used as a jelly or in a sauce for lamb, but also try that sauce with other light meats, such as veal. Its use with peas is classic, but try simmering snipped mint leaves with tomatoes, summer squashes, or eggplant.

Or take a tip from the Vietnamese, who use it to make refreshing, uncooked spring rolls by combining the fresh leaves with bean sprouts, shredded lettuce, and chopped shrimp, and serve it with a peanut sauce for dipping.

Finally, sprigs of mint belong in iced tea and, of course, in the mint julep, where the aroma of fresh mint disguises the drink's potent kick.

Mojito

SERVES 1

Few drinks are as refreshing as a mojito on a hot day, but be careful—they can sneak up on you. Feel free to try other flavor mint leaves, like chocolate mint.

When muddling (crushing) the mint, the best advice is to "muddle like you mean it."

2 sprigs mint
2 ounces silver rum
2 tablespoons simple syrup (see Tips)
Juice of 1 lime
Mint ice cubes (see Tips)
Club soda
Lime wedge

Muddle the mint sprigs with the back of a tablespoon in the bottom of a tall glass. Crush them well. Add the rum, simple syrup, lime juice, mint ice cubes, and top with club soda (Canada Dry has a good, strong fizz). Stir once with a long spoon, add the lime wedge, and serve.

TIPS: To make simple syrup, combine equal parts of water and superfine or regular sugar, heat to dissolve the sugar, then cool.

The key to keeping a mojito from diluting is to use ice cubes made from spearmint tea. Brew a light spearmint tea and freeze the tea in ice cube trays.

Moroccan Mint Tea

MAKES 6 CUPS

Sweetened mint tea has long been the libation over which social interaction occurs in North Africa.

2 cups loosely packed fresh spearmint leaves, plus more for garnish
1/4 cup sugar
2 tablespoons green tea leaves

In a tea kettle, bring 6 cups of water to a boil. Place the mint, sugar, and tea in a teapot and add the boiling water. Let it steep for 10 minutes. Strain the tea through a fine-mesh sieve into cups, then garnish the cups with fresh mint sprigs.

OREGANO AND MARJORAM

SEASON: midsummer

GOOD VARIETIES: Greek oregano, Italian oregano, sweet marjoram

WHAT TO LOOK FOR: When buying the herbs fresh, make sure the leaves are perky and the stems aren't browned or shriveling.

STORAGE AND PREPARATION TIPS: Fresh herbs will store in the fridge in a plastic bag for a week. Both herbs also store well dried; store dried oregano and marjoram in airtight containers for up to 6 months.

NUTRITIONAL HIGHLIGHTS: vitamin C; small amounts of calcium

GO WELL WITH:

Oregano: eggplant, onions, sausage, tomatoes

Marjoram: carrots, chicken, eggplant, pork, potatoes, summer squash, tomatoes, veal

The difference between these two related herbs is instantly recognizable when you taste them side by side. Oregano's taste is more bitter, with a strong, sharp quality. Marjoram shares a similar aroma, but on the palate has a sweet pungency, with a spicy note. In appearance, oregano has a more open habit, with slender but tough, almost woody, stems. Marjoram has twisty, almost knotted-looking leaves on more herbaceous stems.

Having several plants of oregano and marjoram is an absolute must in any herb garden. If you have a sunny windowsill, marjoram will overwinter nicely there in a generous pot. If you're an apartment dweller with not enough sunlight, a nice alternative is to pick up bunches of the herbs at farmers' markets in midsummer, when the essential oils are strongest, and hang them in a warm, dry spot out of direct sunlight. The thin, woody branches and stems will dry. Rub the leaves, which will crumble off the stems, and store the dried leaves in an airtight container. They'll keep for up to a year, at which point you can repeat the process. Both oregano and marjoram are more intensely aromatic dried than fresh.

Greek oregano: You may find this at farmers' markets in spring. The leaves have a dark gray-green appearance, and the flavor is stronger than that of other oreganos, with a resinous note.

Uses

Oregano is a natural with fava beans, eggplant, tomatoes, and most tomato-based Italian dishes, such as pastas with marinara sauce, pizzas, calzones, hoagies, sausage sandwiches—and with Greek dishes such as souvlaki. Unlike many herbs, its flavor persists during cooking, so you can add it at the beginning.

Marjoram is good for flavoring vegetables such as carrots, summer squashes, and potatoes. Its sweet spiciness adds a brisk note to salads. It's good in omelets and on light meats. Like oregano, it marries well with tomatoes, beans, and eggplant. But cooking reduces its flavor, so add it at the end.

PARSLEY

SEASON: summer through late fall

GOOD VARIETIES: See below.

WHAT TO LOOK FOR: Buy fresh parsley that is turgid, not limp, and looks just picked. Avoid dried parsley flakes: when parsley dries, it looses most of its flavor.

STORAGE AND PREPARATION TIPS: To store, shake off any excess moisture, wrap parsley in paper toweling, and put it in a plastic bag in the crisper.

NUTRITIONAL HIGHLIGHTS: antioxidants, folate, iron, vitamin A, vitamin C, vitamin K

GOES WELL WITH: eggs, fish, lemon, tomato sauce, vegetables

Italian flat-leaf parsley seems to be gaining favor with cooks for its rich, straightforward flavor and the way it makes little flakes when minced. The curly-leafed types are similar in flavor, if a little milder, and you get little twisty shapes when you chop them up. Either can substitute for the other in a pinch.

There are many cultivars to choose from. Among the curly-leafed types, I prefer Champion Moss Curled, an older type with great production. Among the Italian flat-leaf types, Giant Italian is the one to look for. It has much thicker stems than the curly type, and these can be used like celery. When a recipe calls for only chopped parsley leaves, reserve the flat-leaf stems, tie them in a bundle with butcher's string, and add them to stocks, broths, soups, and stews. Remove them when cooking is finished.

Uses

Parsley may be good for you, but eating a 1-ounce serving (about 1/2 cup loosely packed) is a chore. So I run a handful of parsley through the juicer along with carrots, kale, a beet, and chard leaves. A pint of this juice daily is my super-energizer. You could also mix it with spinach, collards, and other vegetables that juice well.

If juicing isn't your thing, use parsley liberally with just about any cooked or raw vegetable, in omelets, with fish, with lemony sauces, and in risottos and other rice dishes. Use it in pastas, with tomato sauces or slices, and in the classic dish of mussels in white wine, garlic, and parsley. Italian salsa verde relies heavily on parsley. No stuffed, baked mushroom cap would be complete without minced parsley mixed with butter.

While Americans tend to use parsley as a garnish or a finishing sprinkle over fish and other dishes, many cuisines use a lot more of it. It can be paired with basil—or even be used instead—to make pesto (see page 216). It is a chief component of Middle Eastern bulgur salads. The French include parsley in herb mixtures such as persillade, a mixture of minced parsley and garlic that can be tossed into most anything—sauces, eggs, salad dressings, cheese fillings—or mixed with bread crumbs to make a flavorful breading for meat. (To retain its fresh flavor, persillade is ordinarily used just before the end of cooking.) The Italians make a similar flavorful garnish called gremolata: it's the same as a persillade but with the addition of grated lemon zest. Osso buco, or braised veal shanks, positively demands a sprinkling of gremolata over the top to cut through the richness and add a lively flavor.

Chimichurri Sauce

MAKES ABOUT 1 1/2 CUPS

In Argentina, they brush this tangy, spicy sauce over the top of their grilled meats, which they consume in great quantity along with their good red wines. This recipe is from the winery Bodega Catena Zapata of Agrelo, Argentina, maker of excellent Malbecs and other varietals grown on the slopes of the Andes.

1/4 cup champagne vinegar
4 cloves garlic
1 coarsely chopped shallot
1 jalapeño chile, stemmed and seeded
2 teaspoons dried oregano or 1 tablespoon fresh
Salt and freshly ground black pepper to taste
1 cup extra-virgin olive oil
1 cup Italian flat-leaf parsley, minced (loosely packed)

Place the vinegar, garlic, shallot, jalapeño, oregano, salt, and pepper in a blender or food processor and blend to a smooth paste. Transfer to a bowl and stir in the oil and parsley. Freeze any excess sauce, then spoon out as much as needed and let warm to room temperature.

Green Goddess Dressing

MAKES ABOUT 1 1/2 CUPS

It was San Francisco in the 1920s. The famous actor George Arliss was visiting the Palace Hotel while he was in town, starring in the play The Green Goddess at a local theater. The chef cooking for him became inspired, and here's the now-famous result. Store in the fridge and use within a week. Some versions of this salad dressing call for mayonnaise, but this eggless recipe works just fine.

1 cup half-and-half
1/3 cup canola oil
4 anchovy fillets

1 scallion, chopped
2 tablespoons tahini
1 tablespoon chopped fresh chives
1 tablespoon chopped fresh parsley
1 tablespoon tarragon vinegar
1 teaspoon chopped fresh tarragon

Place all the ingredients in a blender and puree until smooth.

PERILLA

SEASON: early summer to mid-fall

WHAT TO LOOK FOR: Red and green perilla is most easily found in Japanese markets by the name shiso. It is becoming easier to find in better food stores. You may also find it in farmers' markets, sometimes even sold as a pot herb (it's easy to grow).

STORAGE AND PREPARATION TIPS: Perilla leaves will store in the fridge for a week.

NUTRITIONAL HIGHLIGHTS: omega-3 fatty acid

GOES WELL WITH: beef, chicken, fish, radishes, rice

Perilla is a member of the mint family. You may not recognize the name, but you've seen its spade-shaped, light green or wine-red leaves with the crimped edges on your plates of sushi and tasted its fruity spiciness in mesclun mixes.

Many types of perilla are grown around the world. The leafy vegetable perillas include both green and red types, with both pinked edges and smooth edges. Red perilla isn't as aromatic as green, but it is prettier. The leaves are deep burgundy, prompting the sobriquet "beefsteak plant." The flavor has something of basil, but much milder.

Uses

Green perilla, or green shiso as it's now often called, has been discovered by chefs for its delicate aroma and refreshing flavor, which combines mint and anise with overtones of cinnamon and citrus. With its increasing popularity, Americans are coming to know this useful herb and to use it in salads, tempura, seviche, as a flavoring for poached and baked fish, white radishes, and even beef and chicken. Chopped green perilla adds a lovely note to cooked rice.

In Korea, they add green perilla to soups, while the Japanese use it for garnish and fry it as tempura. The Japanese also use the pink flower buds in salads and as garnish. Purple-red perilla is used in Japan to color pickled umeboshi plums; other types of the herb are used in Thailand. Different varieties have specific fragrances imparted by their aromatic oils (much like the different mints do).

Perilla oil is being sold as a food supplement because the plant's seeds are a rich source of omega-3 essential fatty acids. Omega-3 is usually provided by

IF YOU LIKE TO GARDEN

Perilla is very easy to grow, whether in an herb garden or in a pot. Just press seeds into the top of the soil and water—but don't bury them, as perilla needs light in order to germinate. The plants grow about 3 feet tall. If you want to grow perilla organically, just type organic perilla seed into your Internet search engine to find a raft of places to purchase it. If you have an herb garden, red perilla will make a charming color contrast with all that green. It's a tender annual. The seeds of red and green perilla make fine sprouts for salads as well.

fish oil, so this is a good source of this heart-protective substance for vegans.

Green Perilla Salad

SERVES 3

This is a refreshingly different salad. Its unique aroma and flavor is provided by green perilla.

1 cup fresh green perilla leaves
1 1/2 cups peeled and thinly sliced cucumbers
1/2 cup peeled, cored, thinly sliced tart green apple
1/4 cup seasoned rice vinegar
Salt to taste

Make a chiffonade of half the perilla leaves by rolling them up and slicing them into 1/8-inch-wide strips. Place the chiffonade, the cucumbers, apple slices, vinegar, and salt to taste in a bowl and toss to mix. Place the mixture on plates and top with the remaining whole perilla leaves.

ROSEMARY

SEASON: year-round

GOOD VARIETIES: Collingwood Ingram, Corsican Prostrate, Huntington Blue, Majorca Pink, Miss Jessup's Upright, Prostratus, Tuscan Blue

WHAT TO LOOK FOR: The stronger the aroma, the better the rosemary. The cut end of the branch should look fresh, not dark or black. In general, straight, long-branched types have more essential rosemary oil, and thus more flavor and aroma, than the curly-branched types.

STORAGE AND PREPARATION TIPS: While rosemary will store fresh in the refrigerator for up to a week, it's best to use it within a day or two of purchase, as it loses its essential oils over time. Avoid dried rosemary.

NUTRITIONAL HIGHLIGHTS: phytochemicals

GOES WELL WITH: beef, chicken, lamb, mushrooms, pork, potatoes, spinach

Rosemary is one of the most tenacious herbs. This lovely plant sails through California's natural summer drought (May or June to October or November) without irrigation, and greets the height of the hot, dry season not with exhaustion but with scads of pale, lavender-blue flowers that call to every honeybee in the neighborhood. Originally from the Mediterranean region, it's now grown all over the world, wherever the climate is supportive. If you're so inclined, you can take cuttings for the kitchen at any time of year—its aromatic properties never diminish.

Uses

My favorite use for rosemary is to slip pinches of the needle-like leaves into shallow slits cut in the thin layer of fat remaining on a frenched rack of lamb, slip garlic slices into other slits, and roast the rack at 425°F for exactly 25 minutes—it comes out smelling like a dream, perfectly done (see recipe, page 242).

Use rosemary sprigs as a brush to spread marinades such as chimichurri sauce (see recipe, page 225) on your grilled beef or barbecue sauce on your baby back ribs. I have had pieces of chicken thigh skewered on rosemary sticks and grilled to a juicy perfection.

Chopped rosemary leaves can be added to or sprinkled on top of breads, focaccia, and crackers. If you grow your own rosemary, the flowers make pretty little light blue stars sprinkled on a salad. Chopped rosemary, sage, parsley, thyme, sweet marjoram, and summer savory make a Provençal herb blend to add to braising liquids for slow-cooked meats such as lamb shanks—but go easy on the rosemary, because its strong flavor doesn't diminish much during cooking and can dominate.

Add a pinch of rosemary to fava beans, or a tad to mushrooms, roast pork, and oven-roasted potatoes. Italians use it to flavor veal, and it has a strange but likable affinity for spinach.

Rosemary branches: These strong, resinous twigs impart a wonderful, volatile note to whatever they're cooked with. I like to lay tough, woody stems of rosemary under meats such as chicken, steak, or butterflied leg of lamb on the gas grill. The rosemary smoke adds a pleasing, smoky-rich note, rather than the harsher flavor of the fresh leaves.

Rosemary Pesto

MAKES ABOUT 1 1/2 CUPS

Who says pesto has to be made with basil? You can make it with parsley—or you can make a robust and highly flavored version with rosemary that will carry you back to that night in Tuscany. Place a big spoonful on a plate of hot, organic, whole-wheat pasta, stir, shake on some red pepper flakes, and you've got a meal.

3 tablespoons pine nuts
2 cups lightly packed Italian flat-leaf parsley, chopped
1 cup lightly packed fresh rosemary leaves
2 cloves garlic
1/2 cup extra-virgin olive oil, plus extra for storage
1/4 cup grated Parmesan cheese
Salt and freshly ground black pepper, to taste

1. Toss the pine nuts in a small dry skillet over medium heat until toasted light brown. Set aside.

2. Place the parsley, rosemary, pine nuts, and garlic in a blender. Blend to a smooth paste. Add the oil in a very slow, steady stream until the paste is creamy. Pour the mixture into a bowl and add the grated cheese, then salt and pepper to taste.

3. Transfer the pesto to a jar and cover the surface with a thin layer of olive oil. Seal the jar with a tight-fitting lid and refrigerate for up to 2 months, or freeze indefinitely.

Rosemary Chicken Toscana

SERVES 4

Not just in Tuscany, but all over northern Italy, you can find versions of this delicacy. I found the inspiration for this dish in Verona.

4 bone-in, skin-on chicken breasts
1 1/2 tablespoons minced rosemary leaves
Salt and freshly ground black pepper
24 peeled cloves garlic (1 1/2 to 2 heads)
2 tablespoons extra-virgin olive oil
1 cup chicken stock
2/3 cup dry Italian white wine, such as Orvieto

1. Preheat the oven to 475°F.

2. Loosen the skin on the breasts by running your fingers under it, then insert 1/2 teaspoon of the rosemary leaves under each skin. Sprinkle each breast with a little salt and pepper. Place the breasts in an ovenproof skillet or flameproof baking dish, skin side up.

3. Mix the garlic, oil, and 1 teaspoon of the remaining rosemary together in a small bowl. With a spoon, lift out the garlic cloves and arrange them evenly around the chicken. Drizzle the remaining oil and rosemary over the chicken. Put the skillet in the oven and roast for 15 minutes.

4. Add the chicken stock to the skillet, being careful not to spatter the hot oil. Continue to roast until the chicken is cooked through, another 5 to 7 minutes.

5. Remove the skillet from the oven and transfer the chicken to individual plates; keep warm. Place the skillet over high heat, bring the liquid to a boil, and add the wine. Boil for 1 to 2 minutes to reduce the pan juices and evaporate the alcohol, scraping the bottom to loosen any clinging bits. Spoon the reduced liquid over the breasts and serve.

SAGE

SEASON: spring through fall

GOOD VARIETIES: Golden, Green Pineapple, Purple, Three-Colored

WHAT TO LOOK FOR: The leaves should be blemish free and the cut ends should be freshly cut.

STORAGE AND PREPARATION TIPS: Sage is easy to dry, and its flavors and aromas intensify when the leaves are dried. To dry, tie the stem ends of the sprigs together and hang the bundle from the ceiling in a warm, dry place out of direct sun. When the leaves are crisply dry, break them up by rubbing them together with your palms and store in an airtight container.

NUTRITIONAL HIGHLIGHTS: antioxidants, calcium, manganese

GOES WELL WITH: Parmesan cheese, pork, poultry, sausage, turkey stuffing, veal

---

Sage, in all of its colorful varieties, is as pretty in the organic garden as it is useful in the kitchen. It's one of the aromatic herbs of Provence and the Mediterranean basin, and, like thyme, rosemary, and oregano, likes poor, dry soil if it's going to produce the most flavorful leaves.

Besides common green garden sage, with its nubbly texture, there are plenty of attractive varieties: Golden sage's leaves have green and gold markings. The bright red flowers of pineapple sage do taste a bit like pineapple, but the beautiful buds are mostly used to add color to salads. Purple sage sports dark greenish purple leaves. Three-colored sage's leaves have green, white, and pink variegations. But for cooking and that appealing sage flavor, no cultivar beats the plain old green variety. The fresh leaves have a friendly spiciness and a musky, even medicinal scent.

Uses

The most common culinary use for the herb in America is for flavoring the Thanksgiving turkey's stuffing—but that's just the most obvious use. Sage tea has been used as a sovereign remedy for colds, sore throats, and tonsillitis, and as a digestive aid. Its genus name, Salvia, meaning "to save," reflects its medicinal history. In ancient times, it was even thought to promote wisdom.

Ordinary green sage is quite potent, especially when dried, so use it judiciously. It pairs well with other strongly flavored herbs, such as rosemary and oregano, as well as the lemon herbs—lemon balm and lemon verbena. Sage exalts fatty meats such as pork, sausage, veal, and poultry. Stuff a rolled pork roast with a mixture of chopped sage and apples. It also makes a warm partnership with liver and onions. (Mix minced sage and parsley and add it to the batter you use to make fried onion rings.) Tie fresh sage in a bouquet with parsley and thyme and add it to soups and stews, removing it before serving.

Sage has an affinity for Italian dishes such as pizzas, focaccia, pastas, and gnocchi. It adds a pleasant herbal note when used in small quantities with mild cheeses. Chop it fine and use it in your cornbreads and biscuits. Use it to flavor bean, lentil, and pea soups.

Add a fresh sage leaf to other herbal teas when you brew them to augment and enhance their flavor. Add a pinch to tuna salad, to seared ahi, and to baked or poached ocean fish.

Saltimbocca

SERVES 4

This classic Italian dish should jump into your mouth if the name is true, for that's what saltimbocca means. If you have an aversion to veal, use chicken breasts pounded to 1/2-inch thickness or pork cutlets. However, organic veal is humanely raised—by law.

4 organic veal cutlets, pounded 1/2 inch thick
8 thin slices prosciutto
4 slices Fontina cheese
2 tablespoons butter
1/4 cup dry white wine
1/2 teaspoon fresh minced sage
1/4 teaspoon Dijon mustard

1. Top each of the veal cutlets with two slices of prosciutto and a slice of Fontina. Roll them up, turning in the sides so the filling is completely enclosed. Secure them with toothpicks, but don't let the ends of the toothpicks stick out too far, as it will make it impossible to brown the rolls all over.

2. Preheat the oven to its lowest setting. Place a skillet over high heat for 1 to 2 minutes, then add the butter. When the butter is sizzling, add the rolls. Cook for 5 to 7 minutes, turning them frequently, until well browned all over. Remove the skillet from the heat and place the rolls in a serving dish; keep warm in the oven. Put the pan back on the heat; add the wine and cook until the alcohol is evaporated, scraping up any browned bits. Add the sage and mustard and mix well. Pour this sauce over the rolls.

TARRAGON

SEASON: summer and fall

GOOD VARIETIES: French tarragon

WHAT TO LOOK FOR: Make sure you are buying true French tarragon and not the inferior Russian species, which is almost tasteless by comparison. Pull off a leaf and crush it. It should smell and taste like spicy anise. The leaves should be glossy and pointed; smaller leaves should be rounded at the tips.

STORAGE AND PREPARATION TIPS: Store fresh tarragon in the refrigerator in a plastic bag for 3 to 5 days.

NUTRITIONAL HIGHLIGHTS: phytochemicals

GOES WELL WITH: chicken, fish, leafy greens, other herbs

Somewhere, at some time—nobody knows for sure when, except that it was a long time ago—a native Siberian perennial form of tarragon produced a sterile subspecies with a sweet anise aroma and a pronounced anise flavor. Because it produced no viable seed, the only way for its owner to grow more was to take stem cuttings and root them or to divide the plant's brittle white roots and replant the separated pieces.

The owner must have done one or the other, because the plant spread, moving south to the Arab lands (probably in classical times), whence it was carried west to North Africa and then up to Spain during the Moorish invasion. Finally it reached France. The French adopted it with such enthusiasm it came to be called French tarragon and became an indispensable part of their national cuisine. Despite the fact that it had been divided or stem-rooted thousands of times, it was still the same seedless plant.

Other tarragon plants also developed. One grew taller than French tarragon, with dull, rather than shiny leaves, a bitter taste, and little of the sweet anise flavor that makes French tarragon so cherished. This weedy plant has come to be known as just plain tarragon, or sometimes Russian tarragon.

Uses

French tarragon is a featured player—along with parsley, chervil, and chives—in the fresh herb blend called fines herbes, which you can use to flavor the poaching liquid for fish or add at the end of cooking to brighten a dish. A few leaves of fresh tarragon will add a licorice note to salads. Because of the herb's assertiveness, less is more. It's excellent for flavoring shellfish, light fish such as sole and salmon, and white meats. Spinach becomes a whole new vegetable when a little tarragon is sprinkled among its leaves before steaming. You can also make tarragon vinegar. Loosely pack a mason jar with French tarragon, then fill it with a white vinegar (I like the mild, unseasoned rice vinegar), screw the cap on, and let it sit in a cabinet for 3 months. Pour off the vinegar into a fancy bottle and add a fresh sprig of tarragon. Use it in homemade tartar sauce, in marinades, and to baste chicken or fish. Tarragon vinegar has a special affinity for mushrooms, adding a light, high note to the mushrooms' earthy base. In a vinaigrette, it has an anise assertiveness that combines well with tomatoes and basil.

Tarragon Chicken

SERVES 4

Seek out a fresh-killed organic chicken for this classic. It will be worth it. This is a simple dish and the tarragon flavor is not lost in the cooking.

This recipe uses chicken breasts, legs, and thighs. Use the rest to make chicken stock.

One 2- to 3-pound chicken
1/2 cup all-purpose flour
1/4 cup minced fresh tarragon
1 teaspoon salt
1/2 teaspoon freshly ground black pepper
6 tablespoons tarragon vinegar
1/4 cup extra-virgin olive oil

1. Cut the chicken into 2 legs, 2 breasts, and 2 thighs. Reserve the wings, giblets, and backs for stock.

2. Combine the flour, tarragon, salt, and pepper in a plastic bag. Put the vinegar in a shallow bowl. Dip the chicken pieces in the vinegar until entirely wet, then place them in the bag. Shake until the pieces are coated. Shake off any excess.

3. In a large skillet, heat the olive oil over medium heat. When hot, add the chicken pieces and cook on both sides until nicely browned, 15 minutes total. Pour any remaining vinegar over the chicken, reduce the heat to medium-low and continue to cook and turn the pieces about 25 minutes, or until the chicken is done and a fork can be easily inserted into each piece.

THYME

SEASON: Mid-spring through fall

GOOD VARIETIES: See below

WHAT TO LOOK FOR: Fresh thyme should lightly scent your hand when you brush it across the leaves.

STORAGE AND PREPARATION TIPS: Thyme stores well dried. To dry, tie bundles at the base of the stems and hang them in a warm, dry place out of direct sun until the leaves crumble off easily. Store the crumbled leaves in a closed container in a dark cabinet. Save the empty stems to use as a "brush" for adding marinades to almost anything.

NUTRITIONAL HIGHLIGHTS: vitamin A, vitamin C, small amounts of calcium, copper, fiber, iron, manganese

GOES WELL WITH: carrots, cheddar cheese, chicken, fish, goat cheese, legumes, meat, onions, tomatoes

For me, thyme is the central herb—the one around which all others revolve. Its spicy, peppery aroma, its slightly resinous taste that leaves the mouth refreshed, its ability to hold its essential oils when dried, and its perfumed smoke are the very essence of goodness.

Garden or common thyme: A low-growing, shrubby, woody plant that reaches about 1 foot. This is the basic thyme for most recipes.

Lemon thyme: Easily found at herb stands, farmers' markets, and nurseries, where you can also find a cultivar called Lemon Mist. It's a perfect flavoring agent for fish, light stocks, pastries, salads—anywhere a light and lemony herbal touch is needed. You can make a tea from it as well by pouring a cup of boiling water over 4 or 5 sprigs.

Caraway thyme: Native to the islands of Corsica and Sardinia, it has overtones of caraway in its thymol scent. (Thymol is the herb's essential oil.)

Mother-of-thyme: A highly scented, low-growing, creeping form of thyme with very tiny leaves. Its little lavender flowers are beloved of honeybees.

Uses

Thyme does so much in so many ways. It goes with almost all meats—fish and chicken, beef, lamb, and pork, and game such as rabbit and venison. It goes with sweet vegetables, such as carrots, and cooked onions and tomatoes, and even sweet fruits such as figs. It's wonderful with beans and other legumes and with tangy cheeses such as chèvre and cheddar. It flavors soups and stews and ragouts.

Thyme Pizza

SERVES 2

Pizza has a thousand variations, but this one tastes truly Italian because of the garlic and the herbs. You can make pizza dough from organic flour or buy one of those ready-made, organic, sprouted-wheat pizza shells available at many organic grocery stores. Some stores also now sell pre-made raw pizza dough.

One 12-inch pizza shell, or any pizza dough rolled into a 12-inch circle

2 tablespoons extra-virgin olive oil

6 tablespoons marinara sauce, preferably homemade

1/2 cup chopped fresh garlic, finely chopped

2 tablespoons chopped fresh thyme

1 tablespoon chopped fresh oregano

1/2 cup shredded mozzarella (about 2 ounces)

1/2 cup freshly grated Parmesan (about 2 ounces)

Preheat the oven to 500°F and position a rack at the top of the oven. Place the pizza shell on a large baking sheet. Brush the pizza shell with the olive oil, then spread on the marinara sauce. Sprinkle on the garlic, thyme and oregano, and cheeses, in that order. Bake for 12 minutes until the cheeses are bubbling and browning.

CHAPTER 6

Meat, Fish, Dairy, and Eggs

To its credit, the organic movement—farmers, merchants, and consumers alike—have included humane treatment as part of what it means to produce organic meat, milk, and eggs. This isn't the place to enumerate the cruelties with which conventional meat and milk animals and laying hens can often be treated. Suffice it to say that when you buy organic, you know the animals have been raised humanely. The idea is to give them conditions that in some ways account for their natural likes and dislikes.

When you buy organic meat, you are getting some great big bonuses. Grass-fed organic beef, for instance, has more of the conjugated linoleic acid (CLA), which we need for good health. But just as important is what you're not getting. Organic beef cannot by law be fed animal offal, which is how mad cow disease is spread. You're not getting the routine use of antibiotics, which can cause antibiotic resistance among disease organisms that infect human beings as well as farm animals. You're not getting hormones that unnaturally spur growth and stimulate the overproduction of milk. No genetically modified organisms can be fed to organic farm animals. Organic meat cannot be irradiated. And studies have shown that the many chemicals and bioactive substances used in conventional agriculture are of particular danger to developing fetuses and young children. Once again, organic food is preventive, protective, nourishing, and extra flavorful.

CERTIFIED ORGANIC

What does the label "certified organic" signify for meat and other farm-raised animal products? The National Organic Program emphasizes the humane treatment of animals, which gives them a chance to at least savor most, if not all, of the pleasures their natures may offer. Ducks kept for meat may not be able to fly, but at least they can have a pen with water to play in. Veal calves may not be able to run freely, but they can have pasture and the pleasure of suckling their mothers rather than living in a cage and being fed milk substitutes.

No antibiotics, hormones, or chemicals: The animals raised by organic certified farmers are never given antibiotics or hormones, or doused with pesticides. For chickens, this is true from the moment they crack out of their eggs. For beef cattle and hogs, this is true for pregnant mothers from the last trimester of gestation on. During their entire lives, the animals receive only 100 percent organic feed or pasture.

(Although the use of antibiotics or drugs isn't allowed in animals that are sold as organic, this is not to suggest that the animals' health problems are ignored if they become sick. If an animal at an organic farm falls sick and must receive antibiotics, it is removed from the organic herd or flock and treated. After a suitable time, it may be reinstated.)

Clean living conditions: Conventional feedlot cattle not only wallow in their own manure but when they are slaughtered, the meat is often irradiated using radioactive isotopes to kill any bacteria. But filthy slaughterhouses are still filthy, even if the meat is irradiated. And while the feeding of cattle parts to cattle is now banned due to the danger of mad cow disease, beef parts may still be fed to chickens and hogs, and parts of those animals may be fed to cattle. In addition, conventional beef cattle can be fed genetically modified grains, growth hormones, and antibiotics, and be chemically wormed to kill parasites. Under organic rules, none of these practices is allowed.

Benefits in flavor: All of this not only makes farming more pleasant but raises the quality of the meat products they yield. Animals raised according to organic principles of animal welfare are allowed space to express their nature, and that greatly reduces stress. Stress creates imbalances and disease and results in meat of lesser quality. Animals that are stressed before slaughter can yield pale, soft meat that exudes sour lactic acid. If you've ever raised chickens, or if you buy eggs from chickens raised in a healthy environment—with a yard where they can scratch and peck bugs or worms—you know that these eggs barely resemble factory farm eggs.

MEAT

BEEF

GOOD BREEDS: Angus, Polled Hereford, Beefalo

WHAT TO LOOK FOR:

Beef: Meat should be a deep red color with white rather than yellow fat.

Veal: Meat should have a pinkish color; pale or white meat comes from anemic calves that were subjected to cruel conditions prior to slaughter.

STORAGE AND PREPARATION TIPS: Refrigerate meat at 42°F or below; it will keep for two to three weeks. If beef develops mold on the skin, it can be sliced off and the meat underneath eaten if it still smells sweet. Check with your butcher for exact details on how long to store it.

NUTRITIONAL HIGHLIGHTS: B vitamins (including vitamin B_{12}), conjugated linoleic acid (especially from grass-fed cows), copper, iron, phosphorus, zinc

GOES WELL WITH: marsala, mushrooms, onions, sherry

Cows are meant to graze on grass. Organic farming raises cows in as close to a natural state as possible, which is healthier for the cows and yields healthier, better-tasting beef. Cattle that are finished on grains eat an unnatural diet that produces excessive amounts of fat in their muscle tissue and promotes the growth of harmful bacteria in their rumens. Grass-fed meat contains greater amounts of healthful fatty acids than grain-finished animals (see below).

Grass-fed beef: There are two basic kinds of organic beef. One comes from animals that are 100 percent grass fed, meaning that the animals are pastured until slaughter. The other kind involves taking the animals to feedlots for the last months of their lives, where they're fed a diet rich in grains, which fattens them up for slaughter. Grass-fed is a much more natural way for cattle to finish their days. The four stomach compartments of a cow are designed to digest grass, not grains, and feedlots, even organic feedlots, can be smelly, messy places. Between these two kinds of organic beef, 100 percent grass fed carries a premium.

Grass-fed beef contains less saturated fat than cattle finished on grains. Grass-fed beef also contains more of the essential fatty acid omega-3, as well as CLA, an essential fatty acid that helps regulate the way our bodies deal with other fats, boosts the immune system, fights cancer, and has other health benefits.

Grass-fed beef is not as tender as beef from animals finished on grain, but if the meat is aged by hanging for a period of time in a cooler, the aging process will tenderize it. Ask your butcher about aging. For more information about what the various labels for beef

HERITAGE FOODS

Almost all the beef cattle in the U.S. are just three breeds: Angus, Hereford, or Simmental, yet there are thousands of heritage breeds of cattle around the world. Some organic-minded farmers are returning to raising those rare and endangered breeds that offer superior flavor, even at the expense of sheer quantity of meat.

Heritage foods are foods derived from such rare breeds of American livestock—as well as certain crops with strong genetic authenticity and well-defined production methods. They range from the naturally mating American bronze turkey to hand-harvested wild rice from the upper Midwest's lakes and marshes. These foods are part of the identity of this country, yet risk extinction if demand for them does not increase soon.

To help preserve these rare animal breeds and place-specific plants, a group called Heritage Foods USA is devoted to working with farmers and communities where these foods are still produced and helping to bring them to a wider audience of consumers.

One of Heritage's biggest victories, and the reason it first formed, was to help double the population of heritage breeds of turkeys across the United States. Due to its efforts, one breed of turkey, the Bourbon Red, moved up from "rare" to "watch" status on conservation lists. The label allows consumers to track their food on the Heritage Foods USA's Web site (www.heritagefoodsusa.com), from which these foods can also be ordered.

mean, visit the Consumer Union's online guide (www.eco-labels.org).

Cook grass-fed ground beef lightly and cover the pan. The best way to cook steaks is to sear both sides, then finish the them in a 350°F oven for 10 or 15 minutes, depending on the thickness of the steak and the degree of doneness you want—but grass-fed beef is best rare.

Veal: The meat from calves is avoided by many people because they believe the calves are raised inhumanely, confined to crates, unable to nurse, fed "milk replacer" instead of their mother's milk, and become close to anemic because they get no hay to chew. On conventional farms, such a malnourished condition is, in fact, the goal, because there's a market for the pallid white veal that results. This kind of veal is called special fed by the industry. It is to be shunned by people who care about animal welfare.

Not all conventional veal is raised by such cruel methods, however. What's more, organic veal is raised humanely.

The calves are turned out to pasture with their mothers so they can suckle and nibble a little grass, too. This produces a pinker meat, but a meat that still has the qualities of good veal: a subtle flavor, and lots of juicy gelatin that results from the collagen in the meat dissolving in liquid during cooking, which makes veal perfect for creating the sauce bases of classic French cuisine.

Producers of humanely raised veal are generally small, and many are associated with dairy farming, running what's called a cow-calf operation. To continue lactating, a dairy cow must calve once a year. Much veal comes from male calves born from dairy cow mothers.

Organic Advantage

All organic beef is raised and slaughtered in less stressful conditions, which makes for more healthful and savory meat. Because organically raised cattle are not given antibiotics, hormones, or other unnatural substances, they grow strong and healthy on their natural diet. This allows the development of strong, mineral-rich flesh and bones. Their healthy diet makes for healthy animals, and that's transferred to the humans who consume them. (I have done side-by-side taste tests of organic and conventional steaks, and the organic meat is firmer and tastier.)

When animals are given routine antibiotics, only the antibiotic-resistant microorganisms survive. They then can attack humans, and our own antibiotics are less likely to kill them. Doctors consider this a big problem. Hormones given to cattle to force excessive growth can pass to humans, influencing our endocrine systems and causing problems such as feminine characteristics in young males. Children are especially vulnerable.

These are the labels you're likely to encounter when buying fresh meat:

Antibiotic and hormone-free: These animals have not been treated with antibiotics to prevent disease or hormones to increase growth or milk or egg production. Without the name of a certifying agency, however, you have to take these claims on faith. Certified organic foods are guaranteed not to contain antibiotics or hormones.

Certified organic: A certifying agency, usually named on the label, has visited the farm and guaranteed that the farmer has complied with organic rules. Meat from cattle raised on small farms may be organically grown or simply be produced by a farmer who takes great care to raise his animals in a humane, environmentally friendly way. It may not be USDA certified organic, due to the costs and paperwork involved in achieving certification. In such cases, you will have to trust the source.

Certified humane: An agency such as Certified Humane guarantees that the animals have been raised and slaughtered according to strict humane standards. If the certifying agency isn't named on the label, then the words don't guarantee much.

Dry aged: Beef that's hung for a certain number of days to allow enzymes in the meat to begin to soften the tissues and add an extra layer of flavor. Grass-fed beef is lean and especially benefits from aging to tenderize it.

Grass fed: Even organic beef is not necessarily grass fed. Grass-fed cows and sheep have not been fed grains during the last few months of their lives, but rather are pastured until slaughter.

Natural or naturally raised: There is no governmental standard or meaning for these terms; they are essentially meaningless.

Sloppy Joes

SERVES 4

You can get the prepared sloppy joe mixes and ordinary hamburger and white bread buns—or you can make this simple dinner the organic way.

1 pound lean ground grass-fed beef
1/2 cup chopped onion
1 cup chili sauce
1 tablespoon dark brown sugar
1 tablespoon freshly squeezed lemon juice
1 tablespoon white vinegar
1 tablespoon Worcestershire sauce
1 teaspoon Dijon mustard
1 teaspoon paprika
Salt and freshly ground black pepper, to taste
4 whole-wheat hamburger buns

In a heavy skillet over medium-high heat, sauté the ground beef and onion until the meat is no longer pink, about 7 minutes, stirring frequently to break up clumps. Stir in the chili sauce, brown sugar, lemon juice, vinegar, Worcestershire sauce, mustard, paprika, and salt and pepper to taste, and cook over low heat, stirring occasionally, until thickened, about 15 minutes. Fill the buns with the sloppy joe mixture and serve.

LAMB

SEASON: spring

GOOD BREEDS: Hebridean, Manx, Navajo-Churro

WHAT TO LOOK FOR: Look for young lamb—legs less than 5 pounds, racks with small bones—with rich, red meat and white, not yellow, fat.

STORAGE AND PREPARATION TIPS: Lamb should be refrigerated until use, and used as soon after purchase as possible. For leg of lamb, trim the excess fat, then rub the surface with mashed garlic, salt, and pepper before roasting.

NUTRITIONAL HIGHLIGHTS: B vitamins (including vitamin B_{12}), conjugated linoleic acid, copper, iron, phosphorus, zinc

GOES WELL WITH: garlic, mint, Pinot Noir, rosemary

Yes, there is a season when lambs arrive. Spring (late February through June) is

PROFILE OF AN UNCERTIFIED GRASS-FED BEEF FARMER

The Hudson Valley Farmers cooperative in Dutchess County, New York, is a small-scale beef producer that supplies some of the best restaurants in New York City. It was once certified organic, but dropped organic certification when the USDA took over the National Organic Program. Director Steve Kay explained to me, "For the organic rules to be successful, we had to get the government out of the process. But that didn't happen. The rules were written for the big growers—it's all about the label, not small farmers like us."

Although uncertified, some small farmers can be even more careful about their husbandry than large certified producers—you just need to know the producer and his or her product.

The Hudson Valley Farmers coop follows the grass-fed-is-best philosophy and is constantly testing its meat for omega-3 and the cancer-fighting conjugated linoleic acid (see page 252) to see how grass affects their levels in the tissues of the animals.

"I used to grow potatoes," Kay says. "I cared for them like they were my pets. Now I grow beef—Angus and Shorthorns. I used to finish the animals on grain, but now that I've seen the health benefits for the animals—and for humans—from grass fed only, I finish them on pasture." He says the meat is more intensely flavored but denser: muscle is leaner, and the fat cooks away more quickly, so the meat must be cooked more carefully.

"The reason I farm," Kay adds, "is to produce the best possible product, not to follow rules for farming set up by the government, of all people. Under the USDA organic rules, you can finish beef animals on grain in a feedlot, where they are wallowing in their own manure, and still call it organic. My animals never see a feedlot."

A big problem with finishing beef on grain is that their digestive systems simply aren't meant to digest corn. It renders their digestive tracts acidic and hospitable to E. coli and other pathogenic bacteria. Hence there's a need in conventional beef production for more antibiotics and the risk (and reality) of promoting the evolution of antibiotic-resistant bacteria.

"I avoid the word organic," he said. "It's a regulated word now. The rule makers don't understand meat production. If I'm driving and see a farm with fabulous hay, I'll stop and buy it right off the fields. I insist on giving my animals the best possible feed."

Steve Kay represents the kind of independent, stiff-necked Yankee farmer who isn't going to be told what to do or how to do it by the government. He may not be certified, but he farms with the organic spirit. His clients include top-flight New York City restaurants like Blue Hill, Il Buco, and Savoy. "They know me," he said. "I supply them with well-grown beef that tastes better and is clean." That's the organic ideal.

lambing time in North America. The hills of western Sonoma County turn green with the first significant winter rains and by early spring the birthing of the lambs begins. The lambs stay with their mothers, suckling and then eating grasses and wildflowers.

Organic Advantage

Organic lambs are born to mothers given no chemical parasite dips or chemical worming agents. Therein lies a problem for organic sheep and lamb producers, as intestinal worms need to be dealt with. Studies have shown that safe worming agents that would otherwise be allowed, such as garlic, herbs, and diatomaceous earth (containing the sharp-edged skeletons of minute sea plants and animals), simply don't work.

So ingenious organic farmers have developed methods of dealing with the parasites by understanding their life cycles. The parasites tend to move toward the tips of grass blades when they're wet with morning dew, so lambs are turned onto new pasture in the afternoon when the grass is dry. They are also rotated more frequently through new pastures to head off trouble. And far fewer animals occupy any given acre of organic pasture than under conventional systems, lessening the population density and making infection less likely. In addition, certain breeds of sheep seem to be less prone to infection by intestinal parasites than others, and organic farmers have taken note. As for parasites of the wool or skin, there are organic insecticides made from plants, such as sabadilla, a kind of lily, and pyrethrum, a kind of chrysanthemum, that can be dusted on the animals.

All these measures add to the cost of producing organic lamb, but the cost is worth it for health-minded people who know that humanely raised organic lamb is clean and flavorful.

During spring lambing season, American organic lamb is widely available. New Zealand lamb, which arrives six months later, may also be organic. Ask your butcher, or see Sources (page 287) to locate producers of naturally raised, grass-fed organic lamb near you.

Garlic and Rosemary Rack of Lamb

SERVES 2 TO 3

A scrumptious synthesis of flavors results from combining lamb, garlic, and rosemary. It's savory and mouthwatering. Serve it with creamed spinach and potato chunks browned in the fat you remove from the rack.

1 rack of lamb (1 1/2 to 2 pounds), chine bone removed, frenched (see Tip)
3 cloves garlic, sliced into thin rounds
1 sprig fresh rosemary
Salt and freshly ground black pepper

Preheat the oven to 425°F and prepare a roasting pan with a slotted top rack.

Using the point of a sharp knife, make horizontal slits in the fat covering the "eye," or solid meat portion of the rack, about 2 inches apart in all directions. Alternately, insert slices of garlic and pinches of rosemary leaves into the slits. Place the lamb fat side up on the slotted top of the roasting pan. Roast for exactly 25 minutes. Carve the rack into chops at the table.

TIP: You can ask your butcher to french a rack of lamb for roasting, but you can also do this yourself. Cut away the layers of fat from the bones back to where the eye of the rack begins. Slice the connecting tissue between the bones, removing the fat and tissue back to but not into the eye. Remove the layer of fat and the thin bit of meat from the top of the eye, leaving a covering of white fat on the eye.

PORK

GOOD BREED: Berkshire

WHAT TO LOOK FOR: Meat should be a pleasing pink color; avoid grayish meat. Pork tenderloins should be pinkish red. The fat layer covering roasts and chops should be thin and even, not thick. Organic hams—fresh or smoked—should have a water content of 10 percent or less. (Water content often appears on the label; if not, ask the butcher.)

STORAGE AND PREPARATION TIPS: Like lamb, pork should be refrigerated and used soon after it is purchased. Trim the excess fat before cooking it.

NUTRITIONAL HIGHTLIGHTS: B vitamins (including vitamin B_{12}), iron, phosphorus, potassium, protein, selenium, zinc

GOES WELL WITH: sweet fruits like apples; sour foods like sauerkraut

Pigs are not naturally filthy animals. In fact, given proper care, they are rather clean. They like to wallow in mud on a hot day because they have no sweat glands, and evaporating water from the mud cools them down.

They also like to hunt for roots, corms, and tubers. A field infested with yellow nutsedge—a tough, invasive weed with small, juicy tubers (called nutlets)—can be cleaned up by running hogs in the field and letting them root the nutlets out, which they naturally love to do.

In the fall when wild apples, acorns, and mast (beech seeds) are dropping in meadows and forests, hogs that have access to this kind of land will eat massive quantities of them. On this kind of natural diet, pork becomes wildly flavorful. The last time I ate at the French Laundry restaurant in California's Napa Valley, I had such a piece of pork: its flavor and tenderness were exquisite. Chef Thomas Keller said the animal had been fed apples on the Pennsylvania farm where it had been raised. In fact, before 1950, turning pigs out to forage was generally considered a part of good animal husbandry, as it provided the animals vitamins and minerals. That practice ended as hog farming became technologized and focused on mass production.

Besides fresh cuts of pork and cured hams, cured organic Italian-style pork products, such as prosciutto, pancetta, mortadella, and coppa are available, made by domestic producers such as Applegate Farms (carried in most stores with organic sections). You may find imported Italian prosciutto that's organically produced, as Italy is one of the leaders in the European Union's organic movement.

Organic Advantage

For the most part, conventional pigs get a steady diet of corn and soybeans. Organic pigs are given access to pasture spring, summer, and fall. They're also supplied with organic feed. Pigs are tough on pasture, tearing up the soil to get at roots, especially if too many animals are put out on an acre. Organic culture keeps the forage pressure low. Conventional farmers who pasture pigs may clamp a ring through their noses to prevent them from rooting up pasture; when they do try to root, the pigs are hurt. Organic hog producers consider this mutilation and consequently inhumane.

There are other rules contributing to healthy living conditions for the pigs. They can't be housed on 100 percent slatted floors, which are used in conventional operations so excrement and urine fall through the slats and into a holding pit; instead, some flooring is not above manure, and that floor is cleaned daily. All their feed and bedding has to be certified organic. Early weaning is not allowed, so piglets get the benefit of mother's milk and closeness to mom longer, leading to less stress, more hog happiness—and ultimately better meat.

At least 55 percent of their feed has to come from their own farm, or be certified by another organic grower. Routine confinement in crates or boxes—a cruel but common practice in conventional hog operations—is prohibited. Fresh air and daylight have to be provided. Spacious sleeping and resting areas with adequate bedding must be provided. On organic farms, the pig manure is turned into compost and incorporated into the soil in an environmentally sound manner. In fact, organic manure management minimizes soil and water degradation and optimizes the recycling of nutrients back to the land where the hog feed is grown. All this is in addition to the usual prohibitions on genetically modified feed, routine antibiotics, drugs, pesticides, animal by-products, chemically extracted feeds, and other agricultural chemicals.

Will pork raised organically be more expensive than conventional? Of course. But the cost of conventional pork doesn't include the hidden costs associated with it: erosion of depleted and chemically-treated soils, fouling of waterways with runoff from manure piles, and chemicals in the meat that cause illness in human beings.

Uses

Pork cutlets make a good substitute for veal in scaloppine. Pork tenderloins can be stuffed with mashed fruit and then cooked. Pork loin roast is 100 percent meat and therefore economical. Smoked ham hock adds character to bean and pea soups and stews.

Pork Loin Roast with Dried Fruit and Sweet Spices

SERVES 5

Pork is a sweet meat, and its flavor blends beautifully with dried fruits and spices. Try this for a special occasion dinner. You'll need butcher's string and a sharp knife.

One 3-pound rolled pork loin roast
Freshly grated nutmeg
4 cups finely chopped dried fruits such as raisins, cherries, figs, pitted prunes, and/or mangoes
$^1/_2$ cup canola oil
2 cups apple cider
1 tart apple, peeled, cored, and roughly chopped
3 tablespoons butter
1 tablespoon ground cinnamon
Salt and freshly ground black pepper

1. When you buy the roast it will be tied with butcher's string. Cut these strings away. The cylindrical roast will spread open into two connected halves. With a sharp knife, slice into each half at a shallow angle, but not all the way through, so that the roast opens out into a rectangle of pork.

2. Lightly dust the interior surfaces with nutmeg (don't overdo this). Spread $1^1/_2$ cups of the chopped fruit over the surface of one half and another $1^1/_2$ cups over the surface of the other half. Close the two halves up, spreading the final cup of fruit between them. If any fruit is sticking out of the ends or the seam, stuff it back in. Retie the roast with butcher's string where it was tied before, so that it's a secure cylinder.

3. Preheat the oven to 400°F. Heat the oil in a heavy ovenproof skillet or flameproof baking dish. When it's hot but not smoking, put in the roast and brown it all around, but not on the ends. Remove the meat to a plate, pour off the oil from the skillet, return the roast to the skillet, place it in the oven, and roast for 1 hour and 20 minutes.

4. After you've put the roast in the oven, combine the apple cider, chopped apple, butter, and cinnamon in a saucepan and bring to a gentle boil. Reduce the heat and simmer for 30 minutes, or until the apple chunks are soft.

5. When the roast has been in the oven for 50 minutes, pour all of the cider mixture over it. Push any apple chunks off the surface of the roast into the liquid in the skillet. Sprinkle the roast with a little salt and pepper. Roast

the meat for the final 30 minutes. Let rest for a few minutes out of the oven, and serve with the apple cider sauce.

TIP: Pork no longer needs to be cooked until well done. Scientists have discovered that the trichina parasite, which causes trichinosis, is killed at 137°F, well below the 160°F reached when pork is cooked to medium. And pigs today—both organic and conventional—are raised under conditions and fed foods that decrease the possibility of trichina infection. Additionally, pigs today are leaner than they once were; as a result, cooking them to well-done results in chewy meat. So I suggest cooking pork to medium. To be safe, medium rare to raw pork should still be avoided.

POULTRY

GOOD BREEDS:

Chicken: Orpington, Rhode Island Red

Duck: Muscovy

Turkey: heritage breeds such as American Bronze, Blue Slate, Bourbon Red, Jersey Buff, and Narragansett

WHAT TO LOOK FOR: The fat should be yellow, not white, and the bird should appear plump. Pass over birds that look scrawny, or if their skin has serious tears (skin helps seal in juices).

STORAGE AND PREPARATION TIPS: Poultry should be cooked the day you buy it, although it can be stored in a twist-tied plastic bag—but for no more than 2 days.

OTHER MEATS

For what it's worth, the best-tasting red meat I've ever eaten is reindeer, prepared by Philippe Jeanty, who was then chef at Domaine Chandon in the Napa Valley. Antelope living naturally on huge expanses of acreage in New Mexico comes in second. Organic bison meat, often labeled buffalo, is becoming more widely available in supermarkets. Tiensvold Farms in Nebraska is one such purveyor. Bison are raised on pasture, and their meat is very flavorful, low in fat, and devoid of any gamey taste. Elk, caribou, wild boar, and other specialty meats are available, and most probably natural but not certifiably organic.

NUTRITIONAL HIGHLIGHTS: B vitamins (including vitamin B_{12}), iron (dark meat only), niacin, phosphorus, protein, selenium, zinc

GOES WELL WITH:

Chicken: bacon, cream, garlic, mushrooms, rosemary, thyme, wine

Duck: apples, black currants, cherries, citrus, figs, tamari

Turkey: celery, cranberries, ham, prunes, sage, sherry, thyme

What's the difference between poultry labeled natural and organic? According to USDA guidelines, poultry may be labeled natural if it doesn't contain any additions to its natural state, such as artificial flavorings, colorings, chemical preservatives, growth hormones, or stimulants. Organic goes well beyond those restrictions. Poultry producers must provide humane conditions, use organic grains in their feed, and slaughter the birds humanely in order to be granted the organic seal.

Organic Advantage

Chickens: In addition to their organic, antibiotic-free diets, organic birds are treated well in other ways. They cannot be permanently confined and must have access to sunlight, fresh air, and a scratch yard. They get eight hours of darkness at night. They are also slaughtered slightly older than conventional broilers.

Contrast this with the common conventional situation. Chickens are raised two birds to the square foot: up to forty thousand birds in an intensive chicken house. The building is often windowless, with almost constant lighting to speed growth. Stress levels are high, and antibiotics are used to keep the birds alive.

Growth-promoting drugs and stimulants force such a rapid rate of growth that their legs often can't support their bodies. Fans exhaust the ammonia-laden air. At six weeks of age, they are slaughtered—and the inhumane practices at conventional slaughterhouses don't bear repeating.

Ducks and geese: Ducks and geese are waterfowl, of course, and become depressed and dirty if they can't swim and play in the water every day. So organic duck and goose production, which requires a water source, is an expensive method of raising these animals. Organic waterfowl farming is still in its infancy. Slow Food USA is involved in preserving two rare breeds of heritage geese—the American Buff goose and the Pilgrim goose.

Turkey: Of the four hundred million turkeys consumed in the United States each year, all but ten thousand are one variety, the Broad Breasted White. Raised conventionally, these birds are overbred for white breast meat and have lost the ability to run, fly, or breed naturally. According to Slow Food USA, many are unhealthy, never see natural sunlight, and have their beaks shaved off so they don't injure one another in their cramped, stressful environment. Organic turkeys, by contrast, have the same rights to fresh air, sunlight, and pasture as organic chickens.

Other poultry: Other small-scale organic poultry operations include the farming of Coturnix quail for eggs and meat. These quail are very efficient producers of eggs, requiring only two pounds of feed to make a pound of eggs, in contrast to chickens, which require three pounds. Pheasant, squab, and guinea fowl are available, but their organic provenance is usually guaranteed by a local farmer rather than a national certification agency.

Southern Fried Chicken

SERVES 4

My mom was from Kentucky and claimed that down South, the women were beautiful but the men so-so; up North, the women were so-so but the men were handsome. She would impart these pearls of knowledge while setting a plate full of fried chicken on the table. To me, it was the chicken that was beautiful.

1 cup buttermilk
1 large egg
1 cup all-purpose flour
1 cup finely crushed herbed crackers
1 tablespoon minced fresh parsley
1/2 tablespoon dried thyme
2 teaspoons salt
2 teaspoons freshly ground black pepper
2 cups canola oil
3 tablespoons bacon fat
1 frying chicken (about 3 pounds), cut into 8 pieces

1. Preheat the oven to 350°F. In a medium bowl, whip together the buttermilk and egg. In a separate bowl, mix the flour, crushed crackers, parsley, thyme, salt, and pepper.

RABBIT

As a boy, I went hunting for rabbits with my buddies every fall, and we came home with plenty. They were gamier than domestic rabbits, but delicious. We had to check them carefully for parasites, but no one to my knowledge ever got sick from eating wild cottontails.

While most people don't cook rabbit at home, it frequently appears at high-end restaurants. And it can be purchased. Most store-bought rabbits today are raised by specialty growers using specific meat breeds. To get the organic seal, they can't be raised in permanent cages. They must be allowed the company of other animals. They must get a minimum of eight hours of daylight each day. And if given access to pasture, each rabbit must have five square meters of room.

Breeding does (moms) must not have more than six litters per year (they really do breed like rabbits), and the kits (babies) must be allowed at least thirty-five days with their mothers before being weaned.

2. Select a heavy frying pan deep enough to hold the oil and bacon fat, and large enough to hold all the chicken pieces. Add the oil and bacon fat to the pan and heat over medium heat. When the oil is hot, starting with the dark meat pieces, dip each piece of chicken

in the buttermilk mixture, coat them well in the dry ingredients, and carefully add to the frying pan, using tongs to avoid spattering the hot fat on you. Don't let the pieces touch each other.

3. Fry the chicken for 5 minutes on each side, then reduce the heat to medium-low and continue frying for 15 more minutes, turning once, or until nicely browned. Drain the chicken on paper towels. Check for doneness by slicing into the thickest part of the chicken: there should be no pink and the juices should run clear. Check the white meat first. If more time is needed, place the chicken pieces on a baking sheet in a 350°F oven and check every 5 minutes.

SEAFOOD AND FRESHWATER FISH

WHAT TO LOOK FOR: It pays to know your fishmonger. Don't be afraid to ask when the fish was delivered: fresher is always better. It's hard to tell how old fish filets or salmon steaks are, but if you can see a whole fish, look it in the eye. It should be bright and clear and well defined. Find out when deliveries are scheduled and pick up your seafood the day it's brought in. Oysters, mussels, scallops, and clams should be as fresh as possible—you'll have to rely on your merchant to give you accurate information.

NUTRITIONAL HIGHLIGHTS: B vitamins, magnesium, omega-3 essential fatty acids, phosphorus, potassium, protein, selenium

GO WELL WITH: bacon, butter, chiles, lemon and lime juice, onions and shallots, white wines

Fish supplies are dying out.

It doesn't seem so long ago that the Grand Banks southeast of Newfoundland were considered an inexhaustible source of cod as well as other species of fish—numbers beyond imagining. Yet by 1995, all major cod fisheries on the Grand Banks were closed. Fished out. Canada imposed a 200-mile no-fishing limit along its Maritime Provinces coastline to allow fish stocks to recuperate. And then oil was found beneath the underwater plateaus that make up the Grand Banks. Oil development is now proceeding. So much for the Grand Banks as a resource for fish. Around the world, stocks of certain ocean fish are similarly threatened.

It's imperative, then, that organic-minded folks choose their seafood wisely, with an eye on sustainability—that is, fishing at levels that don't deplete stocks but sustain or even increase current fish stocks.

A second concern is mercury. Mercury levels in certain fish, caused by industrial pollution, are dangerously high. It's especially important for young women of childbearing age, pregnant women, and young children to avoid fish species with high levels of mercury because of that element's role in developmental abnormalities. Among the most contaminated fish are king mackerel, shark, swordfish, and tilefish from the Gulf of Mexico. While light tuna is acceptable, white tuna (albacore) has levels of mercury elevated enough to warrant limiting intake. The Center for Food Safety and Applied Nutrition, a division of the Food and Drug Administration (FDA), provides a complete listing of fish and shellfish mercury levels on its Web site (http://www.cfsan.fda.gov/~frf/sea-mehg.html).

More than three dozen projects to produce genetically engineered fish are underway, and the FDA has also received an application to allow the marketing of a salmon engineered to grow thirty times faster than a wild salmon, according to the Center for Food Safety. Researchers affiliated with Slow Food at Purdue University have found that due to their larger size, genetically engineered fish have a mating advantage over native fish, meaning that they will be more successful fertilizing the eggs of native females. But the mortality rate of the offspring of genetically engineered fish is one-third greater than that of native fish, due to the impact of the added genetic material. Some scientists predict that the introduction of genetically engineered fish could cause the extinction of native species, such as Atlantic salmon (already endangered) within only a few generations.

Remember that the government so far refuses to permit labeling of genetically modified organisms—plant or animal foodstuffs—and therefore is actively blocking consumers' ability to identify genetically engineered foods. If these Frankenfish find their way into supermarkets, the average consumer won't know about it. Visit the Center for Food Safety's Web site (www.gefish.org) for further information.

Organic Advantage

Because of the stress the world's wild fish stocks are currently under, fish farming is becoming more and more prevalent. As of this writing, there is no organic fish farming in the United States because the Department of Agriculture's organic rules don't cover farmed fish, although a Florida firm has achieved organic certification for its farmed shellfish. You may find farmed fish labeled organic certification pending, as the USDA is being pressured to adopt rules for organic farmed fish. Canada and Scotland are working to achieve organic certification, too. The problem is the water. Controlling it would be enormously expensive. But without such controls in place, fish farmers just can't certify that their fish don't contain contaminants.

Ocean fish: While wild Pacific salmon can't be labeled organic because there is no way to certify where the fish have been or what they've been eating, these cold-water salmon eat their natural diet and swim the cold, clean waters of the North Pacific, and are natural, even if they can't earn certification. The same

A SUSTAINABLE APPROACH TO BUYING FISH

The Audubon Society and the Monterey Bay Aquarium in California issue cards that tell you at a glance which fish are caught in an environmentally sound manner, which stocks aren't depleted, which are questionable, and which should be avoided because of their mercury content, endangered status, or because the way they're caught depletes or injures other species, including cetaceans. You can download these cards from the organizations' Web sites (http://seafood.audubon.org or www.montereybayaquarium.org/cr/seafoodwatch.asp).

The fish are ranked according to three categories: best choices, proceed with caution, and avoid. Among best choices are farmed catfish, farmed caviar, farmed crawfish, stone crab, wild-caught Alaskan salmon, tilapia, and Pacific halibut. The avoid list includes Atlantic and Icelandic cod, Chilean sea bass, grouper, Caribbean lobster, orange roughy, queen conch, swordfish, imported shrimp, red snapper, shark, and Gulf of Mexico tilefish.

holds true for halibut, petrale sole, and other Pacific fish, and for wild Atlantic fish as well.

Shrimp: Certified organic shrimp are beginning to make their way to markets; some are even available by mail order (see Sources, page 287). Organic certification for shrimp means that the company breeds its own pathogen-free, post-larvae shrimp until they are big enough to move to the grow-out ponds. There they're nurtured with organic feed processed from organically-raised tilapia. Certification also means that the shrimp are grown without antibiotics, hormones, dyes, or chemicals—which tells us something about the way non-organic shrimp and fish are raised. Organic shrimp production discharges no wastewater into the environment; water is biofiltered through a series of vegetation filters and reused.

Shrimp Risotto Supreme

SERVES 4

This risotto combines an interesting mix of flavors that has real synergy. My wife Susanna asks for her fix of this dish about every six to eight weeks.

1 pound medium shrimp
1 bunch asparagus
2 ears fresh corn, shucked
1 1/2 quarts chicken stock
1/4 cup extra-virgin olive oil
1 1/3 cups Arborio rice
1/2 cup dry white wine
1 jalapeño chile, stemmed, seeded, and minced
1/2 teaspoon freshly ground black pepper

2 limes
1/2 cup grated Parmesan
2 tablespoons chopped fresh flat-leaf parsley

1. Shell and devein the shrimp, then steam them in a basket over boiling water until they are just cooked through, about 3 to 5 minutes. Remove and coarsely chop. Chop off the top 2 inches of the asparagus tips and reserve. Save the remaining asparagus for another use. Add the tips to the steamer and gently steam until just tender, about 5 to 7 minutes. Boil the corn for about 3 minutes, or just until the kernels are tender; when cool enough to handle, cut the kernels off the cob and reserve.

2. In a 2-quart saucepan, bring the chicken stock to a simmer, then reduce the heat to low and keep warm.

3. Heat the olive oil in a large, deep heavy skillet over medium heat. When the oil is fragrant, add the rice and stir for 2 minutes until it turns opaque. (This prepares the rice to absorb the chicken stock.) Add the white wine and stir until the liquid is fully absorbed.

4. Add chicken stock, a half cup at a time, stirring constantly, adding another half cup as all the liquid is absorbed. After about 15 minutes of cooking (the rice grains will still have a chalky center), add the corn, jalapeño, and black pepper. When the rice is almost cooked through (about 20 minutes of cooking total), add the shrimp and asparagus tips. When the rice grains are just al dente, tender with perhaps the slightest bite in the center, juice the limes straight into the skillet, add the cheese, stir thoroughly and remove from the heat.

5. Sprinkle with the chopped parsley; serve immediately.

DAIRY

MILK

WHAT TO LOOK FOR: Milk labeled organic means that the milk is not from cows given bovine growth hormone or routine antibiotics. If you can find milk that's also labeled grass-fed, so much the better.

NUTRITIONAL HIGHLIGHTS: B vitamins, calcium, conjugated linoleic acid (especially milk from grass-fed cows), iodine, magnesium, phosphorus, protein, selenium, vitamin A, vitamin C, vitamin D, vitamin E, zinc

GOES WELL WITH: bananas, cherries, chocolate, coffee, rum, strawberries, vanilla

Cows are ruminants—natural grazers—and their four stomachs are exquisitely designed to metabolize grass. In nature, grains are a minimal part of a grazer's diet. Feeding them grain throws their metabolism into high gear—thus they produce more milk, with more milk fat in the milk, just as feeding steers grain in the confinement pens called feedlots fattens them up for slaughter. Grass-fed cows don't produce as much milk, but it's better milk, with more vitamins,

MILK NUTRITIONAL CHART

	MILK FAT %	PROTEIN %	CARBOHYDRATE %	CALCIUM MG	PHOSPHORUS MG	VITAMIN C MG
Cow	3.5	3.5	4.9	118	93	1.0
Goat	4.0	3.2	4.6	129	106	1.0
Sheep	7.0	6.0	5.3	193	n/a	2.5
Human	4.0	1.1	9.5	33	14	5.0

CLA, a beneficial fatty acid, and a richer flavor—as nature intended.

CLA protects against cancer in lab animals and shows promise against breast and prostate cancer in humans. Studies show that the more CLA in the milk, the less the risk of breast cancer in those who drink it. Milk from grass-fed cows has been found to contain five times higher levels of CLA than milk from cows fed supplements of corn kernels and corn silage.

Nevertheless, not all organic milk comes from grass-fed cows. The debate over grass-fed versus grain-fed is ongoing in the organic farming community. You can keep up to date on this and other organic farming issues by visiting the Rodale Institute's Web site (www.newfarm.org).

Organic Advantage

The difference between conventional milk and organic milk from grass-fed cows is striking. I used to buy milk from a lady who ran a very small dairy in the hills of eastern Pennsylvania. You brought your own bottles and she filled them from 5-gallon milk cans. Her cows were pastured except for the twice-daily milking. The milk was raw, unpasteurized, and not homogenized. I could skim the cream from the top of each bottle. Although most of us do not have access to such a dairy, organic milk from grass-fed cows is starting to appear in some markets, so keep your eyes open.

While the ideal of the happy cow grazing her lush green pasture is a pretty picture, it too often is an idealized one. When the National Organic Program was established, access to pasture for organic cows was written into the rules. This was to protect small dairy farmers and prevent large confinement dairies from taking over the organic milk business. It was also to promote the health of the dairy animals and increase the quality of organic milk and milk products. But the USDA, which has responsibility for enforcing the organic rules, is not enforcing the access to pasture rule because the word pasture is not defined in the rules—and is therefore, it claims, unenforceable. Most organic dairy farmers allow their

ONE ORGANIC DAIRY FARMER

One might think that milk is just milk and that organic milk can't be that different from ordinary milk. But then, you probably haven't heard of Mark McAfee, a third-generation dairy farmer, and his Organic Pastures Dairy in Fresno, California. Thousands of people have visited this dairy because it is so unusual. Instead of using confinement sheds, where cows wallow in their own manure, necessitating washing before milking (a practice Mark tells me only washes bacteria down to the udder and into the milk), Mark puts his cows out to permanent pasture. Instead of building a milking barn where the cows are concentrated together, Mark devised a milking parlor on wheels that he drives out to the pastures. He can milk a cow in 10 minutes and then turn it back to pasture. He rotates the cows from pasture to pasture on a regular basis, but they are never confined. This means that manure doesn't build up—visiting his dairy farm, one detects very little of that cow-country smell that arises from cows in close quarters.

McAfee raises Jersey cows, whose milk is richer in butterfat than milk from Holsteins, which are favored by conventional dairy farmers because they produce copious amounts of milk. And his milk is unpasteurized and raw. While the idea of raw milk sounds scary, most of the fine cheese of America and Europe is made from raw milk. McAfee told me he tests each batch of his milk for disease-causing salmonella, E. coli, and listeria, and that in more than six years of doing his organic pastures program, he's never found a human pathogen in the milk. He has even had researchers introduce such bacteria to test samples, and the pathogens have been unable to reproduce. In the varied ecosystem within Mark's milk, the competition from healthy bacteria stifles them. In a recent incident, listeria was found in a batch of his raw milk, but it was from milk he bought from another farmer to augment his supplies. He now tests any milk from outside his farm for all known pathogens.

He explained that a healthy balance of bacteria in the milk comes from a healthy cow, and a healthy cow comes from a healthy farm. And so he has designed what he calls a "pro-cow environment." As cows dry up at the end of their lactation cycle, they are taken out of rotation for fifty days before they are impregnated again. As they dry up for good, they are put out to pasture but never slaughtered. Most dairies would say all of this is uneconomical, and it is—if you think of animals as production units.

Conventional wisdom would say that he'd have a tough time making a decent living, but just the opposite is true. Although his production per cow is low (40 pounds of milk per day per cow compared to 100 at the big commercial dairies), and he has to care for old, dry cows, people are willing to pay more for his milk, and he's doing just fine. His cows are doing fine. And his customers are happy to get raw, organic milk with all its nutrients and enzymes in place.

cows to graze pasture anyway, at least in spring through fall. In winter the cows are in the barn and fed corn, silage, or hay.

Organic milk, especially milk from cows fed solely on pasture or hay, is a true success story. And not just because of 25 percent jumps in sales each year for several recent years, to about $300 million in 2004, while conventional milk consumption fell 10 percent in 2003. In 2006, total sales of organic dairy products (including milk, butter, yogurt, and cheese) reached $2.5 billion.

Uses

We use organic nonfat milk around my house, but I've found that it has different cooking qualities than milk with more fat—especially cream. The more fat, the less likely the milk is to curdle at high heat. This is true of organic as well as conventional—or even evaporated—milk.

Nondairy milks can be made from nuts and seeds. Puree almonds, hazelnuts, Brazil nuts, or other nuts or seeds in the blender until powdered, then mix with water and strain through a cheesecloth-lined colander. Don't use these milks to cook at high heat, or they will separate. (They will be good on your morning granola.)

Sheep's milk is richer in fat and higher in protein and minerals than other milks. Interestingly, human milk has one-quarter of the protein and twice the carbohydrates of other milks, plus much more vitamin C. That stands to reason because other animals have the ability to manufacture vitamin C within their bodies, while humans don't. Nature has compensated by giving human mammary glands the ability to synthesize vitamin C.

Citrus Panna Cotta

SERVES 6

After I tasted the best panna cotta of my life, I prevailed on Christopher Herrera, then the talented pastry chef at Jardinière in San Francisco, to give me his recipe, and here it is. Serve this with fresh seasonal fruits.

2 teaspoons powdered gelatin (2/3 of a packet)
1 cup heavy cream
1 cup sugar
Grated zest of 1 orange (well scrubbed if not organic)
Grated zest of 1 lemon (well scrubbed if not organic)
Grated zest of 1 lime (well scrubbed if not organic)
2 cups (1 pint) sour cream

1. In a small bowl, combine the gelatin with 1/2 cup of cold water to soften; let sit 5 minutes.

2. In a medium saucepan, combine the heavy cream, sugar, and zests, and bring to a boil. When the cream begins to boil and the sugar is entirely dissolved, remove from the heat and allow

it to stand for 2 minutes, then strain through a very fine sieve into a bowl to remove the citrus zest.

3. When the gelatin is entirely dissolved, whisk it into the cream. Whisk in the sour cream until well combined. Pour the mixture into six 6-ounce custard cups, ramekins, or other small molds. Chill at least 6 hours. To unmold, set the molds in a shallow pan of hot water for a few seconds so the *panna cotta* releases. Invert onto plates.

CHEESE AND OTHER DAIRY PRODUCTS

WHAT TO LOOK FOR: Artisanal cheeses—made in small batches by local artisan cheesemakers—have the most flavor and character. When they use raw milk, even more flavor characteristics are preserved. When the milk is organic, that's a big bonus. And when the milk is raw, organic, and from grass-fed cows, it doesn't get any better than that. To find organic cheese, shop in the cheese section of better stores and look for the USDA organic seal on domestic cheeses. European cheeses may be labeled biologique or by other terms, depending on the country. Visit Organic-Europe's Web site (www.organic-europe.net) for access to organic certifiers and movements in various European countries.

NUTRITIONAL HIGHLIGHTS: calcium, conjugated linoleic acid (especially in milk from grass-fed cows), niacin, phosphorus, protein, riboflavin, selenium, vitamin A, vitamin B_6, vitamin B_{12}

GO WELL WITH: mustard, nuts, red and white wines

Cheese is one of life's exquisite bounties. And like wine and bread, cheese is a fermented feast. At the dawn of agriculture, when wild cattle, sheep, and goats were first domesticated, milk was a perishable product. Left sitting around for a few days, it turned naturally into curds and whey, and when the first farmers drained off the whey and pressed the curds, they got cheese.

It's still made that way, except that the curdling agents are rennet and specific strains of bacteria. In other words, it's still a natural product, a collaboration between animal, human, and bacteria. Conventional cheese makers have developed a slew of additives to preserve and texturize their processed cheese food. But as you might suspect, organic cheese is not only additive-free but is made with milk from organically raised animals that are fed organic feed of the kind nature intends for ruminants.

Organic Advantage

Just as with milk (see page 252), cheese from grass-fed cows is five times higher in CLA, a potent cancer fighter, than from dairy cows fed grains. Nutritionists encourage people to get more omega-3 into their diet. Finding a source of grass-fed organic cheese is a way to do so. Pasture grass with some weeds present contains more omega-3 than omega-6 essential fatty acids, while corn and soybeans (the grains usually fed to cows) contain far more omega-6 than omega-3. That's why cheese from grass-fed cows has an excellent ratio of these two essential nutrients.

Organic cheese from grass-fed cows also has higher levels of beta-carotene and other vitamins than cheese from grain-fed animals. Cows are meant to

DANGERS IN CONVENTIONAL DAIRY PRODUCTS

The FDA says recombinant bovine growth hormone, or rBGH, created by Monsanto, is safe, even though it's banned in Canada and Europe. (McDonald's, by the way, serves organic milk at all its outlets in England.)

Sometimes called rBST, it increases milk production in cows about 20 percent by raising the blood levels of IGF-1 (insulin-like growth factor) in the cows' blood. As a result, the cows sometimes suffer reproductive difficulties and mastitis, an infection of the udder. Worse, a study of U.S. women published in The Lancet, the British medical journal, showed a seven-fold increase in breast cancer among premenopausal women who had the highest levels of IGF-1 in their bodies. Elevated levels of IGF-1 have also been associated with higher risks of colon and prostate cancers.

The IGF-1 found in rBGH milk is not destroyed by human digestion. Instead, it is readily absorbed through the intestinal wall, and can be absorbed into the bloodstream, where it can affect other hormones. Some scientists studying IGF-1 believe it's likely that IGF-1 promotes the transformation of normal breast cells to breast cancers, and that IGF-1 maintains the malignancy of human breast cancer cells, including their invasiveness and ability to spread to distant organs.

IGF-1 is found in organic milk—and human breast milk—because it's a growth factor that helps babies grow. But it's not found at nearly the concentrations found in milk from rBGH cows. Cows that get rBGH show as much as a 44 percent increase in IGF-1 levels over cows that don't receive the hormone. Adults have stopped growing, so excess growth hormones floating in adult blood streams may find cancer cells and encourage their growth. IGF-1 in milk is not destroyed by processing or pasteurization, and therefore will even be found in elevated amounts in yogurt, butter, ice cream, cheese, and other milk products made from the milk of cows that receive doses of rBGH.

Organic milk comes from cows that are not given rBGH.

eat fresh grass or hay in the winter. Fed the diet nature intends for them, they give less milk, but better milk. Better milk makes better cheese.

Cow, sheep, goat, and water buffalo cheeses are produced organically (with certified organic milk), both here in the United States and in Europe. As more and more dairy farmers switch to organic production to capitalize on the premiums paid for organic milk, finding such cheeses is becoming easier. The Organic Valley co-op, for example, has introduced a line of organic cheeses. In Europe, myriad farmstead cheeses have been made naturally for thousands of years, so the imported cheese you buy—especially the artisanal ones—may be naturally organic. But more and more, European cheese makers are seeing the value in obtaining organic certification, which reassures buyers that the milk does not contain growth hormones or cause mad cow disease. Virtually any kind of cheese—from cow, goat, sheep, or even buffalo—can be organic, as long as the milk is organic and no artificial flavorings, texturizers, or other such ingredients are added.

Uses

Cheese, like wine, is a huge subject. Have fun exploring it. One way to do that, especially at dinner parties, is to insert a cheese course between the main course and dessert—a noble tradition in France, but not much seen in American homes, where the tradition has been to serve cheese and crackers as hors d'oeuvres before dinner. We now have a huge selection of artisanal and farmstead cheeses available in our markets from which to choose. Serving it after the main course allows dinner guests to refresh their glasses of wine or start a different bottle.

Sometimes sheep's milk ricotta is available in our area. After the curds are drained, the whey is cooked (ricotta is Italian for "recooked," just as panna cotta is Italian for "cooked cream") until ricotta forms. I find sheep's milk ricotta to be enormously superior to most cow's milk ricotta on the market. Blintzes stuffed with sheep's milk ricotta filling and served with strawberry jam and sour cream are a dream come true. (If cows' milk ricotta is all you can find, blintzes are still a dream.)

In the classic insalata caprese, slices of mozzarella are paired with vine-ripened tomatoes and basil and drizzled with a little extra-virgin olive oil (but please, no balsamic vinegar or lemon juice). If you are lucky enough to have a source of fresh, organic water buffalo mozzarella, you will find it indispensable in all sorts of Italian dishes—spaghetti, gnocchi, eggplant parmigiana, calzone, and pizza. It will melt into tomato sauce and give whatever it touches a rich, delicious texture and taste.

Besides cheese, other forms of dairy products made from organic milk are butter, yogurt, cottage cheese, buttermilk, sour cream, cream cheese, ice cream, gelato, crème anglaise, custards, ricotta, quark, and crème fraîche.

Make your own crème fraîche by stirring 2 tablespoons of buttermilk into 1 cup of heavy cream and letting it stand at room temperature for 8 to 12 hours, or until it thickens. Spoon some over fresh fruit, or use it to make creamy soups.

Add sour cream, quark, or crème fraîche to biscuit and pancake batter, to the eggs when you are coating meats or fish with a batter for frying, or to coffee cakes. All of these products provide the cook with chances to be creative.

EGGS

WHAT TO LOOK FOR: Check eggs to avoid buying any that are cracked—a cracked egg may not only be going bad, but may be contaminated with salmonella. If any egg has an off odor or looks strange in any way, discard it. A small spot of blood in an egg is normal, and actually a sign of freshness.

STORAGE AND PREPARATION TIPS: Fresh eggs from the store will last two weeks.

NUTRITIONAL HIGHLIGHTS: biotin, folate, iodine, iron, pantothenic acid, phosphorus, protein, riboflavin, selenium, tryptophan, vitamin A, vitamin B_{12}, vitamin D

GO WELL WITH: Eggs hold many baked goods together—breads, cakes, and pastries of all kinds. Eggs go well with grains and fruits, with bacon, cheeses of all kinds, milk and butter.

The first time I used fresh organic eggs from free-range hens was in a cake recipe that required me to separate four eggs. The whites were not runny, but clear and viscous, holding together in a thick, jelly-like mass. The yolks were deep orange and gave the cake batter a rich, warm color. The yolks were also plump, and when I beat the batter with a fork they clung to the tines of the fork; I had to squeeze them off with my fingers. Then they clung to my fingers, they were so thick and sticky. There is no substitute for eggs like these.

Compare such eggs to eggs from a factory farm, where hens spend their lives cooped up in tiny cages under 24-hour-a-day lighting, fed genetically modified and pesticide-sprayed corn, and are routinely treated with antibiotics to prevent the diseases that would otherwise flourish in these smelly, noisy, inhumane conditions. I've been in such egg factories, and they are a vision of chicken hell. Forced to lay too many eggs, fed as cheaply as possible, and living in unnatural conditions, factory hens lay eggs that may have rough and ridged shells; loose, light yellow yolks; and watery whites. In the kitchen, this translates into poor performance in what eggs are supposed to do: bind ingredients, add body, and support light, well-risen cakes, among other functions.

When shopping for eggs, here are some other labels you may encounter:

Cage-free: The chickens live in a room somewhere—they're not confined to cages—but most likely still have no access to the great outdoors. These shenanigans aren't allowed with hens laying organic eggs.

Certified humane: Ostensibly, this means that chickens are not cooped up three to a small cage, the way they are in egg factories. But who's doing the certifying?

Free-range: Hens can scratch around in a yard outside in the fresh air. But for how long each day? Your guarantee that hens have access to the outside is when their eggs are certified organic.

Hormone-free: These hens have not been injected with hormones to increase egg production. Organic eggs are automatically hormone free.

Natural: The word natural is not covered by any rule, governmental or otherwise. Disregard it.

Omega-3: This simply means that flaxseed has been added to the hens' feed to boost the amount of omega-3 essential fatty acid in the egg.

Organic: Eggs laid by chickens that are raised humanely. The birds have access to the outdoors and are not forced into heavy egg production by 24-hour-a-day lighting. They are fed only organic grains, and so are far less likely to be contaminated with agricultural chemicals.

Vegetarian: The hens are not fed any animal by-products.

Organic Advantage

Organic hens eat only organic feed, so the danger of the bioaccumulation of pesticides and other toxins in their eggs is minimal. Humane treatment, healthy diet, and lack of stress translate into eggs that perform beautifully in the kitchen, including functions such as coagulation, foaming, emulsification, and browning. Compared with a conventional farm, an organic farm is like chicken heaven. According to the standards for the National Organic Program, "All organically raised animals must have access to the outdoors.... They may be temporarily confined only for reasons of health, safety, the animal's stage of production, or to protect soil or water quality."

This means that organic eggs come from hens with a scratch yard. Notice it says they can be shut in the henhouse only temporarily—in other words, they are truly free-range birds. (That doesn't mean they can fly out of the scratch yard and start living under the hydrangea. Laying hens and roosters usually have their flight feathers clipped so they can't fly.)

BROWN VS. WHITE EGGS

Some people think brown eggs are better or more nutritious in some way than white eggs, but it's a myth. Eggshell color is determined strictly by the breed of hen. Araucana chickens, incidentally, produce gorgeous light blue eggs. When crossed with other breeds, they may produce eggs in a variety of light pastel colors.

Uses

You'll find the use of eggs in recipes scattered throughout this book. I will only repeat, for your own sake, for the sake of the birds that provide us with eggs, for the sake of the organic farmers who are striving to raise them properly, and for the sake of the earth: find a source of organic eggs.

TIP: In years past, unsanitary conditions led to fecal contamination of some eggs with salmonella, which caused food poisoning. Today, contamination of eggshells with salmonella is very rare, according to the USDA. (Most salmonella today comes from sick hens whose ovaries and ovarian tracts are infected with salmonella and whose eggs are infected before the shell is formed.) Healthy hens are unlikely to become sick with salmonella. Even so, it's wise to cook eggs, which destroys salmonella, rather than eat them raw.

CHAPTER

7

Kitchen Staples

Today it's easy to find organic forms of kitchen staples—foods that aren't typically grown by local farmers—such as olive oil, butter, stocks, coffee, chocolate, flours and meals, and wine.

Why is it worth searching out the organic brands? Many reasons, including the higher quality that organic producers tend to put into their products. They know their products command a premium and that those products had better deliver high quality in freshness and flavor. Another reason is the benefits for those who produce the foods, such as chocolate and coffee producers. Most organic brands are fair-trade brands: the farmers and producers, many of them in the third world, are given a fair wage for their work.

Still another reason is that organic farmers are more responsible stewards of the land, replenishing the soil, working with nature rather than against her. Organic grape growers are proud of the quality of the wines made from their grapes and go to great pains to ensure that quality. Organic wheat farmers know that a rich organic soil holds more water than a poor, chemically-treated soil and is better able to withstand drought. All the organic kitchen staples you buy contribute to methods of farming and production that protect the earth and increase the health of all involved.

BOUILLONS AND BROTHS

Read the labels carefully when you buy bouillons, bouillon cubes, broths, canned soups, or dry soup mixes. If you use commercial stock, check the salt levels on the label. Most contain a superabundance of salt, which is a great argument for making your own. I look for no-salt-added stocks when I buy commercial stock.

And unless they are organic, these handy bases could contain substances dubbed excitotoxins. These substances, added to many processed foods—especially to savory flavor enhancers such as bouillon—may cause damage to nerve cells, which is of particular concern to parents of growing children. There are a number of other problems linked to many additives found in soup mixes as well. Yeast extract, for example, which is the base for most dry soup mixes, bouillons, and other conventional products, may be made with genetically manipulated starters. Other additives common to these mixes include monosodium glutamate (MSG) and aspartame (NutraSweet).

Some additives have natural-enough sounding names, although their makeup is far from natural. If hydrolyzed vegetable protein sounds like it might be allowed in organic products, one only has to look at its manufacturing process to see why it's not. According to Dr. Russell Blaylock, a professor of medicine at the University of Mississippi, this substance is made from junk vegetables that have been deemed unfit for sale. The protein is extracted by hydrolysis, which involves boiling the vegetables in acid; the acid is then neutralized by treating the vegetables with a caustic basic soda. The resulting product, a brown sludge that collects on the top, is scraped off and allowed to dry into a brown powder high in three known excitotoxins: glutamate, aspartame, and cystoic acid. The powder appears in many types of bouillon, as well as food products ranging from canned tuna to baby food.

Will eating excitotoxins hurt you? Anyone interested in learning more about excitotoxins should read Blaylock's book *Excitotoxins: The Taste That Kills*. It pays to be educated about what we are eating and feeding our children, to read food labels carefully, and to understand what we are reading. Buying organic products avoids these problems altogether, because they can contain no genetically modified ingredients or chemical additives.

The list below includes a set of highly vague ingredient terms that make frequent appearances on processed food labels. These may be perfectly natural and safe, or they may have been created through questionable processes and may contain excitotoxins. There is no way of knowing; just be aware when reading food labels:

- Autolyzed yeast
- Calcium caseinate
- Enzymes
- Glutamate
- Hydrolyzed oat flour
- Hydrolyzed plant protein
- Hydrolyzed protein
- Hydrolyzed vegetable protein
- Malt extract
- Malt flavoring
- Monosodium glutamate
- Natural beef or chicken flavoring
- Natural flavoring
- Seasoning
- Sodium caseinate
- Soy protein concentrate
- Soy protein isolate
- Spices
- Textured protein
- Whey protein concentrate
- Yeast extract

COFFEE

GOOD VARIETIES: Choose arabica over robusta.

WHAT TO LOOK FOR: Buy triple-certified (see below) arabica beans, the beans usually grown by organic and fair-trade coffee plantations. Avoid beans labeled robusta, which are of inferior quality and often grown on monoculture plantations that damage the environment and cause immense social disruption in the areas where they are raised (see Certifying Coffee, page 267).

STORAGE AND PREPARATION TIPS: Store coffee away from light or in a light-barrier bag in a cool dry place; do not refrigerate. Freeze coffee only if you will be storing it less than a month, as it changes the coffee's flavor as well as the way it grinds.

Many coffee grinders have a mechanism to change the grind from coarse to extra fine, allowing you to grind your beans to the grind recommended for your type of coffeemaker. The finer the grind, the stronger the coffee will be. The longer coffee is brewed (steeped), the coarser the grind can be. For drip coffeemakers or percolators, medium to fine grinds work well. Espresso machines require a grind about halfway between fine and medium.

NUTRITIONAL HIGHLIGHTS: phytochemicals

GOES WELL WITH: brandy, chocolate, cream, vanilla, whiskey

Coffee is the world's most popular beverage—after water. An estimated four hundred billion cups are consumed worldwide every year. Nestor Osorio, executive director of the International Coffee Organization, made this pronouncement in 2007: "Coffee is considered to be the second largest traded commodity in the world, after oil. Indeed we estimate that more than 85 billion dollars are involved in the annual trade of coffee."

I don't know about you, but I start my day with a freshly brewed cup—organic, of course.

Organic Advantage

It's often said that when we buy organic products, we are voting for a clean, environmentally safe agriculture with our dollars. When we elect to buy organic coffee, we help the impoverished families who grow this beverage in some of the most economically deprived places on earth as well.

When organically grown within the shade of a rain forest, coffee trees don't need the chemical fertilizers and insecticides required when coffee is grown conventionally as the single crop on sprawling plantations. The reason is that mammals, insects, fungus, and the many other life forms that inhabit the rain forest create a healthy biodiversity that eliminates or keeps pestiferous insects and fungi at bay—the coffee plants are simply part of the ecosystem, and pesticides and other agricultural chemicals aren't necessary.

But there's more. The great diversity of life in the rain forest includes migratory birds that summer in the United States and Canada and winter in the American tropics. Populations of migratory birds that overwinter in Central and South American rain forests are being seriously depleted by clear-cutting for, among other things, full-sun coffee plantations. This has caused the Smithsonian Migratory Bird Center at the National Zoo to encourage us to drink "bird-friendly coffee," or coffee grown on environmentally sustainable farms.

A healthy, biodiverse ecosystem that includes coffee trees protects not only migratory birds but the entire ecosystem of plants, animals, and even the fertility of the soil and the integrity of water supplies. In the tropics, nutrients don't build up in the soil the way they do in cold winter regions. If a leaf falls to the ground, it does fertilize the soil, but the tropical vegetation is so dense that after decomposing, the nutrients are sucked up by plant roots and used to build trees, vines, and other life forms. In a rainforest, nutrients tend to be stored "upstairs" in plant and animal life rather than in the soil. So, when a rain forest is clear-cut, almost all the nutrients stored in its ecosystem are decimated. If the land is replanted entirely with coffee trees, those nutrients must be supplied in the form of chemical fertilizers. Because the natural enemies of the coffee pests will have been destroyed along with the rain forest canopy, they are free to multiply in monoculture plantations consisting entirely of their favorite food, and so pesticides need to be applied and reapplied. Because the shading, sheltering canopy has been removed, groundwater supplies dry up. Nutritionless soil with hardly any organic matter becomes exposed to tropical sunlight and hardens.

The world coffee market is now being flooded with cheap, inferior coffee grown in such full-sun plantations around the world, especially Vietnam. This coffee drives prices so low that

CERTIFYING COFFEE

The highest grade of coffee is arabica, a bean that thrives in shaded mountain regions. Today the market is being flooded with lower-quality robusta which comes mostly from Vietnam and Brazil. Don't buy it. In addition to being of poorer quality, it's causing immense social disruption in coffee-growing countries.

Truly good coffee should meet certain requirements. It should be grown at high elevations (mountain grown) and be specialty-grade arabica. However, as with wine, you can have an award-winning coffee from a plantation one year, and the next year the beans from the same plantation will produce an unremarkable brew. The best bet is to find a company whose product you know, like, and trust as truly organic, shade-grown, and high-grade arabica, and stick with it—until you find something you like even more. Look for coffees that are certified by all three organizations listed below. Through triple-certified coffee, the consumer makes a direct connection with the people and places where the coffee is grown.

These certifications represent a landmark standard for the food industry. (See Sources, page 287, for a list of companies that sell triple-certified coffees, both by mail and in major retail outlets.)

1. **CERTIFIED ORGANICALLY GROWN AND PROCESSED BY QAI:** Quality Assurance International is a worldwide organic certification agency.

2. **CERTIFIED FAIR TRADE BY TRANSFAIR USA:** Fair trade cooperatives help to support 550,000 of the world's top coffee-growing farms. The average third-world family farmer supporting a family of five lives on the equivalent of $500 to $600 per year! The premium put on organic-certified coffee alone is about 15 cents more per pound. In a market that pays only 30 to 50 cents per pound, that premium will not go very far toward improving farmers' lives. Fair trade currently guarantees to the farmer a minimum of $1.26 per pound ($1.41 if organic), regardless of the market price.

3. **CERTIFIED SHADE GROWN BY THE SMITHSONIAN INSTITUTION:** Coffee has a symbiotic relationship with canopy trees: coffee trees do better when grown under a canopy of shade (ideally with 50 to 60 percent shading). While shade-grown coffee is not as productive in terms of the amount of fruit each plant produces, it ripens more completely, with more nutrients in each fruit, creating a richer, fuller flavor. There is only one meaningful certification for shade-grown trees, and that is Smithsonian's. A Smithsonian certification means that the coffee plantation is inspected annually for optimal biodiversity. It requires that everyone from farmer to roaster be independently audited. Most shade-grown coffee, however, is broker or roaster certified, using loose standards or no standards at all.

many small coffee farmers receive less than the cost of production for their beans, which drives them off their land. The land may then be bought by corporations that clear-cut in order to plant full-sun coffee plantations. TransFair USA, a nongovernmental organization that tries to provide growers with a fair price for their products, (www.transfairusa.org or www.fairtradecoffee.org), attempts to pay enough to keep indigenous coffee farmers on the land so they can grow their coffee under the rain forest canopy. While this helps, too many coffee farmers are watching their income shrink and life is becoming untenable for them. Even during the good years, when crops do well and prices are high, growing coffee provides barely enough income to sustain a family. In bad years, things grow desperate.

More and more organically minded coffee businesses in the United States are trying to help desperately poor coffee farmers. Sustainable Harvest Coffee Importers of Portland, Oregon, works directly with family-owned coffee farms in Central America to ensure they can uphold stringent standards to produce premium-quality coffees, for which they are paid premium prices. Allegro Coffee Company of Thornton, Colorado, a subsidiary of Whole Foods Market, forges relationships with its growers, requiring that they use sustainable and traditional coffee growing techniques in return for a guaranteed fair price, and bringing members of coffee co-op farms and family farms to Denver from Guatemala, El Salvador, Mexico, and even India so they can see how their coffees are roasted and marketed. The JBR Coffee Company, a subsidiary of JBR Gourmet Foods of San Leandro, California, has developed a program called Source Aid to help organic coffee growers in Central America through the efforts of its green bean buyer, Pete Rogers (to find out more, visit www.organiccoffeecompany.org).

When you choose triple certified shade-grown coffee, you're protecting a valuable ecosystem, including the human beings who live in it and from it. For more general information about specialty coffees and some of the important issues related to coffee growing, visit the Specialty Coffee Association of America's Web site (www.scaa.org). I guarantee that a trip through its pages will be an eye-opener regarding your daily cup of joe.

Tiramisù

SERVES 6

Good tiramisù (meaning "pick me up" in Italian) starts with good espresso. If you don't have an espresso machine, buy a half-cup (about four shots) of espresso at a coffee shop, but bring your own ceramic or glass jar, or the espresso will taste like cardboard by the time you get it home.

1/2 cup freshly brewed espresso
1/2 cup sugar
2 tablespoons brandy
16 ladyfingers
3 large egg yolks
1/4 cup freshly squeezed orange juice
1 cup (8 ounces) mascarpone cheese
1 tablespoon orange liqueur, such as Grand Marnier
1 teaspoon freshly grated orange zest (well scrubbed if not organic)
1/2 cup heavy cream
1/4 cup grated semisweet chocolate (2 ounces)
1 teaspoon ground cinnamon

1. In a large bowl, combine the espresso, 1/4 cup of the sugar, and the brandy, and mix well.

2. Grease a 9 × 9–inch glass baking dish. Quickly dip 8 of the ladyfingers in the coffee mixture and lay them in the bottom of the dish. Don't let them soak up too much liquid or they will get mushy. Reserve the remaining espresso mixture.

3. In the top of a double boiler, whisk the egg yolks until smooth. Add the remaining 1/4 cup of sugar and the orange juice. Fill the bottom of the double boiler with water (don't let the water touch the top part of the double boiler) and bring to a boil. When it boils, reduce the heat down to simmer. Place the top over the simmering water. Cook, whisking the mixture evenly and lightly, for 4 minutes, until the egg yolks are thickened and light yellow in color. Don't let the yolks curdle. Remove the top of the double boiler from the heat and continue whisking until the mixture is just warm.

4. Beat the mascarpone until it's light and airy and add it to the egg yolk mixture along with the orange liqueur and orange zest, mixing thoroughly. In a separate bowl, whip the cream to soft peaks and gently fold this into the egg mixture until well incorporated. During the last few turns of your rubber spatula, fold in the grated chocolate.

5. Spread two-thirds of this mixture over the ladyfingers in the baking dish, smoothing it flat. Soak the remaining ladyfingers in the remaining espresso mixture until all the liquid is soaked up. Lay them on top of the baking dish, then cover them with the remaining mascarpone mixture. Place the dish in the refrigerator and chill for at least 2 hours, then dust the top with cinnamon.

CHOCOLATE

GOOD VARIETIES: Chocosphere (www.chocosphere.com) is an excellent Web site devoted to listing sources of organic chocolate from around the world, both for eating and for baking and other culinary uses.

WHAT TO LOOK FOR: As with conventional chocolate, organic chocolate ranges in quality from mediocre to excellent. It's a lot like coffee in that it grows best under the canopy of a rain forest (see page 266), so look for chocolate that is certified rain forest grown, fair trade, and organic.

STORAGE AND PREPARATION TIPS: Store chocolate tightly wrapped in a cool, dark place.

NUTRITIONAL HIGHLIGHTS: antioxidants (see Nutrients in Chocolate?, at right)

GOES WELL WITH: cherries, coffee, mint, nuts including almonds and peanuts, orange, raspberries, strawberries, vanilla

---

Suddenly organic chocolate is everywhere. And if you think we've got a good selection here, you should see what they have in the United Kingdom. But what's so good about organic chocolate?

The monoculture setup of conventional chocolate plantations encourages the spread of disease. As with coffee plantations, clearing away swaths of rain forest to grow cacao trees kills off the naturally occurring organisms that fight off pests, fungi, and diseases, forcing farmers to use chemical pesticides and fungicides in their stead. This means that if a disease manages to gain a toehold, it has the potential to devastate the entire plantation, which is exactly what happened in South America in the 1990s, when a virulent fungus wiped out whole plantations of cacao trees—and the incomes of workers who labored on the plantations.

Organic Advantage

Organic chocolate is grown in a diversified ecosystem less prone to epidemics of pathogenic organisms. Jupara, a local nongovernmental organization in Bahia, Brazil, taught the landless workers how to grow cacao in its natural habitat of lowland rain forest under the canopy of taller trees, using organic techniques. This helps preserve the native canopy trees as well as the livelihoods of the workers. The midges—small gnat-like insects—that pollinate cacao require the humid shade of the rain forest and a wide range of plant species and decaying matter on the ground. These insects have no reason to leave their natural habitat and venture into the sunny, dry, cultivated groves of conventional cacao. That's why there is a very low rate of pollination of the tree's flowers on big cacao plantations. Grown organically in its natural habitat, the pollination rates are much higher. This means more pods per tree and therefore fewer trees—and environmental disruption—needed for the same amount of cacao bean crop.

Naturally grown cacao has over four hundred distinct smells (compared to fourteen in roses and seven in onions). Cultivated conventional cacao has only a small percentage of those smells, making it even harder for the pollinating midges to find the flowers. So, what's so great about organic chocolate? Richer flavor expression from beans, and cacao trees grown in ways that protect, and do not threaten, the fragile tropical ecosystem.

After learning how to enrich the soil naturally and use other nature-friendly practices, the farmers—who now call themselves agroecologists—sell their cacao to green markets around the world. The organic cacao, certified by the Brazilian Instituto Biodinâmico de Desenvolvimento, brings a price 40 percent higher than conventional chocolate. This kind of success is being repeated in the Caribbean, Central America, and other parts of South America where cacao is grown. On the Caribbean island of Grenada, for example, the Grenada Chocolate Company gained organic certification in 2004. The cacao is grown in the island's tropical rain forest and the chocolate is roasted and ground on-site in a solar energy-powered facility.

Once this organic cocoa gets to manufacturers, it is turned into what we think of as chocolate through a process known as conching—a constant sloshing and stirring that triggers an oxidation process that reduces the natural bitterness of cacao beans. Many conventional chocolate manufacturers conche for 3 or 4 hours. The highest quality chocolate makers, by contrast, will conche their chocolate for up to 72 hours, producing an extra-silky texture and premium flavor. Instead of white sugar, organic producers often use organic whole cane sugar, which layers in another subtle flavor.

Soy lecithin is used as an emulsifier in conventional chocolate making, and much soy lecithin comes from genetically modified soybeans. And organic cocoa isn't treated with potassium carbonate to alkalize it, as is done in the manufacture of Dutch-processed chocolate. (The alkalizing makes the chocolate easier to dissolve in liquids, but it does nothing for the flavor.)

NUTRIENTS IN CHOCOLATE?

Chocolate has some nutritional pluses. Flavonoids that are found in cacao (and the darker and more concentrated the chocolate, the more the flavonoids) have several positive health effects. First, flavonoids are antioxidants that block arterial damage caused by free radicals. Second, cacao flavonoids inhibit platelet aggregations—clumps of blood cells—that can block blood vessels, causing heart attack or stroke. And there are studies that suggest cacao flavonoids relax the blood vessels, which inhibits an enzyme that causes vessel wall inflammation. (The body responds to such inflammation by covering the surface with plaque. Plaque clogs the blood vessels. As its opening shrinks, blockage by blood clots becomes ever more possible.)

Uses

Chocolate has a thousand uses in all types of sweets—candy, pastry, cake, ice cream, pudding, and many others.

Dark Chocolate–Peanut Butter Sauce

MAKES 1½ CUPS

Mart Buck ran a soda shop near my high school, and his signature topping for ice cream was this chocolate–peanut butter sauce. A generation or two of kids grew up on this delicious stuff. It's best on vanilla ice cream.

1 cup firmly packed dark brown sugar
2/3 cup heavy cream
2 ounces unsweetened chocolate, chopped coarsely
1/2 cup creamy peanut butter
1 1/2 teaspoons vanilla extract
1/8 teaspoon salt

Stir the sugar and cream in a saucepan over medium heat until the sugar dissolves. Add the chocolate and continue to stir until the chocolate melts and the mixture is smooth. Allow it to come to a boil, still over medium heat, and cook for 8 minutes, stirring occasionally to prevent scorching. Remove from the heat, allow it to cool for 2 minutes, then stir in the peanut butter, vanilla, and salt until smooth. Let the sauce cool completely before covering or it will turn grainy.

FLOURS AND MEALS

GOOD BRANDS: Arrowhead Mills, Champlain Valley Mills, Community Mill and Bean, Cooks Natural Products, Giusto's; see Sources (page 287) for mail-order suppliers of organic flours

WHAT TO LOOK FOR: Whether barley, corn, millet, quinoa, rice, spelt, wheat, or any other flour or meal, look for the labels whole-grain and organic. That doesn't mean you have to go without your all-purpose flour or pastry flour for making delicate baked goods—although whole-grain baking is increasingly popular, and there are now some excellent cookbooks on the subject.

STORAGE AND PREPARATION TIPS: Store whole-grain flour or meal in the freezer. It contains the oil-rich germ that can go rancid if left at room temperature.

NUTRITIONAL HIGHLIGHTS:

Whole-wheat flour: B vitamins, fiber, magnesium, manganese, phosphorus, selenium

Processed white flour: B vitamins, calcium, folate, iron, manganese, selenium

Not only do organic flours and meals offer the kind of full flavor that comes from grains grown in soils rich in organic matter, but they are often used in whole-grain form, which increases their flavor and nutrition even more.

Kathleen Weber, who runs Della Fattoria, one of the best organic bakeries in California's wine country, describes why organic bread is so good:

> Commercially grown wheat sends out shallow roots that only absorb the chemical fertilizers given to it. Organic wheat roots have to go deep, where they get what they need to add richness and flavor to the grain. It makes better flour. Over-processed flours from chemically grown grain are gray, not gold and warm and beautiful like organic flour.

The gold color Kathleen praises comes from an abundance of carotene—the precursor of vitamin A—in the organic wheat. Great taste and great nutrition is the winning combination that careful bakers like Weber achieve by using organic flours and meals.

Organic (and Whole-Grain) Advantage

Whole-grain flours and meals contain complex carbohydrates that contribute to good health. Whole grains are made up of the bran, the fibrous covering of the grain; the germ, the seed's embryo; and the endosperm, the protein-rich starchy part. Refining removes the bran and the germ—and most of the trace elements and vitamins. Most often the endosperm is ground to flour by hammer mills or roller mills that create quite a lot of heat. The heat destroys enzymes and further reduces nutrients. Bleaching to turn the flour white further reduces nutrients. Refining removes 80 percent of wheat's magnesium, 70 to 80 percent of its zinc, nearly 90 percent of its chromium and manganese, and 50 percent of its cobalt—trace elements the body uses to function properly. It also removes most of the thiamine, riboflavin, and niacin, which the government mandates be put back, but are invariably added back chemically.

Organic stone-ground whole-wheat flour, on the other hand, contains all the bran and germ. It is not bleached. The stone milling creates much lower temperatures than the high-speed mills, preserving nutrients. There's a great deal of evidence of the benefits of whole-wheat flour. One study, called the Nurses' Health Study, surveyed 65,173 women's diets. Among the results are lower rates of heart disease, less obesity, less diabetes, and healthier digestion among those who ate whole-wheat products regularly.

Uses

When baking bread, use organic flour ground from whole wheatberries—that way you get the maximum nutritional content. When I bake bread, I use some

AN UNADDRESSED PROBLEM

It may be a good idea to slice your bread and store it in the freezer. Baked goods, especially moist breads such as cakes, pastries, and corn bread, turn moldy if allowed to sit out for more than a few days. In fact, the mold is growing in the bread before it becomes visible to the naked eye! Freezing bread delays the growth of mold, and frozen slices or portions can be quickly thawed in the toaster or a warm oven.

Is a little bread mold a problem? Wasn't penicillin derived from bread mold?

As it turns out, mold on wheat, corn, and other food grains—or anything made from their flours and meals—may be a huge problem, or it may not be. The problem is unaddressed. Yes, penicillin is derived from a certain species of bread mold, but it's just one of an array of molds and fungi that produce substances called mycotoxins. (They also cause the toxic—sometimes lethal—effects of poisonous mushrooms.)

According to The Canadian Journal of Physiology and Pharmacology, one such mycotoxin, ochratoxin A(OC), which occurs in certain grains and cereals, is highly toxic to the kidneys and liver, is potentially carcinogenic and immunosuppressive, and may cause birth defects. Its effects and dangers are being studied by several health institutes. Aflatoxin is a highly carcinogenic mycotoxin found on grains, corn, and peanuts, among other foodstuffs. And there are many others. Most of them are not destroyed by processing grains into flour, nor by the heat of baking.

I asked Brendan McEntee, owner of Cooks Natural Products, an organic flour supplier in San Francisco, if the grain used to make his flours is tested for the presence of mycotoxins. "Organic grains are tested the same as conventional grains," he said. "When the grain is delivered from a farmer to the grain elevator, the receiving agent takes a sample and checks it by sight, feel, and smell, and tests it for percentage of protein—but detailed toxicology? No."

Such traceability is at least reassuring. Should an outbreak of mycotoxicosis occur in organic flour, the product can be traced back to a specific mill, grain elevator, and farm, and the problem area pinpointed. Nothing like this happens with conventional grain because everything tends to get mixed together. What's not reassuring is that no testing is done for mycotoxins in our food supply, whether conventional or organic. Support for this testing needs to be encouraged.

whole-wheat and some all-purpose organic flour, which produces a lighter loaf than if the dough is entirely whole wheat; the proportions depend on the kind of loaf I'm after. For a light loaf, I use perhaps a 7:1 ratio of all-purpose to whole-wheat flours; for a whole-wheat loaf, a ratio of 5:2 makes an acceptable loaf. And I usually toss in a little rye flour for flavor—but rye doesn't have the gluten needed for a good rise, so I use it sparingly. (Gluten is a complex protein whose elasticity allows the carbon dioxide produced by yeast to be trapped in dough as bubbles, creating a light, chewy loaf.)

Sourdough: Some folks allow the naturally occurring yeast and bacteria in the air to colonize a mixture of rye flour and water, creating what's often called a sourdough culture. Depending on where you live, these starter cultures (a more accurate term) might indeed be sour, but they also might yield bread that's tangy, tart, vinegary, milky, mellow, or complex. In the San Francisco Bay Area, naturally occurring bacteria called *Lactobacillus sanfranciscensis* and yeast called *Candida milleri* work together to produce a starter culture with a strong sour taste that really can't be duplicated in other regions of the country where these microorganisms don't exist together.

Wherever bread is baked, however, the loaves that the French call *pain au levain*—made with an indigenous starter culture—have something of the taste of the place they are made, along with the quality of the flour they're made from. That's why organic breads are so superb. From the wheat fields through the milling process to the bakery with its homegrown starter culture, someone cares deeply enough about the product and the customer to add quality at every step. That gives this kind of bread terroir—a term for the idea that the product has the signature taste of the place it's from.

Whole-Wheat Black Walnut Quick Rolls

MAKES 6 ROLLS

These little rolls are quick and delicious. Warm from the oven, they make an ordinary dinner into something special.

1 cup chopped black walnuts (see page 187), or regular walnuts
2 cups whole-wheat flour
1 cup all-purpose flour
1/4 cup packed dark brown sugar
1 teaspoon baking soda
1/2 teaspoon salt
4 tablespoons (1/2 stick) unsalted butter, chilled

1 cup chilled buttermilk

1 large egg

2 tablespoons pure maple syrup

1. Preheat the oven to 375°F. Lightly toast the walnuts in the oven until just aromatic. Lightly flour a 15 × 10 × 3–inch baking sheet.

2. In a large bowl, stir together the flours, brown sugar, baking soda, and salt. Using two knives, cut the butter into the dry ingredients until it's reduced to small bits and the mixture resembles coarse meal. Add the walnuts and mix to incorporate.

3. In a separate bowl, whisk together the buttermilk, egg, and maple syrup until well blended. Gradually add the wet ingredients to the dry ingredients, stirring until a dough forms and everything is well incorporated.

4. Lightly flour a board and turn the dough onto it. Knead the dough for 1 minute, giving it a quarter turn after every push. Cut the dough into 6 equal pieces and form each into a ball. Space them on the baking sheet and flatten each into a 3-inch round. Using a sharp blade, cut an X into the top of each round. Bake them for about 30 minutes, or until golden brown and a toothpick inserted into the center of one comes out clean. Let them cool on a rack until just warm.

COOKING OILS AND FATS

WHAT TO LOOK FOR:

Oils: Despite the low-fat, no-fat craze that persists in our culture, judicious amounts of the right kind of fats do promote health. But toss out your polyunsaturated fats such as safflower oil and corn oil. And avoid any products that contain hydrogenated or partially hydrogenated vegetable oils—the notorious trans-fatty acids—such as margarine and vegetable shortening. Stick with monounsaturated fats such as extra-virgin olive oil for low-heat cooking or cold use. Almond oil, canola oil, and peanut oil are great for high-heat cooking, such as frying.

The highest quality olive oil is labeled extra-virgin and has a fruity, peppery, almost bitter flavor. When olives are picked green, their flavor is quite intense—though maybe a bit throat-gripping for most Americans. Those peppery, aggressive oils have the most antioxidants—polyphenols and tocopherols—which help keep bad cholesterol from clogging the arteries. For a list of good organic olive oils, see Sources (page 287).

Fats: Use saturated fats such as butter in moderation. When using a solid fat is necessary for culinary reasons, those trying to keep saturated fat to a minimum or who do not eat dairy products have a wide range of organic nondairy butter substitutes to choose from. Here's what you should look for:

Certified organic: The package will have the USDA organic seal.

Non-GMO: Because it's organic, it will contain no oils from genetically modified plants.

Non-hydrogenated: A hydrogenated fat such as regular margarine will contain harmful trans fats created when hydrogen is bubbled through liquid oil to render it semisolid at room temperature.

At least 80 percent fat content: This makes the product good for cooking and baking as well as spreading. One tablespoon of spread (one serving) is 11 grams. Nine of those grams should be from fats. A lower percentage of fat means that too much water or filler has been added, which will affect your baked goods.

Balanced fats: Check the ratio of fats: the spread should have approximately one-third each of saturated fat, polyunsaturated fat, and monounsaturated fat.

Oil content: You'll usually find a mix of palm, soybean, canola, and olive oils, plus soybean powder and lecithin.

NUTRITIONAL HIGHLIGHTS: Unfortunately, corn, safflower, walnut, sesame, soy, and sunflower oils, while rich sources of omega-6, don't have much omega-3—if they have any at all.

Canola oil: Some folks are leery of canola oil because they may have heard it contains erucic acid, which studies show causes heart lesions in lab animals. It's an old finding. Canadians began a series of hybridizations of the rape plant—the source of canola oil—after World War II that led to varieties with less than two percent erucic acid. Today's canola (for Canadian oil) has acceptable levels of erucic acid.

Fish oil: Fish such as anchovies, cod, mackerel, salmon, and sardines are excellent sources of omega-3, and if you use a lot of oils rich in omega-6 in your cooking or on your salads, you might want to consider fish oil for omega-3 supplementation. That's why Mom made sure you got your cod liver oil. In the old days, you got your daily dose from a spoon. Today, fish oil supplements are sold in convenient gel capsules.

Flaxseed oil: Flaxseed oil is especially good because of its greater amount of omega-3 than omega-6, which will balance some of the excess omega-6 we get in our Western diet. It should not be heated, however, but used cold, on salads, as a dip, in homemade mayonnaise, in smoothies and shakes, or straight up.

Olive oil: There's no denying the benefits of extra-virgin olive oil. The essential fatty acid in olive oil is omega-9, so consuming olive oil won't upset the balance of omega-6 and omega-3 in the rest of your diet. Omega-9 fatty acids are important monounsaturated fats and one of the chief reasons why the olive oil-rich Mediterranean diet contributes so splendidly to cardiovascular health. Olive oil has been proven to lower bad cholesterol and raise good cholesterol, and it has more antioxidants than any other oil. According to *Science News* for April 15, 2000, biochemist Hiroshi Maeda and his colleagues at Kumamoto University School of Medicine in Japan surveyed a range of cooking oils and discovered that "unprocessed olive oils were especially effective in scavenging the free radicals" and "quashing their destructive abilities."

STORAGE AND PREPARATION TIPS: Cooking oil that has reached its

OLIVE OIL CLASSIFICATION

At the store, you'll find many olive oils labeled extra-virgin. Why "extra"? Because there is a classification called simply virgin olive oil, although it's not seen on the market as often. Virgin oil can contain up to 3.3 percent acidity, which means the oil is becoming rancid. (As olive oil turns rancid, its acidity goes up.) Extra-virgin means low acidity, which in turn means that the oil is fresh. Most extra-virgin oils state a percentage of acidity on the label. By law it must be less than 1 percent, and is usually less than .5 percent. To be labeled extra-virgin, the oil also has to score at least 6.5 out of a possible 9 quality points with the International Olive Oil Council's tasting panel in Madrid for European oil, or with the recently formed California Olive Oil Council's tasting panel for California oil.

Extra-virgin oil can show no defects, such as mustiness. It can contain no additives, nor can heat treatments be used to get extra oil from the olive pulp.

THE OMEGA-3 BENEFIT

Oils such as canola contain the important omega-3 and omega-6 essential fatty acids necessary for proper growth in children and the maintenance of cardiovascular health, brain and visual function, and cell replacement in adults. But there's a catch.

Recent studies suggest that the ratio of omega-6 to omega-3 fatty acids may be the most important factor to consider in oils regarding their health benefits, such as lowering blood pressure. For example, if your intake of omega-6 fats is too high, it competes with the omega-3 fats and prevents them from doing their beneficial work, which may lead to an omega-3 deficiency. For a healthy balance, the ratio of omega-6 to omega-3 in your diet should be 3 or 4 parts omega-6 to 1 part omega-3. The typical Western diet has a ratio estimated at 20:1.

The following table shows the ratios of omega-6 to omega-3 in various vegetable oils.

smoke point loses flavor, nutritional value, and many of its health benefits, and can transition into trans-fatty acids. All cooking oil should be stored at a cool temperature in a dark cupboard or closet. Olive oil will start to solidify when refrigerated—when it starts to warm up, moisture in the air condenses inside the bottle, the fatty acids in the oil separate, and it starts turning rancid. Unopened in proper storage, extra-virgin olive oil will stay fresh for about a year because of its antioxidants. Once opened, oil will last from six weeks to two or three months, depending on storage conditions.

NUTRITIONAL HIGHLIGHTS: varies by oil or fat

OIL RATIOS (OMEGA-6:OMEGA-3)

Canola	3:1
Corn	8:0
Flaxseed	2:7
Hemp seed	3:1
Olive	1:0
Peanut	4:0
Safflower	8:0
Sesame	6:0
Soy	7:1
Sunflower	8:0
Walnut	5:1
Wheat germ	7:1

Source: Spectrum Naturals

BUTTER SUBSTITUTES AND SHORTENINGS

I agree with Dr. Joan Gussow, the well-known nutritionist, who, when asked about the butter versus margarine debate, said, "I trust cows more than chemists."

For those who eschew dairy, there are new kinds of organic margarines (such as Earth Balance) that remain firm at room temperature yet contain no hydrogenated or trans fats. Instead, what gives this margarine its soft but solid consistency is palm fruit oil, which is also called palm oil. It is a semisolid, non-hydrogenated oil. Note that this is different from palm kernel oil or coconut oil, both of which are significantly higher in saturated fat. Palm fruit oil is used worldwide as a cooking oil. Studies on human health have shown that it helps reduce LDL (bad) and increase HDL (good) cholesterol, and its antioxidants scavenge free radicals that can cause a number of diseases.

Organic Advantage

Finding a good source of organic oils for culinary use is essential for several reasons:

- Many mass-produced cooking oils such as canola, soy, corn, and cottonseed are from plants that have been genetically engineered to resist damage by herbicides or to incorporate the gene that expresses the toxin produced by *Bacillus thuringiensis*—a self-defeating practice since spreading the toxin throughout crops only encourages pests to become resistant.

CHOOSE THE RIGHT OIL FOR KITCHEN USE

When oil used for frying or sautéing gives off smoke, it not only emits an acrid smell, but healthy fats in the oil can be transformed into unhealthy trans fats. In addition, free radicals form that can oxidize cholesterol in the blood to create artery-clogging plaque. Discard any oil that has reached its smoking point. Use this table to determine which oil is the best to use for your purposes.

HIGH HEAT OILS

For high-heat cooking such as frying and sautéing.

Oil	Smoking Point (°F)
Avocado	510
Almond	495
Apricot kernel	495
Sesame	445

MEDIUM-HIGH HEAT OILS

For lower-heat sautéing and baking.

Oil	Smoking Point (°F)
Canola	425
Grape seed	425
Walnut	400
Coconut	365
Soy	360
Peanut	355

MEDIUM HEAT OILS

Full-flavored, unrefined oils for sauces and salad dressings and for medium-heat sautéing when the oil's flavor is integral to the dish.

Oil	Smoking Point (°F)
Sesame, toasted	350
Sesame, unrefined	350
Olive, extra-virgin	325
Corn, unrefined	320
Coconut, unrefined	280

NO-HEAT OILS

Unrefined oils with a robust flavor and a fragile structure for use on a finished dish or blended into a dressing or sauce without heating.

Oil	Smoking Point (°F)
Borage	225
Evening primrose	225
Flaxseed	225
Wheat germ	225

Courtesy of Spectrum Organic Products, Inc.

- Sewage sludge containing heavy metals may have been used on the fields where the conventional oil-producing crops were grown and thus taken up by the plants. Or if the fields were fertilized with chemical fertilizers, they may be depleted of trace minerals and organic matter, which can affect the quality of the oil-producing crops grown on them.
- Agricultural chemicals such as pesticides have a tendency to accumulate in plant fats and so may be concentrated in the resulting oils. (The chemicals also accumulate in the fatty tissues in our bodies—female breast tissue, for instance.)
- Bulk oils are usually extracted by a process that utilizes hexane, a petroleum by-product and nervous system toxin. While the hexane evaporates at the end of the extraction process and is said to be completely gone from the oil it extracts, it poses a risk to workers. And while the FDA vouches for the safety of chemically extracted oils, its assurances are not reassuring to everyone.

All these worries are void if I buy organic oil. It's not hard to find organic oils these days. Spectrum Naturals, the nation's largest supplier of a variety of organic culinary oils, reports that its business is growing about 25 percent a year; it grossed about $50 million in 2004.

Uses

In baking, a liquid oil will generally render a different taste and texture than a solid fat. A good rule of thumb is to substitute a solid fat for another solid fat—say, butter for vegetable shortening (a hydrogenated fat that should be avoided), and a liquid oil for another liquid oil, such as olive oil for corn oil. Lard is 100 percent fat, rendered from hogs. There are many sources of organic lard, easily found through an Internet search. Be on the look out for leaf lard—it's the internal fat lining a pig's stomach and kidneys and is said to make the most tender, flakiest pastries. It's not usually sold in markets, but you might be able to buy some from a butcher, or contact an organic pig farmer.

SWEETENERS

My take on sweeteners is that we should use them sparingly, and the most natural ones take preference over the refined sorts. I long ago swore off soft drinks, although I do think longingly of a cold

Coke on a hot day—and occasionally indulge. I've found that a container of unsweetened tea brewed from green tea and mint tea in the fridge is completely thirst quenching after work in the garden, or to sip while working or relaxing.

Here are the eight kinds of organic sweeteners, a list of their benefits, and suggestions for how I use them.

Honey: The product of bees, honey is a natural substance, if not organic. Look for raw, unprocessed honey, which will contain all the enzymes, pollen, and other nutrients that the bees gave it. As a liquid, honey dissolves more readily in cold drinks than white sugar. Some people mix honey, lemon juice, and cider vinegar in water as a cold remedy. In baking, honey not only sweetens breads, cakes, and pastries, but adds its flavor and keeps them moist as well. Figure that honey has about 35 percent more sweetening power than an equivalent quantity of white sugar.

Maple syrup: This is our regular sweetener. I use it in my morning coffee, on breakfast cereals, on pancakes, French toast, waffles, and anywhere the sweetener doesn't have to be in hard, crystalline form. Some people prefer Grade B because it is the darkest and most mapley. We prefer the lighter Grade A medium or Grade A fancy because we don't want everything tasting like maple. About 250 years ago, when sugar from the Caribbean was a scarce commodity in New England and maple syrup was the sweetener of necessity, the lighter grades were most prized for the same reason.

Molasses: When white sugar is refined out of sugar cane juice, molasses is what's left over. It's high in iron and other minerals. Organic molasses is produced without the use of chemicals and will be unsulfured.

Stevia (rebaudiana and stevioside): This sweet native Paraguayan herb is used extremely sparingly because of its intense sweetening power and odd flavor. It has few calories and can be used by diabetics because it's not a sugar. The dried leaves are ten times sweeter than sugar, while extracts made from it, called steviosides, are three hundred times sweeter. You can find it in the vitamin departments of natural and organic food stores. You can also grow it in your backyard unless you live in the very coldest zones.

Sucanat: A brand name for organically grown sugar cane juice that has been dried, it contains all the natural substances of sugar in the juice. There are no additives. Brown sugar contains .5 percent of naturally occurring mineral salts, while Sucanat (a contraction of *su*gar-*ca*ne-*nat*ural) contains 3 percent mineral salts, including calcium, iron, magnesium, zinc, copper, and chromium. It also has traces of B vitamins. It can be substituted for refined white sugar, or light or dark brown sugars, on a 1-to-1 basis.

White, dark, confectioners' sugar: Whether refined or unrefiined, all sugar can be organic, meaning it comes from organically grown sugar cane and no synthetic chemicals are used in its processing. Even the popular Domino brand of sugar sells an organic version these days.

WINE

And much as wine has played the infidel,
And robb'd me of my robe of honor—well,
I wonder often what the vintners buy
One half so precious as the stuff they sell.
—*The Rubaiyat,* OMAR KHAYYAM

NUTRITIONAL HIGHLIGHTS:
phytochemicals

WHAT TO LOOK FOR: Organically grown wines include Lolonis and the Bonterra label from Fetzer, which produces close to one hundred thousand cases per year. Organic New York State wines include Silver Thread Vineyards, Four Chimneys, and Swedish Hill. In Oregon, there are Amity, Archery Summit, Brick House, Cameron, Cattrall Brothers, Cooper Mountain, and St. Innocent. More organic vineyards and wineries are coming online all the time. At least eight wineries in California and Washington produce organic wine: Badger Mountain, China Bend, Coturri & Sons, Frey, H. La Rocca Vineyards, Nevada County Wine Guild, Organic Wine Works, and Orleans Hill.

GOES WELL WITH:

White wine: cheeses, chicken, freshwater fish, seafood, shellfish

Red wine: cheeses, chicken, red meat, tomatoes

Do you like Frog's Leap Zinfandel? It's organically grown. Kenwood Cabernet? Organically grown. Phelps, Lolonis, Fetzer, Bonterra, Coturri, Niebaum-Coppola, Z-D Wines, Morgan—all organically grown. And the list goes on and on. But you wouldn't necessarily know it from their labels.

The reason is that, years ago, some wine producers who were more focused on the political implications of organic wines than the quality of the beverage itself made some pretty poor wines with the word organic prominently displayed on the label. Organic wine became synonymous with mediocrity. Meanwhile, many fine wineries wanted to grow their grapes organically because they knew that a biologically active soil would produce better-tasting grapes; they didn't want their vineyard workers exposed to harmful chemicals; and they wanted to preserve the purity of the beautiful country where fine wine grapes flourished. But they didn't want to put organic on their label, because that would hurt sales.

Happily, the reluctance to use the word organic is finally changing. The demand for organic wine has resulted in a boom in organic viticulture in California, where total organic acreage has zoomed from 178 acres in 1989 to approximately 18,000 acres in 2005. It's becoming easier and easier to find organic wine (and organically grown grapes in supermarkets).

One of the world's largest organic wineries is Boisset of France, with sales of $330 million in 2003 and exports to eighty countries. Bill Arbios, one of Boisset's winemakers, says, "Around the world, Boisset has numerous ventures and they are taking all of their projects biodynamic or organic. It is all predicated on maximizing quality in the vineyard rather than in the winery, when it's too late" to improve the quality of the grapes themselves. Many other top wineries worldwide are increasingly using organic or biodynamic techniques in their vineyards as well.

WHAT IS BIODYNAMIC WINE?

In addition to seeing wines labeled organic, you'll frequently come across bottles labeled biodynamic. Biodynamic agriculture follows theories laid down in the 1920s by Rudolf Steiner, founder of the Waldorf School system. His metaphysical approach involves connecting agriculture to a higher, spiritual wisdom through the preparation of certain soil- and plant-enhancing natural sprays, attention to auspicious and inauspicious days for farm activities, and a basic understanding of life processes. Although it sounds fetishistic to some, biodynamics can show good results and satisfy a longing in many individuals for a deeper connection to the earth. And all biodynamic farms are organic.

Organic Advantage

Grapevines are sturdy plants that don't need to be drenched in chemicals to perform their task. Soil for growing wine grapes shouldn't be too rich or too moist, or the plant will respond with big berries. Since almost all the flavor components of wine are in the skins, small berries mean a higher ratio of skin to juice—and consequently more flavor in the wine. Small berries result when vines are forced to struggle for water and nutrients. A little compost, a meager sip of water from irrigation lines—that's about all they get. If mildew threatens early in the year when it rains, organic culture allows vineyardists to spray with naturally occurring sulfur.

Insects are handled without lethal pesticides. Rows are planted with clover and other cover crops that harbor beneficial insects as they add nutrients to the soil. Gophers and other rodents are kept down by owl and raptor boxes placed among the vines. Bats are encouraged by the placement of bat houses, as these creatures help keep mosquitoes and other insects under control. All the pressed skins and seeds are composted and returned to the soil, creating a closed system that promotes the establishment of a site-specific mix of microorganisms in the soil and in the air. This in turn promotes terroir—the term for the unique flavor of a specific place that emerges in wine and other food products produced from that place.

Many wineries that are not certified organic practice a form of sustainable grape growing that is organic in just about everything but name. The Mondavi winery is one of them. "We've learned over the years," Tim Mondavi told me, "that every time we had a choice between a repressive technology such as the use of pesticides, or an inspired technology such as the use of cover crops to help establish beneficial insects that control pests naturally, the inspired technology proved to be a better method. It addresses the fundamental vineyard and winemaking problems, and not just the symptoms. Technology should help you look into life to see how and why it works as it does, not to slaughter it."

Stores like Whole Foods Market sometimes have a special section just for organic wines, and wine shops are increasingly creating sections devoted to organic and biodynamic wines. But snooping around a wine shop for organic wines can be confusing. Here's how to tell what's what.

American labels: Organically grown or made from organically grown grapes on an American wine label means that the vineyards have been handled in accordance with the USDA National Organic Program and with the organic certifying agency of the state in which they were grown as well. Such wines may, however, have sulfur dioxide added to preserve the wine.

Labels from overseas: If you find the words *organic* or *organically grown* on a label on a bottle from overseas (Europe, Australia, South Africa, South America) the wine is probably what it purports to be; the name of a certifying agency, such as EcoCert or another body affiliated with the International Federation of Organic Agriculture Movements (IFOAM), will sometimes be found on the label as well. But many long-time organic producers, especially in France, refuse to get certification—out of tradition or sheer obstinacy.

No sulfites added: This does not necessarily mean the wine is free of sulfites. The fermentation process creates sulfites in small amounts. What's more, the daily process of digestion in the human body produces about the same amount of sulfites as can be found in one hundred bottles of wine, according to MKF, a consulting firm specializing in the wine business. White wines contain about twice the sulfites of reds, although in almost all cases less than 80 parts per million of sulfur dioxide. So, if you're sensitive to red wines, it's probably not the sulfites that are causing the reaction. European winemakers, especially the French, tend to use significantly more sulfites in their wine than American producers.

Transitional: Wine labeled transitional means that the vineyards are handled organically, but the necessary three years since conventional culture has ceased have not yet passed.

Organic wine: The fruit is certified organic and no sulfites have been added.

Biodynamic: All biodynamic farms must meet not only the USDA and state certification standards but also be certified by the Demeter organization, an internationally recognized certification agency for biodynamic agriculture.

See Sources, page 287, for a list of resources for organic wines (and beers, too).

Sources

LEARNING ABOUT ORGANIC FOOD

Read about organic foods and their production, about the environmental consequences of conventional farming methods, and about related topics at the following Web sites.

www.caviaremptor.org

Caviar Emptor

"Let the connoisseur beware." Deals with environmentally sound alternatives to fishing Caspian Sea sturgeon, which are growing increasingly endangered.

www.factoryfarm.org

GRACE (Global Resource Action Center for the Environment) Factory Farm Project

A New York–based nonprofit organization that works to oppose factory farming and to promote a sustainable food production system that is healthful, humane, economically viable, and environmentally sound.

www.iatp.org

Institute for Agriculture and Trade Policy

A Minneapolis-based nonprofit organization that supports sustainable family farms, farm communities, and ecosystems around the world. A good site to visit if you want to support organic agriculture.

www.ifg.org

International Forum on Globalization

Learn more about the role of globalization on the production of foodstuffs.

www.naturalhub.com

The Natural Hub

An interesting Web site about natural foods in the strictest sense of that term—that is, foods our Paleolithic hunter-gatherer ancestors might have eaten. Not everything listed is organic, but much is.

www.newfarm.org
The New Farm
Up-to-date info on organic farming from the Rodale Institute.

www.organicconsumers.org
Organic Consumers Association
A public-interest organization dedicated to environmentally safe and sustainable food production. It posts news reports covering issues of food safety, chemical and biotech agriculture, corporate accountability, and environmental sustainability.

www.slowfoodusa.org
Slow Food USA
The U.S. arm of a worldwide nonprofit educational organization dedicated to supporting food traditions and finding viable alternatives to the globalization and homogenization of the world's tastes. Slow Food supports local, farm-fresh produce and keeps you in touch with the practitioners thereof.

www.vividpicture.net
The Vivid Picture Project
This site is devoted to nothing less than the transformation of the entire state of California's food industry into a sustainable system. It's a project of the Roots of Change Fund (www.rocfund.org), a collaborative of foundations and experts that supports the transition to a healthier food system and healthier environment in California, and Ecotrust Food & Farms (www.ecotrust.org).

www.organictobe.wordpress.com
Organic To Be
A cyberforum hosting some bloggers (including Jeff Cox, Gene Logsdon, Dave Smith, Jesse Cool, and others) with whom organic-minded people can interact to ask questions, make comments, get ideas, or do research. Lots of fun, recipes, and organic chat.

LOCATING ORGANIC FOOD

Learn about farmers' markets and farmers who sell from their farms located near you by investigating these Web sites. Here are also large retailers that sell organic food. The list is far from exhaustive.

http://afsic.nal.usda.gov
Alternative Farming Systems Information Center
This government-sponsored site is the place to start if you're looking to buy organic produce through *community supported agriculture,* a system that links buyers to local organic farmers

for regular purchases of seasonal produce. Other sites that can connect you with participating local farms are the Biodynamic Farming and Gardening Association (www.biodynamics.com) and the Rodale Institute's New Farm farm locator (www.newfarm.org/farmlocator/index.php).

www.eatwellguide.org

Eat Well Guide, Wholesome Food from Healthy Animals

Enter your zip code and up comes a list of suppliers of organic and natural meat products in your area. There's also a list of national mail-order meat suppliers.

www.localharvest.org

Local Harvest

Links to farms and farmers participating in community supported agriculture, farmers' markets, food co-ops, and organic restaurants all over the United States. Information about online ordering of organic foods from their member farms, too.

www.omri.org

The Organic Materials Review Institute

This organization posts its list of subscribers, which include regional organic farmers' associations, organic certifiers, and state departments of agriculture, to which you can turn to find sources of local organic foods.

www.eatwild.com

EatWild.com

One of the best sources of information and access to pasture-based farming and grass-fed organic meats (including bison and lamb) and dairy.

www.ecofish.com

EcoFish

Track down sustainable, low-mercury fish and organic shellfish. EcoFish distributes seafood from environmentally sustainable fisheries to over one thousand natural and organic food stores.

Fancy Meats from Vermont

A co-op of fifty farmers producing lambs, pigs, humanely raised veal, venison, goats, rabbits, eggs, and specialty cheeses. Individuals must pick up the meat at the slaughterhouse.
2604 East Hill Road
Andover, Vermont 05143
(802) 875-3159; fax (802) 875-3159

www.seasonalchef.com

Seasonal Chef

A listing of what's in season and when in California, with links to farmers' market listings nationwide.

www.vermontfresh.net

The Vermont Fresh Network

Lists farms, food producers, restaurants, and distributors in Vermont.

www.wholefoodsmarket.com

Whole Foods Market

A supermarket chain emphasizing organic products. With 195 stores and over 39,000 employees, it has plans to expand to four hundred stores nationwide and in the UK by 2010.

www.ams.usda.gov/directmarketing

USDA Farmer Direct Marketing

The U.S. Department of Agriculture's Agricultural Marketing Service has created the National Farmers' Market Directory, which lists farmers' markets and farmers' market associations across the country. The site also lists which markets accept food stamps.

MAIL-ORDER SOURCES, GENERAL

Mail-order shippers of a range of organic foods can be found at these Web sites.

www.diamondorganics.com

Diamond Organics

Carries an array of organic products.
1272 Highway 1
Moss Landing, California, 95039
(888) ORGANIC or (888) 674-2642

www.earthydelights.com

Earthy Delights

What began as a service to professional chefs, shipping produce overnight to anywhere in the country, is now available to the general public. It's a sort of natural-foods Dean & Deluca, offering fiddlehead ferns, fresh morel and chanterelle mushrooms, caviar, foie gras, artisanal cheeses, pastas, grains, beans, truffles, fruits, nuts, fresh seasonal produce, and more. Carries many organic gourmet products.
1161 East Clark Road, Suite 260
DeWitt, Michigan 48820
(800) 367-4709 or (517) 668-2402;
fax (517) 668-1213

www.forestfarm.com

Forest Farm

Thousands of ornamental and edible plants available.
990 Tetherow Road
Williams, Oregon 97544-9599
(541)846-7269; fax (541)846-6963

www.theorganicpages.com

The Organic Trade Association's *Organic Pages*

The Organic Trade Association's Web site contains a huge amount of information on mail-order suppliers of all kinds of organic products, plus info on organic restaurants, farmers, retailers, and others.
60 Wells Street, PO Box 547
Greenfield, Massachusetts 01302
(413) 774-7511, ext. 13;
fax (413) 774-6432

www.rockcreekorganics.com

Rock Creek Organics

Purveyors of everything you need for organic baking, including whole-wheat flour, golden-wheat flour, wheat bran, almond butter, almonds, walnuts, pecans, pistachios, fruit spreads, pancake mix, muffin mix, and more.
PO Box 255
Idleyld Park, Oregon 97447
(866) 571-NUTS (6887) or
(541) 496-4705; fax (541) 496-4266

www.shopnatural.com

Shop Natural

Based in Arizona, this site carries a wide variety of foods, personal care, and pet items, with many links to information on organics.

www.sunorganic.com

Sun Organic Farm

Packaged organic food products, dried fruits, and vegetables—even wines.
411 South Las Posas Road
San Marcos, California 92078
(888) 269-9888 or (760) 510-8077;
fax (760) 510-9996

www.truefoodsmarket.com

True Foods Market

Online retailer of natural and organic foods, beverages, and cleaning supplies.
(866) 436-1390

MAIL-ORDER SOURCES, SPECIFIC FOODS

Mail-order shippers of specific or hard-to-find organic foods are listed under this heading.

A wide variety of organic dried fruits are available online. Type *organic dried fruits* into your search engine. You may turn up more than you're looking for.

VEGETABLES

www.auxdelices.com

Marché aux Delices of New York

A great source for crosnes, or Chinese artichokes; it also carries fresh and dried wild mushrooms.
(888) 547-5471; fax (413) 604-2789

www.seaweed.net

Mendocino Sea Vegetable Company

Recipe books and a catalog of seaweed products harvested from clean coastlines.
PO Box 1265
Mendocino, California 95460
(707) 895-2996

FRUIT

www.proflowers.com/cherrymoonfarms

Cherry Moon Farms

A source for organic fruits, including pineapples.
5005 Wateridge Vista Drive, Suite 200
San Diego, California 92121
(800) 862-9958

www.froghollow.com
Frog Hollow Farm
An excellent source of tree-ripened organic peaches, nectarines, pluots, Asian pears, and other fruit, as well as peach conserves, chutneys, marmalades, and more.
PO Box 2110
Brentwood, California 94513
(888) 779-4511

www.melissas.com
Melissa's World Variety Produce, Inc.
Specializes in a wide range of organic fruits and vegetables, including specialty items like loquats. Its recent publication, *Melissa's Great Book of Produce* (John Wiley & Sons), is a compendium of the fruits and vegetables it purveys.
PO Box 21127
Los Angeles, California 90021
(800) 588-0151

www.oasisdategardens.com
Oasis Date Gardens
Carries several varieties of organic dates, as well as other dried fruits and nuts.
59-111 Highway 111, PO Box 757
Thermal, California 92274
(800) 827-8017

www.redlandorganics.com/saw_mill_farm.htm
Saw Mill Farm
While longans are not yet a well-known fruit, this farm near Miami sells them, as well as lychees, and will ship.
(305) 252-2357

www.vivatierra.com
Viva Tierra Organic
Viva Tierra carries a number of organic apple varieties that you won't find in most stores—but only as long as the harvest lasts!
922 Third Street
Sedro-Woolley, Washington 98284

Citrus

There are many mail-order sources for organic citrus. The ones below are some of the best. Surely there will be many more by the time you read this.

www.localharvest.org/store
Beck Grove, Fallbrook, California

www.unclematts.com
Uncle Matt's Organic, Clermont, Florida

www.newharvestorganics.com
New Harvest Organics, Patagonia, Arizona

http://purepakinc.com
Purepak, Inc., Oxnard, California

www.stxorganics.com
South Tex Organics, Mission, Texas

The following firms don't have their own Web sites, but more information about them can be found through online search engines.

Kelly Hall Groves, Port St. Lucie, Florida

Ladera Fruit Company, Fillmore, California

Sutherland Produce Sales, Inc., El Cajon, California

NUTS

www.black-walnuts.com
Hammons Products Company
A great source of deliriously delicious Eastern black walnuts.
105 Hammons Drive, PO Box 140
Stockton, Missouri 65785
(888)-4BWNUTS; fax (417) 276-5187

www.maisiejanes.com
Maisie Jane's California Sunshine Products
Soft-shelled almonds, plain and processed.
1324 Dayton Road
Chico, California 95928
(530) 899-7909

www.molokai-aloha.com/macnuts
Purdy's Natural Macadamia Nuts
A source for organic macadamia nuts.
PO Box 84
Ho'olehua, Hawaii 96729
(808) 567-6601

www.rejuvenative.com
Rejuvenative Foods
Sells many kinds of organic nut and seed butters, including a really delicious pumpkin seed butter.
PO Box 8464
Santa Cruz, California 95061
(800) 805-7957; fax (888) 363-8310

www.eco-natural.com
Spirit Bear Bodycare
Numerous organic products, but a particularly good source for pumpkin seed oil.
PO Box 585
Kaslo, British Columbia, V0G1M0
Canada
(250) 353-7680; fax (250) 353-7677

Walnuts

The following companies sell organic walnuts. You can look for these names on packages in stores or search for their Web sites online and order directly from the nut farms.

Baker Walnut, Modesto, California

Dixon Ridge Farms, Winters, California

Ferrari Farms, Linden, California

Gibson Farms, Hollister, California

John Potter Specialty Foods, Patterson, California

Poindexter Nut Company, Selma, California

Sierra Orchards, Winters, California

Tufts Ranch, Winters, California

GRAINS

www.ansonmills.com

Anson Mills

A source for Carolina Golden rice, as well as organic corn products and whole-wheat flours.
1922-C Gervais Street
Columbia, South Carolina 29201
(803) 467-4122; fax (803) 256-2463

www.lundberg.com

Lundberg Family Farms

One of the largest purveyors of organic rice. Sixty percent of Lundberg products are certified organic; the company also offers "eco-farmed" products, which use innovative environmental practices to sustain and preserve the ecosystem.
5370 Church Street, PO Box 369
Richvale, California 95974-0369
(530) 882-4551; fax (530) 882-4500

www.lowellfarms.com

Lowell Farms

A source for organic jasmine rice.
4 North Washington
El Campo, Texas 77437
(888) 484-9213

www.mcfaddenfarm.com

McFadden Farm

A source for organic wild rice.
Potter Valley, California 95469
(800) 544-8230

www.northernnaturals.com

Northern Naturals

Quinoa and amaranth, as well as almonds, dried shiitakes, pumpkin seeds, millet, and spices.
Box 1182 Main Street
Middletown Springs, Vermont 05757
(888) 293-3985

MEATS

www.nimanranch.com

Niman Ranch

Niman Ranch started business nearly thirty years ago in Marin County, California. They still raise cattle on the original ranch but have expanded to sell pork and lamb, too. They now work with over three hundred independent family farmers nationwide who raise livestock according to strict protocols. Niman Ranch products are available through its Web site, as well as in retail stores.
(866) 808-0340

www.hillsfoods.com

Hills Foods Ltd.

Suppliers of certified organic meats, game meats, and specialty poultry. Custom smoking and sausage making. Cash and carry.
1-130 Glacier Street
Coquitlam, British Columbia
Canada
(604) 472-1500

www.lasatergrasslandsbeef.com

Lasater Grasslands Beef

Grass-fed beef from one of America's pioneers of eco-minded cattle farming.
(866) 4LG-BEEF or (719) 541-2855

www.meadowraisedmeats.com

Meadow Raised Meats

Frozen meat shipped to New York, Vermont, New Hampshire, northeast Pennsylvania, and western Massachusetts.
PO Box 103
East Meredith, New York 13757
(315) 829-5437

www.valleyfarmers.com

Valley Farmers Marketing Cooperative

A farmers cooperative of producer-members in New York's Hudson Valley committed to "grass-based" ecological agriculture, humane animal management, and high-quality, clean meats.
PO Box 38
Stanfordville, New York 12581
(845) 868-1826

www.vtqualitymeats.com

Vermont Quality Meats Cooperative

A cooperative representing thirty-eight small family farms, predominantly in Vermont, that raise premium-quality lamb, goat, pork, veal, venison, rabbit, chicken, free-range turkey, and game birds.
PO Box 116
Rupert, Vermont 05768
476 Route 7B North
North Clarendon, Vermont 05759
(802) 394-2558 or (802) 747-5950; fax (802) 747-5994

OLIVE OIL

www.theolivepress.com

The Olive Press

High-quality California organic olive oils and Limonato—olive oil paired with Meyer lemon juice. They also carry Lunigiana Estate, a small-production Tuscan-style (very peppery and bitter) oil made from olives grown in Sonoma County, California.
14301 Arnold Drive
Glen Ellen, California 95442
(800) 965-4839

www.apollooliveoil.com

Apollo Olive Oil

One of the world's greatest olive oils, and so named by prestigious organizations in Italy and Germany. Its secret is the olive oil extraction machinery developed by Professor Marco Mugelli that keeps air out of the system, preventing rancidity. The oil is incomparable—and entirely organic.
PO Box 1054
Oregon House, California 95962
(530) 692-2314

www.davero.com

DaVero Sonoma, Inc.

Stone-ground and pressed the old-fashioned way at a ranch in the Dry Creek Valley near Healdsburg in Sonoma County, California. Its fruity, peppery oil has won a gold medal at the Sonoma County Harvest Fair.
1195 Westside Road
Healdsburg, California 95448
(888) 431-8008 or (707) 431-8000; fax (707) 433-5780

www.mcevoyranch.com

McEvoy Ranch

A very peppery, bitter, green-gold extra-virgin oil in the Tuscan style.
(866) 617-6779, (707) 769-4122, or (707) 778-2307

www.spectrumnaturals.com

www.spectrumorganics.com

Spectrum Naturals

The Arbequina olives used to make this organic oil are grown in Spain and Argentina. It's a mild oil good for cooking, and relatively inexpensive. Many other organic cooking oils are also available.
(800) 995-2705 or (707) 778-8900

www.stellacadente.com

Stella Cadente

Although they are not certified organic, the olives are pesticide free and hand picked at Stella Cadente ("shooting star" in Italian), Sue Ellery and Tom Hunter's ranch in Mendocino County, California. Their oil has won numerous awards, including Best Domestic Olive Oil at the Los Angeles County Fair.
Shooting Star Ranch
Boonville, California 95415
(707) 895-2848; fax (707) 895-9556

CHOCOLATE AND COFFEE

www.chocosphere.com

Chocosphere

An Internet-only chocolate shop based in Portland, Oregon. There are many organic and sustainable brands among the thirty-seven carried.
(877) 99-CHOCO (992-4626)

www.grenadachocolate.com

Grenada Chocolate Company Ltd.

One of the best organic chocolates on the market.

www.rapunzel.com

Rapunzel Pure Organics

An eco-friendly and farmer-supportive company that sells delicious organic chocolate as well as organic baking yeast, yeast extracts, bouillons and broths, and 100 percent shade-grown organic arabica coffee.

ORGANIC WINE

www.chartrandimports.com

Chartrand Imports

Paul Chartrand imports and distributes organic and organically grown wines from Australia, Europe, New Zealand, and the United States.
PO Box 1319
Rockland, Maine 04841
(800) 473-7307 or (207) 594-7300

www.organicvintages.com

Organic Vintages

Certified organic wines, sparkling wines, and beers.
(877) ORG-ANIC (674-2642)

www.ecowine.com

Organic Wine Company

Imports organic French wines to the United States.
(888) ECO-WINE (326-9463)

www.organicwinepress.com

The Organic Wine Press

Organic wines from around the world.
175 Second Street
Bandon, Oregon 97411
(541) 347-3326

ORGANIC BEER

www.BeerTown.org

The Brewers Association

Here's a Web site that can help you find small-scale beer producers.
736 Pearl Street
Boulder, Colorado 80302
(888) 822-6273 or (303) 447-0816; fax (303) 447-2825

www.breworganic.com

Seven Bridges Cooperative

Organic ingredients and supplies for home brewing, as well as certified organic green coffee.
325A River Street
Santa Cruz, California 95060
(800) 768-4409

MAJOR ORGANIC PRODUCERS AND DISTRIBUTORS

These are some of the most prominent wholesale producers of reliable organic foods. Distributors are companies that buy their raw materials (like fruits, vegetables, and milk) from independent farmers and then distribute them to stores under their own label. They can usually be found in the organic sections of supermarkets. This list is not comprehensive—a perusal of your organic supermarket will turn up many more wonderful brands.

www.anniesnaturals.com

Annie's Naturals

Carries one of the widest arrays of organic condiments, such as mustards and organic salad dressings, as well as other pantry items.

www.albertsorganics.com

Albert's Organics

A full-service, wholesale distributor of a year-round line of certified organically grown fruits and vegetables, along with regional lines of organic dairy products. Albert's distributes to five thousand natural stores nationwide.

www.ebfarm.com

Earthbound Farm

Started by husband and wife Drew and Myra Goodman as a roadside stand selling raspberries and lettuces, Earthbound Farm now farms over 13,000 acres of organic land, and sells over one hundred different organic fruits and vegetables year-round, shipped across the country in refrigerated trucks.

www.edenfoods.com

Eden Foods

This company has been around since 1968, when it was founded in Ann Arbor, Michigan, to supply the macrobiotic community. You've undoubtedly seen its Edensoy soy milk boxes, but its catalog holds about two hundred products, from pastas to fruit juices to condiments to sea vegetables.

www.greatspice.com

The Great Spice Company

If your devotion to organic food extends to your spice cabinet, you probably are well stocked on the products of the Great Spice Company. The spices come from seven continents and are certified organic.

www.horizonorganic.com

Horizon Organic Dairy

A nationwide distributor of organic milk, other dairy, egg, and juice products.
PO Box 17577
Boulder, Colorado 80308
(888) 494-3020

www.kingblossomnatural.com

King Blossom Natural

Organic growers with their own controlled-atmosphere storage facility that ensures year-round availability of their apples and pears.
PO Box 2952
Wenatchee, Washington 98807
(888) 959-5464 or (509) 664-8855

www.oceanboyfarms.com

Ocean Boy Farms, Inc.

Ships fresh (never frozen) shrimp from July through December and individually quick frozen shrimp year-round. Its products are available through distributors and retail stores.
2954 Airglades Boulevard
Clewiston, Florida 33440
(863) 983-9941; fax (863) 983-9943

www.organic-planet.com

Organic Planet

A wholesaler who imports and sells organic ingredients from around the world to retail stores in the United States. Products are certified by Quality Assurance International and include many types of seeds and nuts, spices, oils, and other kitchen staples. It's definitely a wholesale operation—there's a one-ton minimum order—but there are undoubtedly many products on your kitchen shelves that have come through Organic Planet.
231 Sansome Street, Suite 300
San Francisco, California 94104
(415) 765-5590; fax (415) 765-5922

www.organicvalley.coop

Organic Valley Cooperative

A source of organic meat, dairy, produce, and other products. Formed in 1988 by George Siemon and a few other organic farmers in the Midwest, the cooperative now encompasses 450 organic farms in seventeen states from Oregon to Maine and from Florida to California. One of the largest organic brands in the nation, Organic Valley is the only one to be solely owned and operated by organic farmers. These farmers today are at the heart of the organic revolution in agriculture. The

Web site can help you find a local store that sells Organic Valley products, but it is not a mail-order site.

www.sheltons.com

Shelton's Poultry, Inc.

"Our chickens don't do drugs." Processed organic poultry products sold through retail stores (there's a directory of stores on the site).
204 North Loranne
Pomona, California 91767
(800) 541-1833 or (909) 623-4361

www.cfarm.com

Small Planet Foods

The pinnacle of organic big business. The company includes Cascadian Farms, an organic food processor in Washington State, as well as Muir Glen, a line of nationally distributed tomato and marinara sauces. In 1999, Small Planet was bought by the multibillion-dollar food giant General Mills.

www.sunopta.com

SunOpta

Canada's leading distributor of fresh organic produce for the last fifteen years, distributing brands such as Pro Organics and Wild West Organics. It offers a complete line of certified organic products year round, with distribution points in Burnaby, British Columbia; Toronto; and Montreal.

www.trade-organic-wine.com

Trade Organic Wine

A business-to-business site with a large variety of organic wine.

www.unfi.com

United Natural Foods, Inc.

UNFI is an umbrella organization that procures organic foodstuffs from thousands of vendors around the world and sells them to seven thousand conventional supermarkets, natural and organic food stores, and independent retail stores. It's a huge operation and the first coast-to-coast certified organic distributor.

www.walnutacres.com

Walnut Acres

Located in Penns Creek, Pennsylvania, this was the granddaddy of all organic mail-order services, but it recently dropped its mail-order business in favor of sales through retail outlets. From its humble beginnings selling homemade apple butter, Walnut Acres has grown into one of the largest and most trusted purveyors of organic foods in the country.

Bibliography

Aaron, Chester. *Garlic is Life: A Memoir with Recipes.* Berkeley: Ten Speed Press, 1996.

_____. *The Great Garlic Book: A Guide with Recipes.* Berkeley: Ten Speed Press, 1997.

Arora, David. *All That Rain Promises and More...: A Hip Pocket Guide to Western Mushrooms.* Berkeley: Ten Speed Press, 1991.

Ash, John, with Sid Goldstein. *From the Earth to the Table.* New York: Dutton, 1995.

Bailey, Liberty Hyde, and Ethel Zoe Bailey. *Hortus III.* New York: Macmillan, 1976.

Blaylock, Russell L. *Excitotoxins: The Taste That Kills.* Santa Fe: Health Press, [1998], c1997.

Bomhard, Gloria M. *Simply Irresistible.* Kearney, NE: Morris Press Cookbooks, 2002.

Brissenden, Rosemary. *Asia's Undiscovered Cuisine.* New York: Pantheon, 1982.

Child, Julia, Simone Beck, and Louisette Bertholle. *Mastering the Art of French Cooking.* New York: Alfred A. Knopf, 2001.

Corum, Vance, Marcie Rosenzweig, and Eric Gibson. *The New Farmers' Market.* Auburn, CA: New World Publishing, 2001.

Cox, Jeff. *From Vines to Wines: The Complete Guide to Growing Grapes and Making Your Own Wine.* Pownal, VT: Storey Books, 1999; [Harper & Row, orig. 1985].

Davidson, Alan et al. *The Oxford Companion to Food.* New York: Oxford University Press, 2006.

Dornenburg, Andrew, and Karen Page. *Culinary Artistry.* New York: John Wiley & Sons, 1996.

Dornenburg, Andrew, and Karen Page. *The New American Chef.* New York: John Wiley & Sons, 2003.

Facciola, Stephen. *Cornucopia II.* Vista, CA: Kampong Publications, 1998.

Fallon, Sally. *Nourishing Traditions.* Washington, DC: New Trends Publishing, 2001.

Foster, Gertrude B., and Rosemary F. Louden. *Park's Success with Herbs.* Greenwood, SC: Geo. W. Park Seed Co., 1980.

Fruit Facts, Vols. 1 & 2. Fullerton, CA: California Rare Fruit Growers, undated.

Gorman, Marion. *Cooking with Fruit.* Emmaus, PA: Rodale Press, 1983.

Griffiths, Sally. *Hot & Spicy Sauces & Salsas.* New York: Rizzoli, 1995.

Hamersley, Gordon. *Bistro Cooking at Home.* New York: Broadway Books, 2003.

Hazan, Marcella. *Essentials of Classic Italian Cooking.* New York: Alfred A. Knopf, 1998.

Herbst, Sharon Tyler. *The New Food Lover's Companion.* 3rd ed. Hauppauge, NY: Barron's Educational Series, 2001.

Horn, Jane, Ed. *Cooking A to Z.* Santa Rosa, CA: Cole Group, 1992.

Kilarski, Barbara. *Keep Chickens!: Tending Small Flocks in Cities, Suburbs, and Other Small Spaces.* North Adams, MA: Storey, 2003.

Kochilas, Diane. *The Food and Wine of Greece.* New York: St. Martin's, 1993.

Lappé, Frances Moore. *Diet for a Small Planet.* New York: Ballantine, 1991.

Lorenz, Oscar A., and Donald N. Maynard. *Knott's Handbook for Vegetable Growers.* 3rd ed. New York: John Wiley & Sons, 2006.

Madison, Deborah. *Local Flavors.* New York: Broadway Books, 2007.

Martinez, Zarela. *Foods from My Heart.* New York: Macmillan, 1992.

McCue, Susan, Ed. *Specialty and Minor Crops Handbook.* 2nd ed. Davis, CA: University of California Division of Agriculture and Natural Resources, 1998.

Morash, Marion. *The Victory Garden Cookbook.* New York: Alfred A. Knopf, 1982.

Morse, Kitty. *Cooking at the Kasbah.* San Francisco: Chronicle Books, 1998.

Norman, Jill. *Herbs & Spices.* New York: DK Publishing, 2002.

Patraker, Joel, and Joan Schwartz. *The Greenmarket Cookbook.* New York: Viking, 2000.

Pittenger, Dennis R., Ed. *California Master Gardener Handbook.* Davis, CA: University of California Division of Agriculture and Natural Resources, 2002.

Richter, Henry. *Dr. Richter's Fresh Produce Guide.* Apopka, FL: Try-Foods International, 2000.

Robinson, Jancis, Ed. *The Oxford Companion to Wine.* New York: Oxford University Press, 2006.

Rombauer, Irma S., Marion Rombauer Becker, and Ethan Becker. *Joy of Cooking.* New York: Scribners, 2006.

Schneider, Elizabeth. *Vegetables from Amaranth to Zucchini.* New York: William Morrow, 2001.

Torres, Marimar. *The Catalan Country Kitchen.* London: Addison-Wesley, 1992.

Tucker, Arthur O., and Thomas DeBaggio. *The Big Book of Herbs.* Loveland, CO: Interweave Press, 2000.

Vaughan, J. G., and C. A. Geissler. *The New Oxford Book of Food Plants.* New York: Oxford University Press, 1998.

Waldin, Monty. *Organic Wine Guide.* London: Thorsons, 1999.

Waters, Alice. *Chez Panisse Fruit.* New York: HarperCollins, 2002.

Waters, Alice. *Chez Panisse Vegetables.* New York: HarperCollins, 1996.

Index

C

N

O

P

Q

R

T

U

V

W

Y

Z